SALAFISM IN YEMEN

LAURENT BONNEFOY

Salafism in Yemen

Transnationalism and Religious Identity

HURST & COMPANY, LONDON

First published in the United Kingdom in 2011 by
C. Hurst & Co. (Publishers) Ltd.,
41 Great Russell Street, London, WC1B 3PL
© Laurent Bonnefoy, 2011
All rights reserved.
Printed in India

A Cataloguing-in-Publication data record for this book
is available from the British Library.

ISBN: 9781849041317 *paperback*

This book is printed using paper from registered sustainable
and managed sources.

www.hurstpub.co.uk

CONTENTS

ACKNOWLEDGEMENTS

This book, from its inception to its publication, would not have been possible without the input and support of a variety of institutions, colleagues, friends and family members. I am ever grateful for their trust and their patience during the time of research and writing, either in Yemen, Saudi Arabia, France or the Levant. Each in their own way have transformed these past years into much more than a strictly academic adventure.

Large segments of this research on the Salafi movement in contemporary Yemen were carried out in the framework of my doctoral thesis at the Institut d'Etudes Politiques de Paris. Bertrand Badie supervised my dissertation, which I defended in October 2007, and gave me most useful advice on matters of methodology and theory. His support and encouragements continue to bear fruit.

I am also profoundly indebted to François Burgat who introduced me to Yemen, to fieldwork, to the complex academic world and to many of the issues addressed in the following chapters. As a *mudîr*, a colleague and a friend his dynamism, his generosity and his confidence have been constant sources of inspiration.

Additional field work in Yemen in 2008 and 2009, in the course of a postdoc, was made possible through funding by the French Agence Nationale de la Recherche and support by the Institut de Recherches et d'Etudes sur le Monde Arabe et Musulman in Aix-en-Provence. Consultancy for the International Crisis Group also allowed me to gather data, particularly on the issue of Zaydi revivalism.

Review of English writing of the manuscript and translation of certain segments by Jeffrey Lewis, in the United States, was funded by the aforementioned Agence Nationale de la Recherche as well as by the Centre Français d'Archéologie et de Sciences Sociales de Sanaa, whose director Michel Tuchscherer generously supported the project. I also wish to thank Michael Dwyer of Hurst & Co. who has given me multiple opportunities to publish my work and who repeatedly trusted me, as well as the two anonymous reviewers for their most useful comments on the initial manuscript.

Along the way, discussions and debates with a number of academics proved inspiring and gave way to conferences, publications, but also, in certain cases, long-lasting friendships. Madawi Al-Rasheed, Valérie Amiraux, Claire Beaugrand, Frédéric Charillon, Ahmad al-Daghshî, Fatiha Dazi-Héni, Renaud Detalle, 'Abd al-Fatâh al-Hakîmî, Noorhaidi Hasan, Bernard Haykel, Joost Hiltermann, Sa'îd 'Ubayd al-Jamhî, Gregory Johnsen, Stéphane Lacroix, Roel Meijer, Pascal Ménoret, Franck Mermier, Yahya Michot, 'Aydarûs al-Naqîb, Bernard Rougier, Olivier Roy, Ahmad Sayf, Mohamed Sbitli, Eric Vallet, Gabriele Vom Bruck and Nâsir Yahyâ have all guided me, helped me persevere and were able to show me how much academic research is most of all a collective enterprise.

During the four years I spent in Yemen, the Centre Français d'Archéologie et de Sciences Sociales de Sanaa provided me with a most stimulating place. Although constraints and threats (not always coming from where one would think!) are on the rise and mobility in the country is no longer what it used to be, the CEFAS still remains an invaluable gate to Yemen. Its team and its researchers, especially Rémy Audouin, Marylène Barret, Rémy Crassard, Samy Dorlian, Etoto, 'Abd al-Hakîm Farhân, Sylvaine Giraud, Juliette Honvault, Muhammad Jâzim, 'Abd al-Qâdir al-Qubâtî and Roman Stadnicki, whatever their task or discipline, have truly been an asset. I am particularly indebted to Mounir and Emmanuelle Arbach who have become more than friends, much like family. Marine Poirier has too turned into a marvellous research companion with whom it will always be a pleasure to work.

The Center for Yemeni Studies in Sana'a, with 'Abd al-'Azîz al-Maqâlih at its head and Khâlid al-Surayhî as my main contact, has provided institutional shelter and helped me deal with the local administration. In Saudi Arabia, the King Faisal Centre for Research and Islamic Studies, particularly Yahyâ Bin Junayd and 'Awadh al-Bâdî have too opened the doors of a society that is in its own way full of surprises and often misunderstood.

In addition to a fantastic case study, the faculty of Education of Lab'ûs in Yâfi' provided me with comfortable board and lodging for months. This proved a unique experience and I am grateful to the faculty's Dean, 'Abd al-Rahmân al-Wâlî, for accepting to help me. The discovery of the depth of his hospitality

ACKNOWLEDGEMENTS

and generosity as well as that of all the teachers and students who patiently answered my questions, let me attend their classes or invited me into their families was without doubt a life-changing experience. I sincerely hope the following pages do not betray them and that, if they ever read them, they will continue to consider me worthy of their trust and consideration.

Above all, over the course of my research in Yemen and Saudi Arabia, an incalculable number of people provided me with useful advice and information. Often in an informal way and through their own individual trajectories, many of them embodied the centrality of transnational connections, while a smaller number made tangible the development of new religious practices labelled Salafism. 'Alî Badr, Munda'î Dayân, 'Alî Fadhl, Sâmî Ghâlib, Sâlim al-Hajrî, Muhammad al-Jandal, Anwar Khadhr, Shihâb al-Dîn al-Muhammadî, 'Alî al-Muharramî, Fâris al-Saqqâf, Nabîl al-Sûfî, Wahîb al-Sa'adî, Khâlid al-Sûma'î, Muhammad Thâbit, Walîd al-Yâfi'î, Sirâj al-Dîn al-Yamânî and Ahmad Zayn have all in their own way offered me the chance to take a glimpse at the complexity and human richness of the Arabian Peninsula. 'Alî al-Ward, patient and generous as he was, helped me work on Salafi sources and introduced me to the many subtleties of religious and Salafi vocabulary, debates and history.

Nabîl Subay', in addition to his invaluable friendship, has offered me a stimulating counterpoint on my subject and a fascinating gateway to the other end of society than the one I was studying: one made of songs, tolerance, poetry, debates and exciting qat chewing afternoons and evenings. Wamîdh Shâkir and Nabil's brothers Jamîl and Murâd, as well as his son, Wahb, are the future of Yemen.

So are Khâlid al-Khâlid and Munâ who in Sana'a, al-Muhâbisha and then in Paris saw this research develop and evolve. They were always available to help me escape the countless traps of Arabic language. Mis-translations and mistakes that may remain in this manuscript are my responsibility alone.

Finally, I wish to thank those in my family and among my friends who, although they did not always understand what exactly I was doing spending months away from them in the Yemeni mountains, never doubted my work and gave me all of their affection. My parents, parents-in-law, Ségolène, Marie, Anne-Marie, Rémi and Octavio were surely in the forefront. Above them all, Jeanne has consistently brought me happiness, stability and creativity. Although a stranger to the academic world, it is her daily support and her precious time that have made these pages possible. Colombe too has been patient, letting her 'papa' work on a book project that will most likely never be able to compete in her heart with *Noah's Ark*, *La petite taupe* or *Totoro*. And she is probably right, in comparison to these characters, Salafis are no match!

GLOSSARY

Dramatis Personae

'Abd Allâh al-Ahmar (1933–2007): Yemeni politician and tribal shaykh. Serving as paramount chief of the Hâshid tribal confederation, he played a leading role in securing the support of the tribes of the northern highlands to the republican system. Doubling as the leader and founder of al-Islâh party, he maintained strong links with the Saudi ruling family and was one of the key proponents of the equilibrium between the different political actors in contemporary Yemen.

Muhammad Nâsir al-Dîn al-Albânî (1914–1999): Prominent transnational Salafi scholar of Albanian and Syrian origins. His emphasis on the study of the *hadîth* continues to have a great impact on shaping the quietist Salafi movement or *salafiyya da'wiyya*.

Salmân al-'Awda (born in 1955): Leading figure of the *Sahwa islâmiyya* movement in Saudi Arabia he was among the main opponents of the Saudi monarchy during the first half of the 1990s. Released from prison in 1999, he gradually made compromises with the regime and has emerged as one of the scholars valued by the *salafiyya munazzama*.

Muhammad Bin 'Abd al-Wahhâb (1703–1792): Cleric of central Arabian (Najdî) descent. His works on *tawhîd* and his political alliance with the Âl Su'ûd helped shape the successive Saudi monarchies. His various teachings are at the source of what is labelled Wahhabism.

'Abd al-'Azîz Bin Bâz (1910–1999): Prominent Salafi scholar of Saudi origin. Although consistently supporting the Saudi monarchy (he served as *muftî* of the Kingdom until his death) he retained a pivotal position and was respected for his knowledge by Islamist circles in Saudi Arabia and beyond.

GLOSSARY

Yahyâ al-Hajûrî (born in the mid-1960s): Yemeni cleric, former student of Muqbil al-Wâdi'î, upon the latter's death, he took over the management of Dâr al-Hadîth in Dammâj. Since then, he has taken a hard line defending the Salafi creed.

Husayn al-Hûthî (1956–2004): Son of a prominent Yemeni Zaydi scholar, he founded the *Shabâb al-Mu'min* and served as member of Parliament (1993–1997). Tensions between his movement and the government gave way in 2004 to the Sa'da war opposing the so-called 'Hûthî' supporters to the national army. He was killed in the first months of the war but is still seen as a reference of Zaydi revivalism.

Taqî al-Dîn Ibn Taymiyya (1263–1328): Levantine Islamic scholar, his teachings have been considered instrumental in the fostering of reformist movements. Although respected beyond these circles, he qualifies as one of the major sources of contemporary Salafis of all trends.

Muhammad al-Imâm (born in 1960): Cleric, former student of Muqbil al-Wâdi'î, he has emerged as one of the most charismatic sources of quietist Salafism in Yemen since the latter's death. He heads the Salafi teaching institute in Ma'bar, south of Sana'a.

Muhammad Amân al-Jâmî (1927–1996): Salafi scholar of Ethiopian origin, he spent most of his life teaching in a variety of Saudi religious institutes, including the Islamic University of Medina. He is deemed the founder of the *Jâmiyya* trend of Salafism who fiercely opposed on religious grounds both the Muslim Brotherhood and the *Sahwa islâmiyya* movement and called for loyalty to the rulers.

al-Habîb 'Alî al-Jifrî (born in 1971): Sufi scholar of Yemeni origin, he is among the founders of the Dâr al-Mustafâ institute and a member of the Bâ 'Alawiyya brotherhood. His connections with a number of Arab rulers and the support he has found among Muslim populations in Europe and North America has seen him emerge as a charismatic figure of transnational Sufi movements.

Rabî' al-Madkhalî (born in 1931): Salafi scholar of Saudi origin. Companion of Muhammad Amân al-Jâmî, he too taught at the Islamic University of Medina and emerged as one of the hardliners of quietist Salafism stigmatising other Islamist trends and movements. In doing that he has come to be one of the leading sources of transnational quietist circles.

Muhammad al-Mahdî (born in the 1950s): Yemeni Salafi cleric, educated in Saudi Arabia (particularly in the city of al-Burayda) and former companion of Muqbil al-Wâdi'î, he was among those who established the Hikma association in 1991.

Abû al-Hasan al-Ma'ribî (born in 1958): Former student of Muqbil al-Wâdi'î, Egyptian-born Salafi scholar. He heads the Dâr al-Hadîth institute near the town of Ma'rib in Yemen but was the object of much controversy within the quietist Salafi movement, being accused of engaging in political activities after al-Wâdi'î's death.

Ahmad Hasan al-Mu'allim (born in 1953): Yemeni Salafi scholar, former companion of Muqbil al-Wâdi'î with whom he studied in Saudi Arabia. He too was imprisoned and expelled from Saudi Arabia for his relations with Juhaymân al-'Utaybî. He left for Kuwait only to come back to his native Hadramawt region after Yemeni unification. He is among the leading figures of the Hikma Salafi association and of the *salafiyya munazzama*.

'Alî 'Abd Allâh Sâlih (born in 1942): Yemeni politician inspired by Arab nationalism, he served as President of the Yemen Arab Republic between 1978 and 1990 and then as President of unified Yemen from 1990 onwards.

Muhammad al-Shawkânî (1759–1834): Yemeni scholar of Zaydi background who engaged in his writings in an important re-evaluation of the importance of the *hadîth*. His teachings have numerous similarities with that of Muhammad Bin 'Abd al-Wahhâb (whose heirs he nevertheless challenged on political grounds as they attacked Hadramawt) and he remains a much revered source by contemporary Salafis.

Muhammad Surûr Zayn al-'Abdîn (born 1938): Religious scholar of Syrian origin, he has played a leading role in bridging the political doctrine of the Muslim Brotherhood and the literalist interpretations of the Salafis. Founder of *al-Sunna* review, living in Birmingham after spending years in Saudi Arabia and Kuwait, he is at the head of the so-called *Surûriyya* trend and is an important source of the *salafiyya munazzama*.

Juhaymân al-'Utaybî (1936–1980): Saudi former companion of Muqbil al-Wâdi'î in the *Jamâ'a al-salafiyya al-muhtasiba*, he took the leadership of the November 1979 uprising in the Meccan shrine, later being sentenced to death.

Muhammad al-'Uthaymîn (1925–2001): Prominent Salafi scholar of Saudi origin. Much like Bin Bâz, he remained until his death a pivotal actor of the Saudi Islamist field as well as that of transnational Salafi movements.

Muqbil al-Wâdi'î (circa 1930–2001): Founder of the Yemeni Salafi movement, he was educated in Saudi Arabia before being expelled from that country. Back in Yemen, he established Dâr al-Hadîth in the early 1980s in Dammâj, in the suburbs of Sa'da city. His charisma as well as his independence of speech and his uncompromising doctrine allowed him to emerge as an important source of quietist Salafism inside of Yemen and beyond.

'Abd al-Majîd al-Zindânî (born in 1942): Yemeni politician, prominent member of the radical branch of the Muslim Brotherhood and of the Islâh party, he was trained as a pharmacist in Egypt. He played an important role, in connection with Saudi Arabia, to mobilise Yemenis against the Soviet Red Army in Afghanistan. Often described as a companion of Usâma Bin Lâdin, he established in 1993 the Îmân religious university in Sana'a. His endorsement of party politics has made him a foe of quietist Salafis.

Institutions, Organisations, Movements

Ahl al-sunna wa al-jamâ'a: Literally 'people of the Tradition and of the Group', formulation often used by the Salafis to describe their movement and to emphasise their filiations with Prophet Muhammad and his community. This nomination is however disputed by other groups, particularly the Sufis.

Committee of Senior 'Ulamâ': In Arabic *Haya' kibâr al-'ulamâ'*, refers to a Saudi assembly of religious scholars created in 1971 and nominated by the government. It is headed by the *muftî* of the Kingdom, currently 'Abd al-'Azîz Âl al-Shaykh, and supervises the General Presidency of Scholarly Research and Ifta (*al-Ri'âsa al-'âma lil-buhûth al-'ilmiyya wa al-iftâ'*) which publishes official *fatâwâ*.

Dâr al-Hadîth: Literally, 'house of the *hadîth*', Salafi teaching institute established in the early 1980s by Muqbil al-Wâdi'î in Dammâj (North Yemen), close to the Saudi border. Other branches were later established in Yemen by his companions and former students.

Dâr al-Mustafâ: Sufi teaching institute established in 1996 by al-Habîb 'Alî al-Jifrî and other scholars in the city of Tarîm in Hadramawt. Since then, it has played a leading role in the Sufi revival in contemporary Yemen.

Al-Hikma: Full name 'Jami'yya al-hikma al-yamâniyya al-khayriyya', literally the 'Yemeni Wisdom Charity Association'. It was established in 1991 by former students and companions of Muqbil al-Wâdi'î who favoured a more political approach to Salafism than that of their former mentor. The strongholds of this representative of *salafiyya munazzama* are found in Ibb and Ta'iz.

GLOSSARY

Al-Ihsân: Full name 'Jami'yya al-ihsân al-khayriyya', literally the 'Benevolent Charity Association'. Officially established as an offshoot of al-Hikma in 1996, its strongholds are in the former governorates of South Yemen.

Jamâ'a al-salafiyya al-muhtasiba: Literally 'the Salafi Group that Enforces Virtue and Prevents Vice', emerged in the mid-1960s as a radical group that sought to fight moral corruption in Saudi society. Among the members were Juhaymân al-'Utaybî, Ahmad Hasan al-Mu'allim and Muqbil al-Wâdi'î and many of the *Ikhwân* (Brothers) who participated in the Great Mosque uprising in November 1979.

Al-Islâh: Full name 'al-Tajammu' al-yamanî lil-islâh', literally 'Yemeni Congregation for Reform' established in 1990. This political party, described as the Yemeni branch of the Muslim Brotherhood, draws together different trends of Islamists, tribal shaykhs and conservative businessmen. Participating in government between 1993 and 1997, it has joined the opposition since then and has established an alliance with other opposition movements against the rule of 'Alî 'Abd Allâh Sâlih. Its connections with the Muslim Brotherhood have made it an important antagonist of quietist Salafis.

P.D.R.Y.: People's Democratic Republic of Yemen, also South Yemen. Established in 1970, it remained the only socialist regime of the Arab world until unification of North and South Yemen in 1990.

Sahwa islâmiyya: Literally 'Islamic awakening', movement that emerged from the 1970s in Saudi Arabia in opposition to the ruling family and to the constant compromise of the leading religious scholars. As a political and religious alternative to the state religious institutions, it sought to merge the political approach of the Muslim Brotherhood with the literalist Salafi doctrine.

Salafiyya da'wiyya/'ilmiyya: Literally 'missionary' or 'scholastic' Salafism, describes the quietist branch of Salafism that openly rejects political participation and calls for automatic loyalty to the rulers. It is also labelled 'shaykhist' or may be called *Madkhaliyya* or *Jâmiyya* in reference to two of its references, Rabî' al-Madkhalî and Muhammad Amân al-Jâmî.

Salafiyya jihâdiyya: Jihadi branch of Salafism which advocates and legitimises on religious grounds use of violence against the state, minorities and its enemies. Although some of its sources might be shared with the two other branches of Salafism, it is nevertheless distinct and is characterised by its own set of scholars and concepts.

Salafiyya munazzama/harakiyya: Literally 'movement' or 'activist' Salafism, describes the political branch of Salafism that accepts to engage in political and charitable activities while continuing to put emphasis on literalist interpretations of the religious texts. It is at times referred to as the *Surûriyya*.

Shabâb al-mu'min: Literally, the 'Believing Youth', political organisation established in the early 1990s by Husayn al-Hûthî and others to support Zaydî revivalism in the northern Yemeni highlands, particularly against Salafi encroachment. Since 2004, it has taken the leadership of the so-called 'Hûthî' movement in the war against the Yemeni government and its tribal allies.

Scientific Institutes (*Ma'ahid 'ilmiyya*): Network of Saudi-funded schools established in North Yemen during the mid-1970s to counter the socialist ideological offensive. These para-public teaching structures placed emphasis on religious teaching and were controlled by activists close to the Muslim Brotherhood and as such accused, until their disappearance in 2002, of spreading a radical version of Islam.

Tablîgh: Missionary Islamic movement of South Asian origin. Sharing much in matters of literalism and of rejection of direct political participation with Salafism, Tablîghî activists nevertheless refer to specific sources of jurisprudence and of creed. As such, they are also stigmatised by Salafis.

Y.A.R.: Yemen Arab Republic, also North Yemen. Established in 1962 it merged with South Yemen on 22 May 1990 to create the Yemen Republic.

Zaydism: Branch of Shi'ite Islam found specifically in Yemen. Around a third of the Yemeni population is nominally Zaydi (including a large proportion of the ruling elite and of some Salafi leaders, including Muqbil al-Wâdi'î) of which only a small minority continues to refer to that religious sect, while the vast majority prefers to refer to a wider Muslim identity. Since the 1980s however, Zaydi revivalists have tried to give new meaning to their identity.

Concepts

'Aqîda: Islamic dogma or creed that defines the Islamic faith.

Bid'a (pl. *bida'*): Literally 'innovation'. According to Salafis, religious practices that came to pollute the original and pure Islamic creed as defined by the first generations of Muslims, the *salaf al-sâlih*.

Da'wa: Literally 'call'. Action of spreading the Muslim faith.

Fatwâ (pl. *fatâwâ*): Juridical advice given by '*ulamâ*' in answer to specific questions. Building on religious sources, the *fatâwâ* are meant to specify the social practice or attitude that is in conformity with the religious teachings as found in the Qur'an and the *hadîth*.

Fitna: Literally 'dissension' or 'chaos'. For Salafis, defines the state of division and strife of the Muslim community caused by political activities. Focus on *da'wa* rather than on politics is then perceived as the way to fight *fitna*.

Hadîth: Sayings and deeds of Prophet Muhammad as collected by its companions and transmitted from generation to generation to form the Tradition (*sunna*). With the Qur'an, the thousands of *hadîth* (classified according to their trustworthiness) form the only two sources of jurisprudence used by the Salafis.

Hizbiyya: Literally 'factionism' or 'spirit of party'. For quietist Salafis, defines the process through which individuals engage in political activities, give their allegiance to man-created institutions rather than to God, and spread dissension or *fitna* among the Muslim community.

Jarh wa ta'dîl: Literally 'refutation and rectification'. Concept used by Salafis to justify their public criticism of other Muslims and in certain circumstances of political rulers. It is the object of much debate among Salafis, particularly as to who can legitimately resort to *jarh wa ta'dîl*.

Jihâd: Literally 'effort'. By extension, has come to define holy war to spread or defend Islam.

Kafîl: Literally 'sponsor'. Designates in the Gulf countries the mandatory person employed by the migrants to serve as an interface between them and the administrations of their host countries.

Khawârij (sing. *khârijî*): Literally 'one who has gone out', name given to partisans of the Fourth Caliph, 'Alî, who turned back against him after the battle of Siffîn, seceded and later assassinated him in 661. By extension it is used by Salafis to designate their opponents and to put into question the reality of their belonging to the Muslim community.

Khurûj: Literally 'exit'. Designates the process of revolt against the ruler, something that is forbidden by quietist Salafis. It is perceived by them as an important source of dissension among the Muslim community. In the specific Yemeni context, refers particularly to Zaydism which considers *khurûj* against an oppressive ruler a central right.

Land of the Two Holy Places (*Ardh al-haramayn*): According to the context may designate the Hejaz (region around Mecca and Medina where the two holiest shrines of Islam are located) in what is now south-west Saudi Arabia or, by extension, Saudi Arabia as a whole. Such a nomination is considered by many Salafis as more legitimate than that of Saudi Arabia.

Madhhab (pl. *madhâhib*): School of Islamic jurisprudence that provides methods to interpret Islamic sources. Usually designates the four Sunni schools (Hanbali, Shafi'i, Hanafi and Maliki) that were established in the centuries following revelation to Prophet Muhammad. The Salafi doctrine claims to reject the *madhhab*.

Mahjar: In Arabic, refers to the land to which one migrates either for socio-economic or religious reasons.

Manhaj: Literally 'method'. For the Salafis, designates their own literalist approach to Islamic sources and their focus on matters of creed rather than on jurisprudence (*fiqh*).

Muftî: Literally designates one who produces *fatâwâ* and interprets Islamic law. By extension has come to designate the highest religious Sunni authority nominated by governments, usually to endorse and legitimise in religious terms their own policies.

Qabîlî (pl. *qabâ'il*): Literally 'tribesman', refers to the most numerous status group in the traditional social hierarchy of Yemen. Tribesmen are usually sedentary, most are peasants and throughout history have doubled as armed men ready to fight or defend the regime.

Qâdhî (pl. *qudhâ*): Literally 'judge', refers to a marginal group in the Yemeni traditional hierarchy whose role was mainly to produce *fatâwâ* and develop knowledge of religious sources.

Râfidhî (pl. *rawâfidh*): Literally 'defector', usually refers to those who reject legitimate Islamic authority. By extension it has come to designate for most Salafis, the Shi'ites who rejected the authority of the first three Caliphs Abû Bakr, 'Umar and 'Uthmân.

Sayyid (pl. *sâda*): Member of the group that claims descent from Prophet Muhammad through his grandsons Hasan and Husayn. May also be referred (although with slight nuances) to as Hashemites or Ashrâf. In the Zaydi highlands of Yemen, the *sâda* exercised monopoly over political leadership and at least partially excluded *qabâ'il* from access to religious knowledge until the 1962 revolution.

Shaykh (pl. *shuyûkh*): According to the context may refer to a tribal leader, an old and respected man, or a revered religious scholar.

Takfîr: Practice of designating others as 'unbelievers' (*kâfir*, pl. *kufâr*). The issue of the religious legitimacy of *takfîr* or excommunication is much debated among Salafi scholars.

Taqlîd: Literally 'imitation'. Practice rejected by the Salafis of blindless imitation of the various *madhhab* or of past *fatâwâ*.

Tawhîd: Literally 'unicity'. Refers to the unicity of God, its qualities, its attributes and sovereignty. The concept gained prominence with the publication in the mid-eighteenth century of *Kitâb al-tawhîd* by Muhammad Bin 'Abd al-Wahhâb and was intended as a means of rejecting practices of *shirk* (literally 'association') which associate things and people with God.

'Ulamâ' (sing. *'âlim*): Religious scholars.

Waqf (pl. *awqâf*): Islamic endowment or property whose production or benefits are meant to finance religious activities.

TRANSLITERATION

I have used throughout this book a simplified transliteration system of Arabic. Although I have persistently distinguished long vowels from short ones, used ' for *'ayn* and ' for the *hamza*, I have not used diacritical marks and not distinguished lunar from solar letters when writing the article (*al-*). The *tâ' marbûta* was marked only when followed directly by an annexation or a name. Also, when transcribing expressions or formulations from colloquial Arabic, I have adapted these to the standard Arabic pronunciation (*qalam* and not *galam* as pronounced in the northern Yemeni highlands, or *muhâjir* and not *muhâgir* as referred to in the south and in Yâfi'). A few words, names of organisations, groups, places and concepts that have become common in English retained their English spelling, among these al-Qaeda, jihadi, Aden, Sana'a imam, Sufi and Salafi.

When writing Bin or Ibn (son of), I chose to stick to the dominant formulation so the former *muftî* of Saudi Arabia is named Bin Bâz while the the fourteenth-century Levantine scholar is referred to as Ibn Taymiyya, while *Abû* (father of) has been preferred to *Abî*. May 'orthodox' Islamologists and linguists excuse these few liberties.

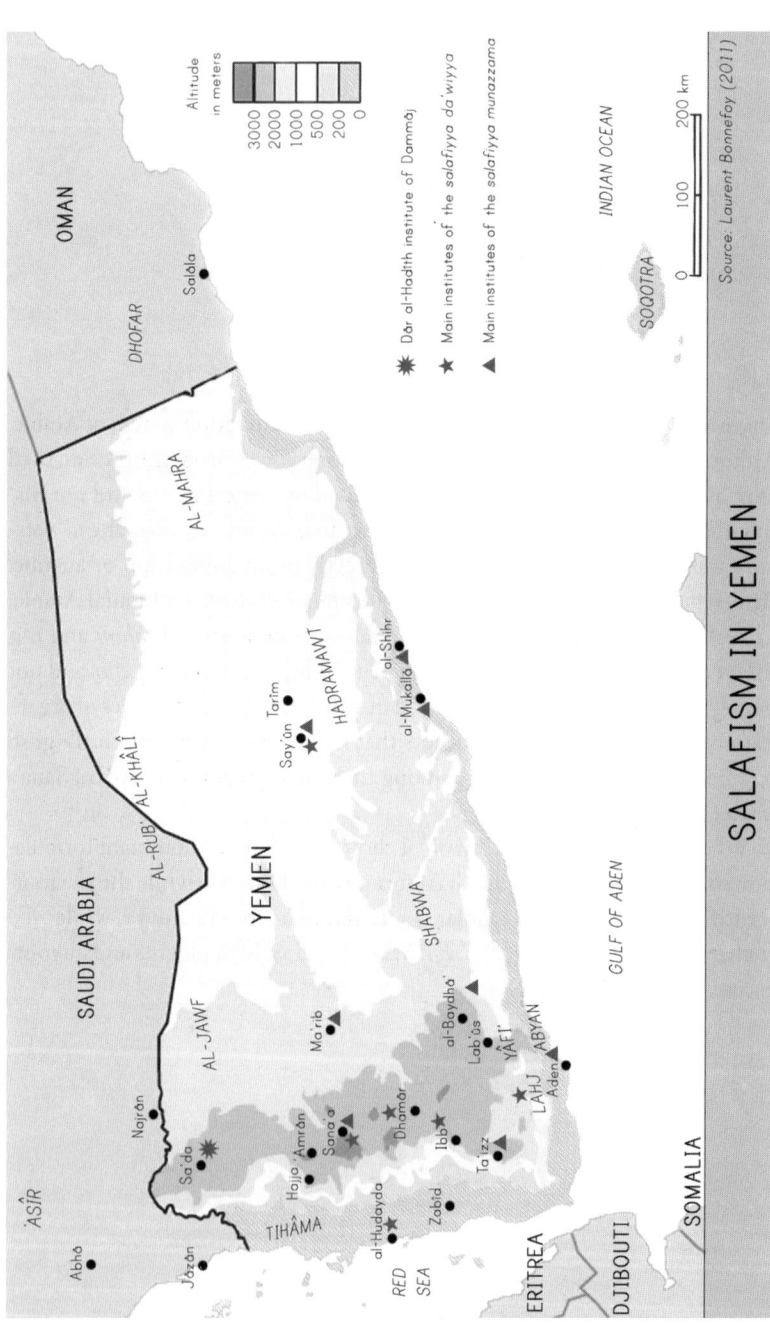

SALAFISM IN YEMEN

Altitude
in meters
3000
2000
1000
500
200
0

✳ Dār al-Hadīth institute of Dammāj
★ Main institutes of the salafiyya daʿwiyya
▲ Main institutes of the salafiyya munazzama

Source: Laurent Bonnefoy (2011)

0   100   200 km

INDIAN OCEAN

SOQOTRA

OMAN

DHOFAR

Salāla

AL-MAHRA

HADRAMAWT

al-Shihr
al-Mukallā

Tarīm
Sayʾūn

SAUDI ARABIA

AL-RUBʿ AL-KHĀLĪ

YEMEN

AL-JAWF

SHABWA

GULF OF ADEN

Najrān

Maʾrib

al-Bayḍāʾ

Laboʿs
YĀFIʿ
ABYAN
LAHJ
Aden

ʿASĪR

Abhā

Jāzān

Saʿda

Hajja
ʿAmrān

Sanʿāʾ

Dhamār

Ibb
Taʿizz

TIHĀMA

al-Hudayda

Zabīd

RED
SEA

ERITREA

DJIBOUTI

SOMALIA

INTRODUCTION

At the turn of the twenty-first century, the international border between Yemen and Saudi Arabia still appears as a kind of 'grey zone', a space that is largely beyond the state's control and influence. Cutting across high mountains and arid deserts, this 1458km long border zone is said to be a place where plots and smuggling or trafficking activities flourish. In one way or another, all involve some sort of violence. Drugs, weapons, explosives, banned goods, anti-American propaganda, 'subversive' religious ideologies, 'terrorists', alien immigrants, and trafficked women and children cross this border everyday more or less illegally. For being so porous, the border is increasingly described as a threat to regional and international stability.

The announced merger of the Yemeni and Saudi branches of al-Qaeda in January 2009 and the establishment of al-Qaeda in the Arabian Peninsula, apparently headed by Yemeni militant, Nâsir al-Wihayshî, only confirmed such an impression. To many, it symbolised the emergence of Yemen as a possible launch-pad for operations outside of the country, particularly in Saudi Arabia but also around the globe with an American citizen of Yemeni origin, Anwar al-'Awlaqî, allegedly pulling the strings. Undeniably, this stretch of land is perceived as a security threat, as transnational flows of people are blamed for undermining state power and stability. In the context of the 'Global War on Terror', the border has become the object of much concern on the part of Yemenis, Saudis and Westerners alike. As such, its surveillance has become a central issue.

For more than sixty-five years, until 2000, a latent border conflict set Yemen against Saudi Arabia. In 1934, a brief war occurred between the Yemeni Zaydi Imamate[1] and the young Saudi monarchy. The Saudis eventually prevailed and

[1] Historically, Yemeni society has been divided into two main religious identities.

gained control over three contested provinces: Najrân, Jâzân and ʿAsîr. During the following decades, despite the 1934 Tâʾif peace agreement, the border was only demarcated in its western sector, from the plain of the Tihâma, on the coast of the Red Sea, to the oasis of Najrân. The rest of the border, that is, its largest part, remained legally undetermined, and numerous clashes occurred between border guards of both countries and among tribesmen.

On 12 June 2000, the signature of the Jeddah Treaty by the governments of Yemen and Saudi Arabia formally ended the conflict but tensions remained between the two rival states of the Arabian Peninsula. The treaty sought to normalise the situation by definitively delineating the border and reducing its porosity.[2] It was supposed to open a new era in the—until then complex—relations between the two parties. Yet less than four years after the signature of the

---

Shafiʾis are Sunni while Zaydis are a branch of the Shiʾa often described as moderate in its jurisprudence, distinct from the Twelver Shiʾas found mainly in Iran, and close to Sunnism in many aspects. Zaydism appeared in 740 in Mesopotamia and Central Asia around Zayd Bin ʿAlî al-Husayn. It was later institutionalised in Yemen by al-Hâdî Ilâ al-Haqq Yahyâ Bin al-Husayn (d. in 911). The elites of this religious sect, which claimed to be descendants of the Prophet Muhammad (the *sâda*), have ruled, under the authority of the imam, over parts or the whole of the Yemeni territory for over a millennium, until the 1962 Republican revolution. Throughout the twentieth century the religious divide eroded considerably. No accurate and trustworthy statistics exist, but Shafiʾis are usually considered to represent the clear majority of the 25 million Yemenis, while Zaydis form around 35 per cent of the population, their bastions being located in the north. Owing to recent changes, among which are internal and external migration, the individualisation of religious identities, along with the improvement in education levels, most Yemenis now consider the sectarian divide as being mostly symbolic. Since then, Zaydism has been in crisis and has experienced important theological and political developments, some of which blunted the main features that distinguished it from Sunnism, while others triggered a significant revivalist phenomenon. Bernard Haykel, *Revival and Reform in Islam. The Legacy of Muhammad al-Shawkânî*, Cambridge: Cambridge University Press, 2003; Gabriele Vom Bruck, *Islam, Memory, and Morality in Yemen. Ruling Families in Transition*, New York: Palgrave, 2005; ʿAbd Allâh Bin Muhammad Hamîd al-Dîn, *al-Zaydiyya* [Zaydism], Sanaʾa: Markaz al-Râʾid, 2004; Samy Dorlian, *Les filières islamistes zaydites au Yémen: la construction endogène d'un universel politique*, Mémoire de master, IEP d'Aix-en-Provence, 2005.

[2] Renaud Detalle (ed.), *Tensions in Arabia: The Saudi-Yemeni Fault Line*, Baden Baden: Nomos Verlagsgesellschaft, 2000; Askar al-Enazy, *The Long Road from Taif to Jeddah: Resolution of a Saudi-Yemeni Border Conflict*, Abu Dhabi: Emirates Center for Strategic Studies, 2005.

Jeddah Treaty, tensions re-emerged, following a terrorist attack in Riyadh on 8 November 2003. Rejecting any domestic responsibility for the event, the Saudi government sought out convenient culprits. It naturally turned to Yemen, its long-time rival, and accused its government of not controlling its border and population well enough, providing al-Qaeda with easy access to weapons. The results of the investigation established that the explosives used during the attack had been bought in Yemen and smuggled into Saudi Arabia. The Saudi rulers then announced a project to build a fence across the desert to protect their country from its allegedly 'dangerous' and 'chaotic' Yemeni neighbour. In late January 2004, Yemeni diplomats and politicians firmly opposed the fence project, stressing the fact that it violated the Jeddah Treaty.[3] At the same time, several Yemeni groups, including the powerful Wâ'ila tribe, whose shaykh, Muhammad Bin Hamad Bin Shâja', known to be one of the most vocal opponents of the Jeddah Treaty, had died in a mysterious car crash in early March 2002, asserted that the new barrier would encroach upon their territory and that they would therefore defend their rights by all means, including resorting to violence. It took the visit of Yemeni President 'Alî 'Abd Allâh Sâlih to Riyadh on 17 February 2004 to persuade the Saudis to abandon the project, for the time being at least. Each party then promised to co-operate to improve control of the border through patrols and bilateral committees.

Four years later, in early 2008, the newly-elected French President Nicolas Sarkozy went on an official visit to Saudi Arabia. As always he was accompanied by a delegation of French businessmen and was meant to facilitate the signature of some lucrative deals. Like President Chirac two years before him, he hoped, in addition to selling the Rafale fighter aircraft and Areva nuclear plant, to promote the expensive border surveillance project proposed by French arms companies. The so-called Miksa project, with an estimated cost of $10 billion, promised to fill the order books of the Thalès European consortium (or of its competitor EADS) for several years. Western 'arms dealers' presented the control of Saudi Arabian borders as a top priority of the 'Global War on Terror'. This electronic surveillance system would indeed allegedly prevent infiltration from its southern neighbour and protect the Kingdom, in the context of the war in Iraq, from spillover from that conflict. The barrier project was a much

---

[3] *al-Quds al-'Arabî*, 30 January 2004. Symbolic of the persistence of the ambiguous status of the Yemeni-Saudi border, a mere ten years after the signature of the border treaty, erroneous maps were still being published, even in serious international magazines and newspapers. These maps amputated from Yemen tens of thousands of square kilometres and drew a border line that was never recognised internationally.

debated issue and as of early 2011 no final decision had yet been taken by either government.

Over the last decades, Yemen and Saudi Arabia appear to be two brothers sharing the same history, with comparable populations and demographic trends, and a relatively homogenous ethnic and religious composition: and yet they are so different. Republic vs. kingdom, rural vs. urban populations, 'poverty' vs. 'opulence', the gap between the rusting oil barrel on which the Yemeni customs officer perches and the air-conditioned and computerised office on the Saudi side of the border is probably one of the most striking in the world. Such a contrast is reflected not only in their differential revenues, but also in terms of access to services and infrastructures, whether private or public, like roads, schools and hospitals. The World Bank's figures are telling: in 2009, the per capita GDP of Saudi Arabia was estimated at $23,429 in purchasing power parity while that of Yemen was ten times less. In 2009, the Saudi Human Development Index was ranked fifty-ninth worldwide, while that of Yemen occupied the 140th position out of 177 countries.

Of course such a differential needs to be qualified. Indeed, the southern provinces of Saudi Arabia (some of which are still considered by some as 'culturally Yemeni' as they were seized by the Saudi monarchy during the 1934 war) are less valued than others since they are poor in natural resources and job opportunities. Furthermore, the dominant narrative of an opulent Saudi society is far from accurate: inequalities are prevalent and therefore give room for comparisons between the two societies. Mass unemployment in Saudi Arabia and the crisis of the welfare state since the 1990s have affected the livelihoods of many, thereby deconstructing the common image of an ever-wealthy state and society.[4]

Nevertheless, the international border seeks to separate two distinct social, economic and political spaces and it has few equivalents elsewhere in the world (except maybe the border between the United States and Mexico).[5] It is widely agreed among local actors and foreign academics that, especially since the 1960s and King Faysal's reign (1964–1975), the Saudis have pursued a consistent

[4] Pascal Ménoret, *L'énigme Saoudienne: les Saoudiens et le monde (1744–2003)*, Paris: La Découverte, 2003, pp. 187–190.

[5] For a study of the transnational relations occurring near the border between Mexico and the United States see Michael Kearney, 'Borders and Boundaries of State and Self at the End of Empire', *Journal of Historical Sociology*, vol. 4, no. 1, 1991, pp. 52–74 and Joseph Nevins, *Operation Gatekeeper: The Rise of the Illegal Alien and the Remaking of the US-Mexico Boundary*, New York: Routledge, 2002.

strategy aimed at maintaining a certain instability in Yemen by financing and arming rebellious tribes and by 'exporting' a kind of fundamentalist Islam, which is either labelled 'Wahhabism' or 'Salafism'.[6] The latter, understood as a radical reformist movement whose aim is to reinstate an authentic practice of Islam and which came to take on particular meaning in the Yemeni context from the 1970s onwards, is the main focus of this book. I aim here to question the materiality as well as the efficiency of the relations linking the emergence of the Salafi movement in Yemen to Saudi proselytisation policies.[7]

In the contemporary Yemeni context, the Salafis and their adversaries alike acknowledge that Salafism is in some way a novelty disrupting the local environment. For its supporters, the emergence of Salafism is a kind of renaissance that put an end to a deviation characterised by corruption and theological misinterpretations. Conversely, for its adversaries, it is an anomaly that clashes with the Yemeni culture and history. Although its name is an explicit reference to the first generations of Muslims (al-salaf al-sâlih—the pious ancestors) living all over the Arabian Peninsula, and in spite of the fact that some of the Salafis' sources of inspiration were originally from Yemen, the development of Salafism in Yemen as a significant and well-organised political and religious movement dates back to the early 1980s. The Salafi movement was mainly organised by a charismatic figure, Muqbil Bin Hâdî al-Wâdi'î who died in July 2001 and had spent many years in Saudi Arabia before going back to Yemen to establish his own network of teaching institutes.

Narratives of 'Saudisation'

In a more or less explicit way the dominant discourse in the media as well as among academics and politicians asserts that the emergence of Salafism in Yemen is directly related to relations with Saudi Arabia and its domination of

---

[6] Paul Dresch, *A History of Modern Yemen*, Cambridge: Cambridge University Press, 2000, p. 141.

[7] Salafism in Yemen has been the object of academic articles by François Burgat and Mohamed Sbitli, 'Les salafis au Yémen ou ... la modernisation malgré tout', *Chroniques yéménites*, no. 10, 2003, pp. 123–152 and by Bernard Haykel, 'The Salafis in Yemen at a Crossroads: An obituary of Shaykh Muqbil al-Wadi'i of Dammaj', *Jemen Report*, no. 2, 2002, pp. 28–31. In Arabic, Sa'îd 'Ubayd al-Jamhî, *Tanzîm al-qâ'ida: al-nashâ, al-khalfiyya al-fikriyya, al-imtidâd. Al-Yaman namudhajân* (al-Qaeda organisation: establishment, ideological background, contiguity. The example of Yemen], Cairo: Madbûlî, 2007 offers an interesting angle on the Salafi movement in Yemen.

the Yemeni state and its society. The transnational dimensions of the Salafi movement are analysed as expressions of Saudi power and are connected to the unequal structure of these bilateral relations. Since the 1960s and despite the tensions linked to the border issue, the Saudi state and elite have played a central role in the politics and economics of Yemen. During the civil war following the 1962 revolution in North Yemen, Saudi Arabia backed the royalists supporting the Zaydi Imamate against the Egyptian-sponsored republicans.[8] It was only on 27 July 1970 and after long negotiations that had started in April of the same year, that Saudi Arabia officially recognised the republican regime of North Yemen.[9] The compromise reached by the Saudi Monarchy and the new Yemeni Arab Republic implied, among other things, that the Saudi government would officially contribute to North Yemen's budget. According to Gregory Gause, who described the Saudi foreign policy of that time as 'riyal-politik' (referring to the Saudi currency), the Kingdom's direct participation first reached $20 million.[10] During a bilateral meeting in Jeddah in August 1975, the heir apparent, Prince Khâlid, was said to have offered 810 million riyals (around $200 million) to North Yemen. In 1976, a special body, the Saudi-Yemeni Co-operation Council, was even created to monitor Saudi donations and manage development projects. According to official Yemeni figures, between 1971 and 1983, an average of 43 per cent of the North Yemeni budget was financed by foreign aid, most of it being of Saudi origin. Over the same period of time, Yemeni society as a whole, whether in North Yemen or in the socialist South Yemen, was also highly dependent upon remittances sent by its

---

[8] According to Fred Halliday, the 26 September 1962 Revolution in North Yemen worried the Saudi government as it feared contagion and was also facing unrest: 'The North Yemeni revolution of September 1962 found a strong echo in the Saudi armed forces: the air force had to be grounded when nine pilots defected to the Nasserites, and US planes had to be brought in to provide a substitute air defence'. Fred Halliday, *Arabia Without Sultans*, Harmondsworth: Penguin Press, 1974, p. 67. On the Saudi monarchy's diplomatic reaction and its policy during the Yemeni civil war: 'Abd al-Wahhâb al-'Uqâb, *Tatawwur al-'ilâqât al-yamaniyya al-su'ûdiyya 1948–1970* [Evolution of Yemeni-Saudi relations, 1948–1970], Aden: Isdârât jâmi'at 'Adan, 1998.

[9] For a detailed and lively account of the reconciliation between North Yemen and Saudi Arabia in the early 1970s by some of its main protagonists: Mohsin Alaini, *50 Years in Shifting Sands*, Beirut: Dar an-Nahar, 2004, p. 384 and 'Abd Allâh Bin Husayn al-Ahmar, *Mudhakirât* [Memoirs], Sana'a: al-Afâq, 2007.

[10] Gregory Gause, *Saudi-Yemeni Relations. Domestic Structures and Foreign Influence*, New York: Columbia University Press, 1990.

numerous migrants working in Saudi Arabia and other Gulf countries. In the mid-1980s annual remittances reached a peak of around $4 billion. The Saudi government's funding kept on rising until the 1990–1991 Gulf War, when united Yemen adopted a neutral stance in the conflict, therefore setting it at odds with Saudi foreign policy. Until the mid-1990s therefore the Saudi payments, along with those of the other Gulf monarchies, decreased dramatically before rising again. To date, official Saudi donations continue to finance mainly development projects and infrastructure.

Over the years, Saudi rulers have also intervened in Yemen through less transparent means, sponsoring opposition groups and rebellious tribes, discretely working against the unification of the Yemens, developing client-patron relations and undermining the central government's power.[11] In 1990 it was alleged that the Saudi Minister of Foreign Affairs, Prince Su'ûd al-Faysal, had visited Aden and promised an aid package of one billion dollars to the socialist rulers of South Yemen if they sabotaged the unification process with North Yemen.[12] Furthermore, salaries continue to be paid on a trimesterly basis to a vast number of Yemeni tribal shaykhs, and Saudi passports have been distributed to many communities living close to the border or to other specific groups. During the 1994 war between the United Yemeni government and secessionist elites in the south of the country, the Saudis financially backed the latter, regardless of the socialist background of some of them, and implicitly recognised the Democratic Republic of Yemen they proclaimed.

These political manoeuvres illustrate the complexity and the inconsistency of the two states' bilateral relations. They also highlight the multiple character and heterogeneity of the state and its interests, as elements associated with the state apparatus may not always be in tune with the government policies.[13] Far from being the sole result of a rational decision taken by a specific ruler, foreign policy is often a combination of actions and policies put forward by organisa-

---

[11] Isa Blumi, *Chaos in Yemen. Societal Collapse and the New Authoritarianism*, New York: Routledge, 2010, p. 147.

[12] Quoted by Mohamed Zabarah, 'Saudi Relations Gone Awry' in Joseph A. Kechichian (ed.), *Iran, Iraq, and the Gulf States*, New York: Palgrave, 2001, p. 270. See also Khadîja Ahmad al-Haysamî, 'al-'Ilâqât al-yamaniyya al-su'ûdiyya 1990–2000 [Yemeni Saudi Relations]' in *al-Yaman wa al-'âlam* [Yemen and the world], Cairo: Maktabat Madbûlî, 2001, pp. 176–177.

[13] Fred Halliday, *Rethinking International Relations*, London: Macmillan, 1994, pp. 81–82. For a systematic approach of the state as a multiple actor: Graham Allison, Philip Zelikow, *The Essence of Decision. Explaining the Cuban Missile Crisis*, New York: Longman, 2nd edition, 1999.

tions, bureaucracies and individuals which may compete with one another and possess a partial rationality and limited patterns of intervention. Such an approach to foreign policy and the role of the state in world politics does not imply that decision makers and rulers are powerless. They (like analysts) have to take into consideration other actors, among whom some might be identified with the state and yet still contradict some of its policies. As a result, associating diplomacy and state, or diplomacy and nation becomes irrelevant. While governments may intervene in the name of the nation and claim to have the monopoly of its representation in world politics, they mostly act for themselves and pursue their own particular interests. Although it is conceptualised in strong and widely accepted narratives, this monopoly is an illusion.[14]

Apart from the above-mentioned complex strategies and dependence, it is often claimed that the Saudi proselytism and religious intervention play a fundamental role in the emergence of new religious groups, whether in Yemen, or in Europe and North America at a more global level. The Saudis are said to sponsor mosques and religious institutes, bribe decision makers, grant scholarships or distribute a specific religious propaganda that is then blamed on for the development of Salafism worldwide. In this framework, Salafi actors often appear as mere agents of a wider process of 'Saudisation' of Islam, a process meant to serve the Saudi national interest. According to the same interpretation, such a 'Saudisation' takes different forms whether theological, physical or cultural: Salafis favour Saudi 'ulamâ' (religious scholars, sing. 'alim) appear to dress like Saudis, support the Saudi government and reject local traditions. These over-simplified narratives are based on the idea of the Saudis exporting an individual and collective religious practice. Such forms of discourse, deconstructed and criticised in other contexts by post-modern theorists,[15] assign a specific function to social change and a particular intentionality to the process.[16]

---

[14] James Rosenau, Mary Durfee, *Thinking Theory Thoroughly: Coherent Approaches to an Incoherent World*, Boulder: Westview Press, 1995, pp. 57–69.

[15] A vast body of literature exists on narratives, constructivism and post-modernism, among these: Kate Nash, *Contemporary Political Sociology. Globalisation, Politics and Power*, London: Blackwell, 2000; Alexander Wendt, *Social Theory of International Politics*, Cambridge: Cambridge University Press, 1999; and François Cusset, *French Theory*, Paris: La Découverte, 2005.

[16] On this specific issue: Prasenjit Duara, *Rescuing History from the Nation: Questioning Narratives of Modern China*, Chicago: University of Chicago Press, 1995; and David Campbell, *Writing Security: United States Foreign Policy and the Politics of Identity*, Minneapolis: University of Minnesota Press, 1998.

Within this stunted framework, Salafism emerged only to satisfy Saudi Arabia's thrust for control, to maximise its interest and to protect its sovereignty.

According to the so-called 'realist' paradigm of international relations, the pursuit of national interests is the main variable of world politics. The shape of international relations is then seen as the result of conflicting interests pursued by different actors and powers. Each of them possesses various instruments of power: some of them are deemed objective, like population, wealth, natural resources, army, and so on. Others are less direct such as ideology, culture, image or what Joseph Nye once called 'soft power'.[17] All are used to pursue the national interests and defend one's sovereignty. From such a perspective, Salafism appears as an indirect means of power or an instrument of 'soft power', one that is allegedly able to shape the allegiance of Yemeni citizens to Saudi Arabia's advantage. Consequently, Salafism is perceived as an inevitably exogenous phenomenon, alien to the Yemeni society for it has been 'exported' or 'imported'—depending on which side you look at—through mechanical Saudi proselytising policies. These narratives more often than not happen to be quite normative as they assume that the 'authentic' and endogenous religion in Yemen is moderate and peaceful while the 'alien', 'deviant' and imported one is characterised by its fundamentalism and its radicalism. Foreign intervention is regarded as a kind of contamination that in the end is to be blamed for episodes of violence. Early nineteenth-century accounts by Dutch diplomats already highlighted the role of 'Wahhabis' coming from Mecca in the transformation of Indonesian Islam and what were perceived as the 'corruption' mechanisms of the *hajj* which would confront Indonesian individuals to religious interpretations that were alien to the allegedly 'innocent' and 'peaceful' Islam of their country of origin.[18]

The narratives connecting social practices to political domination are obviously not specific to Salafism when looking at Saudi-Yemeni relations. Whether in the Islamic world or not, dominant perceptions tend to obscure the truly transnational and grassroots dimensions of religious actors by focusing on state power and its supposed capacity to actually manipulate and control non-state actors. Fundamentalist protestant churches and sects in Latin America and West Africa are frequently considered as bridgeheads of North American

---

[17] Joseph Nye, *Bound to Lead. The Changing Nature of American Power*, New York: Basic Books, 1990.

[18] On the issue of Indonesian Islam and foreign influences; Martin van Bruinessen, 'Global and Local in Indonesian Islam', *Southeast Asian Studies*, vol. 37, no. 2, 1999, pp. 158–175.

domination.[19] The jihad in Afghanistan during the 1980s is largely analysed within the same framework and often linked to the broader issues and confrontations of the Cold War.[20] Today many people would acknowledge that al-Qaeda is a kind of by-product of American foreign policy. The Lebanese Hizbullah is also said to take its orders straight from Tehran, and the Taliban in Afghanistan in the 1990s are often seen as mere creations of the Pakistani and Saudi secret services.[21] Further afield, in Latin America for example, Ariel Colonomos has analysed how transnational Protestant churches were long seen as deviant puppets of Washington's domination and how the transnational dynamics that explain their development were viewed as yet another sign of their illegitimacy.[22]

In Yemen, a whole literature, often published by Zaydi intellectuals, has specialised in exposing the reasons as well as the dangers of the development of Salafism, most often labelled 'Wahhabism'. A great deal of intellectual work went into constructing and legitimising this narrative. Despite their biased and often simplistic views, these publications have contributed to forging the dominant representations of the Salafi movement, portraying it as a Saudi export. Such a perspective has been regularly reproduced by academics and the media, whether in Yemen or abroad. As early as 1979, Muhammad 'Alî al-Shihârî published *al-Matâmi' al-su'ûdiyya al-tawassu'iyya fî al-Yaman* [The Saudi expansionist ambitions in Yemen]. This was followed by an even more explicit volume written by 'Abd Allâh al-Sayânî and published under the pseudonym of Amîn Abû Zayd: *al-Wahhâbiyya wa khataruhâ 'alâ mustaqbal al-Yaman al-siyâsî* [Wahhabism and its danger for the future of political Yemen]. As stated in the first pages, the objective of the author was to:

Inform the Arab reader of the rulers' plots against the peoples and have him aware of the role of the Âl Su'ûd family in the growing oppression of the Yemeni people. In

---

[19] Bruno Fouchereau, 'Les sectes, cheval de Troie des Etats-Unis', *Le Monde Diplomatique*, May 2001.

[20] John Cooley, *Unholy Wars: Afghanistan, America and International Terrorism*, London: Pluto Press, 3rd edition, 2002.

[21] Jason Burke, *Al-Qaeda: Casting a Shadow of Terror*, London: I.B. Tauris, 2003, p. 108: 'Political opponents within Afghanistan claim the Taliban were little more than proxies of Pakistan and Saudi Arabia, their success entirely due to the support of foreigners'. On that issue see Mariam Abou Zahab and Olivier Roy, *Islamic Networks: The Pakistan-Afghan Connection*, London: Hurst, 2003.

[22] Ariel Colonomos, *Églises en réseaux: trajectoires politiques en Europe et Amérique*, Paris: Presses de Sciences Po, 2000, pp. 69–70.

doing so we hope that other peoples will not be mislead by the Wahhabi doctrine used by the Saudi rulers.[23]

In an interview, Ahmad Muhammad al-Shâmî, General Secretary of the conservative Zaydi party al-Haqq, attacked Wahhabism and Saudi Arabia and asserted:

Wahhabism is a child of imperialism. It is the imperialist spear-head in our country. Both are one and the same thing. How do we stand up against an enemy we don't see? We are seeing imperialism in our country in its Islamic guise. In reality, we are fighting something which is more dangerous than imperialism: its legitimate son. Wahhabism is preparing the ground to colonize us indirectly for the imperialist cause.[24]

Elsewhere, Ibrâhîm al-Wazîr, a Zaydi intellectual from one of the former ruling imamate dynasties explained in *al-Balâgh* weekly magazine:

To penetrate the country, Saudi Arabia has different strategies: money, to help creating movements and broadcast its ideas; the introduction of doubt among Muslims by accusing them of being deviant; the threat of *takfîr* (excommunication). [...] The Wahhabi brothers in Yemen, and particularly their '*ulamâ*', have become a factor of division and conflict that aims at breaking down the national and Islamic unity of Yemen.[25]

Obviously, inside the political and religious spectrum, the Zaydis are not the only ones linking the development of Salafism (or 'Wahhabism' as they say) to Saudi imperialist ambitions. In a probably less virulent and direct way, the affiliates of the Muslim Brotherhood are also eager to portray their Salafi competitors as an illegitimate group, alien to Yemeni society. They accuse them of being at the root of terrorist violence and of focusing on minor theological issues.[26]

Sufis, socialists, Nasserites, liberals, Zaydis, as well as government officials all have their say on the Salafi phenomenon, usually claiming its development is the result of Saudi proselytisation policies that aim at destabilising Yemen. Denouncing Salafism, Wahhabism, Saudi *da'wa* (proselyte) activities and foreign policy at the local as well as the national level, is also a widespread and

---

[23] Amîn Abû Zayd, *al-Wahhâbiyya wa khataruhâ 'alâ mustaqbal al-Yaman al-siyâsî* [Wahhabism and its danger for the future of political Yemen], Beirut: Mu'assasa al-basâ'ir, 1991, p. 4.

[24] Interview with the *Yemen Times*, 1 July 1992 quoted by Bernard Haykel, *Revival and Reform in Islam. The Legacy of Muhammad al-Shawkânî*, op. cit., p. 227.

[25] *al-Balâgh*, 30 September 1992.

[26] Ahmad al-Daghshî, *Ahl al-sunna wa al-jamâ'a: ishkâl fî al-fahm am fî al-mafhûm?* [The ahl al-sunna wa al-jamâ'a: Problem of comprehension or of concept?], Sana'a: Markaz al-'Ubâdî, 2003.

popular activity among independent and opposition journalists in Yemen.[27] 'Saudi-bashing' can yet be a dangerous activity as journalists may face harassment or even be sued by the Yemeni authorities for negatively affecting the bilateral relations. Such was the case of independent journalist Nabîl Subay' in December 2004 when he referred in an article to the 'Kingdom of Terrorism (*al-mamlaka al-irhâbiyya*)' instead of the 'Kingdom of Saudi Arabia (*al-mamlaka al-su'ûdiyya*)'. In April 2008, *al-Wasat*, an independent weekly newspaper, famous for its anti-Saudi stance, was temporarily closed by the Ministry of Information for supposedly 'undermining the country's highest interests through harming the warm relations with brotherly countries'.[28]

For their part, Yemeni republican elites, although only rarely being Salafis themselves, appeared to tolerate this movement if not support its rise since the 1980s because of its antagonism with Zaydi royalists and revivalists and due to its appeal for automatic loyalty to governments.

When taken for granted, the representation of Salafism or any other forms of extremism as necessarily alien to Yemen is not exempt from essentialism, a tendency that may turn to be ridiculous. Such is the case of an American journalist who in praising Yemen's potential for tourism, stated:

My days in Sana'a made me wonder how someone like Osama Bin Laden, with his vengeful, inflexible Muslim Puritanism could have come from Yemen, a contradictory society of *khat*-chewing, industrious, welcoming people. I concluded that Bin Laden is not only the black sheep of his family, he's a Yemeni anomaly—more a product of Saudi extremism.[29]

Behind such a simplistic discourse lies the direct accusation of Saudi Arabia, more precisely of the royal family and of the Saudi elites, described as evil actors responsible for the spread of 'Wahhabism' and other violent and intolerant interpretations of Islam that tend to focus on 'holy war (*jihâd*)' and 'excommunication (*takfîr*)'.[30] Everywhere in the Islamic world, terrorism allegedly

---

[27] See for example: 'Intishâr afghânî bi-himâyya amniyya [Afghan Diffusion Under the Protection of Security Services]', *al-Shûrâ*, 22 June 2005.

[28] 'Wizârat al-i'lâm tulghî tarkhîs al-Wasat' [Information Ministry Cancels *al-Wasat*'s authorisation], *al-Wasat*, 5 April 2008.

[29] Terry Boyd, 'In Yemen, nothing is quite what it seems', *Stars and Stripes*, 10 August 2006.

[30] Among the vast anti-Saudi literature, see for example Laurent Murawiec, *Princes of Darkness: The Saudi Assault on the West*, New York: Rowman, 2005; Dore Gold, *Hatred's Kingdom: How Saudi Arabia Supports New Global Terrorism*, Washington: Regnery, 2003.

finds its roots in the theology of eighteenth-century cleric Muhammad Bin 'Abd al-Wahhâb, 'ideologue' of the Saudi state and ally of the monarchy. Saudi culture, history, education and the country's political system as a consequence are bluntly accused of producing and exporting activists allegedly willing to fight 'infidels' everywhere in the world.

The State, Transnational Relations and Religion

Diverging interests and politics, counter-intuitive behaviour, dubious rumours and the idea of a persistent duplicity seem to have characterised the relations between Saudi Arabia and Yemen since the 1930s. For many, studying these bilateral relations would mean highlighting the capacity of Saudi Arabia to influence Yemen (whether divided or united) and to impose its own choices through domination. One would then be left with the option to analyse whether Yemen is only a vassal state of the Âl Su'ûd. How independent is it really? How effective is the Saudi domination? This particular connection was examined by Gregory Gause in his seminal study of Saudo-Yemeni relations between 1962 and 1982.[31] Assuming the existence of a Saudi design towards both Yemens, he focused particularly on the way different domestic and institutional structures explained why Saudi Arabian elites had been more influential in North Yemen than they had been in socialist South Yemen where a strong ideology enhanced social control by the state.

Yet, if one refuses to consider the state as a unitary actor and accepts the idea that many other actors intervene in the bilateral relations, there is no such a thing as a fixed strategy of Saudi Arabia towards Yemen. Defining the Saudi 'national' interest is a difficult task as the relations between the two countries have taken very different and contradictory forms: financial aid for development projects, private investments, restrictive migration policies, support of the Saudi government to the socialist-led secession of South Yemen in 1994, settlement of the border conflict in 2000, security co-operation after 11 September 2001, backing of unruly tribes, direct military intervention along the Yemeni national army against 'Hûthî' rebels in 2009–10, and so on. Consequently, no predetermined interest seems to be able to structure these relations. While certain trends may seem significant, they should not overshadow other ones. The protagonists of these relations are themselves multiple, at times

---

[31] Gregory Gause, *Saudi-Yemeni Relations. Domestic Structures and Foreign Influence*, op. cit.

antagonistic. Patterns and cultures of businessmen are obviously not the same as those of religious clerics or diplomats and policemen in charge of security matters. Highlighting a specific foreign policy is therefore problematic as such policies often lack coherence and continuity.

Focusing on state-to-state relations only gives an incomplete image of the complex reality of the deep social and transnational relations. Likewise, state power does not necessarily help us understand the policy reversals, momentary and counter-intuitive alliances, the social and historical interpenetration of both populations and the different sometimes contradictory policies endorsed by the state itself.

Despite its obvious limits, the realist state-centred frame of analysis is quite consistently used (whether explicitly or not) when describing the relations between Saudi Arabia and Yemen, which are then reduced to interactions between two governments and to confrontations of unequal powers. As Madawi al-Rasheed and Robert Vitalis state:

The history of Saudi Arabian-Yemeni relations for many is a chronicle of antagonism, conflicts, and border disputes. Political scientists and specialists in international relations have charted the long conflict between the two countries in the twentieth century, from the first war of 1934 to the settlement of the border disputes in 2000. This preferential option for conflict unfortunately steered analysis away from a longer and more complex history of the intertwining of peoples that needs to be recovered.[32]

It is precisely the analysis of these phenomena of social interpenetration that I wish to recover throughout this study of the Salafi movement in contemporary Yemen and its complex and ambivalent relations with Saudi Arabia. Rather than a 'chronicle of antagonism', I intend to write an alternative narrative of the interpenetration of societies and religious fields. I aim to explore a relation that has been frequently talked about and often criticised but very rarely analysed. Through such a narrative, my ultimate goal is to show the coherence and integration of this region: societies in the Middle East are not always passive and controlled by the states and their interests. The 'actor-ness' of non-state-actors and their capacity to write their own history[33] must also be acknowledged. Indeed, history does not limit itself to 'big events' and is not only led

[32] Madawi al-Rasheed and Robert Vitalis (eds.), *Counter-Narratives. History, Contemporary Society, and Politics in Saudi Arabia and Yemen*, New York: Palgrave, 2004, p. 2.

[33] Eric R. Wolf, *Europe and the People Without History*, Berkeley: University of California Press, 1982.

or affected by 'providential' men and women. As such, it cannot either be reduced to the 'geo-political' designs and interests of the victorious and dominant. Minorities, indigenous peoples and contradictory voices must also be heard, even if they contradict the beautiful and coherent mechanism of dominant narratives.

In order to reach this objective, this monograph must go beyond the state-centred approach that only focuses on conflicts and neglects the trivial transnational interactions (or as they are sometimes labelled, 'translocal', then putting even more emphasis on the links between various localities and communities at the sub-national level)[34] occurring at the micro-social level, it must also go well beyond common sense and pretences that see the development of the Salafi movement in Yemen as a Trojan horse of Saudi interests. Indeed, rather than through large historical events and foreign policy objectives monopolised by the state, the transnational relations are more often than not shaped by daily and informal connections between individuals and groups. These links are not always purposely built as they do not systematically intend to satisfy a coherent objective that would, for instance, aim to transform the religious and political identities of targeted groups, try to undermine the control of a state over some of its citizens or seek to enhance the political domination of a foreign power. These transnational actors are not to be considered as mere puppets of state interests: on the contrary, their independence must be acknowledged.

These actors have the ability to bypass states and act within the specific social spaces that have appeared to fill the gaps of inter-state and institutionalised relations. Much of their interactions occur in what Peter Mandaville defines as 'translocality', stressing the local dimension and the 'situatedness' of these actors as well as their capacity to cross territories. These gaps are indeed never fully deterritorialised and disconnected from their local context as they connect places, imaginings, experiences and histories beyond borders. Peter Mandaville asserts:

[34] Although aware of the theoretical implications of the use of one term rather than the other, throughout the book I will more systematically refer to 'transnational relations' rather than to 'translocal' ones. This however does not imply that the geographic and sub-national dimensions of these relations will be ignored, much to the contrary. I refer to the broadest of definitions of 'transnationalism', as originally defined by Robert Keohane and Joseph Nye in 1971: transnational activities are 'contacts, coalitions, and interaction across state boundaries that are not controlled by the central foreign policy organs of governments'. Robert Keohane, Joseph Nye, *Transnational Relations and World Politics*, Cambridge: Harvard University Press, 1972, p. xi.

These new identity spaces are not by any means replacements for the state system as we know it. They do not provide structures for global governance, nor systems for the application of transnational justice. Gaps are not regimes. Rather, they contribute to plurality and hybridity in the world polity. We can also see them as trenches, the bunkers from which marginal identities combat the rigidities of institutionalised hegemony. Fluid creatures leak openly from their dilapidated habitats, mixing and matching as they encounter each other in travel.[35]

Inside these 'translocal spaces' or what James Rosenau once described as 'Frontiers',[36] ideas and norms travel and adapt to the different social, political and religious contexts. The daily individual and collective experience of globalisation then offers new resources and opportunities for the actors to use. Peter Mandaville goes on saying:

Translocality does not refer simply to a 'place', nor does it denote a collectivity of places. Rather it is an abstract (yet daily manifest) space occupied by the sum of linkages and connections between places (media, travel, import/export, etc.). The notion of locality is included within the term in order to suggest a situatedness, but a situatedness which is never static. Translocality can be theorised as a mode, one which pertains not to how peoples and cultures exist in places, but rather how they move through them. Translocality is hence a form of travel.[37]

This idea of transplantation[38] or travel, as formalised in the 1980s by Edward Said in his works on comparative literature,[39] is central to this study as it helps

---

[35] Peter Mandaville, *Transnational Muslim Politics: Reimagining the Umma*, London: Routledge, 2001, p. 97.

[36] James Rosenau defines the domestic-foreign Frontier as 'an under-organised domain with fragile sources of legitimacy, while in other respects nascent structures of authority can be discerned. Put differently, the Frontier is a *terra incognita* that sometimes takes the form of a market, sometimes appears as a civil society, sometimes resembles a legislative chamber, periodically is a crowded town square, occasionally is a battle-field, increasingly is traversed by an information highway, and usually looks like a several-ring circus in which all these—and many other—activities are unfolding simultaneously'. James Rosenau, *Along the Domestic-Foreign Frontier: Exploring Governance in a Turbulent World*, Cambridge: Cambridge University Press, 1997, p. 6.

[37] Peter Mandaville, *Transnational Muslim Politics: Reimagining the Umma*, p. 50.

[38] Developed in the 1980s by sociologists Felice Dassetto and Albert Bastenier, the concept of 'transplantation of Islam' in the European context has been defined as a 20th century 'social innovation' and perceived as problematic by large segments of the population. Felice Dassetto and Albert Bastenier, *L'islam transplanté. Vie et organisation des minorités musulmanes de Belgique*, Antwerp: Editions EPO, 1984.

[39] Edward Said, *The World, the Text and the Critic*, Cambridge: Harvard University

grasp the different dimensions and steps of the dissemination and social innovation processes. The theory that concepts and ideas adapt to their new context and face resistance when they travel is fundamental in my approach to analyse the Salafi movement in Yemen. I intend to show that Salafis are far more than the puppets disconnected from their social environment, which their adversaries describe. In doing so, I also intend to emphasise the 'multiple' and 'messy' dimensions of the 'constituent processes and outcomes'[40] of globalisation and transnationalism.

Through such a process, I mainly analyse these relations from a Yemeni perspective, doing my best to assess the 'intertwining of peoples' and the influence of dominant Saudi Arabia over the Salafi movement in the country. While such a perspective surely creates a bias as it largely overlooks the Saudi viewpoint (without however fully ignoring it), this predisposition allows to better confront the issue of domination with the capacity of certain religious actors to grow autonomous. A range of Saudi actors obviously intervened with the objective of establishing patronage networks through religious actors and with the intention of broadcasting a Salafi practice they deemed more authentic and pure than other interpretations of Islam that were dominant in Yemen. As a consequence, benevolent intentions were not necessarily absent, including among state actors.

Implementing a transnational perspective[41] in the Arabian Peninsula is surely not an easy task. It is a well-known fact that when Middle Eastern politics or societies are mentioned, many stereotypes, nonsense and confusion emerge. Social scientists are then left to go beyond these clichés and paradoxes, highlighting the contradictions of 'common knowledge' and dominant media as well as academic perspectives. Political scientists themselves often tend to consider that, when they have not failed, the Arab states are incomplete, that they are still in the process of construction and do not possess the 'normal' attributes of the modern state.[42] Despite their authoritarianism and their bureaucratic

---

Press, 1983, p. 226: 'Like people, and schools of criticism, ideas and theories travel—from person to person, from situation to situation, from one period to another. [...] Such movement into a new environment is never unimpeded. It necessarily involves processes of representation and institutionalisation different from those of the point of origin. This complicates any account of the transplantation, transference, circulation, and commerce of theories and ideas'.

[40] Steven Vertovec, *Transnationalism*, London: Routledge, 2009, p. 2.

[41] Thomas Risse-Kappen, 'Introduction' in Thomas Risse-Kappen (ed.), *Bringing Transnational Relations Back In*, op. cit., p. 3.

[42] The Arab or Middle-Eastern state has been the object of much debate and literature:

systems, Arab states are seen as incapable of obtaining the primary allegiance of their citizens. Infra-state or transnational solidarities through tribalism, religion and ethnicity directly affect the legitimacy and capacity of these states.

The famous (and yet often quite essentialist) concept of *'asabiyya'* used by Ibn Khaldûn and the works of modern day sociologists who focus on the Arab world and the broader notion of *umma* are used to illustrate one of the failures of the state being bypassed by other types of solidarity.

Quite oddly, when we turn to the discipline of international relations, the dominant approach seems to take for granted the fact that the Middle East is structured around the confrontation and competition between unitary states that seek to defend their national interest—power, influence, wealth—for themselves or for the sake of Western dominant powers that manipulate them through colonisation, the Cold War, domination or neo-imperialism. Despite the numerous studies in sociology, anthropology or political science that have highlighted the plurality of actors and the heterogeneous nature of the state,[43] dominant perspectives continue to only take into consideration the relations between states, wars and 'big events', thereby neglecting the processes of exchange, openness, mobility and change that are analysed by social scientists within these societies. Like the French and British colonial powers and the Ottoman empire that were capable of drawing borders and of creating nations from scratch up until the early twentieth century, Iran, Saudi Arabia or Syria are now regarded as the new driving forces around which regional politics structure themselves.

Nazih Ayubi, *Over-stating the Arab State: Politics and Society in the Middle East*, London: I.B. Tauris, 1995; Fred Halliday, *The Middle East in International Relations: Power, Politics and Ideology*, Cambridge: Cambridge University Press, 2005; Philippe Droz-Vincent, *Moyen-Orient: pouvoirs autoritaires, sociétés bloquées*, Paris: Presses Universitaires de France, 2004; Bertrand Badie, *Les deux États: pouvoir et société en Occident et en terre d'Islam*, Paris: Seuil, 1997; Giacomo Luciani, *The Arab State*, London: Routledge, 1990; Elizabeth Picard (ed.), *La politique dans le monde arabe*, Paris: Armand Colin, 2006 and Kiren Aziz Chaudhry, *The Price of Wealth: Economies and Institutions in the Middle East*, London: Cornell University Press, 1997.

[43] Among many other references on the plurality of actors and informal politics: Diane Singerman, *Avenues of Participation: Family, Politics, and Networks in Urban Quarters of Cairo*, Princeton: Princeton University Press, 1995; Patrick Haenni, *L'ordre des caïds: conjurer la dissidence urbaine au Caire* Paris: Karthala/Cedej, 2005; and Asef Bayat, *Street Politics: Poor People's Movements in Iran*, New York: Columbia University Press.

INTRODUCTION

While states in the Middle East are often deemed incapable of controlling their borders and territory and gaining their citizens' full allegiance, it is paradoxical to consider them as the sole (or even main) actors of regional and world politics.[44] Only taking into account state actors and governments is insufficient. One should therefore focus particularly on the actors that truly shape world politics on a daily basis. These are not necessarily the ones, like the states, that monopolise resources or that are able to 'write' history and shape narratives to their advantage. The domination and pre-eminence of the state, in the Middle East as elsewhere, is largely an illusion. Livelihoods are as often directly affected by informal interactions, commerce, migration and exchange as they are by laws, budgets, state policies or diplomatic meetings. Transnational relations have concrete social and political effects that should not be over-shadowed by inter-state relations or government strategies and objectives.

It goes without saying that these brief observations on the state and transnational relations do not mean that the state is automatically sidelined and should therefore be considered as a marginal actor. State policies, although not always effective, are never absent and play an important role. Consequently I do not over-rate the capacity of grassroots and transnational actors to bypass state decisions and act as moral actors that are 'better' or 'nicer' than states. I simply mean here to stress the importance of taking into account the fact that access to world politics no longer needs the mediation, the authorisation and the control of state actors. Moreover, the divide between inside and outside is no longer to be taken for granted.[45] As a consequence, the well ordered representation (or fiction) forged by the realist paradigm of international relations loses much of its capacity to explain social realities: loyalty to the state does not always prevail, and state control over its citizens can fail. Through highlighting the importance of transnational interactions, I certainly do not mean to regard them as sacred or to praise them simply because of the mere fact that they are 'transnational'.

Although I consider the transnational paradigm of particular interest, I never ignore the existence of other models and other actors, which may constitute useful and thought provoking approaches: I thereby try to avoid the

[44] Morten Valbjorn, 'Toward a 'Mesopotamian Turn': Disciplinarity and the Study of International Relations of the Middle East', *Journal of Mediterranean Studies*, vol. 14, no. 1, 2004, pp. 47–75.
[45] David Held, Anthony McGrew and David Goldblatt et al., *Global Transformations: Politics, Economics, and Culture*, Stanford: Stanford University Press, 1999, and Bertrand Badie, *Le diplomate et l'intrus*, Paris: Fayard, 2008.

pitfall of oversimplifying a complex reality just for the sake of creating an artificial theoretical coherence. States and transnational actors indeed often go hand-in-hand as their co-existence is not a zero sum game. The new security resources accumulated by Middle Eastern states in the post-9/11 context are not, for instance, correlated with any necessary decrease in transnational relations. Since the latter are often informal and take the shape of fragmented networks and representations, they are not automatically in contradiction with greater institutional control over certain specific fields (security, economy, bureaucracy, and so on).

Over the last twenty years, churches, brotherhoods, sects and other proselytisation and charitable religious organisations have increasingly become legitimate objects of analysis by readers of international relations. Buddhists in San Francisco, Muslims in Paris, Hindus in Dubai, Catholics in Tokyo or Mormons in Accra are just examples among many others of the transnationalisation and deterritorialisation of religious identities in an increasingly globalised world. Like multinational corporations, transnational advocacy networks[46] and epistemic communities,[47] religious groups have emerged in the academic discourse as figures of transnationality.[48] North/South migrations, the development of 'New Age' spiritualities or the more aggressive proselytisation actions of Muslim and Evangelical Protestant groups[49] are among the various incarnations of the international dissemination of the major world religions. Such a process is not only linked to a specific appetite and need to gain new followers and conquer new territories, but also the result of involuntary and non-proselytisation diffusion processes, especially through diasporas and migrations. While religious expansion has traditionally been linked to the political hegemony of particular powers or nation-states, as it was the case during the Muslim con-

---

[46] Margaret Keck, Kathryn Sikkink, *Activists Beyond Borders: Advocacy Networks in International Politics*, Ithaca: Cornell University Press, 1998.

[47] Peter Haas, *Knowledge, Power and International Policy Coordination*, Columbia: University of South Carolina Press, 1997.

[48] Among the vast literature on religion and transnationalism: Susanne Hoeber Rudolph and James Piscatori (ed.), *Transnational Religion and Fading States*, Boulder: Westview Press, 1997; Peter Beyer, *Religion and Globalisation*, London: Sage Publications, 1994; Scott Appleby, *The Ambivalence of the Sacred: Religion, Violence and Reconciliation*, Lanham: Rowman and Littlefield, 2000; and Roland Robertson, 'Globalisation, Politics, and Religion' in James and Thomas Luckmann (eds.), *The Changing Face of Religion*, London: Sage, 1989, pp. 10–23.

[49] Susan F. Harding, *The Book of Jerry Falwell. Fundamentalist Language and Politics*, Princeton: Princeton University Press, 2000.

quests, the colonial empires and missionary enterprises, the spread of religious identities nowadays seems much more complex. The individualisation of identities and the low level of institutionalisation and centralisation of the religious movements increase the capacity of these identities to adapt to local circumstances and environments. Consequently, designating a particular cradle or point of origin for these identities is more than often misleading as it ignores such an adaptation process.

The resurgence of religious actors, which few social scientists had anticipated, takes many different shapes and has become a privileged way of contesting both internally and internationally existing political orders. It reshapes individual loyalties, often diverting them from the state and plays a central role in the emergence of new actors, that may not necessarily be powerful, but that have emerged as major disruptors of the contemporary post-Cold War world order.[50]

However, it would be erroneous to consider that the transnationalisation of religion is a new phenomenon. Through pilgrimage, travel and faith have always existed in pairs.[51] Building on contemporary examples, many monographs have focused on the capacity of religious actors to create networks and bypass states, and they have also analysed their connections with transnational economic or political actors.[52] Religious transnational relations are therefore not only the concern of priests, muftis, monks, rabbis or, in a nutshell, religious institutions. One should also take into account larger groups and phenomena that bind religious actors to earthly matters.

Whatever their destination or origin, transnational religious flows are often linked to an expansion process and represent a quest for 'new markets' by religious entrepreneurs. Such a proselytism is designed to spread new norms and thus affect the livelihoods and loyalties of the actors involved. As such, it

[50] Olivier Roy, *Globalized Islam: The Search for the New Ummah*, New York: Columbia University Press, 2004.

[51] Dale Eickelman and James Piscatori (eds.), *Muslim Travellers: Pilgrimage, Migration, and the Religious Imagination*, Los Angeles: University of California Press, 1990.

[52] For such connections in different contexts, see among others: Jérôme Bellion-Jourdan, 'Les réseaux transnationaux islamiques en Bosnie-Herzégovine' in Xavier Bougarel and Nathalie Clayer (eds.), *Le nouvel Islam balkanique*, Paris: Maisonneuve et Larose, 2001, pp. 429–472; Andre Corten and Ruth Marshall-Fratani (eds.), *From Babel to Pentecost: Transnational Pentecostalism in Africa and Latin America*, London: Hurst, 2001; Miriam Cooke and Bruce Lawrence (eds.), *Muslim Networks from Hajj to Hip Hop*, London: University of Carolina Press, 2005 and more particularly Engseng Ho, 'Empire through Diasporic Eyes: A View from the Other Boat', *Comparative Studies in Society and History*, vol. 46, no. 2, 2004, pp. 210–246.

cannot be totally disconnected from the balance of power, the issues of domination and the competition between social and political groups at the international level. Religious actors are not in a vacuum and do not totally escape the contingencies of world politics and inter-state relations. Having said that, the logic that mechanically turns religion into a variable of domination or an instrument of imperialism able to shape allegiances is probably overstated as it underestimates the autonomy of transnational actors vis-à-vis states and national interests. Such a state-centred and over-simplistic approach seeks to reveal the strategy and intentionality that lie behind the religious and spiritual discourse and turns religion into a kind of Trojan horse promoting larger state interests and 'big politics'.

An alternative approach to transnational religion takes transnationalism seriously by recognising the agency of non-state actors and the possibility for them to have a specific agenda, one that is separate from that of the state. Within this framework, in-depth studies of religious movements, particularly of Protestant networks in Latin America and Muslim networks in Western Europe,[53] underlined the multiple and antagonistic effects that the actual 'travelling' had on religious actors: they highlighted the latter's capacity to adapt both their behaviour and their doctrine to the new environment. This research also emphasised the capacity of these religious actors to divert themselves from relations of domination. This alternative and rigorous approach is best suited to help grasp the complexities of religious phenomena including religious expansion, and invitations to reassess the links between states, transnational relations and religion.

The Yemeni Case-Study

In terms of state/religion relations, Yemen appears as a fascinating case study. It allows one to analyse the development of Salafism and transnational religious relations in an environment that remained non-repressive for many years. As such, and probably more than anywhere in the Middle East, it was well into the end of the 2000s decade a privileged post of observation for many academics

[53] Jean-Pierre Bastian, Françoise Champion and Kathy Rousselet (eds.), *La globalisation du religieux*, Paris: L'Harmattan, 2001; Ariel Colonomos, *Églises en réseaux: trajectoires politiques en Europe et Amérique*, op. cit.; Peter Mandaville, *Transnational Muslim Politics: Reimagining the Umma*, op. cit.; Katy Gardner, *Global Migrants, Local Lives: Travel and Transformation in Rural Bangladesh*, Oxford: Clarendon Press, 1995.

who could have access to many different sources without being constantly harassed by the various intelligence services. The same went for the political and religious movements themselves (although not all of them): they indeed had the opportunity to develop in an environment that was not exclusively shaped by violence and confrontation. The high degree of integration of the different components of the political spectrum, as well as the relatively low level of repression against the Islamist 'opposition' (including Salafis, but excluding the Zaydis since 2004 and the Sa'da war), represented two core characteristics of the political system that developed in North Yemen after the end of the civil war of the 1960s. The country was by no means a democracy and suffered from endemic corruption, underdevelopment as well as upsurges of brutality, yet it had not experienced comparable levels of state-sponsored violence, as in the case of Saddâm Husayn's Iraq, or the same deprivation of political liberties, as in the Saudi monarchy. It had not been confronted with massive bloodshed or repression as it happened in Algeria in the 1990s or Egypt in the 1970s, whether from the state, the army or rebel factions. However, things have turned slowly but surely, giving way to brutish repression of its own citizens in the framework of the Sa'da war, in Southern governorates as well as against the opposition, and a shrinking of public freedoms throughout the second half of the 2000s decade.

Since the early ages of Islam, religion has been closely associated with political power in the Yemeni highlands and coastal areas. The fall of the Zaydi imam's monarchy in 1962 marked a great rupture as it put an end to over a millennium of religious ruling and gave way to a more direct separation between politics and religion in Yemen. This secular regime took the shape of a republican system inspired by Jamâl 'Abd al-Nâsir's model in Egypt. Yet the modernisation of the state and society neither in North Yemen nor in South Yemen (though it had experienced until 1967 British colonisation and remained until 1990 the only proper socialist Arab state), did not really undermine the influence of the religious and traditional political actors. The same can be said of the unification of both Yemens in May 1990.

The relationship between the state and the different political groups, particularly the Islamists, and the integration of these various tendencies into public institutions, army, police and universities, to quote but a few, as well as the establishment of patronage links with the main tribes, particularly the Hâshid and Bakîl confederations, were probably the key to understanding the relative political stability of Yemen, something that few would have anticipated when 'Alî 'Abd Allâh Sâlih came to power in 1978. Whether this relatively long-lasting stability had been the result of a deliberate strategy on the part of the regime that aimed at weakening its enemies and dividing political and religious groups or was the unintended outcome of its sheer incapacity, for better or for worse, power-sharing was one of the main features of the Yemeni system up until the late 2000s decade. The presence of a strong traditional 'civil society' in the form of tribal and religious groups largely armed and capable of opposing the state, had persistently undermined the regime's capacity to monopolise all the levers of power and fulfil its authoritarian dreams.

Earlier on, the 1962 republican revolution had been supported by Nasserist Egypt that had sent troops to Yemen for five years in order to fight the Saudi-backed royalist opposition. The republican regime was uncompromising at first, but soon held dialogue with the Zaydi-royalists as well as the tribal groups, especially those who had initially opposed the republic. From 1967 onward, the Yemeni government sought to reintegrate a minority of the former royalists through striking compromises. Some Zaydi clerics were given high positions, including the prestigious rank of *muftî* of the republic.

Affiliates of the Muslim Brotherhood were a central proponent of the system. As in other countries, they focused most of their attention on forging the education system to their advantage. In 1967, one of their leaders, 'Abd al-Mâlik al-Tayyib, was appointed Minister of Education in North Yemen. During the 1970s, a radical member of the Muslim Brotherhood, 'Abd al-Majîd al-Zindânî, was in charge of religious education and Egyptian and Sudanese teachers educated in religious universities, including the famous Cairo-based al-Azhâr, were recruited.

This power-sharing with the Islamists turned more political in the 1990s. While the unification was initially built on a partnership between the two former ruling parties of North and South Yemen, northern elites were eager to find new allies. In 1993, after the first multiparty general elections, 'Abd al-Majîd al-Zindânî became one of the five members of the presidential council, while 'Abd Allâh al-Ahmar, a prominent tribal leader from the Hâshid confederation and the head of al-Islâh,[54] was elected speaker of the parliament

---

[54] *al-Tajammu' al-yamani lil-islâh* (Yemeni Congregation for Reform) or al-Islâh is the main opposition political party in Yemen. It was founded in 1990 and draws together tribal elites along with businessmen around a core of members of the Muslim Brotherhood. Jillian Schwedler, *Faith in Moderation, Islamist Parties in Jordan and Yemen*, New York: Cambridge University Press, 2006; Laurent Bonnefoy and Marine Poirier, 'The Yemeni Congregation for Reform (al-Islâh): The Difficult Process of Building a Project for Change' in Myriam Catusse and Karam Karem (eds.) *Returning to Political Parties? Partisan Logic and Political Transformations in the Arab World*,

thanks to the votes of the ruling General People's Congress (GPC) party's MPs. As tensions arose within the coalition, pitting the socialist leaders against the Northern political establishment, 'Alî 'Abd Allâh Sâlih decided to govern together with al-Islâh. The Muslim Brotherhood directly participated in the successive governments between 1993 and 1997, playing an even greater role after the 1994 war and the complete demise of the socialists. 'Abd al-Wahhâb al-Anisî was appointed Deputy Prime Minister, and other al-Islâh members were entrusted with important ministerial portfolios (justice, education, trade and religious affairs).

While al-Islâh's participation in the government was interrupted in 1997, the integration of all kinds of Islamist groups into the state apparatus continued both formally and informally. Many important positions in the army and security forces were held by individuals identified as Islamists of all streams. This is well illustrated by the case of one of the regime's most controversial figures, 'Ali Muhsin al-Ahmar, a close kin of President 'Ali 'Abd Allah Salih and head of an army brigade based in Sana'a, but who would eventually become of its most resolute opponents in 2011. The repression of Islamist groups, although existing, has long been limited. Salafis, Sufis, some Zaydis, members of the Muslim Brotherhood and even some individuals sympathetic to jihadi doctrines continue, despite the United States' harsh criticism, and have for a long time enjoyed easy access to political and tribal elites. Within such a context, unlike in many other countries, religion, 'values', 'vocabulary' and 'ethics' were not the principal dividing lines between the government and the opposition.[55]

The Saudi leaders have also based much of their rule on their relations with the religious elite. It is generally acknowledged that the Saudi state, as early as the mid-eighteenth century, drew its legitimacy through a pact with a religious group then organised around Muhammad Bin 'Abd al-Wahhâb.[56] This pact is said to still be active and represents a cornerstone of the contemporary Saudi regime and of much of its foreign policy. While such a narrative is probably simplistic, as it ignores the numerous tensions, violence and repression that

Beirut: Lebanese Center for Policy Studies, 2010 and Paul Dresch and Bernard Haykel, 'Stereotypes and Political Styles: Islamists and Tribesfolk in Yemen', *International Journal of Middle East Studies*, no. 27, 1995, pp. 405–431.

[55] François Burgat, 'Le Yémen islamiste entre universalisme et insularité' in Rémy Leveau, Frank Mermier and Udo Steinbach (eds.), *Le Yémen contemporain*, Paris: Karthala, 1999, pp. 236–237.

[56] David Commins, *The Wahhabi Mission in Saudi Arabia*, London: I.B. Tauris, 2006.

occurred between the Âl Su'ûd and the religious 'Wahhâbî' establishment and other religious groups, it gives a sense of the important position clerics enjoyed inside and within the state.[57] As in Yemen, but in a more institutionalised way, the different rulers of the Saudi kingdom have sought to co-opt the religious actors and include them into the state apparatus, whereby they somehow blurred the borders of the opposition. Indeed, in both countries, being an Islamist willing to restore the legitimacy of the religious discourse in politics does not necessarily equate with being an opponent. In this context, governments or, more precisely, some individuals inside the governments have often turned a blind eye or even actually supported the transnational activities of religious activists. Such permissiveness represents a great opportunity for these actors and adds surely a new dimension to the issue of transnationalism that is of great interest to my study. The connections that I am focusing on throughout this research might be seen as being in opposition to the state as much as they can be interpreted as attuned with it.

Salafism in Yemen, Transnational Relations and Social Change

Building on the transnational paradigm of international relations, I intend throughout this book to analyse the diversity of the Salafi movement in Yemen focusing more specifically on its relations with Saudi Arabia, both as a sponsor and as an ideological reference. How 'Saudi' is Salafism in Yemen? How important is the role played by Saudi-proselytising policies in the development of the Yemeni Salafi movement, at the level of both the religious entrepreneurs and the grassroots? Are Salafi activists more loyal to Saudi Arabia than other religious or political actors? The focus here is clearly not on the so-called jihadi fringe of Salafism, one that has received much attention due to its links to al-Qaeda and its participation in various conflicts inside and outside of Yemen. Jihadi-Salafis, whose actions are obviously visible, are nevertheless not easily (if ever) accessible to researchers. Furthermore, their development in opposition to states (although links may have existed) and their antisystemic doctrine imply a different set of questions than the one I have chosen to work on. Focusing on the quietist branch of Salafism that has developed in Yemen around

---

[57] On the state/religion relations in Saudi Arabia: Steffen Hertog, *Princes, Brokers, and Bureaucrats: Oil and the State in Saudi Arabia*, Ithaca: Cornell University Press, 2010; Pascal Ménoret, *L'énigme saoudienne: Les Saoudiens et le monde (1744–2003)*, op. cit. and Alexei Vassiliev, *The History of Saudi Arabia*, London: Saqi Books, 1998.

Muqbil al-Wâdi'î, I would like to question the capacity of dominant states to actually control transnational actors whether inside their own territory or in other countries' territories and societies. Rather than assuming that these transnational actors are only extensions or instruments of a given state-power, I initially hypothesise the opposite, reversing the point of departure of the dominant narratives and stating that they are largely autonomous. Such a stance does not imply that I will consider this autonomy as a given throughout my research. On the contrary, I allow myself as I proceed the scope for re-evaluating the religious actors' position.

The main hypothesis of my work is the following: the interactions between the religious actors in Yemen and Saudi Arabia are not primarily the result of strategies of influence between states or even between societies. Consequently, state-centred approaches focusing on (soft or hard) power and on imperialism (be it cultural or not) are only partial as they omit most of the Saudi-Yemeni contemporary religious relations. Despite manifest proselytism by institutions identified with the Saudi state, the emergence of Salafism in the Yemeni context is mostly the result of transformations, dynamics and recompositions occurring at the local, global and translocal levels. As such, it is important to acknowledge the triviality of the transnational relations, even when these are religious, as they are the result of ordinary and daily interactions rather than being shaped by exceptional/historic events and big politics. Salafis, whatever the extent to which they are affected by the different transnational flows (religious, commercial, migratory, political, and so on) are able to adapt their strategies, practices and actions to the social context in which they are embedded. They therefore swing between the local and the global and sometimes mixing the two, using the resources they have capitalised, juggling with references and transplanting them in different environments, thereby establishing flexible networks.[58]

Obviously, my aim is not to systematically pit an exogenous dynamic (the process of importing or exporting Salafism) against various endogenous phenomena (social and political recompositions) as that would be tantamount to rehabilitating the old, and unhelpful, boundary between domestic and foreign politics. I rather aim at highlighting the complex social dynamics occurring within communities as well as between them. I consider these dynamics as

[58] The transposition of transnational resources at the local level has been the object of much work by Saskia Sassen, *Globalisation and its Discontents*, New York: New Press, 1998 and *The Global City: New York, London, Tokyo*, Princeton: Princeton University Press, 1991.

daily evidences and manifestations of integration in the Arabian Peninsula. The individual experience of migration, the shifts in religious identities, the emergence of translocal elites and the effects of the 'Global War on Terror' are just a few examples among others of the interpenetration and interdependence of societies. Nevertheless, domestic structures and institutions have their importance as they constrain transnational actors. In the case of Salafism, they explain the fact that the partisans of this political and religious doctrine have to adapt to their environment. As a consequence, Salafism does not bear the same significance in Yemen as it does in Saudi Arabia. It is mainly for this reason that the state, however dominant, has trouble controlling its development abroad both at grassroots level and at the level of the entrepreneurs.

The essentialist and simplistic image of Saudi Arabia must be challenged, for example by pointing to the excesses of post-9/11 'Saudi bashing' as an unhelpful distortion of reality. Such a project is not a way of absolving Saudi Arabia, state and society, of its responsibilities, nor does it imply denying the fact its government's policies might have played a role in the development of Islamist groups in a globalised world. It is rather a way of acknowledging the diversity of the Saudi society and state and of taking seriously the non-state actors' independence and capacity to adapt to local contexts. It is finally, as Prasenjit Duara states, a way of 'rescuing history from the nation,'[59] that is, of dissociating as much as possible the emergence of Salafism in Yemen from a largely constructed and at times fantasised Saudi national interest. More bluntly, I wish to go beyond the partial and biased interpretation of the transnational flows as an expression of the power differential between the two states.

The identification of a religious dimension in transnational relations should not be restrictive. Functions are indeed never completely partitioned. Having said that, traders, tourists and workers may well participate in the religious interpenetration of societies, and they play a role in the transformation of religious identities across borders. My focus therefore goes well beyond imams, pilgrims and religious shaykhs. Grassroots actors and anonymous activists are also central to this study as they are the daily vehicles of ideas and practices in the process of transnational relations. In this framework, the analysis of Salafi doctrine is important to understand the transnational relations between Yemen and Saudi Arabia insofar as it is confronted with the different actors' behaviour, as these might well be inconsistent and contradictory. Highlighting the flexibil-

---

[59] Prasenjit Duara, *Rescuing History from the Nation: Questioning Narratives of Modern China*, op. cit.

ity of religious observance is as important as focusing on its coherence and the rigidity of its implementation. The very demanding doctrine of Salafism which perceives itself as being in rupture with society is no exception.

Recent works by François Burgat and Mohamed Sbitli,[60] Bernard Haykel,[61] Olivier Roy,[62] Bernard Rougier,[63] Madawi al-Rasheed,[64] Stéphane Lacroix,[65] Roel Meijer,[66] Thomas Hegghammer,[67] Saba Mahmood[68] and Quintan Wiktorowicz[69] have focused on the Salafi doctrine and its activists in various contexts. Although definitions as well as approaches differ as some do focus more specifically on the issue of violence and terrorism, these publications are all important sources of inspiration. Nevertheless, this book is essentially the result of my own extensive fieldwork in numerous parts of Yemen and more marginally in Saudi Arabia's two main cities: Riyadh and Jeddah.

For different reasons linked particularly to the local and global contexts of the 'War on Terror' and certain specificities of the Salafi doctrine, conducting my research has not always been an easy task. Since June 2004 when I started my work, the brutal war between the Yemeni army and some Zaydi revivalist groups in the north of Yemen has severely limited my mobility in that region.

[60] François Burgat and Mohamed Sbitli, 'Les salafis au Yémen ou ... la modernisation malgré tout', op. cit. and François Burgat, *L'islamisme à l'heure d'al-Qaida*, Paris : La Découverte, 2005.

[61] Bernard Haykel, *Revival and Reform in Islam. The Legacy of Muhammad al-Shawkânî*, op. cit.

[62] Olivier Roy, *Holy Ignorance. When Religion and Culture Diverge*, New York: Columbia University Press, 2010 and Olivier Roy, *Globalized Islam. The Search for a New Ummah*, op. cit.

[63] Bernard Rougier (ed.), *Qu'est ce que le salafisme?*, Paris: Presses universitaires de France, 2008.

[64] Madawi al-Rasheed, *Contesting the Saudi State: Islamic Voices from a New Generation*, Cambridge: Cambridge University Press, 2007.

[65] Stéphane Lacroix, *Les islamistes saoudiens: une insurrection manquée*, Paris: Presses universitaires de France, 2009.

[66] Roel Meijer (ed.), *Global Salafism: Islam's New Religious Movement*, London: Hurst/ Columbia University Press, 2009.

[67] Thomas Hegghammer, *Jihad in Saudi Arabia. Violence and Pan-Islamism since 1979*, Cambridge: Cambridge University Press, 2010.

[68] Saba Mahmood, *The Politics of Piety: The Islamic Revival and the Feminist Subject*, Princeton: Princeton University Press, 2005.

[69] Quintan Wiktorowicz, *The Management of Islamic Activism: Salafis, the Muslim Brotherhood, and State Power in Jordan*, Bloomington: Indiana University Press, 2001.

As a result, I have never been granted access to Sa'da, one of the historical cradles of Salafism in the country, where Muqbil al-Wâdi'î established his institute. Apart from such a restriction on my movements I was able to roam over much of Yemen (in Sana'a, the capital city, but also Aden, Ta'iz, Ibb and Wâdî Hadramawt) over a total of four years. In addition, I focused intensively on Yâfi', a mountainous region, north-east of Aden, where I was able to establish sustained ties with a community of Salafi students from the Faculty of Education in the town of Lab'ûs. In all these regions, without being directly confronted by a combat zone or a dangerous field, I had to adapt my own methodology. Intellectual and physical investment was sensitive and problematic as my work was at times seen as intrusive by the Yemeni authorities who even warned me against Saudi intelligence services as well as the Salafis themselves.

Another parameter came to make the relations I eventually built with Salafi activists even more complex. The apolitical claim of their doctrine and the fact that the Salafis, or at least the quietist fringe I was focusing on, that Quintan Wiktorowicz would formally label as 'purist Salafis'[70] and Bernard Rougier 'literalist'[71] ones, preferred to stay away from a corrupt society, not mingle with politics but rather focus on strictly religious issues were core obstacles in my research as this stance actually limited the interactions and the scope of the discussion with the informants. The interview I conducted with Muhammad al-Imâm, one of the leading figures of the Salafi movement after Muqbil al-Wâdi'î's death, is quite illustrative. Knowing I was not a Muslim, he had reluctantly accepted to talk to me in his office in Ma'bar, 70 kilometres south of Sana'a, and ended up delivering a monologue about the numerous advantages of being Muslim. When I tried to go on with the interview and ask him more precise questions about the Salafi creed, regarding especially the issue of political participation, he bluntly answered: 'These are matters you will eventually learn after you have become a Muslim; they are too complicated for you now'.[72] The conversation was over. Without any political issues (Palestine, American foreign policy, elections, local politics, and so on) as shared entry points, interacting with and being accepted by Salafis was not self-evident or at least much more difficult than it would have been with politicised Islamists, even radical ones. With the Salafis, I wondered: would they even accept to talk to me? On

---

[70] Quintan Wiktorowicz, 'Anatomy of the Salafi Movement', *Studies in Conflict and Terrorism*, vol. 9, no. 3, 2006, pp. 207–239.

[71] Bernard Rougier, 'Introduction' in Bernard Rougier (ed.), *Qu'est ce que le salafisme?*, op. cit., p. 15.

[72] Interview, Ma'bar, October 2004.

which basis could we be in interaction? Would we be able to bridge the gaps? Would they ever consider me as something else than a 'potential convert' or a 'hopeless unbeliever'? Winning their trust in the faculty in Yâfiʿ was surely a challenge, yet not always an unpleasant one, which took weeks, numerous rounds of observation and a lot of energy. As I proceeded, I was fully aware of the great fragility of my access to the field and the actors since one wrong step, one misunderstanding could potentially annihilate months of effort.

Throughout my research, I did my best to stay in close contact with the actors, their daily experiences and life stories. In doing so, I tried to understand why and how a new political and religious practice, deemed exogenous, managed to fit into the Yemeni environment and how embedded it actually was. In exploring this matter, I distinguished different levels and scales. These are perceived as complementary and will often interweave in my chapters. The micro/macro distinction then appears as artificial. Steven Vertovec rightly states that 'the scales, spaces and mechanisms of globalisation and transnationalism are just too entangled to allow such clear abstractions'.[73] The micro, the macro, bottom-up and top-down processes, the individual and the collective overlap, all being interdependent yet they cannot be analysed as completely separate phenomena. The first level is concerned with theorists, emblematic figures and the Salafi entrepreneurs, who are the main agents of the emergence of the movement. Among these, personalities such as Muqbil al-Wâdiʿî, Muhammad al-Imâm, Ahmad Hasan al-Muʿallim or Abû al-Hasan al-Maʾribî are central. Through their *fatâwâ*, controversies and rivalries in the political and religious fields, they have forged the Salafi doctrine and circumscribed a movement whose principles, ideas, practices, roots and relations with Saudi Arabia can be constituted as an object of studies. In order to fulfil that objective, an abundant literature exists (recorded conferences and sermons, pamphlets, essays, magazines, and so on). The one hundred or so audio cassettes[74] and dozens of books I have gathered from Salafi bookshops in Sanaʾa, Aden, Tarîm, Maʿbar, Labʿûs but also Jeddah and Riyadh are fundamental resources

---

[73] Steven Vertovec, *Transnationalism*, op. cit., p. 3.

[74] Dating the publications (books and pamphlets) and audio recordings is a difficult task as data is often missing. Information can be drawn from the context or from what the cleric says, but most often it is impossible to actually tell when the conference was given. Consequently, drawing a precise chronology of the publications and history of the Salafi movement as a whole proved very difficult. Since the 1980s, audio cassette recordings have become a cheap and efficient instrument of propaganda in Yemen, where significant proportions of the population are illiterate.

that were cross-checked and completed by, more or less formal, interviews with academics, journalists, intellectuals and 'ulamâ'.

The second level deals with the anonymous activists and followers of the Salafi dogma. Understanding the behaviour of these sympathisers implies a different type of investigation[75] as their practice is not limited to a doctrine or an ideology. This investigation is analysed within a larger framework of individual trajectories and specific social practices. Such a micro-social approach has only been possible through a lengthy personal investment in the field. The second level, largely structured around informal networks of kinship, friendship or rivalry, also embodies the concrete emergence of Salafism in Yemeni society. It underlines its dynamism, as well as its links with transnational or translocal phenomena. Much of my data derive from first-hand observation and participation in the Faculty of Education in Yâfi': religious classes' attendance, lengthy discussions and qat chews with Salafis (at least those who accept to chew) and their rivals, informal gatherings, short trips in the countryside and longer ones to Aden, and even ping-pong games were among the different (at times surprising) opportunities available that helped me grasp the Salafi universe in all its complexity. These informal means, which may at first sight seem 'unscientific', nevertheless allowed me to sketch an alternative picture of Salafism, one that happens to be different from that which books and formal interviews compiled in an 'ivory tower' would have drawn. My technique of investigation probably builds a less coherent and structured image, but I con-

---

[75] The strict gender separation in Yemeni society in general, and particularly among Salafis, necessarily renders my conclusions male-biased. Indeed, I never had access to the female dimensions of Salafism. This incapacity to gather data on half of Yemeni society cannot be overcome for obvious reasons. I am fully conscious of this shortcoming and would welcome any contribution on the Salafi female perspective to complement, support or qualify my findings. However, I always tried my best to keep in mind that Salafism is in no way an exclusively masculine phenomenon. Numerous female students are present in the different Salafi institutes and some female clerics (the most famous being the wife and daughters of Muqbil al-Wâdi'î) have even published books dealing with matters such as marriage and gender issues. In Egypt, a women's pietistic religious movement, similar to the Salafi fringe I study, has been the focus of Saba Mahmood, *The Politics of Piety: The Islamic Revival and the Feminist Subject*, op. cit. In Yemen, Anne Meneley analysed the transformation of piety and modesty throughout the 1990s and the development of literalist religious interpretations, Anne Meneley, 'Fashions and Fundamentalisms in Fin-de-siècle Yemen. Chador Barbie and Islamic Socks', *Cultural Anthropology*, vol. 22, no. 2, 2007, pp. 214–243.

clude with a narrative that, in my opinion, is true to the Salafis' everyday livelihoods and aspirations. When compared to the first level of Salafi thinkers, the trajectories of these 'ordinary' Salafis reveal the flexibility, fluidity and malleability of their daily practices: hard-core apolitical Salafis may for instance progressively engage in political processes, they may value apparently contradictory references or *'ulamâ'*, find over time daily compromises with the society or build bridges with violent fringes. At the grassroots level, these actors are engaged in a complex process of adaptation that makes them distance themselves from the constraining Salafi model they nevertheless continue to admire. In the end the adherence to the theological principles advocated by the *'ulamâ'* appears to be quite relative. Taking into account such flexible behaviours also enables me throughout the book to demystify Salafism, that is, to see it as a mundane social practice embedded in its environment rather than solely a rigid religious doctrine and a fixed essence. Once again, this emphasis does not imply any attempt to vindicate Salafism from certain upsurges in violence and stigmatisation that do occur.

Travelling Salafism: Mythical Origins and Adapted Practices

The structure of this book is rather straightforward: it follows much of the physical and conceptual process of travel of Salafism, from its mythical origins, its original doctrine and ideal-type to the adapted practices. It builds an alternative approach to the development of Salafism in the Yemeni environment since the early 1980s, reassessing its relations with Saudi Arabia defined as a state, a nation, a society and a reference. As we will see, such a line of travel or 'transplantation' is by no means chronological nor is it linear: the different stages turned into chapters are more often than not simultaneous.

While writing this book, I too have written a story or as I said earlier, a narrative that can and should be scrutinised, deconstructed and contested. Highlighting the role of societies rather than that of states and national interests in the emergence of this religious and political movement is a choice in itself: as a consequence, certain actors and phenomena have been put under the spotlight while others have received less attention. Nevertheless, I have never ignored or obliterated processes simply for the sake of building a coherent narrative that would assert that transnational actors are always independent, that they roam freely and that states are nowadays bypassed and incapable of controlling non-state actors. If the structure of the book intends to be quite simple, the image of the Salafi movement that is sketched throughout the following chapters is one of intense complexity and subtle nuances. Quite clearly, it is not meant to satisfy policymakers in the quest for easy definitions and classifications in which they could categorise friends or foes in the contemporary Islamic world. Salafism in Yemen, despite the existence of an identified core of common practices and concerns, is shaped by contradictory trends, some leaning backwards or towards modernity, others leading to stigmatisation or compromise, dependence or autonomy, peace or violence. As such, it is extremely diverse. Rather than focusing on doctrines and labels, I strove to let individual trajectories and destinies play their role and guide me through. I voluntarily chose to highlight the complexity of the movement, taking into account its diversity, internal debates, fluidity, and, above all, its ability to adapt, as well as its inconsistencies and contradictions. I placed societies and non-state actors in the spotlight, paying attention to actors that are often ignored or deemed marginal.

The 'travel' or spread of Salafism involves three different steps that are mirrored in the three parts and the seven chapters of this book. In the first part, comprising Chapters One and Two, I provide a general presentation of Salafism as an ideal-type, as a point of origin or departure, defining its doctrine and specificities and analysing the main proponents and characters of this religious and political movement. Chapter One is an attempt to define Salafism and allows me to present the different 'players' on the Yemeni Salafi scene. Chapter Two analyses more precisely the way quietist Salafis interact with the state and society, also looking into their relation to violence. Both these chapters draw their data mainly from Salafi publications and put these in perspective with some of the practices of their leaders both past and present.

The second part is devoted to the process of travel of Salafism *per se*. Chapter Three looks at the way Saudi and Yemeni relations, particularly migration flows and phenomena of domination, are central in understanding the development of Salafism in contemporary Yemen. Chapter Four focuses on how transnational flows and dependence on Saudi Arabia are themselves both a resource for the Salafis and something they are trying to get away from. My general argument is then checked against the Yâfi'i case study in Chapter Five in which I analyse at the micro-social level the implantation of Salafism in a small community of students and teachers. My ethnographic findings stress the largely 'spontaneous' development of Salafism in this specific context. Although Yâfi' is far from the Saudi border, informal translocal relations do actually link both spaces and societies. In the absence of any specific Saudi proselytisation policies, without any prominent institutes, institutions, mosques, bookshops or entrepreneurs, Salafism emerged there as a kind of flexible 'sub-culture' that anonymous activists or supporters adopted as a starting point in life before forging their own individual trajectories.

The final section of the book, highlights the adaptation of the Salafi doctrine to the Yemeni environment, in what can be seen as the final stage of the Salafi movement's line of travel. Chapter Six accounts for the important variables that are the other competing religious and political identities present in Yemen, particularly the Zaydis, the Sufis and the Muslim Brotherhood. It focuses on the rivalry between these religious and political actors and looks into the way identity and 'Yemenisation' are central stakes in this competition. Chapter Seven shows that far from being disconnected from today's society, as Salafis claim themselves, Salafism appears to be highly embedded in local issues and to have normalised itself in the Yemeni landscape: internal debates, for instance, are generally Yemeni-centred. The movement, as a result of the efforts by the Salafi entrepreneurs to impose themselves as legitimate endogenous actors, participates in the Yemeni political game, the state having frequently instrumentalised it.

PART 1

DOCTRINE AND PRACTICE

1

FRAMING SALAFISM

I. The Vocation of Salafism

The Salafi Reform Project

Over the last fifteen years, the terms 'Salafism' and 'Wahhabism' have clearly gained a degree of recognition in public discourse in Europe and North America, as well as among academics across the globe. In the context of the Algerian civil war of the 1990s, and in what has been called a post-9/11 world, these two -isms have been taken as constituting a new menace, and as synonymous with terrorism, 'jihadism', or Islamic fundamentalism.[1] The two are often mistaken for each other. Salafism and Wahhabism in this context play to perfection their role as 'rhetorical foils'.[2]

In relation to concepts of 'Islamism' that academic debates and media handling have used up or worn out, assigning it negative connotations and mean-

---

[1] Examples of such stigmatisation of Salafism are numerous. On Feb.26, 2006, speaking to the French National Assembly, Nicolas Sarkozy, at that time Minister of the Interior, said that 'Salafist literature' had been found by police in the house of Youssef Fofana, accused of having assassinated Ilan Halimi. Such a discovery was then implicitly supposed to indicate that the purpose of this hate crime was anti-Semitic. During 2009 and 2010, the public debate in France over a prohibition on wearing a 'face veil' (burqa or niqab) was polarised with regard to the question of Salafism, and with regard to the necessity of countering the development of that political and religious movement in French society.

[2] Alexander Knysh, 'A Clear and Present Danger: 'Wahhabism' as a Rhetorical Foil', *Die Welt Des Islams*, vol. 44, no. 1, 2004, pp. 3–26.

ings that it did not have originally among academics, the terms 'Salafism' and Wahhabism' seem to be part of specialists' jargon, intended to legitimise the one using it. These terms extend and continue the expert discourse of the matter and their continued use creates an argument from authority that is difficult to defeat. However, the terms are not interchangeable, but must be defined as clearly as possible.

Without question, the events of September 11, 2001 have promoted the spread of a certain literature that appears 'scientific' but which tries either to condemn or to rehabilitate a Wahhabi or Salafi ideology that has usually been constructed to serve the purposes of its different authors. In the book *Terror's Source*, for exemple,[3] Vincenzo Oliveti bluntly and without proper qualification assumes that the 'ideology of Wahhabo-Salafism' is at the root of the terrorism of al-Qaeda. Conversely, Natana DeLong-Bas presents readers with the biased and almost hagiographic intellectual biography of the founder of Wahhabism and attempts to portray his thought as modernist and tolerant.[4] By the very fact of their conclusions, so diametrically opposed, these two extremes of the broad spectrum of such publications prove the uselessness of all definitions of Wahhabism or Salafism based solely upon theological or political writings that are several centuries old, without regard for the current or past practices of actors. A more document-based (and certainly more objective) approach can be found elsewhere than in these two essentialist interpretations that create an intrinsic tie between history, certain texts and social behaviours that can be identified today. Knowing whether Muhammad Bin 'Abd al-Wahhâb was a nice and tolerant person or a power-hungry madman is not pertinent for people who want to understand Usâma Bin Lâdin, terrorism, contemporary Salafism, international relations and the Arabian Peninsula, or just the Saudi state. In other words, such 'texts' cannot suffice to establish an ideology and explain political and social behaviours such as those that disrupt the world at large, especially the Middle East.

If I choose, so early on in the process, to distance myself from the term 'Wahhabism', it is because it does not refer to the social practices I aim to study and which constitute the object of this book. Rather, Wahhabism refers to a historical reform movement begun in the eighteenth century by Muhammad

---

[3] Vincenzo Oliveti, *Terror's Source: The Ideology of Wahhabi-Salafism and its Consequences*, Birmingham: Amadeus Books, 2002.

[4] Natana Delong-Bas, *Wahhabi Islam: From Revival and Reform to Global Jihad*, Oxford: Oxford University Press. See also my own review of this book in *Journal of Islamic Studies*, vol. 17, no. 3, 2006, pp. 371–372.

Bin 'Abd al-Wahhâb in the Arabian Peninsula.[5] The Wahhabi movement can be characterised in theological terms by an emphasis on the singularity or uniqueness (*tawhîd*) of God, by an adherence to the Hanbalî school (*madhhab*) and by a desire to purge religious practice from certain innovations that have arisen since the emergence of Islam. Historically it was supported by its political alliance with the first Saudi state (1744–1818) against its opponents.

One often finds the term Wahhabism to define either the religious institutions of Saudi Arabia, a particular way of practicing Islam, or even a certain religious imperialism associated with the kingdom of the Âl Su'ûd family. As Pascal Ménoret puts it, 'the concept of Wahhabism' has undergone a 'semantic shift that would be anecdotal if it was not associated with a properly essentialist reading of phenomena that are improperly brought under a single term'.[6] In fact, use of the stigmatising concept of Wahhabism is equivalent to ignoring not only the various religious and political disagreements that have occurred during the last 300 years in the Arabian Peninsula, but also the very multiplicity of sources, behaviours and practices that this term is supposed to refer to.

Apart from its intrinsically polemic character, this term leads to a direct identification with what would become Saudi Arabia, since that was the geographical origin of the Wahhabi movement. In the Yemeni political debate certain intellectuals, especially Zaydis like Amîn Abû Zayd,[7] use it in order to associate their competitors with a supposed Saudi origin. In doing this they intend to discredit them, and to support their own claim to be legitimate actors, and authentically Yemeni. In Central Asia, in the ex-Soviet space and in West Africa where the partisans of political Islam are called Wahhabis, the same strategy with regard to the use of this term is being employed.[8] In this context it is obvious that the use of such a label has more to do with political polemics than with identifiable social practices.

In the framework of the present study, the identification with Saudi Arabia proves quite problematic, to the extent that it establishes an automatic con-

[5] David Commins, *The Wahhabi Mission in Saudi Arabia*, op. cit.

[6] Pascal Ménoret, 'Le wahhabisme, arme fatale du néo-orientalisme', *Mouvements*, no. 36, 2004, p. 55.

[7] Amîn Abû Zayd, *al-Wahhâbiyya wa khataruhâ 'alâ mustaqbal al-Yaman al-siyâsî* [Wahhabism and its danger for the political future of Yemen], op. cit.

[8] See especially Igor Dobaev, 'Radical Wahhabism as an Extremist Religious-political Ideology', *Central Asia and the Caucasus*, vol. 16, no. 4, 2002, pp. 128–138; and for West Africa, Richard Warms, 'Merchants, Muslims, and Wahhabiyya: The Elaboration of Muslim Identity in Sikasso, Mali', *Canadian Journal of African Studies*, vol. 26, no. 3, 1992, pp. 485–507.

nection between contemporary practices (Salafism), a historical movement (Wahhabism) and a national origin (Saudi Arabia). But nothing justifies all this *a priori*, and in fact this line of argument will be challenged throughout the chapters of this book.

The term 'Salafism' appears as more neutral and therefore more relevant as it avoids a direct reference to Saudi Arabia, as well as the polemical associations and stigma attached to 'Wahhabism'. In addition, this term is usually accepted by the actors themselves, who call themselves *salafiyûn* (Salafis) or *ahl al-sunna wa al-jamâ'a* (the people of the Tradition and the Group) and can be referred to in this way by others. At the same time, the relationship between religious people called Salafis with the religious current known as Wahhabi is neither unique, nor automatic, nor even univocal. By the same token, the term 'Wahhabi' stands revealed as inapt and misleading, since it tends to obscure a large number of sources and behaviours.

In the broadest sense, Salafism is a Sunni reform movement that originated in the Middle Ages, especially in the teachings of Taqî al-Dîn Ahmad Ibn Taymiyya (died 1328)[9] and gained momentum in the course of the twentieth century. This movement is characterised in theological terms as a return to religious foundations, and the *Encyclopaedia of Islam* refers to it as a form of 'primitive faith'.[10] The devotees intend to return to the practices of the 'pious ancestors' (*al-salaf al-sâlih*; from which the movement's name stems), that is, the earliest generations of Muslims who are treated as models of piety. It is then believed that their religious practice had not yet been altered by any number of later innovations, which Salafis condemn. It is noteworthy that this objective implies that the Salafis claim to bypass the four traditional schools of jurisprudence (*madhhab*) within Sunni Islam (Maliki, Hanafi, Hanbali and Shafi'i schools). The development of Salafism in its various forms since the beginning of the twentieth century has then to do with what some, like Saba Mahmood, have described as the '*post-madhhab*' character of modern religiosity.[11] In fact, the original reform project of Salafism intended to transcend all political, geographical, social and sectarian differences. Consequently this term has an initially positive connotation across Muslim societies. The emphasis of the

---

[9] On the writings of Ibn Taymiyya, see especially the commentaries of Yahya Michot, *Mardin: Hégire, fuite du péché et 'demeure de l'Islam'*, Paris: al-Bouraq, 2005.

[10] 'Salafiyya', *Encyclopédie de l'Islam*, Leiden: Brill, 2nd edition, vol. 8, 2002, p. 931.

[11] Saba Mahmood, *The Politics of Piety: The Islamic Revival and the Feminist Subject*, op. cit, p. 81.

origins of Islam confers a certain image of authenticity and social prestige on Salafis.

But this definition is still too broad to define a set of social practices concretely. It does refer implicitly to an ambition and a project that eventually was shared, more or less explicitly, by thinkers as disparate as Muhammad Bin 'Abd al-Wahhâb (1702–1792) in the Najd, Shâh Wâlî Allâh (1703–1762) in India, Muhammad al-Shawkânî (1760–1834) in Yemen, Jamâl al-Dîn al-Afghânî (1838–1897) in the Ottoman Empire or Muhammad 'Abdû (1849–1905) and Hasan al-Bannâ (1906–1949) in Egypt. The term 'Salafism', repeatedly adapted to different local or historical contexts, gradually came to designate opposed currents. Like the concept of Wahhabism, it then risked losing its explanatory power, by designating very different things.

For example, since the modernising reform of Muhammad 'Abdû, the *salafiyya* movement which the *Encyclopaedia of Islam* retains as the only definition of Salafism,[12] the term's meaning has shifted, to the point where the Yemeni intellectual Ahmad al-Daghshî, close to the Muslim Brotherhood, today maintains that it is being 'monopolized' by sectarian groups.[13] In effect, it has come to refer—in academic discourse and in the discourse of Muslim actors—to certain religious movements that are otherwise labelled 'fundamentalist' or 'extremist', and whose connection with a project of reform and modernisation is not immediately apparent.

In this context, the simple definition of Salafism as a movement whose object is to return to the foundations of Islam or to purify it, appears as too broad and diffuse. In order to define this object it appears necessary to take account of the semantic evolution the term has undergone, and also of its use by certain political, social and religious movements that emerged during the second half of the twentieth century around figures such as Muhammad al-Albânî, 'Abd al-'Azîz Bin Bâz, Muhammad al-Jâmî, Muqbil al-Wâdi'î and Rabî' al-Madkhalî. Preaching, teaching and the aura of these individuals have in fact played the largest role in this appropriation of the term. Beginning with a universalist call that aims to bypass the traditional schools of Islamic jurisprudence, finding its own roots in a reformist project that appeared during the Middle Ages and developed from the eighteenth century onwards, contemporary Salafism has

---

[12] 'Salafiyya', *Encylopédie de l'Islam*, op. cit., pp. 931–940.

[13] Ahmad al-Daghshî, *Ahl al-sunna wa al-jamâ'a: ishkâl fî al-fahm am fî al-mafhûm?* [The ahl al-sunna wa al-jamâ'a: Problem of comprehension or of concept?], op. cit., p. 24.

worked up a doctrine and a specific method (*manhaj*), giving rise to a movement that most agree to label Salafi.

In view of the diversity of interpretations and movements that claim to be Salafi, it is understood that my own definition cannot claim to be exhaustive, especially because I do not examine the theological and historical dimensions of these currents in depth or in detail, and because I restrict my attention to a particular time and region (the contemporary Arabian Peninsula). Consequently the definition I will stick to concerns only a portion of a large spectrum of phenomena, directly involved with the peninsular environment. The actors that concern me most belong to a particular segment, generally described as emblematic of the *salafiyya da'wiyya* (missionary Salafism, also called 'shaykhist', literalist or *salafiyya 'ilmiyya*—scholastic Salafism) that is opposed to jihadi Salafism (*salafiyya jihâdiyya*) and also to activist Salafism (*salafiyya munazzama* or *harakiyya*, sometimes also termed *Surûriyya*). The first tendency is characterised by quietism: it is apolitical in principle, refusing any party system and in theory gives its allegiance to existing authority. The second is specified by the fact it resorts to violence against its enemies, either religious or political and the third is made specific by its tolerance of party politics. All three share the same reformist ambition and a certain literalism towards the founding texts of Islam as well as an emphasis on the issue of creed (*'aqîda*), however all tend to stigmatise and criticise one another in very direct ways, often focusing on apparently minor details. Without denying that connections can exist between the various segments, for example through their shared conception of theological questions (the centrality of the *hadîth* and the *tawhîd*),[14] my efforts here are intended to follow up on the supposed apolitical nature of Salafism as it has developed in contemporary Yemen, specifying the object of analysis in terms of associated social practices and behaviour.

Above all, Salafism, particularly the 'missionary' branch which is here considered as the main ideal-type, is marked by an emphasis on purifying religious practices from local particularities and innovations (*bid'a*) that have managed over centuries to 'pollute' the original Islam, such as it was revealed in the Qur'an and the prophetic Tradition. The quest for the original Islam is often considered by Salafis themselves as the main hallmark of their movement. In a booklet entitled *al-Salafiyya: qawâ'id wa usûl* [Salafism: rules and foundations], published in Cairo, Ahmad Farîd, an Egyptian Salafi author asserted:

---

[14] Bernard Haykel, 'On the Nature of Salafi Thought and Action' in Roel Meijer (ed.), *Global Salafism. Islam's New Religious Movement*, op. cit, pp. 33–50.

Salafism does not represent an individual's conception of Islam; it does not refer to Islam as understood by Ibn Taymiyya or Bin Bâz[15] [...] The objective of Salafism is to defend the faith of our ancestors (*salaf*) and their understanding of the Book and the Tradition [...]. Salafism serves the Tradition as the Prophet commanded us.[16]

This approach, using reform and 'purification' implies a certain decontextualisation of Islam, and a certain literalism on the part of Salafis. The point is to break off the connection to superstitions, celebrations and beliefs that belong to popular Islam, particularly Sufism, which through the cult of saints appears to be guilty of introducing intercession between God and the believer.

Such 'cleansing' also implies that Salafis reject the imitation (*taqlîd*) of the traditional Sunni schools of Islamic law, which serve as the base of jurisprudence (*fiqh*). The Salafi doctrine then prescribes a restriction of the sources of such jurisprudence to only the Qur'an and the prophetic Tradition (*sunna*) contained in the *hadîth* (sayings and deeds of the Prophet Muhammad, as told by his companions).[17] This theoretically leads Salafis to abandon two sources on which the four traditional *madhhab* do rely: the consensus between *'ulamâ'* (*ijmâ'*) and analogical reasoning (*qiyâs*). The restriction of acceptable sources favours emphasis on theology through the assertion of the uniqueness of God (*tawhîd*) and through the study of the *hadîth*. Such a focus is maintained largely at the expense of the study of *fiqh*.

For Salafis, the science (*'ilm*) of the *hadîth* consists essentially in verifying the authenticity of various traditions carried forward along a chain of transmission extending from the companions of the Prophet in the seventh century of our era, up to their inclusion in various collections, the two most important being those of Bukhârî (died in the year 265 of the Hijra calendar—868 AD)

---

[15] 'Abd al-'Azîz Bin Bâz, born in 1910, named grand *muftî* of the Kingdom in 1992, was a pivotal figure of the contemporary Saudi religious establishment. Both a 'servant' of the Âl Su'ûd royal family and a relatively independent figure, he was until his death in May 1999 the beneficiary of an aura that extended well beyond 'Wahhabi' or 'Salafi' circles. For a hagiography of Bin Bâz, see Muqbil al-Wâdi'î, *al-Dîbâj fî marâthât shaykh al-islâm samâhat al-shaykh 'Abd al-'Azîz Bin Bâz* [The silk in the funeral oration of the *shaykh al-Islâm*, his excellency shaykh 'Abd al-'Azîz Bin Bâz], Sana'a: Maktabat al-Idrîsî al-Salafiyya, 1999; and a special issue 'al-Shaykh Ibn Bâz wa sîrat hayâtihi [Shaykh Bin Bâz and his biography]', *al-Faysal*, no. 273, 1999, pp. 2–8.

[16] Ahmad Farîd, *al-Salafiyya: qawâ'id wa usûl* [Salafism: rules and foundations], Cairo: Dâr al-'Aqîda, 2003, p. 11.

[17] On the methodology of the study of hadîths and their scope, see Bernard Rougier, 'Introduction' in Bernard Rougier (ed.), *Qu'est ce que le salafisme?*, op. cit., p. 10.

and Muslim (died in 261 H.—874 AD). From these *hadîth*, which are supposed to represent the practice of the first generations of Muslims, Salafis draw a group of teachings and restrictions that they try to apply as literally as possible, without any contextualisation. The practice of the *salaf al-salih* is thus sanctified, but also circumscribed, that is, mostly contained in a fixed corpus of texts whose relevance is not measured by rational comparison or reference to the teachings or the spirit of the Qur'an, but in relation to the quality of the persons who preserved the *hadîth*. Within this framework the validity of a religious argument is supposed to hang on its conformity to the Book and the prophetic Tradition. Thus, verses and *hadîth* are systematically used by Salafi interpreters in their exegesis and doctrinal thought, in order to validate some prohibition, imperative or piece of advice addressed to both believers and leaders.

Thus the delineation of a closed corpus constitutes an advantage. Salafism offers its devotees an apparently simple and infallible religious doctrine that claims to empower each individual by letting him/her interpret texts and act to create an individual destiny, outside of dominant institutional structures, either partisan or dependent on religious or traditional hierarchies. As such, Salafism can present itself as a faith with equality among believers. Consequently the rationalisation process that is supposed to symbolise Salafi doctrine is also that which makes it seductive and popular.[18]

Literalism implies a particular focus on elements of worship (*'ibâda*: prayer, ablution, fasting, and so on) and dogma (*'aqîda*) that are perceived by the Salafi worldview as more important than the material gains (social justice) that are to be won in the area of politics. The quest for these gains is actually seen as responsible for fomenting division and chaos (*tafarruq* or *fitna*) between believers. Such an interpretation, held mainly by the so-called missionary Salafis, explains why party politics as well as violence are deemed counter-productive. Consequently, this literalist branch of Salafism can be described as quietist and pietist at the same time,[19] inasmuch as it means to detach itself from the context surrounding it.

---

[18] Madawi Al-Rasheed, *Contesting the Saudi State: Islamic Voices from a New Generation*, op. cit., p. 132.

[19] Pietism originally described a Protestant (Lutheran) tendency that appeared in the seventeenth-century, and which was characterised by 'austere piety', a certain literalism and the practice of a worship that was private and personal rather than public. In a broad sense the term applies to several different religious currents marked by an insistence on devotion and faith, not on works or actions. Quietism, in contrast, is part of a more ancient spiritual tradition that has affected Hinduism, Stoicism and

This 'universalist' vocation of Salafism, stating that whatever the time and place, absolute principles must be implemented with no exception, is symptomatic of a disconnection between religious identities as a whole and cultures, or what Olivier Roy labels a 'deterritorialisation of the local' and of 'deculturation'.[20] Among Salafis, such a process is accompanied by a desire to get rid of many innovations that have become part of worship in the course of Islamic history: intercessions between God and the believer, as well as popular rites and beliefs. Paradoxically, by struggling against local particularities and by identifying groups that practise them the Salafis do inject themselves into a particular context and are thus increasingly politicised. They identify their competitors and their critics, and they arrange to stand apart from them, particularly by stigmatising them and publicly denouncing their alleged theological errors. However, quietist Salafis generally refuse the principle of overt excommunication or declarations of impiety (*takfîr*) and engage in more subtle or indirect methods of stigmatisation. This strategy of naming and blaming builds on a particular claim: Salafis perceive themselves as the only Muslim group that will be saved on Judgment Day. The claim to represent the *firqa al-nâjiyya* (saved group), also called the *tâ'ifa al-mansûra*, understandably implies a certain feeling of superiority, even supremacy. Salafi *'ulamâ'* base themselves on a *hadîth* that recalls that the Prophet Muhammad had said that the Muslim community would be divided into seventy-three sects (*firqa*) and among these only one (the one that 'holds the same views as I and my companions have set forth' will be saved from Hell).[21]

Buddhism as well as the three great monotheistic religions. Quietism emphasises the annihilation of self and passive contemplation, which involves becoming indifferent to everything that can affect the world here below. Salafism, through its focus on religious practice and its reluctance with regard to political commitment and involvement in the material world, can reasonably be characterised by both these terms.

[20] Olivier Roy, *Holy Ignorance: When Religion and Culture Diverge*, op. cit., p. 25. The disconnection between religious identities and cultures is also something that is highlighted, building on the case of American born-again Christians, by Susan Friend Harding, *The Book of Jerry Falwell. Fundamentalist Language and Politics*, op. cit., pp. 125–152 in her fifth chapter 'Cultural Exodus'. On the same issue and building on the case of Baptist Christians in Latin America, David Martin writes: 'People are no longer and forever consigned by baptism into a religious identity which is also a national identity. Rather they are exposed to options and alternatives'. David Martin, *Pentecostalism: The World their Parish*, Oxford: Blackwell, 2002, p. 72.

[21] *Sunan Abî Da'ûd*, no. 4596–4597.

Minor Behaviours and Distinctive Practices

A certain number of social practices stem from the religious doctrine and project identified above. These establish a particular *manhaj* that clearly distinguishes the actors that are the object of this research within the Yemeni context. It is on what can be described as their 'minor behaviours' as well as on their specific relationship with political commitments that the quietist Salafis manage to emerge as a distinct group. In fact, their apparently apolitical attitude appears as a structuring factor, both within the movement and between the movement and its competitors.

Quietist Salafis claim to draw from the Qur'an and the *hadîth* a group of precise rules that make up an etiquette, codes and strategies for the 'presentation of the self' which are tantamount to what Erving Goffman labelled 'minor behaviours'.[22] These allow other members of the group to recognise one another; to respect these behaviours is to participate in the community of members. They also make possible the identification of Salafis by other persons not belonging to the faith community.

Clothing is undoubtedly a 'distinctive practice' and the most visible marker for belonging to the Salafi group. In order, as they claim, to adopt the same clothing as the early Muslims, Salafis wear a tunic (*qamîs* or *thawb*) or a skirt (*fûta* or *ma'waz*) that must reach no lower than the ankles and often rests at mid-calf.[23] This restriction holds for all clothing: if a Salafi is obliged to wear trousers while performing some professional activity (this applies especially to teachers in public schools), the cuffs must not hang down below the prescribed level. In the Yemeni context, as well as the Saudi one, such a prescription appears as contrary to the dominant dress codes or the latest globalised fashion that over the last few decades have inescapably transformed the way people dress. In addition to the length of clothes, Salafis are often eager to distinguish themselves through head-dress. Contrary to dominant habits in the Gulf States, the *'imâma* (length of cloth placed on the head, or turban) is worn by most Salafis without an *'iqâl* (a short cord that holds the *'imâma* in place). Apart from all justification of a religious nature, this specific detail of the Salafi costume has to do with the desire of men of science (*'ulamâ'* or *ahl al-'ilm*) to be distinguished from cattle-raising Bedouins.[24] In fact the *'iqâl* was originally the cord

---

[22] Erving Goffman, *Interaction Rituals. Essays in Face-to-face Behavior*, New Jersey: Transaction, 2005, p. 139.

[23] This rule is justified by the *hadîth* found in Bukhârî's collection, vol. 7, book 72, no. 678: The Prophet said, 'whatever is below the ankles will be in the Hell-fire'.

[24] On the symbolic and historic role of the *iqâl* in Saudi Arabia, see Abdulaziz Al-Fahad,

used by herders to hobble sheep, goats and dromedaries, and then later it became an element of male dress in the Arabian Peninsula. Since the *'iqâl* is not part of traditional Yemeni dress, the Salafis in that country generally continue this distinctive practice by wearing, in the manner of Saudi religious individuals, the *'imâma* (also called *shmâgh, sumâta, shâl* or *kashîda* depending on the region), merely placed on the head, and not tied as is usually the custom in Yemen. Other examples of 'distinctive practices' include wristwatches worn on the right wrist, because the left is considered impure, or even change of first names.[25] The beard should not be shaven or even cut, but moustaches are worn short and away from the lips, in conformity with the prophetic Tradition. Nonetheless, as Muqbil al-Wâdi'î, founder of the Yemeni Salafi movement, said at a conference entitled *al-Radd 'alâ al-mukhâlafîn* [The answer to transgressors] that was circulated on audio cassette:

> It is not enough to wear the *'imâma*, to trim one's moustaches, and to wear the *thawb* above the ankles. All that is positive but it is not the whole of the Tradition. It is necessary for each one to know his religion and the Tradition. It is also necessary to be able to distinguish authentic *hadîth* from those that are weak.

In addition to these vestimentary codes, there are a number of rules and procedures for behaviour, and Salafis give them a great deal of attention: there are for example formulas for thanking and greeting that are judged to be more pious than the ones generally used by other groups. While the traditional and popular ways of saying 'good morning' and 'good evening' are *sabâh al-khayr* and *masâ' al-khayr*, Salafis systematically replace these with the formula *al-salâm 'alaykum*, peace be with you, or simply 'peace' (*salâm*) if the addressee is not Muslim. For the ordinary formula for 'thank you', *shukran*, Salafis substitute *jâzak Allâh khayr*, 'may God reward you'. From sleep to mealtime, every act in daily life is thus codified and calls for particular invocations that may well be contained in little booklets or printed on posters so that the members of the community do not forget them.

'The *Imama* vs. the *Iqal*: Hadari Bedouin Conflict and the Formation of the Saudi State' in Madawi Al-Rasheed and Robert Vitalis (eds.), *Counter-Narratives. History, Contemporary Society and Politics in Saudi Arabia and Yemen*, op. cit., pp. 35–75.

[25] A Yemeni Salafi born under the socialist regime recalled how upon arriving to study in the main Salafi institute in the early 1990s, he had been asked to change his first name (Sâm), deemed un-Islamic, to one that emphasised his religiosity (Shams al-Dîn). Interview, Sana'a, April 2008.

This literalism, aimed at putting a stop to innovations, is accompanied by a great number of prohibitions and refusals (something that is reminiscent of the rigid rules and 'clean break' enforced by 'straight-edge' teenagers[26] as well as Protestant movements in Latin America).[27] Based on the Book and the prophetic Tradition, Salafis do not, for example, permit the writing of insurance policies, since these are supposed to imply that the believer doubts the goodness of the destiny God has decreed for him. To the extent that they are bad for one's health, qat,[28] cigarettes and hookahs (*shîsha*) are also banned. Music, including religious psalmodies (*nashîd*), is considered illicit, and only recitations of the Qur'an are allowed. Since all forms of figuration, representation of human beings and anthropomorphism are prohibited, television, drawing, theatre and sculpture are banned as well. The rejection of all mediation between God and believers gives way to defiance with regard to popular Islam (specifically Sufism) as exemplified by the cult of saints, visits (*ziyâra*) to their tombs and celebrations of the birthday of the Prophet Muhammad (*mawlid*). This desire to imitate and repeat practices from early Islam creates an arrangement that is apparently coherent: every question receives an irrefutable answer,

---

[26] Ross Haenfler, *Straight Edge: Hardcore Punk, Clean Living Youth, and Social Change*, Piscataway: Rutgers University Press, 2006.

[27] On Pentecostal ethics in Latin America, David Martin writes: 'The clean break offered through Pentecostalism and through other evangelical groups cuts the ties with the carnival, with the fiesta, and with godparenthood, as well as with the politico-economic system of clientage [...]. This in turn means cutting free from the world of alcohol, of deals in bars, and of football and the weekend male spree. [...] The contrast of 'faith' with 'world' needs persistent reinforcement'. David Martin, *Pentecostalism: The World their Parish*, op. cit., p. 72.

[28] Qat is a mild narcotic that is chewed daily by a large percentage of people in Yemen in the afternoon during the *maqyal*. The distribution of qat, chewed fresh, across the entire country by means of regular delivery routes makes it an important part of Yemen's national identity. On this subject, see especially: Daniel Varisco, 'The Elixir of Life or the Devil's Cud: The Debate over Qat (Catha edulis) in Yemeni Culture' in Ross Coomber and Nigel South (eds.), *Drug Use and Cultural Context Beyond 'The West'*, London: Free Association Books, 2004, pp. 101–118. For Salafi argumentation against the consumption of qat, see: *Fatâwâ fî tahrîm al-qât wa abhâth hawlahu li'ulamâ' al-Yaman* [Legal opinions on the prohibition of qat and studies of the matter by Yemeni 'ulamâ'] posted online: http://www.sahab.ws/3069/news/4338.html?print=1 (accessed 8 August, 2006) or the work by Muhammad al-Imâm, *Tahdhîr ahl al-îmân min ta'âtî al-qât, al-shamma wa al-dukhân* [Warning to people of faith against qat, shamma and cigarettes], place, publisher and date unknown.

because it has been decontextualised and mainly focuses on procedures.[29] Sequences of queries sent to '*ulamâ*' and recorded on audio cassettes with their answer or collections of *fatâwâ* thus play a fundamental role in the diffusion of Salafi doctrine and the etiquette associated with it.[30]

These characteristics are not merely anecdotal, but they are undoubtedly less important within the Salafi trend than the question of the relationship to the state and to politics. Studies on contemporary Islamism have often overlooked a fundamental movement. Over the past decades, plenty of research has been carried out on politicised groups whose central aim is to seize power and control the state, or at least put significant pressure on it, whether through peaceful or violent means. On the contrary, quietist or supposedly apolitical religious actors who focus exclusively on cult, purification or religious guidance have not frequently drawn the attention of political scientists or anthropologists.

The Muslim reformist current gave rise not to one, but two Islamist ideal-types whose distinguishing characteristic is a divergent relationship to politics. For one category, represented particularly by the Muslim Brotherhood, the priority for action is the quest for a kind of social justice via the reform of society, which leads them to prioritise intervention in the political arena. The second is represented by Salafi elements known as quietist, or by the transnational movement Tablîgh;[31] the emphasis is placed on taking one's distance from the social and political world that is said to foster nothing but corruption and division. Like any ideal-typical category, these two groups cannot be con-

[29] On the *fatwâ* system and its connection with political power in Yemen, see Brinkley Messick, *The Calligraphic State*, Berkeley: University of California Press, 1993. In another publication the same author considers, in passing, *fatwâ* that concern legal and theological questions worked out for problems that are closer to the daily life of believers: Brinkley Messick, 'Media Muftis: Radio Fatwas in Yemen' in Muhammad Khalid Masud, Brinkley Messick and David Powers (eds.), *Islamic Legal Interpretation: Muftis and their Fatwas*, Cambridge: Harvard University Press, 1996, pp. 310–320.

[30] On the function of recorded sermons and conferences within the Islamist realm: Charles Hirschkind, *The Ethical Soundscape. Cassette Sermons and Islamic Counterpublics*, New York: Columbia University Press, 2006, p. 55. He writes: 'As one of the few media able to circulate beneath the radar of state surveillance and regulation, sermon tapes emerged as the privileged medium of an Islamic opposition discourse. [...] Silence the speaker, but his words would still proliferate and acquire agency through the actions of listeners within the electronic network'.

[31] Khalid Masud (ed.), *Travellers in Faith. Studies of the Tablîghî Jamâ'at as a Transnational Islamic Movement for Faith Renewal*, Leiden: Brill, 2000.

sidered as completely separate or mutually exclusive. Bridges exist between them and they may be found on the same side in some respects, for example among the various jihadi movements or within the *Sahwa islâmiyya* fringe that developed in Saudi Arabia since the 1970s.[32]

The characteristic of the particular brand of Salafism that my research focuses on primarily has to do with a certain uneasiness with regard to any direct involvement in the political sphere. The fear of division (*fitna*) among believers caused by factionalism or partisan activity (*hizbiyya*) or even by participation in charity associations is in fact a structural element in the Salafi field. By refusing to participate in elections, whether by proposing candidates or by voting, quietist Salafism indicates its objective, to establish 'Islamised' spaces through preaching (*da'wa*, literally, 'call to God') and not through assuming actual political power.

The fear of seeing the community of the faithful suffer dissension and chaos has brought contemporary Salafism to pledge its allegiance to political leadership (*walî al-amr*) as long as that leadership is not exposed as clearly impious (*kufr bawâh*). Consequently Salafis stand apart from political parties or institutionalised movements of Islamist opposition, and also from street demonstrations, revolutions and coups d'état. The attitude of the Saudi religious institution, and especially of 'Abd al-'Azîz Bin Bâz, grand *muftî* of the Kingdom, during the Gulf War of 1990–1991, when he legitimised the presence of an 'unholy' or impious American army on Saudi territory,[33] clearly illustrates this option of allegiance to existing political authority.

Although often accused by their adversaries of resorting to *takfîr*, the quietist Salafi movement as such generally rejects it as a matter of principle. A severe critique of the teachings of Sayyid Qutb,[34] whose writings legitimise excommunication of government and of society itself, in fact constitutes an important characteristic of the contemporary quietist version of the Salafi doctrine. Rather

---

[32] On the development of the *Sahwa islâmiyya* in Saudi Arabia, see Stéphane Lacroix, *Les islamistes saoudiens: une insurrection manquée*, op. cit.; and Madawi Al-Rasheed, *Contesting the Saudi State*, op. cit.

[33] The Gulf War caused intense debate among religious actors; see especially Yvonne Yazbeck Haddad, 'Operation Desert Storm and the War of Fatwas', in Muhammad Khalid Masud, Brinkley Messick and David Powers (eds.), *Islamic Legal Interpretation. Muftis and their Fatwas*, op. cit., pp. 297–309.

[34] Olivier Carré, *Mystique et politique. Le Coran des islamistes. Lecture du Coran par Sayyid Qutb Frère musulman radical (1906–1966)*, Paris: Editions du Cerf, 2004; John Calvert, *Sayyid Qutb and the Origins of Radical Islamism*, London: Hurst, 2010.

than *takfîr*, this *da'wa* asks '*ulamâ*' to offer advice (*nasîha*) to the leaders, in theory in a discreet or secret manner, in order to fulfil the objective of 'promotion of virtue and prevention of vice (*al-amr bil-ma'rûf wa al-nahî 'an al-munkar*)'.[35] Public disagreements—via the principle 'of refutation and rectification' (*jarh wa ta'dîl*)—and open criticism directed at governments are in theory only authorised after the first stage of consultation has taken place. Salafi entrepreneurs claim to offer allegiance without conditions, as long as leaders (president, king or imam) are not clearly proven to be impious, and as long as they do not declare themselves apostate.

Nonetheless, such conditions obviously favour great flexibility. Consequently, stigmatisation by Salafis of other religious, social or political groups, and even of foreign governments, sometimes in quite violent terms, causes the principle of refusal of *takfîr* to be rather weak and dependent on circumstances. For example, Muqbil al-Wâdi'î, the tutelary figure in Yemeni Salafism, made a play on words when speaking of the partisans of *Jamâ'at al-takfîr* (a generic name he uses to refer to the so-called jihadi groups) accused of practicing excommunication of leaders and segments of the population, calling them *khawârij*.[36] Resorting to such a label clearly amounts to calling into question their belonging to the Islamic community, although he never employs the term *kâfir*.[37]

The use of ancient categories, inherited from disputes that occurred during the first centuries of Islam, cannot completely conceal the fact that the various actors involved, although they might deny any implication in politics, are competing with one another and sometimes end up fragmenting the Islamic community around political issues. As the Yemeni case study will show, the practices of Salafi actors, even at the core of the quietist movement, are particularly varied. As such, their patterns of action cannot be characterised in a one-sided fashion either by violence and fundamentalism or by their principles of pacifism, apoliticism, quietism or pietism.

[35] On this notion see in particular Michael Cook, *Commanding Right and Forbidding Wrong in Islamic Thought*, Cook, Cambridge: Cambridge University Press, 2001. For a more contextualised approach, see also Saba Mahmood, *The Politics of Piety: The Islamic Revival and the Feminist Subject*, op. cit., in particular Chapter 2 'Topography of the Piety Movement'.

[36] Plural of *khârijî* ('one who has gone out'), name given to partisans of the Fourth Caliph, 'Alî, who turned against him after the battle of Siffîn, seceded and later assassinated him in 661.

[37] Muqbil al-Wâdi'î, sound recording, *I'lân al nakîr 'alâ jamâ'at al-takfîr* [Notification of the atrocity of the *Jamâ'at al-takfîr*].

II. The Political and Religious Context of Yemeni Salafism

The Central Figure of Muqbil Bin Hâdî al-Wâdi'î

In Yemen, quietist Salafism as an ideologically structured movement, organised in networks of centres, bookstores and around specific entrepreneurs, emerged in the beginning of the 1980s.

It revolved mainly around the figure of Muqbil Bin Hâdî al-Wâdi'î and his institute, Dâr al-Hadîth (the 'House of *hadîth*') located 250 kilometres north of the capital, Sana'a, in the village of Dammâj, just outside Sa'da city. The dominant branch of Yemeni Salafism he established is generally considered close to the *Jâmiyya* movement (so-called after the name of Muhammad Amân al-Jâmî, a scholar originally from Ethiopia but based in Saudi Arabia, where he died in January 1996) and to the current movement led by Rabî' Bin Hâdî al-Madkhalî (a Saudi, born in 1931, native of the Jâzân area near the border with Yemen and long a prominent member of the Islamic University in Medina).[38]

Allegedly, as discussed previously, this branch represents a Salafism that is particularly hardline with regard to doctrine and practices, but also maintains in principle an apolitical stance, and as such can be considered as less uncompromising than other Islamist groups who are direct opponents of the regimes and governments.

Born in the late 1920s (or perhaps early in the 1930s—he was not sure himself) in the region of Sa'da in northern Yemen, Muqbil Bin Hâdî al-Wâdi'î came from a Zaydi tribe, al-Wâdi'a, which belonged to the large but loose tribal confederation, Bakîl, which extends from the area around Sana'a to the Saudi border. He belonged to the category of *qabâ'il* (tribesmen), the most numerous in the semi-rigid system of social stratification of the Yemeni highlands that still structured social life during Muqbil al-Wâdi'î's youth (and to a certain degree is still relevant in contemporary Yemen). Although some fluidity may have existed at the margins, tribesmen, who had been providing soldiers for the regime of the Zaydi imam for many centuries, were topped by the religious and political elite of the *sâda* (descendants of the Prophet or Hashemites, singular *sayyid*) and also by the category of the *qudhâ* (judges, singular *qâdhî*), guarantors of law.

---

[38] Sa'd al-Faqîh, 'I'tirâdhât al-salafiyîn 'alâ al-dîmûqrâtiyya [The Salafis' objections towards democracy]' in 'Alî al-Kuwârî (ed.), *Azmat al-dîmûqrâtiyya fî al-buldân al-'arabiyya* [The crisis of democracy in Arab countries], Beirut: Dâr al-Sâqî, 2004, pp. 67–93.

In a society still shaped by traditional structures and status groups, the subordinate position of Muqbil al-Wâdi'î in the social hierarchy theoretically, according to him, prevented him from having access to religious knowledge. Such inferiority of status probably sheds light on al-Wâdi'î's lifetime resentment towards the higher categories and his adherence to a doctrine, Salafism, that claimed to explicitly reject traditional social hierarchies and hereditary power.

When he finished his basic education at the beginning of the 1950s, Muqbil al-Wâdi'î left for Saudi Arabia, and found work as a doorkeeper (*bawâb*) of a building in Mecca. He stayed there about five years. According to his autobiography, by reading a number of Sunni-oriented religious works lent or given to him by Saudis or fellow Yemenis, he discovered the alleged theological errors indulged by his Zaydi upbringing. After returning to Sa'da, he tried to study in al-Hâdî mosque, one of the major Zaydi teaching centres, but he claimed his situation there was uncomfortable: he was stigmatised by the '*ulamâ*' because of his tribal origin, and he was disregarded by the *sâda* 'aristocrats'. Nonetheless, he pursued his theological studies while neglecting the specificities of Zaydism and diverging from his sect of origin. Confronted by negative perceptions from fellow students and teachers, al-Wâdi'î claimed to focus mainly on grammar studies so he could escape from the 'brain wash' that the Zaydi clerics from al-Hâdî mosque wanted to impose on him.[39] The fact that he had preserved in the face of opposition coming from his own family, his own tribe and the local, Zaydi-dominated environment in general was something al-Wâdi'î later felt proud of: he compared himself to Muhammad Nâsir al-Dîn al-Albânî,[40] who had known his own destiny as a teenager, and had defied his father, leaving home to continue religious studies.[41]

[39] Muqbil al-Wâdi'î, sound recording, *As'ila 'an hayât al-shaykh Muqbil al-Wâdi'î wa sîratuhu* [Questions about the life of shaykh Muqbil al-Wâdi'î and his biography].

[40] Muhammad Nâsir al-Dîn al-Albânî, who died in October 1999, was one of the great figures of transnational Salafism. Of Albanian origin, he was a student in Syria, and then briefly lived in Saudi Arabia. He was once close to the monarchy, but their relations gradually became strained during the 1970s. He then returned to live and work in Damascus and Jordan. His many publications essentially focused on the *hadîth*. Al-Albânî still represents the main reference point for quietist Salafism insofar as it has been able to remain de-politicised and independent from political power. Stephane Lacroix, 'Between Revolution and Apoliticism: Nasir al-Din al-Albani and his Impact on the Shaping of Contemporary Salafism' in Roel Meijer (ed.), *Global Salafism*, op. cit., pp. 58–80.

[41] Muqbil al-Wâdi'î (ed.), *Tarjamat Abî 'Abd al-Rahmân Muqbil Bin Hâdî al-Wâdi'î* [Biography of Abî 'Abd al-Rahmân Muqbil Bin Hâdî al-Wâdi'î], op. cit., p. 12.

Following the republican revolution of 1962, Muqbil al-Wâdi'î fled the Yemeni civil war. Sa'da was then a bastion of the royalists defending the Zaydi imamate and al-Wâdi'î took refuge in Saudi Arabia once again. He remained in Najrân, near the border with his home country, for two years, and then spent a few months in Riyadh at a religious institute headed by Muhammad Bin Sinân al-Hadâ'î, a Yemeni, who was able to send him to Mecca, where he stayed for six years. In the holiest city of Islam, he made the acquaintance of some Yemenis and he was joined by his family and managed to find a number of small jobs while deepening his interest for religious literature and for the emerging Salafi doctrine.

The time spent in Mecca appears to have permanently affected his relationship with the Muslim Brotherhood. For a while he was close to them, but he quickly changed his mind, finally concluding that 'their preaching is worldly (*duniyawiyya*)',[42] that is, motivated by material interests rather than a spiritual project. Playing with words and sounds as he would often do, he began to call them the 'Ruined Brotherhood' (*al-Ikhwân al-muflisîn*) instead of *Ikhwân al-muslimîn*. As he would assert later, he was not hostile by nature to the thought formulated by Hasan al-Bannâ, and even found it attractive, but he thought that the institutionalisation of the Brothers was a betrayal of their initial project, and that it had caused them to focus on political questions that were actually of secondary importance. In fact, much like in the Saudi context, this group gradually became an important ideological foil for what was to emerge as Muqbilian Salafism after he came back to Yemen.[43] The Yemeni religious leader says in his biography that the increasing number of members of the Muslim Brotherhood at the institute where he was studying in Mecca forced him to move once more. He then began studies at the prestigious Islamic University of Medina, where in 1976 he received a Master's degree in the sciences of the *hadîth*, and where he attended classes and occasional sermons given by Muhammad Nâsir al-Dîn al-Albânî during his visits to Saudi Arabia, and 'Abd al-'Azîz Bin Bâz, then president of the Islamic University. During his time at the university, Al-Wâdi'î also got to know Rabî' al-Madkhalî, remaining close to him for the rest of his life. According to some sources, he tried to begin doctoral

---

[42] Muqbil al-Wâdi'î, *al-Makhraj min al-fitna* [Leaving dissension behind], op. cit., p. 131.

[43] See especially 'Abd Allâh al-Sayânî, *al-Ikhwân al-muslimûn wa al-salafiyûn fî al-Yaman* [The Muslim Brotherhood and the Salafis in Yemen], Sana'a: Markaz al-Râ'id, 2002.

studies in Egypt, but for reasons that were unclear he quickly moved back to Saudi Arabia, apparently expelled by the Egyptian government.[44] After his return to Saudi Arabia, the intensity and verbal violence of certain theological debates along with his activities with the *Jamâ'a al-salafiyya al-muhtasiba*,[45] of which he became an active member and close aide of Juhaymân al-'Utaybî got al-Wâdi'î jailed for a month and a half in 1978. Shortly before the uprising in Mecca in November 1979, he was arrested again by the Saudi authorities, imprisoned for three months, and then brutally and permanently expelled from that country: 'quicker than a bird, and we didn't even have time to lift our heads up', as he would later recall.[46] The Saudi authorities accused him of being one of the mentors of Juhaymân al-'Utaybî who at the time published pamphlets critical of the monarchy, and who would a few months later lead the *Ikhwân* uprising in the Great Mosque of Mecca.[47]

Upon his forced return to Yemen, al-Wâdi'î attempted to spread his learning, secured financing for the construction of a small mosque, and founded in the early 1980s the Dâr al-Hadîth study centre in the village of Dammâj in his native region, that is, in a majority Zaydi environment that was hostile to him. According to 'Abd al-Fattâh al-Hakîmî, a Yemeni journalist and author of various studies on Salafism, the institution established by al-Wâdi'î, which then bore the name of the Scientific Institute of Dammâj (*Ma'had Dammâj al-'ilmî*), was at first put under the authority of the Bureau of Scientific Institutes (*Maktab al-ma'âhid 'ilmiyya*), a parallel and semi-public network of schools that was established officially in 1977 by Yemen's President, Ibrâhîm al-Hamdî, and directed by groups that were close to the Muslim Brotherhood:

[44] 'Aqîl al-Maqtarî, sound recording, *Wa rahal 'âlim al-Yaman* [And the scholar of Yemen passed away].

[45] On the *Jamâ'a al-salafiyya al-muhtasiba* (literally the 'Salafi group which enforces virtue and prevents vice'), Thomas Hegghammer and Stephane Lacroix, 'Rejectionist Islamism in Saudi Arabia: The Story of Juhayman al-'Utaybi Revisited', *The International Journal of Middle East Studies*, vol. 39, no. 1, 2007, pp. 97–116.

[46] Muqbil al-Wâdi'î, sound recording, *Nasihatî lil-shabâb al-su'ûdî* [My advice to Saudi youth].

[47] On the Great Mosque siege and its context, see: Rifa'a Sayyid Ahmad, *Rasâ'il Juhaymân al-'Utaybî* [The letters of Juhaymân al-'Utaybî], Cairo: Maktabat Madbûlî, 2004; Pascal Ménoret, 'Fighting for the Holy Mosque. The 1979 Mecca Insurgency' in Christine Fair and Sumit Ganguly (eds.), *Treading on Hallowed Ground: Counterinsurgency Operations in Sacred Spaces*, Oxford: Oxford University Press, 2008, pp. 117–139 and Yaroslav Trofimov, *The Siege of Mecca*, New York: Doubleday, 2007.

The honeymoon between shaykh al-Wâdiʿî and the Muslim Brotherhood did not last longer than two years. In fact, in 1982 the shaykh published his famous work *Al-makhraj min al-fitna* in which he clarified what separated his preaching from that of the Brothers.[48]

After many setbacks, some involving the repatriation of his private library from Medina to Dammâj, Dâr al-Hadîth began to grow. Its prosperity was then mainly linked to financing from rich Saudi businessmen of Yemeni origin, and from charitable organisations linked to the Saudi government or to important *ʿulamâ* of the religious establishment who protected it despite its anti-Saudi political stance. Accused by his Zaydi enemies of being financed by foreigners and of living in opulence, al-Wâdiʿî drew parallels between his situation and the early years of Islam, recalling that 'the hypocrites put pressure on rich philanthropists to make them stop supporting the Prophet and his companions'.[49] In order to answer these attacks in a definitive manner, various figures of Yemeni Salafism insisted upon the simplicity of life in Dammâj: 'God knows that the students eat nothing but white rice',[50] said for example ʿAqîl al-Maqtarî, a former student, who also recalled that one building in which students were housed was an old hangar that had also been used as a chicken coop. Another, anxious to make sure that Salafi preaching was not seen as too closely associated with Saudi riches and opulence, said:

The house of the shaykh Muqbil was small, made of clay, and it reminded you of the houses of the companions of the Prophet. He ate with the students and guests, whom he served himself. Money came in from all over, but he never gave much attention to what people gave, because he knew that this world here below is nothing but disorder.[51]

Despite such modesty, gradually, Muqbil al-Wâdiʿî says, and 'without effort' students arrived 'from Egypt, Kuwait, from the Land of the Two Holy Places,[52]

---

[48] Interview, Aden, May 2005.

[49] Muqbil Al-Wâdiʿî (ed.), *Tarjamat Abî ʿAbd al-Rahmân Muqbil Bin Hâdî al-Wâdiʿî* [Biography of Abî ʿAbd al-Rahmân Muqbil Bin Hâdî al-Wâdiʿî], op. cit., p. 143.

[50] ʿAqîl al-Maqtarî, sound recording, *Wa rahal ʿâlim al-Yaman* [And the scholar of Yemen passed away].

[51] ʿAbd Allâh Bin ʿAbd al-Hamîd Al-Khubânî in Rabîʿ Al-Madkhalî (ed.), *Nasîhat al-shaykh Rabîʿ al-Madkhalî li ahl al-Yaman* [Advice of shaykh Rabîʿ al-Madkhalî to the people of Yemen], Tarîm: Jâmiʿ al-Sunna, 2004, p. 14.

[52] The expression 'Land of the Two Holy Places' (*ardh al-haramayn*) refers to the two holiest Muslim shrines, Mecca and Medina. In the vocabulary of the Salafis, this can

the Najd, Aden, the Hadramawt, Libya, Somalia, Belgium and from other countries, Islamic and non-Islamic'.[53] Around al-Wâdi'î there arose an important network of mosques, bookstores and centres, allowing him to distribute his forty books and hundreds of recorded sermons, and to organise conferences even in the remotest of villages. During the 1990s, former students of Muqbil al-Wâdi'î, including Muhammad al-Imâm, Yahyâ al-Hajûrî, Muhammad al-Wisâbî, 'Abd al-'Azîz al-Bura'î, Muhammad al-Sawmalî, Abû al-Hasan al-Ma'ribî and 'Aqîl al-Maqtarî created their own teaching institutes or mosques throughout Yemen.

Although difficult to quantify, especially as regards the participation of women, the Salafi phenomenon expanded in Yemen. At the end of the 1990s, at its height, the centre at Dammâj had almost a thousand students in residence, all of whom received free room and board. In addition to courses in *fiqh* (Islamic law), *tawhîd* (monotheistic theology) and the study of the *hadîth*, residents were taught grammar, calligraphy and techniques of preaching (*ta'lîm al-khatâba*). On its website, the centre at Dammâj set forth conditions for admission:

Students must be Sunni Muslims who will adopt the Salafi method. There is no place for *hizbiyîn* (i.e., 'partisans', members of parties) in this house, nor for *ahl al-bid'a* (innovators). Those who have families must come alone until they are given authorisation to bring their families. Students are not required to be of any certain age, or to supply photos, or identity documents, or diplomas or any other particular qualifications'.[54]

Rapidly, Salafism grew prominent enough in certain regions to compete with traditional religious practices, then emerging as an alternative identity that appeared as particularly attractive to the younger generation. In a short polemic publication entitled *Sa'da limâdhâ?* [Sa'da, why?], published in the early 1990s under a pseudonym, a member of the traditionalist Zaydi al-Haqq party asked himself why an 'offensive on the part of Wahhabis' was being led by the Dâr al-Hadîth centre in a northern Yemeni region normally considered a bastion of the Zaydis.[55] This writer described the pressure his religious group was confronted with, and claimed that the development of Salafism was closely

refer to Saudi Arabia as a whole, but more often refers to the region of the Hejaz only.

[53] Muqbil al-Wâdi'î (ed.), *Tarjamat Abî 'Abd al-Rahmân Muqbil Bin Hâdî al-Wâdi'î* [Biography of Abî 'Abd al-Rahmân Muqbil Bin Hâdî al-Wâdi'î], op. cit., p. 30.

[54] www.muqbel.net/old/dammaj/index.htm (accessed on 9 January, 2006).

[55] Muhammad al-Sa'îdî, *Sa'da limâdhâ?* [Sa'da, why?], Beirut: Dâr al-Basâ'ir, date unknown.

linked with a certain Saudi imperialism. Years later, taking stock of the emergence of something he viewed as a foreign and imported religious identity, the same author (now a member of the socialist party) expressed chagrin: 'Zaydism no longer exists, there is nothing left in our country but Wahhabism!'[56]

In 1990, the unification of the two Yemens and the fall of the socialist regime created new opportunities for the Salafis. In fact, the South, which was seen as having been de-Islamised through the Marxist acculturation process it had undergone, appeared as a territory to be reconquered. The fact that the socialists—often called 'communists' (*shuyû'iyyûn*) by Salafis—still played an active institutional role in the newly unified political system and held important positions (Vice-President and Prime Minister) led the majority of Islamist movements, Muslim Brotherhood and Salafis in the forefront, to oppose the terms of the agreement for unification negotiated between the governments of the North and the South.[57] Some inside Yemen viewed that stance as a result of influence from the Saudi government, which considered the unification of Yemen to be contrary to its own interests. The simplistic notion that Islamists were no more than handmaidens of Saudi policy, however, did not long resist analysis or the impact of events on the ground. In fact the intra-Yemeni war of 1994, during which Islamist militias participated as allies of the government, opposed to 'secessionists' (brought in by socialists and certain of the elites of the Hadramawt, many of whom were supported by Saudi Arabia and other Gulf States and were also linked to Sufi groups) proves that the initial opposition of certain Islamist currents was not dictated by the Saudi patron, but above all by deep hostility toward any political formation influenced by Marxism.

The military victory, which brought about a lasting dismantling of the Yemeni socialist party, increased the space for manoeuvring of the whole Islamist movement, and particularly of the Salafis. In comparison to Zaydism in the north, it was Sufism and (still) socialism that served as the ideological foils to the Salafi current in the regions of the former People's Democratic Republic of Yemen. The destruction of Sufi shrines, especially at the 'Aydarûs mosque in Aden (along with the Sira brewery, the only one in the whole Ara-

---

[56] Interview, Sana'a, April 2006.

[57] See for example, Muhammad al-Anisî, sound recording, *al-Wahda* [Unity] and Muqbil al-Wâdi'î, sound recording, *Nasîhatî lil-sha'abayn al-yamanî al-su'ûdî* [My advice to the people of Yemen and Saudi Arabia] in which he declares: 'The *ahl al-sunna* are not satisfied by unity with the socialists. We have warned the political leaders but they have decided to continue the process they had begun'. Also see another recorded sermon of al-Wâdi'î, *Hukm al-intimâ' ilâ al-ahzâb* [Judgement concerning party membership].

bian Peninsula and a leftover of British colonisation) in the summer of 1994, a short while after the forces of the North and their allies entered the former capital of South Yemen, constituted the symbols of Islam's revival and of the offensive of a new militant brand of religion.

The Salafi Critique of hizbiyya

Despite, or perhaps because, of these dynamics, Salafism in Yemen during the 1990s experienced some internal dissension and conflict between an orthodox core, headed by Muqbil al-Wâdi'î, and a reformist offshoot. Debate largely revolved around the issue of the institutionalisation of the movement and around the assertion of the apolitical nature of the Salafism. Since its emergence—more so than in other national contexts—the denunciation of political participation has occupied a central role in the rhetoric of Yemeni Salafis, differentiating them from other Islamist groups, particularly the Muslim Brotherhood. Such rejection of party politics also implies that the Salafis denounce all formal institutionalisation of their movement, even in the form of charitable associations. Many Salafi publications denounce the form of innovation (*bid'a*) represented by membership in parties, a kind of corruption that leads to what they label *hizbiyya* (factionalism). They also directly criticise democracy, elections and, as they claim, any affiliation to formal organisations that implies some kind of loyalty other than allegiance to God. For Muhammad al-Imâm,[58] the principal heir of Muqbil al-Wâdi'î, *hizbiyya* is 'illicit (*harâm*)', it represents 'a disease', 'one of the greatest calamities' and its 'effects are among the most horrible that Muslims find among themselves'. For him, the various elections organised in Yemen since unification 'tore to pieces the country and the believers'. In a 1996 sermon explicitly entitled *Hurmat al-intikhâbât* [The illicit nature of elections], Muqbil al-Wâdi'î declared: 'Why do we prohibit elections? We prohibit them because they give Yemeni criminals the same rights as Muslims'. Al-Wâdi'î claimed to reject democratic principles to the extent that they 'imply that power lies with the majority, and not with God'. He also said, 'Democracy means that the people rule themselves, and that God rules nothing!'[59] 'Abd

---

[58] See for example Muhammad al-Imâm, sound recording, *Khatar al-tahazzub* [The danger of party politics] and by the same author *Tanwîr al-zulumât bi-kashf mafâsid wa shubuhât al-intikhâbât* [Clearing away obscurity through the revelation of the ravages and the uncertainties of elections], Ma'bar: publisher unknown, 1996.

[59] Muqbil al-Wâdi'î, sound recording, *Liqâ' sahîfat al-bayân al-imâratiyya* [Interview with the Emirati paper *al-Bayân*].

al-'Azîz al-Bura'î, head of the Salafi centre of Mafraq Hubaysh near the town of Ibb, saw elections as 'a waste of time and money that could have been spent to spread the message of the *ahl al-sunna*.'[60]

The focus on the rebuttal of political participation and democracy appears to be directly linked to the actual embeddedness of Yemeni Salafis in their own national context and history. The emphasis on staying away from politics and opposed to all *hizbiyya* can to some extent be explained by the fact that the concept of *hizb* (party) has a negative connotation for most of Yemeni society. For this reason, the two main political formations, the Yemeni Congregation for Reform (*al-Tajammu' al-yamanî lil-islâh*, commonly referred to as *al-Islâh*)[61] and the GPC (in power) do not perceive themselves as parties. In 1986 President Sâlih stated, for example, in a speech given to GPC members: 'The party spirit is treason, fragmentation, the end of peace and national unity, it is clientelism.'[62]

To an even greater extent, the emphasis given to this question of *hizbiyya* by Yemeni Salafis appears as the result of the republican Yemeni context (unique in the Arabian Peninsula) and of the democratisation project formulated at the end of the 1980s in North Yemen and (at least partially) implemented at the moment of unification in 1990. In fact, the development of Salafism took place while Yemen was experiencing multiparty politics and free elections for the first time of its history. The difficulties connected with the transition phase of power-sharing between the elites of the North and the socialists of the South from 1990 to 1994 no doubt affected the outlook of the Salafi actors. This period, characterised by rivalries between elites, political assassinations (particularly of former socialist leaders), dirty tricks and intense partisan activity,

---

[60] 'Abd al-'Azîz al-Bura'î, sound recording, *Tahdhîr min al-fitan* [Warning against dissension].

[61] On the internal dynamics of al-Islâh, see Laurent Bonnefoy and Marine Poirier 'The Yemeni Congregation for Reform (al-Islâh): The Difficult Process of Building a Project for Change' in Myriam Catusse and Karam Karam (eds.), *Returning to Political Parties? Partisan Logic and Political Transformations in the Arab World*, op. cit.; Nâsir Muhammad al-Tawîl, *al-Haraka al-islâmiyya wa al-nizâm al-siyâsî fî al-Yaman. Min al-tahâluf 'ila al-tanâfus* [The Islamist movement and the political system in Yemen. From alliance to competition], Sana'a: Maktabat Khâlid Bin al-Walîd, 2009.

[62] Speech given by Yemeni President 'Alî 'Abd Allâh Sâlih quoted in Sâlih Bin Muhammad al-Yâfi'î, *al-Mawâqif al-râhina fî al-Yaman min tatbîq kitâb Allâh wa sunnat rasûlihi* [The current positions in Yemen as concerns the application of the book of God and the Tradition of his Prophet], Riyadh: Maktabat al-Mu'ayyad, 1993, p. 88.

led to the war of the summer of 1994. This specific context explains much of the emphasis put by the Salafi entrepreneurs on the criticism of party and institutional politics. Since they were operating in a political system that was trying to build legitimacy for itself through elections and multiparty democracy, the rejection of *hizbiyya* became a structural element in the political-religious field of Salafism. At any rate this process of legitimisation was radically different from the one that prevailed in other countries of the region and in the Saudi context. In the latter, an absence of any type of elections (up until 2004–2005) and of socialist, Ba'athist or Nasserist legal opponents, connected to the prohibition on political parties, favoured a general de-politicisation or de-institutionalisation of society, which to some extent caused the question of participation and parties to recede into the background.[63]

In 1990, the unification of the two Yemens, political pluralism, internal debates within the Salafi field and echoes from the Gulf War led to the creation of a charitable association, al-Hikma (Jam'iyyat al-khayriyya al-hikma al-yamaniyya—Yemeni Wisdom Charity Association) by former students at Dammâj, especially Muhammad Muhammad al-Mahdî, 'Abd al-'Azîz al-Duba'î, 'Aqîl al-Maqtarî and Ahmad Hasan al-Mu'allim.[64] This association, whose name is an explicit reference to the famous *hadîth* of the Prophet, according to which 'faith is from Yemen and wisdom is from Yemen (*al-îmân yamân wa al-hikma yamâniyya*)',[65] legitimised the formal institutionalisation of the Salafi current. Well established in the Ta'iz region in the south-western part of the country, this organisation began to provide important social services such as support for orphans, and construction of mosques and schools. Al-Hikma members continued to claim to be following the teachings of Muqbil al-Wâdi'î, although the latter criticised them, rejecting the value and the manner of their social and political interventions. When the leaders of the association explained that their

---

[63] On the phenomenon of de-politicisation in Saudi society, see Pascal Ménoret, 'Le cheikh, l'électeur et le sms: Logiques électorales et mobilisation islamique en Arabie Saoudite', *Transcontinentales*, no. 1, 2005, pp. 19–33; and Madawi al-Rasheed, 'Interdire le politique: le discours religieux wahhabite en Arabie Saoudite' in Abdellah Hammoudi, Denis Bauchard and Rémy Leveau (eds.), *La démocratie est-elle soluble dans l'islam*, Paris: CNRS éditions, 2007, pp. 147–165.

[64] Ahmad al-Mu'allim was acquainted with Muqbil al-Wâdi'î and Juhaymân al-'Utaybî at Medina during the 1970s. Following this he was imprisoned in Saudi Arabia for several years, apparently because of his connections to the group that stormed the mosque at Mecca in November 1979.

[65] *Hadîth* collected in Bukhârî vol. 4, book 56, no. 703; also cited in vol. 5, book 59, no. 671.

benevolent activity also financed scholarships for students to study at Salafi centres, Muqbil al-Wâdi'î responded:

They lie when they claim that they support the students of Ma'bar, Ma'rib and Dammâj [i.e., centres run by Muhammad al-Imâm, Abû al-Hasan al-Ma'ribî and himself]. You won't find one person down there for whom they bought so much as the soap to wash their clothes. [...] The money those associations take in just sits in the banks![66]

In 1992, al-Hikma itself experienced internal division. 'Abd Allâh al-Yazîdî and 'Abd al-Majîd al-Raymî (who directed in Sana'a the Markaz al-da'wa al-'ilmî, Centre for Scientific Preaching) officially founded with other *'ulamâ* and philanthropists an association they called al-Ihsân (benevolence) based in al-Mukallâ in Hadramawt, which limited itself to benevolent activities. The creation of this competing organisation (which did not become active until 1996, and established itself essentially in the governorates of the former South Yemen) however did not provoke an open breach with al-Hikma. The creation of al-Ihsân was the result of a desire to expand in geographical terms the field of action, and to try to get new financing, especially from rich Hadrami businessmen, and also from people close to the Qatari government.

Gradually al-Hikma was drawn into political activity. The *salafiyya munazzama* (activist salafism) it represents is characterised by a rapprochement between the ideology of the Muslim Brotherhood and Salafi references that are quietist or connected to the *salafiyya da'wiyya* of Muqbil al-Wâdi'î. Members of the association consequently maintained a certain number of practices characteristic of the Salafi current, such as wearing the *thawb* above the ankles, not cutting the beard and stigmatising other religious groups. The two publications of al-Hikma, *al-Furqân* (The Qur'anic Proof—which is nicknamed by al-Wâdi'î, *al-Firqa*, the Division), and above all the monthly *al-Muntadâ* (The Forum) exemplify this relationship. Both these publications, for example, respect a variety of Salafi habits or norms, among which is the blurring of faces in photographs. The articles published generally conform to Salafi doctrine as established by al-Wâdi'î and his partisans. Articles critical of Shi'ites and Sufis but also Jews and Christians are common.

Despite such formalism and respect for the principles of Salafism, the break with the canons of Muqbilian Salafism lies in the idea of creating an association

---

[66] Muqbil al-Wâdi'î, *Tuhfat al-mujîb 'alâ as'ilat al-hâdhar wa al-gharîb* [Precious responses to questions from one who is present and one who is absent], Sana'a: Dâr al-Âthâr, 2005, p. 117.

and participating directly in the political sphere. For ʿAqîl al-Maqtarî, who heads an al-Hikma centre in Taʿiz, this formal institutionalisation guarantees a certain independence with regard to governance (through, for example, the payment of membership fees) and it is the only arrangement that permits effective work in preaching.[67] Rather than focus on principles that are disconnected from local issues, the partisans of al-Hikma opt in favour of adapting to the context in which they find themselves, and in favour of direct involvement with society. ʿAbd Allâh al-Sayânî, director of the Zaydi research centre al-Râ'id, and as such hardly likely to be indulgent with regard to Salafism in any of its forms, does concede, for example, that al-Hikma is marked by a certain pragmatism, which clearly distinguishes it from the Muqbilian and orthodox trend of quietist Salafism:

They use modern language, [...] they pass out thousands of brochures [...] and they have specified the strategic objective of their preaching, which is to build an individual who is a Muslim in effect.[68]

The controversy that arose from this division within the Salafi movement expresses the refusal of institutionalisation and political participation. Al-Wâdiʿî, who thought that these schisms were a dead end, said of Muhammad al-Mahdî, the director of al-Hikma, whom he had earlier thought would become a 'great scholar':

I'm afraid he will lose his head one of these days. He is one of the big losers in al-Hikma association. Why? Because the people around him listened to him and respected him but today he is all alone. All he has left is his association. He has lost himself and now has nothing.[69]

In an even more mocking tone, he chided the *esprit de corps* that motivated a feeling of 'exclusive allegiance' within al-Hikma, noting that 'even their plates and silverware are marked with Jamʿiyyat al-Hikma on them!'[70]

The al-Hikma association took a further step in the legislative elections of 1997 and 2003, by supporting and even presenting candidates for certain districts in the south of the country. As ʿAbd al-Fattâh al-Hakîmî recalls, in

---

[67] ʿAqîl al-Maqtarî, sound recording, *al-ʿAmal al-jamâʿî* [Work in associations].
[68] ʿAbd Allâh al-Sayânî, *al-Ikhwân al-muslimûn wa al-salafiyûn fî al-Yaman* [The Muslim Brotherhood and the Salafis in Yemen], op. cit., p. 125.
[69] Muqbil al-Wâdiʿî, sound recording, *Hâdhihi al-surûriyya faihdharuhâ!* [This is the Surûriyya so be careful!].
[70] Muqbil al-Wâdiʿî, sound recording, *Rihlat Yâfiʿ* [Journey to Yâfiʿ].

accordance with Salafi doctrine, the candidates' posters did not have photographs on them.[71] In the matter of political involvement, this group's attitude is however still ambiguous. Nâsir Yahyâ, researcher at the Centre for Strategic Studies, a think-tank associated with the Islâh party, asserted:

The people of al-Hikma are getting closer to political work, they propose co-operating with us [i.e., al-Islâh] but they aren't very clear about their positions and their objectives. Are they a political group? A charity organisation? What are they doing? They don't know themselves![72]

In return, Hasan al-Hâshidî, a member of the editorial committee of *al-Muntadâ* magazine and active member of al-Hikma, claims that the relationship of his association to the political sphere is as clear as can be:

Concerning political work, it is not one of our priorities. There is no project for the establishment of a Salafi political party. Some people claim this but it is false. They would like to see us become a wing of *Mu'tamar* [i.e., the GPC] but we prefer to concentrate on our benevolent activities.[73]

Still, in early 2009, prior to the general elections that were to occur in April of that year (but were eventually postponed repeatedly), the attitude of al-Hikma remained the object of much debate. Many still asked whether it would sponsor independent candidates or openly support candidates from other parties, including those of the ruling GPC. What would be the attitude of this Salafi organisation during elections?[74] In the framework of the 2011 Yemeni uprising, the question still remained to be answered.

The schism led by al-Hikma and al-Ihsân at the beginning of the 1990s embodies a wider shift within transnational Salafism. It represents in the specific Yemeni context the development of a more directly politicised version of Salafism, often labelled *Surûrî*, which acquired wide visibility in the context of the Gulf War. This movement accompanied the development of the *Sahwa islâmiyya* in Saudi Arabia which in the early 1990s built its popularity on criticism of the monarchy and of the religious establishment which had authorised the presence of American military forces on the country's holy soil. The

---

[71] 'Abd al-Fattâh al-Hakîmî, a*l-Islâmiyûn wa al-siyâsa: al-ikhwân al-muslimûn namûd-hajan* [Islamists and politics: the example of the Muslim Brotherhood], op. cit., p. 20.

[72] Interview, Sana'a, February 2006.

[73] Interview, Sana'a, February 2006.

[74] *Abwâb* (Yemeni independent monthly), March 2009 and Muhammad al-Mahdî's interview with *al-Taghiyîr* weekly, 20 March 2009: http://www.al-tagheer.com/news8223.html (accessed 1 September 2010).

Surûrî movement, as it has often been called by analysts and by some of its adversaries, drew its name from Muhammad Surûr Zayn al-'Abidîn, a cleric born in Syria in 1938, and former affiliate of the Muslim Brotherhood. Fleeing repression from Syria, he worked between 1965 and 1973 as a teacher in Saudi Arabia, but he was expelled from the Kingdom because of political activities that mixed the teachings of Hasan al-Bannâ and Sayyid Qutb with Salafi literalism. He then moved to Kuwait and in 1984 to the United Kingdom. In Birmingham, he established the Dâr al-Arqâm centre and the magazine *al-Sunna*, which came to be widely distributed throughout the Muslim world. During the 1990s, this magazine argued in favour of a contextualised and politicised Salafism that would refuse systematic allegiance with existing political authority.

In a seminal article entitled '*al-Islâm al-rasmî* [Official Islam]' and published at the height of the *Sahwa* movement in the early 1990s, Muhammad Surûr asserted that the dependence on existing authority of this 'selective Islam' (*intiqâ'î*), which lacks coherence in its decisions and in the positions it adopts, is indeed 'the sickness (*'illa*) of the Muslim community'.[75]

This *Surûrî* trend was not at all limited to *al-Sunna* magazine nor to Muhammad Surûr himself, but developed in a significant way around figures connected to the Saudi *Sahwa islâmiyya*—especially Salmân al-'Awda, Safar al-Hawâlî, Sa'îd al-Ghâmidî, 'Awâdh al-Qarnî or 'Â'idh al-Qarnî—or groups or parties led by 'Abd al-Rahmân 'Abd al-Khâliq of Kuwait. Following the crisis of the Gulf War of 1990–1991, the current of the *Sahwa* became more structured and managed to exert a wide influence. Through various petitions, it called for important political, institutional and social reforms in Saudi Arabia. Though this movement suffered repression, as well as some prominent members being imprisoned, a segment of the movement gradually found common ground with the Saudi government, especially after September 11, 2001. Some of its figures, among which Salmân al-'Awda and 'Â'idh al-Qarnî, were even more or less co-opted by the government, emerging as leading figures in the Saudi media. Another segment tried to maintain a degree of independence, while a third, an even smaller minority, started to favour the recourse to armed action against the state and against 'Western interests'.[76] The recanta-

---

[75] Muhammad Surûr Zayn al-'Abidîn, "al-Islâm al-rasmî [Official Islam]", *al-Sunna*, no. 21, 1992, p. 5.

[76] On the process of radicalisation of the Saudi Islamists, see Thomas Hegghammer, *Jihad in Saudi Arabia*, op. cit., pp. 83–98 and Stéphane Lacroix, *Les islamistes saoudiens*, op. cit., pp. 180–236.

tion of some former opponents, having often been imprisoned, is today the subject of a number of mocking jokes. Thus the magazine of Salmân al-'Awda, *al-Islâm al-yawm* (Islam Today) is now nicknamed *al-Istislâm al-yawm* (Capitulation Today) by some of its former supporters, who reject its new status as a mainstream publication.

Despite its activism and its dynamism, few Islamists in Saudi Arabia, in Yemen or elsewhere subscribe explicitly to the *Surûrî* label. Still, *al-Sunna* magazine connected to Muhammad Surûr has allowed this movement to spawn and to some extent to theorise about a significant evolution of the transnational Salafi presence by representing the emergence of a relatively homogeneous current in activist Salafism (*salafiyya munazzama*).

The emergence of this new Salafi movement in Yemen, via al-Hikma and al-Ihsân elicited strong reactions from the majority Muqbilian current. In 1999, Muqbil al-Wâdi'î explained these schisms with reference to the desire for gain on the part of those who 'did not persevere in their learning, who could not be satisfied with eating only their proper portion of bread and beans, and who thus turned toward the *hizbiyya*'.[77] He also insisted on their connections with the current of Kuwaiti Salafism, especially with 'Abd al-Rahmân 'Abd al-Khâliq, whom he accused of 'corrupting the *ahl al-sunna* in Yemen, and blinding them with his Kuwaiti dinars rather than by his thoughts'.[78] Criticising the politicisation of the *salafiyya munazzama* and of the *Surûrî* current and their rejection of universal religious references to the benefit of local *'ulamâ'* who, as they claimed, are supposed to take into account the specificities of the political environment, Muqbil al-Wâdi'î explained:

> The partisans of Surûr invite you to refer yourselves to Salafis that understand the situation, for example in the case of Yemen, they claim it's necessary to return to Salafis who are involved with the situation [i.e., they are from Yemen].[79]

In this way he refutes the 'relativist' approach of the *salafiyya munazzama*, explaining that 'the reference points, for the *ahl al-sunna* are the Book and the Tradition', and these apply in all cases regardless of context. Such a position recalls in a direct way the position defended by certain Saudi *'ulamâ'* close to

---

[77] Muqbil al-Wâdi'î, sound recording, *As'ila 'an hayât al-shaykh Muqbil al-Wâdi'î wa sîratuhu* [Questions about the life of shaykh Muqbil al-Wâdi'î and his biography].

[78] Muqbil al-Wâdi'î, *Tuhfat al-mujîb 'alâ as'ilat al-hâdhar wa al-gharîb* [Precious responses to questions from one who is present and one who is absent], op. cit., p. 288.

[79] Muqbil al-Wâdi'î, sound recording, *Hâdhihi al-surûriyya faihdharuhâ!* [This is the Surûriyya so be careful!].

the monarchy, including Muhammad al-'Uthaymîn, 'Abd al-'Azîz Âl al-Shaykh, and Abû Bakr al-Jazâ'irî, whose speeches were collected on an audio cassette entitled *Aqwâl al-'ulamâ 'alâ al-hizbiyya* [Speeches from *'ulamâ'* on membership in parties] that was distributed through Salafi bookstores in Yemen. Responding to a young activist from Yemen who had asked questions about the Islâh party and the fact that members of parties had 'said that Saudi shaykhs do not understand the situation in Yemen', a Saudi scholar, apparently al-'Uthaymîn, said:

Our answer is that the parties are not in conformity with Islam because God said that there is only one party: the party of believers. [...] It is true that I am not Yemeni, and I have never visited that country, but I know that the sickness of the Muslim community is the same everywhere. [...] There is no difference between this country, Syria, Algeria, Tunisia, Libya and Morocco, they are all far from the Salafi method.

This formula captures very well the gap that exists between the two ideal-typical categories of Islamism specified above and which are represented here by the universalist and de-contextualised form of Salafism characterised as quietist, and, with regards to the second category, by a willingness to adapt to contexts and to become more or less directly involved in the political space.

Salafism in Yemen after Muqbil Bin Hâdî al-Wâdi'î

Suffering either from liver cancer or from cirrhosis,[80] Muqbil al-Wâdi'î was hospitalised during the summer of 2000. At this time he delivered his last sermons in Yemen, at al-Khayr mosque in Sana'a, before a crowd of several thousand people.[81] But the severity of his illness required him to seek medical care outside the country. So, he agreed to return to Saudi Arabia. More than twenty years after his expulsion (which he continued to characterise as unjust), he explained his reluctance to return to that country and his desire not to

[80] On 12 July 2001, ten days ahead of the actual event, the Qatari newspaper *al-Râyya* claimed that Muqbil al-Wâdi'î had died from cancer ... of the tongue, something he managed to deny in his last recorded sermon. The reference to the tongue, no doubt intentional in this case appears as an ironic reference to his particular tendency to violently criticise or insult his adversaries during fiery speeches.

[81] According to a journalist from the English-language weekly *Yemen Times*, about 4,000 people attended a conference given by al-Wâdi'î focusing on the prophetic Tradition: 'All About the Founder of the Salafiyah Movement, Moqbel Bin Hade al-Wade and his Followers', *Yemen Times*, 24 July 2000.

appear as having gone back on his previous statements, particularly as regards his criticism of the Saudi government:

More than once people suggested that I ask Prince Ahmad, the Deputy Minister of the Interior [of Saudi Arabia], for permission to make the *hajj* and the *'umra* [and so to ask for a visa to enter Saudi Arabia]. I told them that it was not necessary. I said to myself that I was not going to lower myself to such a thing, and that in the end, thanks be to God, I was happy in my own country among my students.[82]

Owing to the mediation of Muhammad al-'Uthaymîn, member of the Committee of Senior *'ulamâ'* (who would himself die a few months later), Muqbil al-Wâdi'î arrived in Jeddah in late 2000. From there, seriously ill, he was sent to the United States and then to Germany for medical treatment, which ended up being inefficient, and he returned to die in Mecca on 21 July, 2001.[83]

Much like the episode of the Gulf War, the death of Muqbil al-Wâdi'î produced a certain number of rearrangements within the political and religious field of Salafism. His central position and his authority had unarguably made him the symbol of the Salafi movement in Yemen. Consequently, his death engendered fierce quarrel between his heirs, each of whom claimed to represent his valued heritage.

Among these rearrangements, the supremacy of the founding branch of the Dâr al-Hadîth network of religious institutes, in Dammâj, was increasingly contested. In fact, with Muqbil al-Wâdi'î's death, the centre of Ma'bar, located 70 kilometres south of Sana'a and directed by the charismatic Muhammad al-Imâm (his original name: Muhammad Bin 'Abd Allâh al-Raymî), gradually gained prominence, without ever creating an open split. Not only did the Dammâj institute appear as geographically remote (and located in the Sa'da war-torn area from June 2004 onwards) but its new 'director', Yahyâ al-Hajûrî, was seen as unpopular because of his excessive zeal.[84] According to a member of the Hikma association:

---

[82] Muqbil al-Wâdi'î, sound recording, *Mushâhadâtî fî al-Mamlaka al-'Arabiyya al-Su'ûdiyya* [My experience of the Kingdom of Saudi Arabia].

[83] The final months of the life of Muqbil in Saudi Arabia are the subject of a long narrative written by Yahyâ al-Hajûrî and published in a work edited by the wife of al-Wâdi'î, Umm Salama Al-Salafiyya (ed.), *al-Rihla al-akhîra li-imâm al-Jazîra* [The last journey of the imam of the Peninsula], Sana'a: Dâr al-Âthâr, 2003.

[84] In a sermon from 2005 entitled *al-Hajûrî: qunbula wa musîba* [al-Hajûrî: bomb and disaster], Nu'mân al-Watar, a companion of Abû al-Hasan al-Ma'ribî, ferociously criticised the excessive language of al-Hajûrî and accused him of 'soiling the reputation of Salafi preaching'. For al-Watar, 'it is devastating that he should pronounce such evil words in a mosque, they are not fit for the street or the market'.

Al-Hajûrî only talks. Muhammad al-Imâm has a lot more knowledge, and he performs real social and religious work (*'ilmî*) in Ma'bar where he maintains good relations with the tribes.[85]

Still, while losing credit among Yemenis, the Dammâj branch remained popular among foreigners who were searching for authenticity and related to Dâr al-Hadîth's prestigious past.

Over and above processes of internal political recalculation, the death of the founder of the Yemeni movement provoked a second schism and numerous ripples around the person of Mustafâ Bin Isma'îl al-Sulaymânî, known as Abû al-Hasan al-Misrî (the Egyptian) or Abû al-Hasan al-Ma'ribî (from the town of Ma'rib). Born in Egypt, and for a time associated with the violent movement, al-Takfîr wa al-hijra,[86] Abû al-Hasan moved to Yemen at the beginning of the 1980s fleeing repression, and became a student of Muqbil al-Wâdi'î at Dâr al-Hadîth. The briefness of his stay at Dammâj did not prevent him from developing a close relationship with the Yemeni scholar. Later he established his own teaching institute, also called Dâr al-Hadîth, near the town of Ma'rib, 200 kilometres east of the capital. Thanks to the intervention of powerful tribal shaykhs of that region, in 1996 he was granted Yemeni citizenship, something that occasioned a degree of diplomatic tension with the Egyptian government. The creation in 1999 by Abû al-Hasan of a charity organisation called *al-Birr wa al-taqwa* ('Charity and Devotion') provoked arguments but, contrary to what had happened with al-Hikma, this association was not formally criticised by al-Wâdi'î, who from all appearances continued to hold Abû al-Hasan in high esteem.[87] The benevolence of the position taken by the founder of the Salafi movement in Yemen was not entirely incoherent. Al-Wâdi'î indeed claimed to have developed a more subtle doctrine on the issue of the formal institutionalisation of charity activities:

The partisans of the *Surûriyya* say we disapprove of the creation of associations. Who has told you this, my poor children! We disapprove of certain associations that lead to people having party spirit, to exclusive allegiances (*walâ' dhayyiq*) and to robbery.[88]

---

[85] Interview, Sana'a, February 2006.

[86] Interview, Sana'a, April 2008. For a detailed study of this violent Islamist group, see Gilles Kepel, *Le Prophète et le Pharaon: Les mouvements islamistes dans l'Égypte contemporaine*, Paris: La Découverte, 1984, pp. 70–100.

[87] 'Abd al-Fattâh al-Hakîmî, *al-Islâmiyûn wa al-siyâsa: al-ikhwân al-muslimûn namûdhajan* [Islamists and politics: the example of the Muslim Brotherhood], op. cit., p. 21.

[88] Muqbil al-Wâdi'î, sound recording, *Hâdhihi al-surûriyya faihdharuhâ!* [This is the Surûriyya so be careful!].

Despite such asserted flexibility, the combination of the death of al-Wâdi'î in 2001 and the emergence of Abû al-Hasan al-Ma'ribî in the Yemeni Salafi arena led to much debate and in the end produced another schism. This split appeared not only as the result of a quarrel between putative inheritors, but was also related to the larger context of the development of a more politicised Salafism. Regardless of its literalism and its claim to defend a universalist interpretation of the Qur'an and the sunna, the quietist Salafi movement in Yemen was affected by processes of political recomposition that led some to accept involvement in the social and political spheres.

Within the framework of this internal controversy that basically opposed Abû al-Hasan al-Ma'ribi to hardliners headed by Yahyâ al-Hajûrî, each trend attempted to legitimise its own position by citing Saudi references in support. Taking advantage of the vacuum left by a succession of deaths of important Salafi *'ulamâ'*, Rabî' al-Madkhalî, a former companion of al-Wâdi'î and a former faculty Dean at the Islamic University of Medina, waded into the debate and attempted to put himself forward as a new guarantor of Salafi orthodoxy.[89] He published a number of books or booklets explaining in detail various theological and strategic errors committed by Abû al-Hasan al-Ma'ribî.[90] All during 2002 and 2003 he put out, along with other Saudi *'ulamâ'* (especially 'Ubayd Bin 'Abd Allâh al-Jâbirî or Muhammad Bin Hâdî al-Madkhalî) a series of pamphlets attacking Abû al-Hasan and inviting Muslims to stop supporting him.[91]

Since he was about to die without male descent, al-Wâdi'î shortly before he passed away had written a will in which he had made a list of his *ahl al-sunna* heirs, including Abû al-Hasan.[92] Nonetheless, in the context of the second schism that occurred after his death, the status of Abû al-Hasan as an intellectual heir of al-Wâdi'î was called into question by his adversaries. Through a number of pamphlets, conferences and cassettes this group attempted to prove that al-Wâdi'î himself mistrusted Abû al-Hasan, and had begun during his lifetime to separate from him. It was stated that al-Wâdi'î, shortly before his

---

[89] On the position of Rabî' al-Madkhalî within the *Jâmî* or quietist Salafi movement in Saudi Arabia: Stéphane Lacroix, *Les islamistes saoudiens*, op. cit., pp. 256–258.

[90] See, for example, Rabî' al-Madkhalî, *Intiqâd 'aqdî wa manhajî likitâb "al-Sirâj al-wahâj fî bayân al-minhâj"* [Contractual and methodological disapproval of the book 'The bright light of the declaration of method'], Sana'a: Dâr al-Âthâr, 2002.

[91] A list of these anti-Abû al-Hasan books and pamphlets has been published by François Burgat and Mohamed Sbitli, *'Les salafis au Yémen... ou la modernisation malgré tout'*, op. cit., pp. 138–139.

[92] Ibid., p. 152.

death had declared: 'If Abû al-Hasan is able to do it, he will destroy the *da'wa* of the *ahl al-sunna* in Yemen'.[93] In the same vein, the circumstances that surrounded al-Wâdi'î's writing of a will (with the help of a member of his tribe) ten days before his death while in Saudi Arabia have been the subject of debate. Sa'îd al-Mashûshî al-Yâfi'î claimed in a short booklet that the presence of Abû al-Hasan's name in the will was only the result of a misunderstanding, and of manipulation on the part of the 'Egyptian felon' and his partisans. In fact, according to the story he tells about the writing of the will, after having made an initial list of his intellectual heirs without including the name of Abû al-Hasan, Muqbil al-Wâdi'î, in a very weak condition, went to the bathroom. When he returned, the person helping him write the will is supposed to have asked, 'And Abû al-Hasan, what about him?' Al-Wâdi'î is supposed to have replied, 'I forgot him!' For those contesting the status of Abû al-Hasan, this was equivalent to rejection. But the story is that the helper misunderstood this answer and incorrectly added the name of Abû al-Hasan to the list.[94]

Despite such an anecdote, the exclusion of Abû al-Hasan by al-Wâdi'î during his lifetime is nonetheless improbable. In fact, he remained close to the founding father of the Salafi movement in Yemen until he died, and was even part of the small group that accompanied him during his medical treatment in Saudi Arabia.[95] In this context, the attempts to prove that the founder of the Yemeni Salafi movement rejected his association with Abû al-Hasan appear to lack consistency.

In this heated debate, the Egyptian origin of Abû al-Hasan has been used as a means of discrediting him. His opponents always refer to him as '*al-Misrî*' (the Egyptian) and not '*al-Ma'ribî*' as he calls himself. Rabî' al-Madkhalî, one of the main perpetrators of the transnationalisation of the controversy, referred

[93] Pamphlet distributed by the Muhammad Bin 'Abd al-Wahhâb bookstore in Tarîm in the spring of 2005.

[94] Sa'îd al-Mashûshî al-Yâfi'î, *Anbâ' al-fudhalâ'* [News of noble people] Sana'a: Maktabat al-Athariyya, 2002.

[95] Despite the violent disagreement between Abû al-Hasan and Yahyâ al-Hajûrî, the latter confirmed the presence of the former in Saudi Arabia at the time when al-Wâdi'î was seeking medical treatment there in 2000–2001: Umm Salama Al-Salafiyya (ed.), *al-Rihla al-akhîra li-imâm al-Jazîra* [The last journey of the imam of the Peninsula], op. cit., p. 17. Concerning Abû al-Hasan al-Ma'ribî, Nu'man al-Watar and Abû Hâtim al-Fâdhlî, Yahyâ al-Hajûrî does add: 'I would like to be able to strike out these three names but [...] as the shaykh [Muqbil] mentioned them, I cannot change anything'. Ibid., p. 15.

to him as 'the guest' (*al-nazîl*) of Ma'rib[96] in order to underline the transitory character of his presence in Yemen. These points are not insignificant as they are directly related to a certain popular animosity towards Egyptians that exists in Yemen. This is based to some extent on abuses linked to the military intervention of Jamâl 'Abd al-Nâsir in support of the republicans during the 1960s. They are also implicit references to things Muqbil al-Wâdi'î wrote in different publications, especially his most famous book *al-Makhraj min al-fitna* [Leaving dissension behind], in which he repeatedly insulted Egyptians and criticised their presence in Yemen.[97]

In addition to these attacks, Abû al-Hasan has been accused of having corrupted the Salafi movement with his hidden political agenda, and even of having renounced al-Wâdi'î's teachings after his death. His association is thus nicknamed *Jam'iyyat al-birr wa al-taqwâ al-hizbiyya* (the partisan) instead of *al-khayriyya* (charitable). The fact that his father, 'Isma'îl al-Misrî', was, according to opponents of Abû al-Hasan, executed in 1966 along with Sayyid Qutb by the Egyptian authorities constitutes a new accusation: 'Abû al-Hasan came

---

[96] Rabî' al-Madkhalî, *Intiqâd 'aqdî wa manhajî likitâb 'al-Sirâj al-wahâj fî bayân al-minhâj'* [Contractual and methodological disapproval of the book, 'The bright light of the declaration of method'], op. cit., p. 3.

[97] See for example Muqbil Al-Wâdi'î, *al-Makhraj min al-fitna* [Leaving dissension behind], op. cit., p. 113. al-Wâdi'î declares: 'Those who corrupted the Muslim Brotherhood in Yemen, were the Egyptians who came to work in Scientific Institutes (*Ma'ahid 'ilmiyya*) and to work for the Bureau of Orientation and Guidance (*Maktab al-tawjîh wa al-irshâd*). Most of them were opportunists. They pretend to adhere with zeal to the Brotherhood in order to gain the confidence of the directors of institutes and get jobs. But most of these Egyptians 'change colour' (*yatalawwanûn*). They are ready to be Sunnites among the Sunnites, Shi'ites among the Shi'ites, and even Sufis among the mystics'. Quoted in François Burgat, *L'islamisme à l'heure d'al-Qaida*, op. cit., pp. 36–37. François Burgat and Mohamed Sbitli, 'Les salafis au Yémen...ou la modernisation malgré tout', op. cit., p. 134 also quote a recorded conference with Muqbil al-Wâdi'î entitled *'Amâ'im 'alâ bahâ'im* [Turban Wearing Asses] in which he states 'I told the Brothers, about these turban wearing asses, I mean the turban wearers of al-Azhâr, whom many consider asses (*bahâ'im*). The degenerate azhârîs who call for unification, we say to them, "Go reform your own country. Don't come here to get 8000 riyals in salary from the Bureau of al-tawjîh wa al-irshâd in order to corrupt our country. Go reform where you come from, in your country of women's exhibitionism (*tabarruj wa-sufûr*), communist parties, wine and every kind of corruption. We can do without you and your red fez, your turban and your robe (*jubba*) that drags on the ground." [...] The government is responsible before God for 8000 riyals that it pays them, while giving 500 or even 400 to Yemenis. The degenerate azhârî gets 8000 riyals. Break their heads, O Yemeni. Expel them from the mosques'.

to Yemen as a disciple of Sayyid Qutb',[98] some say. This reference to the radical thinker of the Muslim Brotherhood allows Abû al-Hasan to be accused of permitting violence, and his former involvement with the *Takfîr wa al-hijra* group can thus be mentioned again. In this context, 'Abd al-'Azîz al-Bura'î, in a pamphlet published in 2004, addresses the partisans of Abû al-Hasan al-Ma'ribî and asks:

Can you hold yourselves apart from Sayyid Qutb, from whose thoughts the explosion just now sounding in the world (i.e., 9/11 attacks) took form? For it is the students and devotees of his books that have done this [...] Abû al-Hasan continues to revere Sayyid Qutb, and justifies this attitude because he was the grandfather of his wife.[99]

This allegation of matrimonial links between Abû al-Hasan and Sayyid Qutb is evidently difficult to verify, but it still allows people to point to a supposed sympathy on the part of the dissident of Egyptian origin with the thought of Qutb, the subject of long refutations from the main figures of quietist Salafism and the *Jâmiyya*.

With regard to accusations of sympathy for Sayyid Qutb, Abû al-Hasan has never formally denounced him (Muqbil al-Wâdi'î himself recognised the interest his books held and their literary qualities)[100] but has emphasised his own unreserved condemnation of violence and terrorism. At the end of 2001, before the controversy that opposed him to other heirs of Muqbilian Salafism, he was accused by the government of Yemen of harbouring in his centre at Ma'rib some foreign members of al-Qaeda. In order to escape repression, he clarified his positions, distanced himself from currents rumoured to be jihadi, and in 2004 in Saudi Arabia published a work entitled *al-Tafîrât wa al-ightiyâlât: al-asbâb, al-âthâr, al-'ilâj* [Explosions and assassinations: reasons, effects, and solutions]. In this book he attempted to bypass quarrels internal to Salafism and he asserted his allegiance to the existing government. In his view, the supporters of illegitimate armed action against the state are to be considered zealots (*ghulû*) whose behaviour is illicit. He also wrote that it 'is necessary for all reasonable people to be patient when faced with oppression and the tyranny

---

[98] 'Abd al-Rahmân Bin Muhammad Âl 'Umaysân, *al-Hajaj al-salafiyya lidahad shabh Abî al-Hasan al-hizbiyya* [Salafi arguments to refute those who would argue that Abû al-Hasan favours attachment to parties], place, publisher and date unknown.

[99] 'Abd al-'Azîz al-Bura'î, *Takâtuf al-mutasâqitîn* [The alliance of losers], place and publisher unknown, 2004, p. 4.

[100] Muqbil al-Wâdi'î, *Ijâbat al-sâ'il 'alâ ahamm al-masâ'il* [Answer to those who ask the most important questions], op. cit., p. 398.

maintained by those who hold power (*walî al-amr*).[101] Thus, in accordance with the concept of *wasatiyya* (moderation), violence against Muslim governments is for Abû al-Hasan strictly prohibited.

In this context of recomposition for Yemeni Salafism, particularly along political lines, the two dissident Salafi trends, structured around al-Hikma and Abû al-Hasan al-Ma'ribî, once mutually opposed, show progressive signs of reconciliation. Interestingly, such a process also involves certain currents within the Muslim Brotherhood. In August 2004 a joint conference was organised in the city of Say'ûn in the Hadramawt by Abû al-Hasan and Ahmad Hasan al-Mu'allim, the representative of al-Hikma in the region. In a booklet entitled *Takâtuf al-mutasâqitîn* [The alliance of losers], 'Abd al-'Azîz al-Bura'î presents this trend as proof that Abû al-Hasan now follows the *hizbiyya* system, although previously he and his partisans had condemned al-Hikma unequivocally. So he declares:

Before the *fitna* created by Abû al-Hasan, we were united against these deviant groups [i.e., the Muslim Brotherhood, members of al-Hikma or al-Ihsân associations] and we all thought they were on the wrong path.[102]

Gradually Salafis that have been excluded or ostracised in the course of these quarrels have regrouped and sought some form of merger between dissidents. In July 2009, 'Abd al-Majîd al-Zindânî, the controversial figure of al-Islâh and head of the radical Muslim Brotherhood wing of the party, participated in the graduation ceremony of students of a religious summer school organised by al-Hikma. In Sana'a, at the Maktabat al-Idrîsî bookstore, allied with Abû al-Hasan, but located just next to the main Salafi centre in the capital, the Masjid al-Khayr (directed by Muhammad al-Sawmalî, who has remained associated with the orthodox Muqbilian trend), people speak of the difficulties of co-existence:

We can go to pray at masjid al-Khayr but some of our people have problems, they refuse to say hello to us, or they insult us. If necessary, we can go a little further to the Andalus mosque run by al-Ihsân association.[103]

Probably less significant than the Abû al-Hasan al-Ma'ribî schism, another controversy arose in the late-2000s following the establishment of an institute

---

[101] Abû al-Hasan al-Ma'ribî, *al-Tafjîrât wa al-ightiyâlât: al-asbâb, al-âthâr, al-'ilâj* [Explosions and assassinations: reasons, effects and solutions], Riyadh: Dâr al-Fadhîla, 2004, p. 27.

[102] 'Abd al-'Azîz al-Bura'î, *Takâtuf al-mutasâqitîn* [The alliance of losers], op. cit., p. 4.

[103] Interview, Sana'a, June 2005.

by ʿAbd al-Rahmân al-ʿAdanî, also called al-Marʿî, and his brother ʿAbd Allâh in al-Fayûsh on the outskirts of Aden. The issue initially had to do with land ownership (properties in al-Fayûsh were being sold at apparently excessive rates, particularly to foreign Salafis) and financial problems, and this conflict gave rise to a controversy more ideological in nature. Once again, Yahyâ al-Hajûrî took the lead among opponents of the ʿAdanî brothers who earlier headed an institute on the coast of Hadramawt in al-Shihr, and accused them of enriching themselves, of practicing *hizbiyya* and of betraying the doctrine of Muqbil al-Wâdiʿî. He claimed that their actual objective was to draw people away from Dammâj and to create their own independent movement, a step tantamount to establishing a political party.[104] The violent debate between Salafi entrepreneurs of various leanings had important transnational repercussions, particularly on the internet via al-ʿUlûm forum (aloloom.net). French Salafis, for example, took sides: two opposing blogs were opened, one (ah-je-savais-pas.over-blog.net) defending the position of Yahyâ al-Hajûrî, the other (maintenant-tu-sais.com) that of ʿAbd al-Rahmân al-ʿAdanî. During 2008 and 2009, Rabîʿ al-Madkhalî from Saudi Arabia intervened as he had during the Abû al-Hasan *fitna*, published various texts and commented on the issue but eventually tried to calm things down and reconcile both parties, something that was only partially achieved.

The controversy eventually resulted in a crisis of legitimacy concerning Yahyâ al-Hajûrî, whose enmity towards his rivals, as well as fellow Salafis, and excessive focus on apparently minor issues made him incapable of replacing Muqbil al-Wâdiʿî in the hearts of Salafis from Yemen and abroad. As such, it is clear that Muqbil al-Wâdiʿîʾs death in 2001, the effects of which were bound up in the aftermath of the 9/11 attacks, severely destabilised the quietist Salafi movement and with it the possibility of its recomposition.

This chapter's overview of the founding principles of doctrine and of the main actors of the Salafi movement in Yemen helped contextualise it within a broader Islamist field, encompassing other movements with different strategies, leaders and approaches. As emphasised above through a focus on the ideological production of the scholars as well as through their life-stories, Yemeni quietist Salafism manifests specific characteristics because of its original and uncom-

---

[104] Yahyâ al-Hajûrî (ed.), *Mukhtasar al-bayân al-mawdhah li-hizbiyyat al-ʿAdanî* [Summary of declaration proving the partisanship of al-ʿAdanî], Dammâj: Dâr al-Hadîth, 2009.

promising approach to politics and to Islamic scripture. It has also emerged as a specific group due to a number of high-profile individuals who, in the course of their own personal histories and internal rivalries, have created a vivid and complex movement. Building on such a picture, the second chapter will look more deeply into the concrete interactions between the Salafi movement and its context in contemporary Yemen. It will more specifically address the issue of the relationship of Salafis to politics, the state and violence.

2

THE SALAFIS, THE STATE AND SOCIETY

I. Salafism as Deviance?

The centrality of the critique of *hizbiyya* within the quietist Salafi movement in Yemen has evident implications in terms of the Salafis' relations to the state, as well as to other social actors. Although 'worldliness' is, in their view, supposed to give rise to disorder and *fitna*, aspects of 'the worldly' remain among the main objects of their concern and their debates. In fact, while feigning to turn away from materialism and worldly matters, the Salafi doctrine, in reality, never stops focusing on them. A fine-grained analysis of the relationship to politics of Yemeni Salafism thus cannot limit itself simply to going over sermons and publications by major figures in the movement or to its intellectual history. It is necessary to look more closely at the social practices of Salafi actors and their relationship to various contexts.

Fleeing Corruption

The attitudes of Yemeni Salafis often appear to be quite ambiguous. While wishing to exclude themselves voluntarily from society and from the management of the state in order to avoid certain kinds of corruption, they do in fact try to influence decision-makers and society alike. To the extent that they move back and forth between deviance, condemnation, disdain, instrumentalisation and participation, the apparently apolitical attitude of the quietist Salafi doctrine is largely an illusion. In fact, the statements made by the entrepreneurs of Salafism should not hide the flexibility of actors' practices and their involvement in certain particular dynamics.

Through their controversies, rivalries and denunciations of political involvement, the promoters of quietist Yemeni Salafism have shaped a particular vision of the world and of politics. Their doctrine and practice revolves around a will to escape worldly contingencies. Such a stance is manifest in the so-called minor behaviours highlighted previously and which may in some instances be seen by others as signs of social deviance. The leading figures, entrepreneurs and actors within Salafism appear to face a kind of predicament as they simultaneously advocate 'exit strategies' and automatic allegiance to existing authority.[1] They pride themselves on being both outsiders and insiders, deviants and conformists, both external to the system and a docile ally of the rulers. Through such a difficult stance, Salafis end up 'embedding' themselves into the very context they claim to avoid.

Considering the important role of qat in Yemeni society, its rejection arguably appears as a notable characteristic of devotion to Salafi principles and to the strategy of self-exclusion and social deviance. Muqbil al-Wâdi'î himself thought that the mild narcotic was 'a great calamity' and likened those who chew it to 'cattle'.[2] In order to discredit the founders of al-Hikma association, he accused them of being qat-chewers and smokers (*mukhazzin wa mudakhkhin*).[3] Al-Wâdi'î even deplored the fact that cultivation of qat, which brings in a significant amount of income to farmers and helps direct some of the money in towns and cities towards rural areas, had replaced the cultivation of hot peppers (*bisbâs* in dialect) and fenugreek (*hulba*), which are used in the traditional cuisine of the highlands of Yemen.[4]

In the circles of the political elites, within families and tribes, and among friends, chewing qat plays a significant role. It is an important social marker; it takes up time in the afternoon and represents a dominant source of socialisation and deliberation in contemporary Yemen.[5] During the course of the

---

[1] For analysis of the variety of forms of protest and resistance in the Muslim world and the dilemmas facing political movements, see, Mounia Bennani-Chraibi and Olivier Fillieule, 'Exit, voice, loyalty et bien d'autres choses encore...' in Mounia Bennani-Chraibi and Olivier Fillieule (eds.), *Résistances et protestations dans les societies musulmanes*, Paris: Presses de Sciences Po, 2003, pp. 43–126.

[2] Muqbil al-Wâdi'î makes reference here to the practice of consuming qat, putting young shoots and leaves between cheek and gum, and chewing this mixture for several hours, until a ball is formed, which sometimes can become surprisingly large.

[3] Muqbil al-Wâdi'î, sound recording, *As'ila 'an hayât al-shaykh Muqbil al-Wâdi'î wa sîratuhu* [Questions about the life of shaykh Muqbil al-Wâdi'î and his biography].

[4] Muqbil al-Wâdi'î, *Ijâbat al-sâ'il 'alâ ahamm al-masâ'il* [Answers for those who ask the most important questions], op. cit., p. 297.

[5] Anthropologist Lisa Wedeen highlights the political role of qat chews among elites

maqyal when individuals gather to chew, political, economic and social differences are settled, ideas and opinions are exchanged, alliances are concluded, music is played and poetry is recited.

Consequently, at all levels of society, the refusal to chew qat (and also, though this is less important, the rejection of television that is increasingly watched while chewing and is a dominant source of information) forces Salafis to work out alternative forms of socialisation: circles for the recitation of the Qur'an or learning the *hadîth*, organising conferences in mosques, and so on. Their self-exclusion, added to their disapproval of those who chew qat as well as all other political and religious groups who do not share their intransigent attitudes—is representative of the desire to escape a corrupt (*mufsid*) society.

Furthermore, the establishment of Salafi centres on the outskirts of towns expresses the desire to go against traditional religious powers by occupying a 'virgin' territory that has been recently made part of a town or city and where a kind of religious vacuum exists. It also expresses the objective of escaping from the immorality (*fujûr*) of the city. This is another sign of the privileged choice of self-exclusion by Salafis in the Yemeni environment. A former student from the faculty of Islamic law at the University of Sana'a recalled for example his satisfaction at finally having left the 'corrupt and overgrown city' after finishing his studies, in order to teach in his native village.[6] This reason appears to explain why Dâr al-Hadîth came to be built a few kilometres from Sa'da; why the centre of Muhammad al-Imâm is in the small town of Ma'bar near Dhamâr; and why the centre of 'Abd al-'Azîz al-Bura'î is located in Mafraq Hubaysh, north of Ibb, while the important al-Khayr mosque, its four bookstores and its teaching institute, are located in recently established neighbourhoods in the suburbs south of Sana'a, along the Ta'iz street.

When questioned about the reasons for locating his centre in Ma'bar, Muhammad al-Imâm, not a native of that small town, said that 'the creation in 1996 of the centre at Ma'bar was not part of a particular strategy but the result of the hospitality from the people of the town'.[7] Still, in view of the success of his enterprise, one would say that setting up centres in small urban areas is favourable for the constitution of Islamised spaces that appear almost as quasi-autarkies. In fact, around these centres, institutes and mosques, clusters of

---

and citizens and even compares them to 'public spheres' as described by Jurgen Harbermas: Lisa Wedeen, *Peripheral Visions. Publics, Power and Performance in Yemen*, Chicago: Chicago University Press, 2008, pp. 120–147.

[6] Interview, Lab'ûs, April 2005.

[7] Interview, Ma'bar, November 2004.

Salafi-oriented businesses spring up: sellers of honey, audio cassettes or perfumes, bookstores and shops where people can make telephone calls or eventually log on to the internet and make photocopies. Honey and perfume are both consumer products that carry a particularly positive religious connotation for the whole society and among Salafis in particular. The stores that sell them are usually quite luxurious, and are quite often run by former students of Salafi institutes or by graduates of al-Îman University, headed by radical member of the Muslim Brotherhood 'Abd al-Majîd al-Zindânî. Such stores are thus an important source of jobs for young people whose education has been mostly religious, something that is not in great demand elsewhere in the job market. One Islamist intellectual who had studied for five years with Muqbil al-Wâdi'î in the early 1990s recalled how after 'graduating' from Dammâj he had worked in a Sana'a honey shop for several years before finally becoming a teacher in a public school.[8] In these 'Salafi cluster' shops, flasks of Bohemian crystal filled with perfumes bearing evocative names such as 'Dammâj', the cradle of Yemeni Salafism, and jars of the Hadrami honey of Wâdî Du'ân, said to have many beneficial qualities and ranking among the most expensive varieties in the world, stand alongside cassette recordings of recitations of the Qur'an or sermons.

In Ma'bar, the centre of Muhammad al-Imâm hosts several hundred students, including foreigners from the Horn of Africa, from South-east Asia or from Europe. The buildings are modest, not to say rundown. There are rooms for students and their families, a large library used by the residents of the centre, but also by people who live in the neighbourhood, and a very large mosque, said to be able to hold up to 3,000 of the faithful. Around the institute there are four bookstores whose ideological orientation is made explicit by their names: Dâr al-Hadîth, Maktabat al-Bukhârî, Maktabat al-Salafiyya and Maktabat al-Imâm Muqbil al-Wâdi'î. All sell varieties of books, booklets and collections published in Yemen, Saudi Arabia or Egypt, as well as recorded sermons and conferences given by the main Salafi figures of Yemen and elsewhere.

Beyond the urban corruption that justifies self-exclusion, the tribal system and the traditional social hierarchy of status groups, which together still govern the interaction of a large proportion of the population of the Yemeni highlands, are also denounced by the Salafis. This rejection, however, remains largely formal. In various texts and recordings, promoters of Salafism point out that the tribal system causes divisions between people, and often implies a philosophy of 'supporting one's companion even if he is wrong'.[9] Tribal law is thus

---

[8] Interview, Sana'a, May 2008.
[9] Muqbil al-Wâdi'î, *al-Makhraj min al-fitna* [Leaving dissension behind], op. cit., p. 50.

accused of harking back to the pre-Islamic period, and of conflicting with religious law. The contradictions between tribal law and *sharî'a* concern, for example, bequests and dowries, the amount of which has inflated so much since the 1970s that the average age of people getting married has increased, consequently becoming an issue that Salafis willingly highlight.

In order to escape the material world that causes discord among Muslims, but also to fully apply the notion of equality among the latter, Yemeni Salafism rejects the preeminence of the *sâda*, *ashrâf* or Hashemites (descendants of the Prophet Muhammad), a religious elite that dominated northern Yemen until the revolution of 1962, and was a mainstay of British colonial administration in the South until 1967. The rejection of the claim to power of the *sâda* is shared by the ideology of nationalist revolutionaries and served as the basis of the modern state. On the opposite, criticism of tribalism remained only theoretical as tribal structures still play a prominent role in Yemeni government and economics.

The rejection of tribalism illustrates the desire of this quietist Salafi doctrine, as formulated by Muqbil al-Wâdi'î and other scholars, to go beyond the many contingencies and specificities that characterise what it sees as a corrupt society. By criticising society, Salafis are not only trying to construct Islamised spaces that are differentiated and de-contextualised, but also to spread throughout society the norms that they believe to be in perfect accord with the Qur'an and the Tradition of the Prophet. In some cases, these references may appear to be deviant and contrary to common practice. So, for example, in opposition to a dominant norm in Yemen, Muqbil al-Wâdi'î, without having ever appeared to be progressive as regards the rights of women (he had maintained for example that women should marry as soon as possible, that is, beginning at the age of twelve, and that they should not exercise the slightest political responsibility), maintained that it should not be obligatory for women to cover their faces with the *niqâb*,[10] that they should be allowed to drive cars,[11] that their brothers should not confiscate their portion of a bequest[12] and that dowries (*mahr*) should not be high.[13] In the same vein but in another context, pushed to the

---

[10] Muqbil al-Wâdi'î, sound recording, *al-Ijâba 'alâ as'ilat Yâfi'* [Answers to the questions of Yâfi'].

[11] Cited by 'Abd Allâh al-Sayânî, *al-Ikhwân al-muslimûn wa al-salafiyûn fî al-Yaman* [The Muslim Brotherhood and the Salafis in Yemen], op. cit., p. 115.

[12] Muqbil al-Wâdi'î, sound recording, *al-Ijâba 'alâ as'ilat Yâfi'* [Answers to the questions of Yâfi'].

[13] Muqbil al-Wâdi'î, *al-Makhraj min al-fitna* [Leaving dissension behind], op. cit., p. 137.

point of caricature, the famous *fatwâ* of Levantine Salafi scholar al-Albânî, that called in the early 1990s on the Palestinians to abandon the combat against Israel and to forsake their lands because they were occupied by non-Muslims, and thus imitate the Prophet's *hijra* from Mecca to Medina shows how much the universalist, literalist and de-contextualised vocation of quietist Salafism can influence the leading figures of Salafism, in Yemen and elsewhere, to disconnect from their environment and go against dominant attitudes.

Considering the rejection of certain practices or norms that are widespread among Yemenis, as well as the intention to stand apart from society, Salafism may be seen by others, including fellow Islamists, as a kind of deviance. While their religious knowledge can in some instances be valued, Salafis undeniably are subject to a certain stigmatisation from other social and religious groups. They are frequently referred to by means of various epithets and nicknames that focus on particular physical, historical or moral characteristics, real or imagined: *abû lihiya* is a reference to their uncut beards, *wahhâbî* refers to their alleged connections with Saudi Arabia, *mutawwaʿ* refers to the lowest rung of the Sunni religious 'hierarchy', but also to the 'Saudi religious institution and *irhâbî* refers to their suspected relations with terrorist movements. The position they occupy in the political and religious arena in Yemen, as well as their doctrine itself, more often than not ends up being discounted or caricatured. Late shaykh ʿAbd Allâh al-Ahmar, head of the Islâh party, declared of them: 'They have a guide (*murshid*) in Saʿda called Muqbil al-Wâdiʿî. What he does is declare people infidels and write books against everyone else.'[14]

Nonetheless the Salafis' position in Yemeni society is ambivalent. Despite their self-exclusion and their stigmatisation by other social groups, they manage to play the part of what Howard Becker calls 'moral entrepreneurs'.[15] The 'outsiders' Becker was studying in his research (delinquents, jazz musicians, homosexuals, drug addicts, and so on) did not wish to impose their own norms on everyone, but the Salafis want to reform the society they live in (and from which they separate themselves) in their own image. Their preaching has the specific aim of bringing as many people as possible into their group. The norms they promote, their morality, their struggle against moral corruption and the reform project they support may not always be perceived negatively by the rest of society, but it is usually rejected because its enforcement is often considered

---

[14] Quoted in Paul Dresch, *A History of Modern Yemen*, op. cit., p. 200.
[15] Howard Becker, *Outsiders: Studies in the Sociology of Deviance*, New York: The Free Press, 1973, p. 147.

violent and intransigent. Salafi morality is then confronted with resistance from local public institutions, tribes and other political and religious actors. The allegedly 'imported' character of Salafism, that is, its supposed Saudi origin, adds to the hostility with which this current is faced, almost as if it represented a kind of internal enemy in the country. Stressing such hostility, Muqbil al-Wâdi'î wrote in his autobiography about the difficulties he had had to overcome, related to the Zaydi environment in which he began to preach after his expulsion from Saudi territory at the end of the 1970s:

> When I arrived in Yemen, I returned to my village, I stayed there, and I taught the Qur'an to children. But I felt attacked from all sides, as if I had come to destroy the country, the religion, and the government. At that time I did not know any leaders or any tribal chiefs.[16]

The difficulty he had in getting his library sent to him from Saudi Arabia constituted for Muqbil al-Wâdi'î an illustration of the exclusion to which his current was subjected. He wrote: 'You cannot imagine the penalties paid [i.e., bribes paid to customs agents], the exhaustion and the worry that they made me suffer.'[17]

At the local level, taxes levied on the exploitation of religious endowments (*awqâf*)[18] by traditional actors (mainly Zaydis from the northern part of the country and Sufis in the Hadramawt and on the coastal plain of Tihâma) disadvantage emerging identities, including Salafism. The new religious groups

[16] Muqbil al-Wâdi'î (ed.), *Tarjamat Abî 'Abd al-Rahmân Muqbil Bin Hâdî al-Wâdi'î* [Biography of Abî 'Abd al-Rahmân Muqbil Bin Hâdî al-Wâdi'î], op. cit., p. 27.

[17] Ibid., p. 28.

[18] The rôle of the *awqâf* in Yemeni society is too often neglected. They constitute a most important source of financing for religious and traditional actors and are at the basis of what in many respects appears as an endogenous civil society. In a study of the system of *awqâf* in Sana'a, Robert Serjeant and Husayn al-'Amrî reckoned that at the beginning of the 1980s, about two-thirds of the buildings and most of the old city of Sana'a were placed in this category in one way or another. Because of this, their use or rental allows an important amount of money to be collected, which is managed by different actors working for the state and by communities. Money can then be used for benevolent ends or for building mosques, or for paying those who perform worship services. Consequently, recourse by religious actors to external and private financing appears as a secondary question, even a marginal one. Robert Serjeant and Husayn al-'Amri, 'Administrative Organisation' in Robert Serjeant and Ronald Lewcock (eds.), *Sanâ' an Arabian Islamic City*, London: World of Islam Festival trust, 1983, p. 151. On the social and administrative organisation of Sana'a, see also Franck Mermier, *Le cheikh de la nuit. Sanaa: organisations des souks et société citadine*, Arles: Actes Sud, 1999.

are forced to find sources of external funding, which often have the effect of reinforcing their deviant and foreign character in the eyes of third parties and their opponents.

The imaginative character of certain critiques aimed at the Salafis is belied by the often modest facilities found at their institutes, mosques and bookstores—and also by their rudimentary level of organisation. Consequently, the dominant image of brand-new religious buildings, bookstores well-stocked with low-price publications (since they allegedly are subsidised), the smell and bling of petrodollars everywhere and so on, has little to do with the reality. From a strictly material point of view Salafism bears no material advantages in comparison with other political or religious movements in Yemen. In Aden, for example, large modern mosques (such as al-Ridhâ', deemed close to the Yemeni government) constructed or restored during the 1990s, whose uniform architecture recalls Riyadh or Abu Dhabi more than the traditional architecture thought of as 'authentically' Yemeni, were financed through the Hâ'il Sa'îd An'am foundation of Yemen, founded by an important merchant from Ta'iz.[19] These grandiose mosques, managed directly through the ministry of Awqâf, represent for the people of Yemen a form of modernity, which cannot be assigned a particular political function. In comparison the Salafi-affiliated mosques, often in cheap barracks in shanty suburbs could carry neither the same meaning nor the same flamboyant image.

Irrelevant Governments and Politics

Deviants and moral entrepreneurs at the same time, Salafis do not seem in their various publications and conferences to care much for governments. Based on their quietist principles, they consistently assert that they will never try to obtain state power. In their view, decisions by the government must be respected in order to preserve the unity of the believers. However, such a principle is not systematically enforced and the government remains widely ignored to the extent that it is ineffective and has no particular role to play. Consequently, Salafis may end up actually criticising state decisions and not appearing as loyal as their doctrine commands them to be. Overt participation in state activities and taxation, which is described as an innovation of the modern 'westernised'

---

[19] On the mosques of Aden, see: Amîn Sa'îd Bâ Wazîr, *Halqât al-qur'ân al-karîm wa majâlis al-'ilm fî masâjid 'Adan* [The Qur'anic circles and the scientific assemblies in the mosques of Aden], Sana'a: Markaz al-'Ubâdî, 2005.

state, are among the various points of contention. During a recorded conference entitled *'Awâqib al-zulm* [The consequences of oppression] Muhammad al-Imâm, for instance asserted that taxes were 'a form of oppression of our times', and opined that the religious tax, the *zakâ*, should be sufficient for the minimal functioning of the state. Muqbil al-Wâdi'î went further as he even discouraged his followers from joining the army or the police, because they would be required to shave their beards. In this way he reminded people that it is forbidden to work at a job that leads one to transgress against the prohibitions imposed by religion.[20]

The relationship to the state prescribed by the quietist Salafi doctrine is moreover characterised by a certain disdain for political power. Political authority is accused of concerning itself only with material things and secondary matters, and of turning out to be ineffective. Muqbil al-Wâdi'î explained his lack of interest in political matters by claiming that 'the victory of Islam today is happening in the mosques'.[21] That is, the victory of which he speaks is not the result of actions by Arab or Muslim governments. Elsewhere in the same text, he remarked that the United States, Russia and the enemies of Islam are more afraid of 'those who are involved in their religion, Islamic renaissance men' than of 'leaders (*zu'ama*) and kings [...]. They are not afraid of our tanks, our planes or our defense. They are afraid of Islam and of those who are engaged in the call to Islam'.[22] To justify his claim to universal truth and to an apolitical attitude, speaking to his disciples, the *ahl al-sunna*, he declared:

Your doctrine is clear, the political leaders know that you do not want political positions (*karâsî*) and that you give no importance to material things, that you have no intention of starting a revolt (*khurûj*) against them because your doctrine does not ask you to disobey a Muslim government. So, I pay the customs duties on my car although I believe that these taxes are illicit (*harâm*) but it is the responsibility of the state to set taxes, not mine.[23]

Lack of interest and disdain for governments means that quietist Salafis think that these governments are incapable of actually solving the problems that face Muslims today, even if these governments are Islamic. A former student of al-Wâdi'î puts it this way:

---

[20] Muqbil al-Wâdi'î, *Ijâbat al-sâ'il 'alâ ahamm al-masâ'il* [Answers to those who ask the most important questions], op. cit., p. 222.

[21] Ibid., p. 223.

[22] Ibid., p. 225.

[23] Muqbil al-Wâdi'î, sound recording, *al-Madhhab al-zaydî* [The Zaydi school].

If you ask a partisan of political action, great or small, what the reasons are for the failure of the Islamic State and for dissension among Muslims, he will answer you: 'The power is not in the hands of *'ulamâ'* or pious people'. If you then ask him: 'Why?' He will answer: 'because the leaders work for the West or the East, not for us'. This answer is stark proof of their ignorance, because the real reason is the presence of innovations (*bid'a*) [...] and the presence of groups and parties that do not follow the Book, the Tradition and the path traced by our pious ancestors.[24]

Such an interpretation of the source of the problems of the world clearly illustrates the opposition between the two afore-mentioned Islamist ideal-types: the first being concerned above all with social justice, while the second believes that respect for the letter of religious worship is the highest priority. This 'schism' is thus based on a divergent interpretation of the role of *'ulamâ'* and their capacity to transcend particular contexts.[25] The first is marked by a certain relativism and contextualisation, the second considers that men of religion are delivering a universal message that transcends all contexts, local, national or regional.

Despite the apparent rigidity of the Salafi doctrine, social and political behaviours and the daily practices of the activists and religious entrepreneurs often vary. When facing a situation they consider not to be in conformity with their Islamic ideal, Salafi actors do not simply head for the exits, or retreat within automatic allegiances, but often appear to go beyond a doctrinally apolitical stance by adopting more severely critical positions, which can under certain circumstances even lead to violence.

II. Allegiance and Violence

Loyal Salafis

An apparent disinterest for political matters (undoubtedly coupled with fear of state repression) leads the major figures of quietist Salafism to claim that they support existing authority and oppose violence against the state in principle (as long as the state is considered Muslim, that is, as long as the persons who hold temporal power pray, and do not give obvious signs of being impious).

---

[24] 'Abd Allâh Bin 'Abd al-Hamîd al-Khubânî in Rabî' al-Madkhalî (ed.), *Nasîhat al-shaykh Rabî' al-Madkhalî li ahl al-Yaman* [Advice of shaykh Rabî' al-Madkhalî to the people of Yemen], op. cit., p. 24.

[25] On the question of the social and historical role of *'ulamâ'*, see especially Michael Gilsenan, *Recognizing Islam. An Anthropologist's Introduction*, Sydney: Croom Helm, 1982, pp. 27–54.

In the Yemeni context where it holds particular historical and political meaning, the Salafis are more specifically opposing a concept, that of *khurûj 'alâ al-hâkim al-zâlim* (literally, to rise against an oppressive ruler), which is part of the basis of the Zaydi political doctrine of the imamate. For over a millennium, up until 1962, the imam as the spiritual and political leader of the Zaydis and of the territory that eventually became North Yemen was chosen from among the descendants of the Prophet, and had to satisfy fourteen particular conditions having to do with his soundness in body and mind. In the context of this doctrine, when faced with an oppressive imam, it was legitimate for the Zaydis, headed by the imam-to be, to revolt against such leadership, using force if necessary, and to install a just and legitimate imam.

Basing themselves on the aphorism of Ibn Taymiyya, who espoused that 'sixty years of an oppressive (*zâlim*) imam are preferable to one night without one', the Salafis declare that in theory they are opposed to revolutions and coups d'état. In fact, they have argued such revolts often cause Muslims to kill one another, and they give rise to chaos and dissension among the believers. In claiming that, they explicitly react to *khurûj* and denounce a religious concept that played a central role in Yemeni politics and still appears as a divisive notion. Muqbil al-Wâdi'î in one of his texts recalled that revolutions can create a greater evil than the one they are supposed to fight against. To support this interpretation, he took the example of Egypt, where the coup against King Fârûq gave way to the rule of Jamâl 'Abd al-Nâsir, whom he despised, and the example of South Yemen, where a revolution against British colonisers gave rise to the 'impious communist' regime of South Yemen.[26]

During the 1980s, faithful to his ambition to be the counsellor of rulers rather than their opponent, al-Wâdi'î declared concerning the government of Yemen: 'The *ahl al-sunna* are satisfied with the President and with the absence of elections, but we still ask him to base himself on the Book, the Tradition, and the religion of God'.[27] Later, at the end of the 1990s, despite the democratisation process launched by the authorities after unification, he asserted: 'We still consider our country to be Islamic despite the corruption that rules in it. [...] Democracy has been imposed on us from the outside, even the leaders do not want it!'[28]

---

[26] Muqbil al-Wâdi'î, *Ijâbat al-sâ'il 'alâ ahamm al-masâ'il* [Answers to those who ask the most important questions], op. cit., p. 229.

[27] Muqbil al-Wâdi'î, *Tuhfat al-mujîb 'alâ as'ilat al-hâdhar wa al-gharîb* [Precious responses to the questions of one who is present and one who is absent], op. cit., p. 222.

[28] Muqbil al-Wâdi'î, sound recording, *al-Zindânî wa majlis al-shaykhât bil-Yaman* [al-Zindânî and the assembly of women of Yemen].

Allegiance to Yemeni President 'Alî 'Abd Allâh Sâlih appears to almost be a constant in quietist Salafi discourse in Yemen at all levels. The corruption that affects existing authority is frequently imputed to ministers and other leaders and representatives of the state, rather than to the *ra'îs* himself, judged to be irreproachable by nature. Echoing the position of the *ulamâ'*, a Salafi student put it this way: 'Our President is rather good, but unfortunately he is surrounded by dishonest people!'[29] In this respect the Salafis (much like the members of the ruling GPC itself) appear to be careful not to cross a certain red line by criticising the President directly. In a text entitled *Hâdhihi da'watnâ wa 'aqîdatnâ* [This is our preaching and our doctrine] the founder of the quietist Salafi movement in Yemen set forth thirty-six points important to the genesis of his movement. In paragraph 13, concerning the question of violence in conflict with the state, he asserted:

We do not accept revolt (*khurûj*) against leaders of Muslims, even if they are not perfect. We do not believe that coups d'état can be the source of reforms, rather they bring corruption into society. In return we accept the combat against the leaders of Aden, as long as they continue in atheism and socialism, and call people to worship Lenin, Marx, and other impious leaders.[30]

Building on the same idea, Muhammad al-Imâm explains:

If the leaders are oppressors, the *'ulamâ'* must ask the people to be patient, to pray to God to liberate and defend the country. The people must also be asked to analyse the nature of the oppression, as it could have its source within them.[31]

Furthermore, contrary to what many of their opponents assert, the Salafis' doctrinal framework states that the *'ulamâ'* can in theory pronounce the *takfîr* only against acts, not against persons, unless the persons concerned declare themselves apostate. Thus to clarify his position on the question of excommunication, Muqbil al-Wâdi'î declared in the mid-1990s:

A Muslim is a Muslim even if he is negligent (*muqassir*). If he shaves his beard, wears a long thawb or possesses musical instruments, he is still a Muslim.[32]

---

[29] Interview, Lab'ûs, April 2005.

[30] Muqbil al-Wâdi'î (ed.), *Tarjamat Abî 'Abd al-Rahmân Muqbil Bin Hâdî al-Wâdi'î* [Biography of Abî 'Abd al-Rahmân Muqbil Bin Hâdî al-Wâdi'î], op. cit., p. 136.

[31] Muhammad al-Imâm, sound recording, *'Awâqib al-zulm* [The consequences of oppression].

[32] Muqbil al-Wâdi'î, sound recording, *Nasihatî lil-sha'abayn al-yamanî al-su'ûdî* [My advice to the people of Yemen and Saudi Arabia].

It is especially on this point of the *takfîr* pronounced against society, persons and leaders that the quietist Salafism represented by Muqbil al-Wâdi'î in Yemen and the *Jâmiyya* movement in Saudi Arabia now headed by Rabî' al-Madkhalî stand in diametrical opposition to the doctrines of movements labelled jihadi and to the thought enunciated by Sayyid Qutb. In his writings published in the mid-twentieth century, Qutb went as far as declaring an entire society *jâhilî*, that is, ignorant and pre-Islamic and therefore impious, to the extent that it had shown itself incapable of overthrowing a tyrant who oppressed Muslims. In the end, such an approach provided direct justification for the violent option against political authority and the ruler, as was the case in October 1981 when Anwar al-Sâdât was assassinated.[33]

With the rise of Islamist political contestation in Egypt, Algeria and Saudi Arabia, the issue of *takfîr* of the rulers became a cause of dissension during the 1990s, and then again in the post-9/11 context. Such debate had an effect on Yemeni Salafism, to some extent via certain Saudi clerics such as Sâlih Fawzân al-Fawzân advocating complete support to governments in their fight against al-Qaeda. Thus the work entitled *al-Irhâb wa âthâruhu al-sayyi' 'alâ al-afrâd wa al-umam* [Terrorism and its negative impact on individuals and nations], written in 2003 by Zayd Bin Muhammad al-Madkhalî, a Saudi Salafi of the *Jâmiyya* trend, was again symptomatic of the break between the two ideal-typical Islamist forms. Zayd al-Madkhalî accused the Muslim Brotherhood, Sayyid Qutb and his descendents (including Muhammad Surûr and Salmân al-'Awda, the prominent figure of the *Sahwa islâmiyya* in Saudi Arabia) of being the main cause and the masterminds of terrorist violence. Without ever saying anything about Usâma Bin Lâdin or al-Qaeda, al-Madkhalî explained that 'the terrorists defame the true Islamic community and open wide for the enemies of Islam and Muslims the doors of slander'.[34] In contrast to the dominant canons of anti-imperialist rhetoric, which the politicised Islamist ideal-type, exemplified by the Muslim Brotherhood, Zayd al-Madkhalî never mentioned in his book the alleged state 'terrorism' of the Israeli or American states nor any kind of structural domination on the world scene that would explain violence.[35] On

[33] Gilles Kepel, *Le Prophète et le Pharaon: Les mouvements islamistes dans l'Égypte contemporaine*, op. cit.

[34] Zayd al-Madkhalî, *al-Irhâb wa âthâruhu al-sayyi' 'alâ al-afrâd wa al-umam* [Terrorism and its negative impact on individuals and nations], Cairo: Dâr al-Minhâj, 2003, p. 14.

[35] For an example of this anti-imperialist rhetoric, which consists in responding to accusations of terrorism with accusations of state terrorism perpetrated by Western

the contrary, he only attacked Muslim groups with whom he was in disagreement concerning political and theological points, points that for an outside observer might appear minor but that he considered fundamental. These practices of differentiation by means of a few 'small differences' turn out to be central within the political and religious field of Salafism and may well explain the depth of some schisms.

The structural character of this break over the question of violence against the state is largely ignored by the dominant view in academic and media discourse. These often have too strong a tendency to count as similar a number of 'Salafi' groups that nonetheless attack, exclude and criticise each other, sometimes in harsh and direct terms. In this regard, the dominant position within the Yemeni Salafi field is often caricatured through the assimilation of quietist Salafis to jihadi groups. All during the 1990s, Muqbil al-Wâdi'î was accused by his political adversaries in Yemen and in other countries of giving students military training at the Dâr al-Hadîth centre. His response, not without malice, was as follows: 'We do not have time for military training'.[36] He expanded on this on another occasion:

It would not be forbidden to do it if only we had the money to buy rifles and machine guns, all under the watchful eye of our government of course. The government knows perfectly well what we do. You can see that we are too busy memorising collections of *hadîth* by Bukhârî and by Muslim and reading the commentary on the Qur'an (*tafsîr*) of Ibn Kathîr.[37]

In response to the indiscriminate violence and attacks that were hitting the Middle East, the leading figures of quietist Salafism in Yemen claimed that the position they had adopted was clear and firm. In several speeches, al-Wâdi'î explicitly distanced himself from Usâma Bin Lâdin, to whom he claimed to have written at the end of the 1990s, advising him to reject not only the option of violence against the governments of Muslim countries, but against Western interests as well.[38] In an interview with the Kuwaiti newspaper *al-Ray* from

---

governments, see Muhammad Bin 'Abd Allâh al-Salûmî, *al-Qitâ' al-khayrî wa da'âwâ al-irhâb* [Benevolent associations and accusations of terrorism], Riyadh: al-Bayyân, 2004; Sharaf Luqmân, *al-Irhâb fî muwâjahat al-irhâb* [Terrorism faced with terrorism], place, publisher and date unknown.

[36] Muqbil al-Wâdi'î, sound recording, *Jalsa ma'a al-sahafî al-almânî* [Meeting with a German journalist].

[37] Muqbil al-Wâdi'î, sound recording, *Liqâ' sahîfat al-bayân al-imâratiyya* [Interview with the Emirati paper *al-Bayân*].

[38] Ibid.

December 19, 1998, al-Wâdi'î invited Muslims to stand clearly against Bin Lâdin and his organisation. Otherwise, in another conference, entitled 'Who is behind the attacks in the Land of the Two Holy Places?' [*Min warâ' al-tafjîrât fî ardh al-haramayn?*], insisting upon the priorities of Salafi preaching, he criticised the attitude of the famous Saudi billionaire who refused 'to give 20,000 Saudi riyals for the construction of a mosque, but offered 100,000 riyals to buy machine guns'.[39] This blunt condemnation of Bin Lâdin, motivated by profound theological disagreements, is a clear break with the ambiguous position of much of the Yemeni population, who may well, in a number of instances, be seduced by the anti-imperialist rhetoric of al-Qaeda although disagreeing with its violent methods. Thus quietist Salafi doctrine shows itself to be essentially unaffected by the political, anti-imperialist message delivered by Usâma Bin Lâdin and other advocates of violence.[40] In that framework, quietist Salafi doctrine tends to stand apart from widespread opinion. For a grocer who had studied three years at Dammâj at the end of the 1990s, Bin Lâdin, despite his evident popularity among young people, is nothing but a 'criminal who gives Islam a bad name'. Thus al-Qaeda leaders' political positions do not resonate at all with someone who endorses an apolitical position.[41] Such a stance eventually leads many clerics within the Salafi field to think that the 'enemies of Islam' are in fact those who are responsible for various attacks, especially those directed against Muslim governments. Speaking about the 2003 attacks in Saudi territory, Yahyâ al-Hajûrî expressed surprise that 'the Americans and the British knew about the attacks two or three days before they happened'.[42] Consequently, far from legitimising the option of violence, these operations are seen as directed against Islam, in order to discredit it.

Such opposition by Yemeni quietist Salafis to the jihadis' plans from the 1990s onwards is confirmed by 'al-Qaeda strategist' Abû Mus'ab al-Sûrî in his influential *Da'wat al-muqâwamma al-islâmiyya al-'âlâmiyya* (Global Islamic Resistance Call), a 1,600-page account of jihadi ideology and history.[43] Al-Sûrî

[39] Muqbil al-Wâdi'î, *Tuhfat al-mujîb 'alâ as'ilat al-hâdhar wa al-gharîb* [Precious responses to the questions of one who is present and one who is absent], op. cit., p. 281.
[40] Also see this sermon, recorded before the 9/11 attacks: Yahyâ al-Hajûrî, sound recording, *I'lân al-nakîr 'alâ du'â al-tafjîr* [Announcement of disapproval of preachers of the explosion].
[41] Interview, Lab'ûs, February 2005.
[42] Yahyâ al-Hajûrî, sound recording, *As'ilat Mafraq Hubaysh* [Questions fom Mafraq Hubaysh].
[43] Brynjar Lia, *Architect of Global Jihad: The Life of Al-Qaida Strategist Abu Mus'ab al-Suri*, London: Hurst, 2008.

repeatedly mentions the tensions that existed between Bin Lâdin and al-Wâdi'î, the latter even being accused of scotching Bin Lâdin's plans to open a new front against the socialists of South Yemen in the months after unification. Al-Sûrî recalls how al-Wâdi'î at the time recorded various conferences in which he referred to Usâma Bin Lâdin as the 'head of *fitna* in Yemen' and asserts that al-Wâdi'î's position was to oppose and criticise all other Islamists while supporting President Sâlih.[44] Al-Sûrî claims that he 'once heard Bin Lâdin in front of guests saying that if he was to excuse all those who did him wrong during his life, he would excuse everyone but al-Wâdi'î'.[45]

Obviously such considerations with regard to violence do not imply that there is no connection whatsoever between quietist Salafism and contemporary violent movements in Yemen. Nonetheless, the recourse to armed action does not constitute the primary option for Salafis, and those who consider this option do not seek to justify it in a systematic manner in religious texts. In a certain number of instances, including a few transcripts of Guantanamo detainees' hearings such as those of Muhammad Ahmad al-'Ansî, Fahd 'Abd Allâh Ghâzî and al-Khadhr 'Abd Allâh al-Yâfi'î[46] or in the biographies of other militants such as American convert 'Abd al-Hakîm Muhammad who shot down two soldiers in an Arkansas military recruiting centre in June 2009, the fact that certain militants had studied in Dammâj or in other Salafi institutes may have been highlighted, but the discovery of connections between these teaching institutes and jihadi networks does not constitute sufficient proof of a cause and effect relationship between the doctrine preached by Muqbil al-Wâdi'î and violent action. Individual interpretations and trajectories should also be analysed and contextualised. Evidently, the issue of why individuals chose violence or terrorism is not one that can be solved easily just by referring to a limited number of examples.[47] Evidently a small number of former students

---

[44] Abû Mus'ab al-Sûrî, *Da'wat al-muqâwamma al-islâmiyya al-'alâmiyya* (Global islamic resistance call), 2005, p. 775.

[45] Ibid., p. 776.

[46] For biodata on these individuals, see Andy Worthington, *The Guantanamo Files. The Stories of 774 Detainees in America's Illegal Prison*, New York: Pluto Press, 2007.

[47] On the variety of factors and variables that explain, beyond ideology, radicalisation and violence: Stéphane Beaud and Olivier Masclet, 'Un passage à l'acte improbable? Notes de recherche sur la trajectoire sociale de Zacarias Moussaoui', *French Politics, Culture and Society*, vol. 20, no. 2, 2002, pp. 159–170; Romain Bertrand, 'Plus près d'Allah' L'itinéraire social et idéologique d'Imam Samudra, terroriste et militant islamiste' in Annie Collovald, Brigitte Gaïti, *La Démocratie aux extrêmes: sur la radicalisation politique*, Paris: La Dispute, 2006, pp. 201–222 and Muhammad Hafez,

or quietist Salafi activists have turned violent, but the majority clearly has not. Consequently, to criminalise all the activists and entrepreneurs of Muqbilian Salafism and state that studying in Dammâj is tantamount to terrorism would be to misunderstand the nuances of this movement and also to overlook most of its history.

The Afghan jihad of the 1980s, which was supported by the entire Islamist spectrum, including the quietist Salafis,[48] should not be considered as the only frame of reference for the study of the relationship that various Islamist groups have with armed violence. In the quietist Salafi current, this event, which gave structure in a lasting way to a number of political and religious movements in the Middle East,[49] appears as quite singular, especially because the 'freedom fighters' were also supported by the governments under which Salafis lived. While the initial objective to fight against the Soviet Union and to make it fall was approved of, the final outcome has been criticised. According to different Salafi scholars, the jihad caused intense struggles for power and influence among the participants, and after the retreat of the Red Army, the struggles produced a new war, this time between Muslims, acting against the objectives of the Arab governments. This result reinforced the opposition of the Salafi current to armed action in foreign countries. In a series of conferences recorded in 2001, Rabî' al-Madkhalî says that during the 1980s his position was opposed to that of the grand *muftî* 'Abd al-'Azîz Bin Bâz and to that of Muhammad al-Albânî, particularly popular among the whole of the Salafi spectrum, with regard to the Afghan jihad. According to him, the invitation extended by these leaders to fight in Afghanistan had the effect of 'leaving Saudi Arabia in the hands the leaders of parties (*hizbiyûn*)'.[50] Thus, for Rabî' al-Madkhalî, 'it was the *fatwâ*

Why Muslims Rebel: Repression and Resistance in the Islamic World, Boulder: Lynne Rienner, 2003.

[48] See for example the work by Muqbil al-Wâdi'î, *al-Suyûf al-bâtira li-ilhâd al-shuyû'iyya al-kâfira* [Sharp swords for the impious communist heresy] place, publisher and date unknown, devoted to 'communism' in South Yemen but also in Afghanistan and a clear endorsement of the activities of the *mujâhidîn*.

[49] On the structural effect of the Afghan jihad of the 1980s, see especially Mariam Abou Zahab, Olivier Roy, *Réseaux islamiques: la connexion afghano-pakistanaise*, Paris: CERI/Autrement, 2002; and Jonathan Benthall, Jérôme Bellion-Jourdan, *The Charitable Crescent: Politics of Aid in the Muslim World*, London: I.B. Tauris, 2003. For analysis of the implications of the Afghan war in the Arabian Peninsula, particularly in Saudi Arabia, see Thomas Hegghammer, *Jihad in Saudi Arabia. Violence and Pan-Islamism since 1979*, op. cit.

[50] Rabî' al-Madkhalî, sound recording, *al-Radd 'alâ shubuhat salafiyyatnâ aqwa min*

of al-Albânî that led the Muslims to Afghanistan, not that of 'Abd Allâh 'Azzâm'.[51] Also, at the beginning of the 1990s, Muqbil al-Wâdi'î wrote a book about the death of Jamîl al-Rahmân al-Afghânî, leader of the *Jamâ'at al-da'wa ilâ al-qur'ân wa al-sunna* ('Group for Preaching to the Qur'an and the Tradition'), an Afghan Salafi movement, who was, according to him, assassinated by militants of the Muslim Brotherhood. For al-Wâdi'î, his death was a symbol of the vanity of the internal struggles between *mujâhidîn* seeking power.[52]

As regards the other areas in which jihad was conducted (Bosnia-Herzegovina, Algeria, Chechnya, Iraq), a conference recorded by Yemeni cleric Muhammad al-Imâm entitled *Hay 'alâ al-jihâd... lâkin* [Call for jihad...but] showed how much the option of maintaining allegiance to existing authority remained in general preferred by quietist Salafi actors, at the expense of the confrontational attitude. Organised in the particular context of the American occupation of Iraq in April 2003, this conference confirmed the importance of jihad, which 'is an obligation commanded by God, like prayer, fasting and pilgrimage'. But while holy war had once 'allowed Muslims to destroy Russia', it had also 'brought Evil among the fighters'. According to Muhammad al-Imâm, although the world was confronted with a 'third world war', including an 'alliance between Jews and Christians' for the purpose of destroying Muslims, the conditions were not right to declare jihad in Iraq against the Americans and their allies. In fact, he considered that such a thing could not be legitimate unless it was endorsed by the leaders (*hukâm*) involved:

God does not require peoples to declare jihad. As an individual obligation (*fard 'ayn*) this must be declared by governmental leaders [...] who must then refer the declaration to the *'ulamâ'*. Only then is it obligatory for individuals to fight according to their personal abilities.

---

salafiyyat al-Albânî [Answer to those claiming that our Salafism is stronger than the Salafism of al-Albânî].

[51] The reference to 'Abd Allâh 'Azzâm, the 'imam of jihad', assassinated in Pakistan in November 1989, is an attempt to take account of the internal struggles within the field of Saudi Islamism. For Rabî' al-Madkhalî, a radical member of the Muslim Brotherhood of Palestinian origin like 'Azzâm could not have the influence necessary to lead young Saudis to fight in Afghanistan. In this way he affirmed that, in contrast to the Salafis represented by Bin Bâz and al-Albânî, the Muslim Brotherhood was not a representative movement in Saudi Arabia. For a biography and edited texts by 'Abd Allâh 'Azzâm, see: Thomas Hegghammer 'Abdallah Azzam: L'imam du jihad' in Gilles Kepel (ed.), *Al-Qaida dans le texte*, op. cit., pp. 113–217.

[52] Muqbil al-Wâdi'î, *Maqtal al-shaykh Jamîl al-Rahmân al-Afghânî* [The assassination of shaykh Jamîl al-Rahmân al-Afghânî], Sana'a: Dâr al-Âthâr, 2006.

Following this, he further asserted:

I warn those who go to fight today in the name of jihad [...]. It is not possible for a Muslim to go and fight under the banner of jihad unless this banner has been properly raised, that is, unless the jihad has been organised according to the rules.

In addition, the absence of hierarchisation or of clear-cut objectives from Muhammad al-Imâm's point of view would lead to ineffectiveness and would promote criminal behaviour: those who went to war in Iraq would be 'immediately destroyed by America'. According to him, during the 1990s the disorganised character of such fighting and its illegitimate status also led to the massacre of Muslims in Algeria, and 'left a million and a half victims'. Muhammad al-Imâm understood implicitly that the international context and American pressure prevented Arab governments, including Yemen, from declaring holy war against the United States and its allies, but in order not to appear completely incoherent, he further declared, 'We thus call on Muslim governments to open the doors of jihad'. In this framework the principles of loyalty, allegiance and the literalist dogma led Salafi entrepreneurs to choose a completely de-contextualised approach, which at the same time appeared disconnected from popular expectations.

Violence and Opposition Despite the Doctrine?

This image of a purely pacific doctrine, however, is incomplete, and it obscures many of the practical inconsistencies of the Salafi movement in Yemen. Deeds might at times appear to directly contradict the peaceful and apolitical doctrine. On the one hand, condemnation in principle of armed action by the quietist Salafi movement does not imply the absence of violent practices linked to so-called jihadi networks in Yemen, Afghanistan, Iraq or other countries where there is conflict. In this regard the doctrine often appears to fade into the background, depending on the context in a particular place. On the other hand, the claim of allegiance to the *walî al-amr*, the rejection of *khurûj* and violence do not prevent quietist Salafis from joining in oppositional practices. As such, the assertion of the universal or intangible obligation pronounced in the texts, in sermons and in doctrine must not lead to surinterpretation. On the contrary, it is necessary to confront such an assertion with actors' practices, which sometimes are guided or motivated more by opportunism, chance and a simple desire to stand apart, than by an essence or an ideology. The apolitical principle thus appears as an illusion or a fiction, essentially more flexible than the entrepreneurs of the Salafi field would admit.

It is a fact that in comparison to the condemnation of violence highlighted previously, Salafi individuals have supported actions against various other political and religious groups within the Yemeni realm. Despite the principles of non-violence and the refusal of *takfir*, several violent episodes did mark the development of the Salafi movement in Yemen. Against socialists,[53] Zaydis, Ismailis and Sufis, the Salafis have at times attempted to gain victory for their norms through the use of arms. This was particularly the case in 1994 and 1995 against the Sufis of the 'Aydarûs mosque of Aden. The destruction of tombs by the Islamists—Salafi-affiliated ones, but also many members of the Muslim Brotherhood who had fought alongside the Northern army against Southern secessionists during the summer of 1994—the use of bazookas was encouraged by various political and religious figures. This violent campaign, followed early in 1995 by clashes in Hadramawt[54] and in the Ismaili bastion of Harâz, was followed by strong criticism from people in the government and certain liberal wings in the Islâh party. Despite all this, al-Wâdi'î thought that the destruction of al-Hâshimî and 'Aydarûs shrines in Aden was a positive deed:

That is the best thing we [i.e., the *ahl al-sunna*] have done. [...] This affair did not affect the government, our brothers or our people. But foreign media got the Yemeni leaders to worry about the affair. [...] The Prophet said that he who sees Evil must correct it by force (literally *al-yad*—by the hand), if he cannot do that then he must correct it by speaking (*al-lisân*—the tongue) or else with the heart (*al-qalb*).[55]

In the same conference, he recalled that at the moment when his partisans attacked the 'Aydarûs mosque, police cars patrolled around the scene without intervening and it was only later, as a result of international pressure, that the government dissociated itself from the action.

From time to time the struggle between Salafis and other political and religious groups at the local level gave rise to violent episodes.[56] In February 1998,

---

[53] Muhammad al-Imâm, *al-Hizb al-ishtirâkî fî rubu' qarn* [The Socialist Party during a quarter of a century], Sana'a: Dâr al-Âthâr, 2008.

[54] For background on the tensions and episodes of violence between Sufis and Salafis see Chapter Six of this book along with Alexander Knysh, 'Contextualizing the Salafi-Sufi Conflict (from the Northern Caucasus to Hadramawt)', *Middle Eastern Studies*, vol. 43, no. 3, 2007, pp. 503–530 and Engseng Ho, *The Graves of Tarim. Genealogy and Mobility across the Indian Ocean*, Berkeley: University of California Press, 2006, pp. 5 and ff.

[55] Muqbil al-Wâdi'î, sound recording, *Liqâ' sahîfat al-bayân al-imâratiyya* [Interview with the Emirati paper *al-Bayân*].

[56] For a detailed account of the 'clash of fundamentalisms' between Salafis (labelled

during a visit to Aden, someone tried to assassinate al-Wâdi'î. According to a young Salafi student:

Shaykh Muqbil had planned to hold a conference at al-Rahmân mosque in Aden but someone tried to stop him. One person tried to throw a grenade at him but thanks to God the grenade went back towards the terrorist. [...] God only knows who threw the grenade, but it might have been the socialists.[57]

Also, in the context of intense internal rivalries within the Salafi field, al-Khayr mosque, the main Salafi centre in Sana'a, was struck in April 1998 by an attack. Al-Wâdi'î himself refused to give the names of those he thought were responsible. For the newspaper *al-Ayyâm*, on the other hand, the attack, which caused two deaths, was linked to the controversy between the Muqbilian wing and 'Abd al-Majîd al-Raymî of al-Ihsân association.[58] At the same time, the mosque controlled by 'Abd al-'Azîz al-Bura'î in the town of Mafraq Hubaysh was attacked by those whom al-Wâdi'î labelled '*hizbiyûn*',[59] that is, members of the Muslim Brotherhood. In October 2003, fights between Zaydis and Salafis for the control of a newly constructed mosque caused one death and wounded two in the town of Dhamâr. The brutal rebellion in Sa'da between the national army and a group of Zaydi revivalists headed by Husayn al-Hûthî and later by his kinsmen since June 2004 also highlighted the Salafis' potential for violence while emerging as yet another way for this group to portray itself as an ally of the government (see Chapter Seven).

'Wahhabis') and Zaydi revivalists around the town of Râzih in Sa'da governorate in the early 1990s, see Shelagh Weir, *A Tribal Order. Politics and Law in the Mountains of Yemen*, Austin: Texas University Press, 2007, pp. 296–303. Conflict between both groups occurred in 1992 as local Salafis organised a campaign against the Zaydi religious festival of ghadîr that was to be organised in Râzih. Held each year on the eighteenth day of the Islamic calendar's month of Dhû al-Hija, the ghadîr khumm is the subject of considerable controversy between Sunnis and Shi'ites. It celebrates 'Alî's supposed designation as the Prophet Muhammad's authentic successor and thus rejects the legitimacy of Abû Bakr, the first caliph recognised by Sunnis. The festival therefore is interpreted by Yemeni republicans and Salafis alike as reaffirming the Hashemites' claim to power, as 'Alî was the Prophet's son-in-law and cousin from whom all Hashemites claim descent while Abû Bakr was only one of the Prophet's companions. The celebration was abandoned after the revolution but re-emerged in the 1990s amid Zaydi revivalism.
[57] Interview, Lab'ûs, April 2005.
[58] *al-Ayyâm*, 29 April, 1998.
[59] Muqbil al-Wâdi'î, *Tuhfat al-mujîb 'alâ as'ilat al-hâdhar wa al-gharîb* [Precious responses to the questions of one who is present and one who is absent], op. cit., p. 391.

From a more global perspective, the positions defended by many Salafi clerics regarding the issue of violent jihad outside of their country (or more precisely outside of the Arab world) show that neither an apolitical stance nor a pacific one can be considered automatic choices, as positions are constantly shifting. The further away the problem, the less nuanced the Salafis' positions will appear. As such, the universalist claim of their doctrine is directly constrained by various contingencies of the environment the Salafis live in. A clear example of internal practical contradictions appeared when al-Wâdi'î endorsed holy war in the Molucca Indonesian Islands in 2000,[60] which was compared with his earlier criticism of Yemeni Islâh party clerics who labelled the 1994 war against the socialist-led secession a holy war. For al-Wâdi'î, this was to be rejected because the designation would lead to Muslim civilian casualties.

Although the 9/11 attacks and similar operations were generally considered illegitimate and wrong since they had, in retaliation, fostered further casualties and war in the Muslim world,[61] the condemnation of violence targeting Western interests is in no way systematic. In fact, the principle of confrontation between the West and the Muslim world is usually something that is acknowledged and supported by Salafi scholars and activists. Nevertheless, in the dominant quietist Salafis' perspective, use of violence is considered counter-productive: Muslims are first of all not ready to fight as they are too weak and divided, and Muslim governments have not raised 'the banner of jihad', so fighting would only cause turmoil.[62] In that frame of mind, while the general objective of targeting a

---

[60] Noorhaidi Hasan, *Laskar Jihad: Islam, Militancy, and the Quest for Identity in Post-New Order Indonesia*, Ithaca: Cornell University, 2006, p. 115 and following as well as Noorhaidi Hasan, 'Between Transnational Interest and Domestic Politics: Understanding Middle Eastern Fatwâs on Jihad in the Moluccas', *Islamic Law and Society*, vol. 12, no. 1, 2005, pp. 73–92. In the context of a severe economic crisis, fighting in the Molucca Islands between 1999 and 2002 opposed Muslim and Christian communities. It resulted in the death of thousands and in the displacement of around 500,000 civilians. The involvement of the Laskar Jihad Islamist paramilitary group was endorsed by various Middle Eastern *fatâwâ*, coming either from Saudi Arabia or Yemen, particularly one published by Muqbil al-Wâdi'î in April 2000. In his short handwritten *fatâwâ*, Muqbil al-Wâdi'î (without probably knowing much about the complex situation in Indonesia and while already being ill) claimed that the defence through jihad of Muslims (whom he considered were being attacked) in the Mollucas against the Christians was an individual duty for Muslims in Indonesia and a collective duty for Muslims outside of that country.

[61] Sâlih al-Fawzân, *al-Ijâbât al-muhima fî al-mashâkil al-mulima* [The important answers to the acute problems], 2005.

[62] Muhammad al-Imâm, sound recording, *Hay 'alâ al-jihâd... lâkin* [Call for jihad...

dominant West might be supported, it can only be attained in the long run and all current attempts are then bound to fail and as such are negative. In various instances, al-Wâdi'î showed an anti-imperialist rhetoric not very different from that of al-Qaeda affiliated groups. In a 1996 conference, for example, he asked God to destroy America by sending 'a heroic nation like the people of Afghanistan who destroyed Russia', yet he denied being a terrorist, claiming he 'is even incapable of shooting a gun correctly'. Furthermore, at the same conference, he asserted the Salafis 'are currently preparing the people to fight America through jihad' and recalled how 'America corrupted the nations by supporting the governments and the tribes but never the Salafis'.[63]

Acknowledging these inconsistencies as well as the fact that the potential for violence exists within the quietist Salafi movement despite the doctrine does not mean endorsing the idea that quietist Salafism is by essence, as many assert,[64] the antechamber of terrorism and 'jihadism' or that Muqbil al-Wâdi'î was a 'Salafi leader renowned for his jihadi discourse'.[65] In fact, such an erroneous amalgamation of quietist Salafism and violent Islamist groups turns out to be of little use from an analytical point of view, and it actually interferes with any attempt to understand the real issues involved in the recourse to violence by religious and political actors. Excessive focus on doctrine or on the vocabulary used is often substituted for a detailed study that takes various contexts into account as regards the determining factors in violence or any other practice engaged in by actors (the nature of relations with authority, the personal history of activists, competition between political and religious groups).

The failure of their apolitical project is especially linked to the status Salafis have as 'moral entrepreneurs', which leads them into proselytism and to the desire to impose their own Islamic norms on the whole of society. Consequently they can be neither fully deviant (they would then face repression from the government) nor exclusively loyal (they would then lose all credit). Through

---

but] and Muhammad Nâsir al-Dîn al-Albânî, sound recording, *al-Radd 'alâ al-jihâd al-muzayif* [The answer to counterfeit jihad].

[63] Muqbil al-Wâdi'î, sound recording, *Jawâhir al-sunniya fî al-as'ilat al-faransiyya* [Sunni jewels in the French questions].

[64] Quoted by the *Washington Post*, Muhammad al-Muttawakil, a prominent Yemeni intellectual of Zaydi background, for example states: 'The Salafists and al-Qaeda are like the two faces of the moon. The Salafists are the light face and al-Qaeda is the dark face. They have the same culture', *Washington Post*, 10 February 2010.

[65] Dominique Thomas, *Les hommes d'al-Qaïda: discours et stratégies*, Paris: Michalon, 2005, p. 51.

complex concepts such as the 'promotion of virtue and prevention of vice'—
which applies to the whole population—and the concept of 'refutation and
rectification' (*jarh wa ta'dîl*)—which is relevant to those in power and *'ulamâ'*—
Yemeni Salafis are able to legitimise the oppositional option. Explaining his
own role, Muqbil al-Wâdi'î declared:

> Men of science (*ahl al-'ilm*, i.e., the *'ulamâ'*) should go to see political leaders to com-
> municate to them the claims of the people, because the people are starting to get dis-
> gusted when they see that problems continue.[66]

Various precepts drawn from the religious corpus turn out to be particularly
flexible, allowing individuals to justify a very wide range of behaviours, sometimes contradictory, that change with the context (and especially with the
degree of government repression). The apolitical attitude advocated by quietist
Salafi entrepreneurs runs up against the social, economic and political conditions that are actually experienced by the actors. In this way Yemeni Salafism
becomes an eminently political entity that is distinct from the official Saudi
religious institutions (General Presidency of Scholarly Research and Ifta (*al-
Ri'âsa al-'âma lil-buhûth al-'ilmiyya wa al-iftâ'*) and the Committee of Senior
'Ulamâ') with which it is nonetheless often associated. In the end, this question
of opposition to power constitutes a central element that distinguishes the
Yemeni Salafi movement from others, including the stricter quietist trend long
symbolised by 'Abd al-'Azîz Bin Bâz as well as by Muhammad Nâsir al-Dîn
al-Albânî and by Rabî' al-Madkhalî.

Ready to defend Bin Bâz against the attacks he faced (particularly coming
from the activists of the *Sahwa islâmiyya* after the 1990–1991 Gulf War),
Muqbil al-Wâdi'î still expressed throughout his career several disagreements
with the former *muftî* of the Kingdom of Saudi Arabia. The differences of
interpretation concerned mainly the *jarh wa ta'dîl*, which according to Muqbil
al-Wâdi'î authorised making public disagreements and disputes between
'ulamâ' and with political rulers, while these controversies should remain
secret in the view of Bin Bâz.[67] In the doctrinal framework elaborated by al-
Wâdi'î, it became possible to insult and stigmatise those deemed ignorant in
order to 'shake the people's consciences and correct them', on the one condition

---

[66] Muqbil al-Wâdi'î, sound recording, *al-Madhhab al-zaydi* [The Zaydi school].

[67] Muqbil al-Wâdi'î, sound recording, *As'ila 'an hayât al-shaykh Muqbil al-Wâdi'î wa
sîratuhu* [Questions about the life of shaykh Muqbil al-Wâdi'î and about his
biography].

that the critic himself was a person of knowledge, or had been oppressed in the past by those he criticised (which according to al-Wâdi'î was the case with him, since he had unjustly been expelled from Saudi Arabia). Such an interpretation led Muqbilian Salafis, according to circumstances and contexts, to become reluctant political actors, thus neglecting to some extent their vows of allegiance.

As stated earlier, Yemeni Salafis do indeed appear to expect nothing from political authorities they disdain, but at the same time they implicitly seem to ask governments to let them pursue their activities freely. The evictions of foreign students decided by the Yemeni government in the wake of the 11 September 2001 attacks or arrests of some students in the years after gave rise to protests from the Salafi leaders, who repeated that they posed no threat to the government, as long as the government let them be. Long before the attacks, during a conference recorded in 1995, al-Wâdi'î stated the following:

If I am gagged, there will be strong reactions as happened with al-Mas'arî[68] the insolent (*safîh*) who offended Saudi Arabia, the state and the shaykh Bin Bâz. This is why I advise the government and particularly you, 'Alî 'Abd Allâh Sâlih, not to do it. You were courageous when from the outside you were accused of harbouring terrorists, and you answered, 'No, we have only *'ulamâ'* who teach the Qur'an and the Tradition'. [...] My brothers, I say to you, if the government is smart, it will leave us alone.[69]

Even more clearly, his interpretation of what he called 'the affair of the sanctuary', that is, the uprising of Juhaymân al-'Utaybî, Muhammad 'Abd Allâh al-Qahtânî and their companions of the *Ikhwân* in November 1979 in Mecca, underlines al-Wâdi'î's awareness of the negative effects of repression. Since he had an ambiguous relationship to that event, he explained with regard to Juhaymân al-'Utaybî: 'He was a student whom I knew, he studied at our centre, but he was not one of the best students and his understanding was limited'. Al-Wâdi'î nonetheless refused to condemn him clearly, although he disapproved of his actions and of the attack on Mecca:

---

[68] Muhammad al-Mas'arî was one of the main figures of Islamist opposition to the power of the Âl Su'ûd. Head of the Committee for the defence of legitimate rights (*Lajnat al-difa' 'an al-huqûq al-shar'iyya*) founded in 1993, based in London, he attracted throughout the 1990s the interest of both Arab and Western media. See especially Mamoun Fandy, *Saudi Arabia and the Politics of Dissent*, op. cit., pp. 11–148 and Stéphane Lacroix, *Les islamistes saoudiens*, op. cit., p. 167.

[69] Muqbil al-Wâdi'î, sound recording, *Hâdhihi al-surûriyya faihdharuhâ!* [This is the *Surûriyya* so be careful!].

There is no doubt that they [i.e., the insurgents] were wrong [...] they provoked a bloodbath in Mecca [...] and they carried arms into the sanctuary, which the Prophet forbade.[70]

Still, for the Yemeni Salafi leader, despite the implication and the faults of Juhaymân al-'Utaybî and his followers, the Saudi government was ultimately the responsible party. In fact, for al-Wâdi'î, it was because al-'Utaybî was persecuted and suffered state repression that he began to write letters, and felt encouraged in his radicalisation.[71] Despite saying this, Muqbil al-Wâdi'î absolved himself, and asserted that he was not responsible for the insurgents choosing the option of violence, though he intended to show that it was preferable for governments not to enter the negative spiral of repression.

Furthermore, al-Wâdi'î in his various books and conferences appeared to remain consistent with key elements of the doctrine of the *Ikhwân*.[72] Although the messianic dimension of al-'Utaybî's enterprise and the importance of the *mahdî* do not appear as central for its activists, the Yemeni Salafi movement as originally built around Muqbil al-Wâdi'î shared much with the *Jamâ'a al-salafiyya al-muhtasiba* of which both he and al-'Utaybî had been active members in the 1970s. The fact al-Wâdi'î was accused by Saudi authorities of being the ghost writer of Juhaymân al-'Utaybî's letters reinforces the impression of such doctrinal proximity and might explain the features of Yemeni Salafism. Indeed, criticism of the Saudi state as expressed in al-Wâdi'î's writings during the 1980s and early 1990s (see Chapter Four) echo much of al-'Utaybî's argument in his famous letter 'The State, Allegiance and Obedience' written in 1978: the Âl Su'ûd are considered illegitimate as they are not from Quraysh (descendants of Prophet Muhammad's tribe) and are accused of being allies of Christians.[73] Nevertheless, despite their alleged corruption, the Saudi rulers, like all Muslim leaders, are not to be excommunicated: *takfîr* is thus forbidden. Furthermore, al-Wâdi'î's extreme social conservatism, his rejection of pictures, music and his claim that it was illegitimate for someone to work as a civil servant or in the army of Yemen, as well as some unorthodox interpretations of the texts (regarding for instance the possibility to pray while wearing shoes) were all consistent with al-'Utaybî's practices.

---

[70] Muqbil al-Wâdi'î, *al-Makhraj min al-fitna* [Leaving dissension behind], op. cit., p. 143.

[71] Muqbil al-Wâdi'î, *Ijâbat al-sâ'il 'alâ ahamm al-masâ'il* [Answers to those who ask the most important questions], op. cit., p. 398.

[72] Muqbil al-Wâdi'î, *al-Makhraj min al-fitna* [Leaving dissension behind], op. cit.

[73] Muqbil al-Wâdi'î, sound recording, *al-Ilhâd al-Khumaynî fî ardh al-haramayn* [The blasphemy of Khomeini against the Land of the Two Holy Places].

In a way, the Yemeni branch of Salafism seems to have learned from al-'Utaybî and the *Ikhwân*'s mistakes and adopted an apparently clearer stance towards loyalty to the ruler, particularly the Yemeni leadership, thus escaping from potential repression and abandoning revolutionary plans. Instead of directly confronting the ruler, al-Wâdi'î considered that it was necessary to be loyal to the political system in order to prevent the country from falling into chaos. He then asserted that state policies could be oriented through the secret advice of *'ulamâ'* to the rulers.

Nevertheless, allegiance to a government, such as that of quietist Salafi entrepreneurs, also has limits, like violence itself. Apart from certain statements of a general character, expressing the view that Muslim leaders had become 'the tails of America and Russia'[74] and consequently did not constitute an option for dissent or criticism of the Yemeni *walî al-amr*, Muqbil al-Wâdi'î expressed anger with his own government on a number of occasions. He criticised the spies the Yemeni government was supposed to have sent to Dammâj to watch his teachings and to monitor him. In a conference devoted to the movement of Muhammad Bin Surûr, he declared:

> The Yemeni government considers *'ulamâ'* as if they were cockroaches (*sarâsir*). Look how Bin Bâz is a cleric, and can also deliver authorisations to enter that country [Saudi Arabia]. I tell you, Yemen is communist and Ba'athist, and you can find Christian missionaries all the way to Dammâj.[75]

This critique, certainly not an overt attack on the President of the Republic, was nevertheless a departure from certain principles of allegiance stated in other contexts, as analysed above. As such, it set Yemeni Salafis structured around al-Wâdi'î in a class of their own. The references to communism and especially Ba'athism—a movement 'Alî 'Abd Allâh Sâlih was allegedly once close to—are rather pointed, inasmuch as both ideologies had been condemned by Salafis as impious. The very ambiguous positions of al-Wâdi'î with regard to Saudi Arabia and its government (which shall be studied in more detail below) also illustrate certain contradictions—or adaptations—of the practice of Salafi actors in Yemen.

In contrast to the Saudi case, where political dissidence has long been the only alternative to loyalty to the monarchic power, the Yemeni political field,

---

74 Muqbil al-Wâdi'î, *Ijâbat al-sâ'il 'alâ ahamm al-masâ'il* [Answers to those who ask the most important questions], op. cit., p. 459.

75 Muqbil al-Wâdi'î, sound recording, *Hâdhihi al-surûriyya faihdharuhâ!* [This is the Surûriyya so be careful!].

since it allows a certain freedom of expression, allows a more nuanced position without ever exposing the Salafis to direct state repression. Without overtly opposing the government or becoming its sworn enemies, without even drawing frontal criticism from Saudi *'ulamâ'*, the Yemeni Salafi movement established by Muqbil al-Wâdi'î made use of the relative freedom available to it. Thus the principle of respect for the decisions of *walî al-amr* has a variable geometry. For example, Muhammad al-Imâm, in a recording devoted to democracy, openly criticised the basis of the Yemeni political regime:

I have read the new democratic constitution [for Yemen] and it is not Islamic. Article 4 after revision says that sovereignty belongs to the people. [...] We say that sovereignty belongs to God, over our lives, over our actions, and over our wealth. There is nothing of this in the constitution. [...] I believe that the constitution of Yemen is an impious constitution (*kufrî*), I declare this, and I will maintain it until my death.[76]

The limits of the Salafi apolitical attitude are clear and so are the shortcomings of an approach to Salafism exclusively based on ideology, since it does not take into account the diversity of practices and positions.

Over and above the reality of the flexibility of the actors' behaviours, the apolitical or quietist attitude that is claimed by the Salafis becomes political by its functional character. In fact, the rejection of all participation in the political sphere fulfils a particular function to the extent that it allows the religious entrepreneurs to avoid the responsibilities that the exercise of political power implies, even at a local level. Consequently, by withdrawing from the political field, at least formally, the Salafis do not overuse or dry up their mobilising capacity.

In a study of Salafism in Jordan, Quintan Wiktorowicz saw in the apolitical stance and the refusal of institutionalisation an oppositional technique that allows Salafis to escape state control effectively. By being loosely organised, they would be less exposed than if they were formally structured with a hierarchy.[77] He explains that in Jordan, the quietist Salafis' refusal to organise in

---

[76] Muhammad al-Imâm, sound recording, *al-Dîmuqrâtiyya* [Democracy].

[77] On the Salafis' reasons for rejecting institutional politics, Quintan Wiktorowicz writes: 'The Asad regime's crackdown on visible manifestations of the Islamic movement led al-Bani [ie: Muhammad Nâsir al-Dîn al-Albânî] to issue a *fatwâ* when he first arrived in Jordan, which stated that Muslim activism through organisations is haram. He believed that organisations prompted harsh reprisals from state authorities and therefore stunted the spread of the Islamic message. He instead preferred Islamic work through the traditional structure of lessons, the mosque, and meeting in homes'. Quintan Wiktorowicz, *The Management of Islamic Activism. Salafis, the Muslim Brotherhood, and State Power in Jordan*, op. cit., p. 131.

parties or associations, and the fact that they declare political organisations to be illicit, is a leftover from their experience of repression in Syria under the Ba'athist regime. This idea does account for some of the emphasis on refusal of *hizbiyya* in the Yemeni Salafi field. The apolitical stance is indeed instrumental since it preserves the Salafis from repression and also from the difficulties associated with the exercise of power. Nevertheless, such a role should not be seen only as the result of a strategy. In fact, it is not solely repression, little if any of which is aimed at the Salafis in Yemen, which is the source of their rejection of institutionalisation and politics, but certain ideological principles, particularly flexible, that draw on the specific Yemeni context and on the Salafis' history as a movement that faced competition from overtly political movements and did its best to differentiate itself. Consequently, the divisive role played by the denunciation of the *hizbiyya* in the rhetoric of Yemeni Salafis, which was continued after Muqbil al-Wâdi'î passed away, is an indicator of the extent to which Salafism has adapted to its environment.

The presentation of the Salafi spectrum in Yemen, its doctrines and some of its practices throughout these first two chapters was meant to highlight the complexity and the diversity of the object of this book. While the Yemeni Salafis that emerged around Muqbil al-Wâdi'î, or even those who parted from it like the Hikma association, are neither adepts of so-called jihadi violence, nor unwaveringly loyal or pacific they undoubtedly position themselves into multiple and contradictory dynamics. In the light of the Yemeni case, quietist Salafism can be defined in large measure by its 'minor behaviours', a failed universal and apolitical project, and the apparent reluctance of actors to get involved in the political sphere. The flexibility of oppositional practices, hesitation between deviance, violence and allegiance make the relationship between Salafis and the state and society itself ambiguous. Without managing to operate in an entirely neutral, apolitical and de-contextualised environment, Salafis still hold to their universalist calling, which is intended to extract them from their context and worldly matters. Their apparent lack of interest in power preserves their capacity for mobilisation, but also shows their rejection of the state as an efficient and necessary actor. This relationship in return favours a certain transnationalism of the Salafi current. Consciously or not, they structure themselves around actors who have the capacity to go beyond national boundaries and identities and get involved in a space that is strongly marked by translocal recompositions. As shall be highlighted in the second section of this book, it is essentially by basing itself on these recompositions, rather than on state-related politics, that Salafism has managed to develop in the Yemeni environment.

PART 2

TRANSNATIONAL SALAFISM

3

DOMINATION AND TRANSNATIONAL FLOWS
IN THE ARABIAN PENINSULA

Since the 1970s, attempts by the six Gulf monarchies (Saudi Arabia, Qatar, the United Arab Emirates, Kuwait, Bahrain and Oman) to actually create and popularise a national and regional identity or consistent image[1] that would be clearly distinct from a truly *Khalījī* (Gulf) identity (one that could even qualify as 'Arab-Persian', including Iraq but also Iran) or a larger Peninsular one have only had a limited success. Among other things, such projects have not been able to mask the role played by Yemen in the long-standing integration of the Arabian Peninsula. Thus, despite the continuing exclusion of Yemen from the Gulf Co-operation Council (GCC, established in 1981), for which it has been a candidate for membership since 1996, the Arabian Peninsula appears to be a highly integrated region in terms of flows and shared culture. As such, the arbitrary academic separation between 'Gulf studies' and 'Yemeni studies' does not do justice to the extensive nature of the connections that exist between all the nations and communities of the Arabian Peninsula. The focus of scientific studies on the coastal areas of the Arab-Persian Gulf and on the six monarchies can be explained mainly by the strategic and economic interest of the very large reserves of hydrocarbons the region possesses. Rich in human capital and in history but poor in natural resources, Yemen is supposed to be no more than a peripheral area hardly worth considering except when it comes to security-related issues and to al-Qaeda. Despite these deeply-rooted stereotypes, it

[1] Paul Dresch and James Piscatori (eds.), *Monarchies and Nations: Globalisation and Identity in the Arab States of the Gulf*, London: I.B. Tauris, 2005.

appears that it is undoubtedly necessary for researchers as well as decision-makers to take account of phenomena of interpenetration, and of the fact that the Arabian Peninsula cannot simply be pigeonholed as a space that has little coherence in itself.[2]

For it is in terms of this integration and this shared history, frequently under-valued although profound and meaningful, that the actors and interactions with which the second part of this monograph of Salafism is concerned can be understood. Transnational Salafism in Yemen is in no way disconnected and 'rootless', rather it finds itself filled with meaning in a particular context of domination and flows that predates it in the wider peninsular environment.

International relations theory, dominated by so-called realism, has long neglected the study of individuals. In many respects this scale of analysis continues to be stereotyped as individuals are most frequently portrayed as secondary actors, always subjected to the vagaries of international regimes and overarching structures. The individual is too often described as a passive figure that is tossed back and forth by states and their real or imagined interests.

Nonetheless, since the end of the Cold War the academic discipline of international relations has increased its awareness of the complexity of the world, of the multiplicity of actors and of the plurality of spaces of interaction. Thus alternative paradigms were developed with the intention of 'humanising the international'.[3] By restoring the individual to his or her rightful place, these approaches, which find their roots in liberal theory, recognise the irrational, accidental and unforeseeable character of many events and social behaviours: decision processes do not always produce the expected results and the world is not developing according to a grand design. As a result, the efficiency of state policies and decisions is directly questioned. These approaches, that may be labelled 'a transnational perspective', also highlight cumulative phenomena and the fact that the microsocial level should not be neglected, since through aggregation such events can transform structures. Individuals produce change thanks to more or less informal connections that are made and eventually organised through transnational networks.[4]

---

[2] Sheila Carapico, 'Arabia Incognita: An Invitation to Arabian Peninsula Studies' in Madawi Al-Rasheed and Robert Vitalis (eds.), *Counter-Narratives. History, Contemporary Society, and Politics in Saudi Arabia and Yemen*, op. cit., p. 11.

[3] Bertrand Badie, 'Nouvelles approches des relations internationales et du fait religieux' in Jean-Pierre Bastian, Françoise Champion and Kathy Rousselet (eds.), *La Globalisation du religieux*, op. cit., p. 266.

[4] James Rosenau, *Distant Proximities: Dynamics Beyond Globalisation*, Princeton: Princeton University Press, 2003, pp. 21–22.

Based on these theoretical presuppositions, this second part of the book intends to link together the contemporary political and religious transnational relations between Yemen and Saudi Arabia and the development of Salafism in the Yemeni context. To this end, my approach also aims, insofar as possible, to distinguish these two processes from a third: the domination that Saudi Arabia (along with the other Gulf monarchies, although much less centrally) exercises over Yemen. The idea here is to avoid the predisposition of much work in international relations, which leads scholars to concentrate their attention on political interactions in the international sphere from the point of view of states, state power, so-called 'national interests' and confrontation.

By putting the individual back at the centre of things, the transnational approach allows the connections between the microsocial and macrosocial levels[5] to be grasped, and to go beyond the issues of interests and competition. As such, it focuses more on interactions than on confrontation. At another level, this approach also seeks to answer one of the main challenges in the area of international relations today: to what extent can individuals be considered as relevant actors in the international sphere? Can the aggregation of transnational behaviours be said to be the foundation of macrosocial phenomena?

Going back to the specific issue of Salafism in Yemen, contemporary transnational relations, especially religious ones, do not appear to be guided by an identifiable objective, but remain the result of social and political recompositions. There is no question here of opposing the notion of an endogenous Salafism, born out of local dynamics, to that which is contained in certain influential narratives, which portray Salafism as something imported, the result of Saudi domination. On the contrary, the following pages show how the internal and external factors blend together, especially through migratory trajectories and in what James Rosenau labelled as 'Frontiers'. Through financial flows, economic investments, development aid, commerce, news reports, social narratives and certain individual aspirations, Saudi Arabia, like other Gulf States, plays an important role in the constitution of local identities, whether religious, social or political. The intensification of relations, whether labelled transnational or translocal, particularly in a context of globalisation, brings together spaces that otherwise are considered to be distinct, and turns certain events and phenomena that take place far away into objects of daily conversation. Thus increased traffic (legal or not) across borders and interpenetration

[5] On the issue of micro/macro interactions see, Saskia Sassen, 'Local Actors in Global Politics', *Current Sociology*, vol. 52, no. 4, pp. 649–670.

of certain spaces are no longer perceived as anomalies, but provide a basis for an approach which, rather than concentrating on phenomena of excessive rootedness and territorial purity, emphasises the mobility of actors and ideas, that is, the interaction between what is present and what is absent, between what is near and what is far.

Symbolic and economic exchanges, money transfers, private and public development aid, migrations and the long history that connects Yemen with other states of the Arabian Peninsula all play a direct role in the elaboration and dissemination of an imaginary mindset that is favourable for the development of Salafism. In this regard the Yemeni migratory phenomena promote interdependence, increase the latitude available to non-state actors, and at the same time create the conditions for an interpenetration of societies. The massive amount of remittances from Yemeni workers in Saudi Arabia, sent back to their families during the 1970s and 1980s, for example, allowed society to bypass state control, including for example its management of the banking system.[6] As such, state institutions appear to be globally incapable of forcing individuals to fulfil their own objectives and satisfy their 'national interests'. In the same sense, the porous nature of the borders and phenomena of regional solidarity expose the somewhat imaginary character of sovereignty. States and transnational actors demonstrate a certain structural autonomy with regard to each other, without ever being completely independent and distinct. Consequently the states in the Arabian Peninsula, which are often said to be 'weak' or 'in the process of being constructed' partly because they bring together actors with different or divergent interests, are not always able to attain their own ambitious objectives and to actually control their subjects or citizens.

I. Migratory Trajectories and Transnational Relations

Undoubtedly, Yemeni migratory trajectories towards Saudi Arabia and the Gulf monarchies constitute an important variable in the process of Salafism's development. Migrants are in fact the main actors in contemporary transnational relations, although not the only ones. Migration makes these relations a matter of daily life, and so influences the many aspirations and practices. Counterintuitively, the transnationalisation of the religious sphere appears to take place via the category of expatriates, *mughtaribîn*, and thus by means of

[6] Kiren Aziz Chaudhry, *The Price of Wealth: Economies and Institutions in the Middle East*, op. cit., p. 217.

actors that are not *a priori* designated as religious. Therefore, religious relations cannot be considered specific or directly singled-out and are thus formed and 'carried' along with men, goods and money, but also in the imaginations of individuals.

Despite a long-standing reputation for being closed off and difficult to access, Yemeni territory has long had to deal with outside influences. The ancient incense route, the Rasûlid dynasty in the thirteenth to fifteenth centuries, two Ottoman occupations (sixteenth and twentieth centuries) and then the British colonisation of Aden and its hinterland have shaped society and the state, beyond all doubt. Southern Arabia is a geographical and political crossroads, and is characterised by an ancient migratory and commercial tradition, whose importance has varied through history and by region.

The ancient migrations from the eastern Yemeni province of Hadramawt have been the object of numerous academic studies, including some carried out by Hadramis themselves,[7] but other regions of the ancient land known as *Arabia felix* remain under-analysed. Indeed, much like Hadramawt, these provinces (Shabwa, Yâfi' or Ta'iz to name just a few) were also shaped by the life stories of emigrants and by their remittances but, conversely, they did not experience a kind of proactive investment in a particular identity. Beyond these specific localities, in one way or another, migratory flows have gradually come to involve all Yemenis.[8] For several centuries or more recently, from South-East Asia (Indonesia, Malaysia) to East Africa (Ethiopia, the Comoros Islands), and from the Indian sub-continent to the United Kingdom (Sheffield and Cardiff in particular),[9] to the United States (Detroit, Buffalo, the San Joaquin Valley) and of course to the other countries of the Arabian Peninsula, Yemenis looking for better livelihoods or commercial opportunities have formed significant communities of expatriates, or even what could well constitute a diaspora. In

---

[7] Ulrike Freitag and William Clarence-Smith (eds.), *Hadhrami Traders, Scholars and Statesmen in the Indian Ocean (1750s–1960s)*, Leiden: Brill, 1997; Engseng Ho, *The Graves of Tarim: Genealogy and Mobility Across the Indian Ocean*, op. cit.; Linda Boxberger, *On the Edge of Empire: Hadhramawt, Emigration and the Indian Ocean (1880s–1930s)*, Albany: State University of New York Press, 2002; Mas'ûd 'Amshûsh, *al-Hadhârim fî al-arkhibîl al-hindî* [Hadramis in the Indonesian Archipelago], Aden: Dâr Jâmi'at 'Adan, 2006; and Abdalla Bujra, *The Politics of Stratification: A Study of Political Change in a South Arabian Town*, Oxford: Clarendon Press, 1971.

[8] Jonathan Friedlander (ed.), *Sojourners and Settlers: The Yemeni Immigrant Experience*, Salt Lake City: University of Utah Press, 1988.

[9] Fred Halliday, *Britain's First Muslims. Portrait of an Arab Community*, London: I.B. Tauris, 2010.

return, these communities have had a considerable effect on Yemen, transforming a number of its social structures.

Patterns of Yemeni Migration Inside the Arabian Peninsula

Over the course of the twentieth century, economic emigration to Saudi Arabia gradually replaced the more ancient migratory flows towards South-East Asia or East Africa. Before the 1970s oil boom,[10] the Arabian Peninsula was characterised by an exceptional capacity for integration into its economic, religious and social structures. The vitality of the cosmopolitan port of Jeddah, and then the discovery of oil reserves during the 1950s reinforced this specificity of regional history. In addition, the central role played by Mecca and Medina in the Muslim world made them privileged centres that attracted foreign '*ulamâ*', who often found employment in the official structures of Saudi Islam. Such was the case of prominent figures such as Muhammad al-Amîn al-Shanqîtî, who came from Mauritania (died in 1974), Abû Bakr al-Jazâ'irî—the Algerian (died 1999) and also Muhammad Nâsir al-Dîn al-Albânî. All three, although at different levels, participated in the organisation of Saudi religious institutions during the 1960s. In similar circumstances, several Yemeni figures, including Muhammad Sâlim al-Bayhânî (died 1972), resided during this period in Saudi Arabia but also in Kuwait, receiving religious training and socialising with '*ulamâ*' from other parts of the Muslim world. The Arabian Peninsula was at the time shaped by an authentic transnational tradition and a real cosmopolitanism that remain underestimated even today.

All this notwithstanding, the construction of the Saudi state and economic growth during the 1960s required the importation of a large number of unskilled workers.[11] Fleeing from drought and infertile lands, but also from chronic tribal violence, Yemeni workers fulfilled this requirement *en masse* even before South Asian immigrants arrived. As an indirect result of oil drilling, the extent of Yemeni provinces affected by this migratory call gradually became larger. Zones of Shafi'i origin in which emigration had been going on

---

[10] For a detailed political economy of Saudi Arabia and of the institutional changes occurring after the 1970s oil boom, see Steffen Hertog, *Prince, Brokers, and Bureaucrats. Oil and the State in Saudi Arabia*, op. cit.

[11] 'Abd al-Wahhâb al-'Uqâb, *Tatawwur al-'ilâqât al-yamaniyya al-su'ûdiyya 1948–1970* [Evolution of Yemeni-Saudi relations 1948–1970], Aden: Isdârât Jâmi'at 'Adan, 1998.

for many centuries (particularly the areas of the Hadramawt, Shabwa, Yâfi', Dhâli', Hujariyya and Tihâma) were no longer the only ones involved as migrants of the Zaydi highlands also started to offer their labour on the regional market.

Such experience of migration and the mobility of actors were then part of the foundation of regional integration and the interpenetration of societies. The golden age of Yemeni emigration to the six Gulf monarchies, which extended from 1965 to 1990, was characterised by relative freedom of circulation for workers, and by strong economic growth.[12] As a result of the aggregation of migratory experiences, the presence of the Gulf, and particularly of Saudi Arabia (be it in the form of a state, a society or even a certain collective image in the people's imaginations) where the vast majority of migrants worked, was a daily reality in Yemeni society, including its religious and cultural dimensions.

In Yemen as in other historical and cultural contexts, emigration is to be considered as an important factor in social change. In what can be defined as translocal space, global processes (money transfers, international legislation, economic trends), and local ones (traditions or social hierarchies, for example) interact in such a way as to favour the transformation of both individual and collective practices.[13] Beginning in the 1960s in both North and South Yemen, the increase in emigration brought important changes to social and family structures, especially concerning agricultural work performed by women and the spacing out of births. These changes also helped maintain the model of the extended family.[14] The importance of the experience of migration for young men even came to be assimilated to a rite of passage, something that was actually part of the process of assuming the identity of an adult Yemeni.[15]

---

[12] 'Abd Allâh Sa'îd Bâ Hâjj, *al-Yamaniyûn fî al-Su'ûdiyya khilâl rubu' qarn (1965–1990)* [Yemenis in Saudi Arabia during a quarter of a century (1965–1990)], Sharjah: Dâr al-Thaqâfa al-'Arabiyya, 2002.

[13] For a study of these complex interactions between global space and local space, see in particular Katy Gardner, *Global Migrants, Local Lives: Travel and Transformation in Rural Bangladesh*, op. cit.; and Valérie Amiraux, *Acteurs de l'Islam entre l'Allemagne et la Turquie: parcours militants et expériences religieuses*, Paris: L'Harmattan, 2001.

[14] Thomas Stevenson, 'Migration, Family, and Household in Highland Yemen: The Impact of Socio-Economic and Political Change and Cultural Ideals on Domestic Organisation', *Journal of Cooperative Family Studies*, vol. 28, no. 2, 1997, pp. 14–53.

[15] Thomas Stevenson, 'Migration as a Rite of Passage in a Highland Yemeni Town' in Jonathan Friedlander (ed.), *Sojourners and Settlers: The Yemeni Migrant Experience*, op. cit., p. 37.

Through much of the second half of the twentieth century, large sections of the borders between North Yemen, South Yemen and Saudi Arabia remained ill-defined and unrecognised by international law. This undeniably facilitated the comings and goings of workers and blurred much of the national identities as multiple passports were often held or handed over as a means of putting pressure on the neighbouring governments. Such generosity constituted a tool in the competition between Saudi Arabia and both Yemens along the border: nationality would in the last resort become a way to prove the legitimacy of one's claim over disputed land.[16] Under the Saudi regime, the implementation at the beginning of the 1960s of the *kafâla* system (every foreign guest-worker had to find and pay a private Saudi sponsor who would serve as an interface between him or her and the administration)[17] did not directly affect Yemenis, who benefited from a specific status not enjoyed by the large immigrant population arriving from the Indian sub-continent, from South-East Asia, or from elsewhere in the Arab world (Egypt, Palestine and Sudan in particular). Yemenis in fact did not have to get visas or have a sponsor (*kafîl*) in order to work in Saudi Arabia (as elsewhere in the other small Gulf monarchies who all implemented a *kafâla* system),[18] and were even allowed to start businesses that they could own under their name.

During the 1970s, Yemeni workers from socialist South Yemen, in theory, did not benefit from this exemption in Saudi Arabia. In practice they quite often managed to escape the very constraining and onerous system of the *kafâla*. In fact, the legislation was not systematically implemented, because many 'Southerners' had a passport from the Yemen Arab Republic. Regional networks constituted by those who had long migrated also facilitated the entry of this large group into the Saudi economy.

At this time, pilgrimages to Mecca and Medina were, for all Yemenis from both North and South, a legal means of access to the Saudi job market. The *hajj* or the *'umra* often became an opportunity to spend several months working at a construction site or in a business in a Saudi city, Jeddah in particular, before returning to live in one's village in Yemen.

[16] Thomas Pritzkat, 'The Community of Hadramî Migrants in Saudi Arabia and the Rationale of Investing in the Homeland' in Rémy Leveau, Franck Mermier and Udo Steinbach (eds.), *Le Yémen contemporain*, op. cit., p. 409.

[17] On the *kafâla* system and Saudi nationalism, see Hélène Thiollet, 'Nationalisme d'Etat et nationalisme ordinaire en arabie saoudite: la nation saoudienne et ses immigrés', *Raisons Politiques*, no. 37, 2010, pp. 89–102.

[18] Anh Nga Longva, 'Keeping Migrant Workers in Check: The Kafala System in the Gulf', *Middle East Report*, no. 211, 1999, pp. 20–22.

During the period prior to the Gulf War (which directly put an end to the golden age of Yemeni migration in the Arabian Peninsula), labour appeared as the main export of Yemen and despite the 1990–1991 shock when many of those residing in the Gulf monarchies were forced to return to the Yemeni homeland, they gradually retained their prominent economic role in the course of the 2000s decade. The exact number of Yemeni workers in Saudi Arabia and in the other Gulf states is unknown, and frequently has been the object of controversy. Estimates at the height of the phenomenon in the early 1980s vary between 500,000 and 1.25 million, while in the early 2010s it is likely to be close to one million. According to official figures, revenue sent home by emigrants amounted in 1980 to 40 per cent of the gross national product of North Yemen and 44 per cent of that of South Yemen.[19] But these figures hide important regional disparities and have fallen dramatically since then. With regard to geographical origin, to position in hierarchies of traditional status groups (*sâda, qudhâ, qabâ'il*, and so on) and seniority in emigration, individual trajectories are evidently varied. Furthermore, each region has remained associated with one or more occupational specialties, and this largely conditions its place in the economic and social system of the host country, as well as the possibility of migrant workers staying permanently and eventually obtaining Saudi nationality. For car mechanics from Yâfi', gold sellers and merchants from Hadramawt, or building painters from Khawlân, opportunities nowadays often remain limited and job options are mostly pre-determined. The high cost of living in Saudi cities, especially as regards rent levels, and certain restrictions, for example limitations on foreigners' access to higher education, have made reunification of families and extended time of residency difficult.

The vast majority of Yemeni immigrant workers in Saudi Arabia are therefore limited to unskilled or low-skill jobs, and thus are not meant to become permanent residents. Over the course of the twentieth century, people with substantial commercial interests and some '*ulamâ*' may have succeeded in overcoming these limitations and in obtaining Saudi nationality. Success in migration, made visible both in financial terms and through reputation would also be endorsed by popular vocabulary and denomination in the homeland: through their faraway success simple *mughtaribîn*—expatriates—would become in the eyes of many Yemenis wealthy *tujâr*—merchants. The signature case, and also the most commented on, involved Muhammad Bin Lâdin, who was originally a mason, a man of modest means from Wâdî Du'ân in Hadra-

---

[19] Gwenn Okruhlik and Patrick Conge, 'National Autonomy, Labor Migration and Political Crisis: Yemen and Saudi Arabia', op. cit., p. 556.

mawt, and who rose in thirty years to possess one of the largest fortunes in Saudi Arabia. He founded the largest construction and public works company in the country, the Saudi Ben Laden Group (Majmû'at Bin Lâdin al-Su'ûdiyya). Another man, Sâlim Bin Mahfûz, came to Saudi Arabia also from the Hadramawt region in 1912, took up residence in Mecca and then moved to Jeddah, where he founded in 1953 the National Commercial Bank (Bank al-Ahlî), today the most important financial institution in the Kingdom.

To the extent that the port of Aden declined and Yemeni merchants moved their business to Saudi Arabia, Jeddah actually became in the 1970s the main centre for Yemeni business. This was the place where many merchants originating from that country could be found while still sending portions of their earnings back home, thus contributing to the development of their homeland. However, from the 1960s to the 1990s, the ongoing situation of instability in (and between) the two Yemens, as well as the ideological offensive staged by the socialist regime in the South, limited reinvestment opportunities and money transfers back to the home regions of Yemeni businessmen operating in Saudi Arabia as well as elsewhere in the Gulf monarchies. Despite these limitations, certain notable successes among the migrant businessmen were much talked about in these home regions, and this provided a certain impetus for others to leave. Through the purchase of land, construction of houses, schools, clinics or mosques, and other commercial or industrial investments in the home regions, immigrants also were constructing a positive image of the *mahjar* (the destination of emigrants, in this case, the Gulf monarchies) among other locals, and of the experience they too might have. Thus the transnational dimension constituted a political and economic resource for expatriate actors.

This phenomenon of building an image or reputation through transnational links was in no way restricted to those who migrated to Saudi Arabia, and is not to be considered a recent trend in Yemeni society. In his early 1960s anthropological study of the small town of Huraydha in the southern part of Shibâm, in Hadramawt, Abdalla Bujra found that a similar process had taken place decades before. He explained how the long tradition of emigration from that region, once colonised by the British, had allowed certain groups to build up or maintain privileged positions. At the beginning of the twentieth century, the 'Attâs family for instance had managed to defend its social and religious status thanks to resources obtained through migration and transnational Sufi networks.[20]

---

[20] Abdalla Bujra, *The Politics of Stratification: A Study of Political Change in a South Arabian Town*, op. cit., p. 21.

Since the 1970s, the financing of religious-oriented projects appeared as just one outlet among many others to build one's status. Quite oddly, it only rarely was associated with a conscious desire to proselytise or make a political statement. As such, the funding of Salafi centres such as Dâr al-Hadîth and other centres for Qur'anic instruction found throughout Yemen, provided by Yemeni businessmen operating in Saudi Arabia as elsewhere in the Gulf, appears less as the result of their exposure to the dominant strain of Islam labelled as 'Wahhabi' than as a result of their affluence and their desire to support religious projects that are perceived as beneficial by large proportions of Yemenis. Consequently, the financing of a mosque, including Salafi projects, does not necessarily imply allegiance to its political or religious orientation. The case of the only mosque in the settlement of al-'Umarî in the Lower Yâfi' region supports such a claim. The mosque was built in the mid-1990s thanks to money contributed by a Yemeni, a retired officer in the Qatari Army who had left South Yemen shortly after independence. In the absence of any other trained scholar in the village, the responsibility for this centre of worship was given to a young man who had studied at Dammâj. The reputation for piety of Salafis, along with other characteristics of Islamic knowledge, had a positive connotation and commanded respect, including from parts of the population who, much like the retired officer's family, were not particularly devout. Using this construction, the *mughtaribîn* appeared to be able to take advantage of their position and present themselves as being not only successful in social and economic terms, but in religious terms as well.

Over the course of the second half of the twentieth century, socialisation into Saudi Sunni Islam (which once again must not be limited to the dominant form of Islam promulgated by official religious institutions) undoubtedly influenced the practices of Yemeni immigrants. Over and above the image of a certain economic success, the experience of having gone to Saudi Arabia, frequently accompanied by pilgrimages to Mecca and Medina, granted expatriate workers special religious prestige whenever they returned to their home region in Yemen. As a result, differences in the manner of worship (Zaydis do not pray in the same physical position as Sunni Muslims) were often soft-pedalled and such experiences contributed to a deeper uniform process that bridged Zaydi and Shafi'i Sunni religious identities.[21] However it would be wrong to overestimate the function of these migrations. Among Yemeni workers, such

[21] Laurent Bonnefoy, 'Les identités religieuses contemporaines au Yémen: convergence, résistances et instrumentalisations', *Revue des Mondes Musulmans et de la Méditerranée*, no. 121–122, 2008, pp. 201–215.

transformations do not appear to have led to the development of mass prosely-tisation or activism. In fact, the high rate of illiteracy among this expatriate population and the fragility of their administrative status in the *mahjar* have encouraged neither the politicisation nor the theologically motivated rejection of practices common to popular Islam, a feature that is central in the Salafi doctrine.

However, although marginal in numbers, student grants given by the Saudi state or by para-public institutions for the purpose of pursuing studies at Saudi Islamic universities may have increased the influence of a certain world vision, based on a literalist approach to religious texts and on the stigmatisation of allegedly 'deviant' sects, that directly participated in the development of Salafism or of other forms of militant Islam. Muqbil al-Wâdi'î, Ahmad Hasan al-Mu'allim, 'Abd al-Wahhâb al-Anisî (former Deputy Prime Minister), Ghâlib 'Abd al-Kâfî al-Qurashî (Minister of Religious Affairs from 1993 to 1997 and a former student at the Islamic University of Medina), Muhammad Bin Muhammad al-Mahdî (prominent member of the Hikma association) and also 'Abd al-Majîd al-Zindânî are without doubt the most illustrious examples of this socialisation into Saudi Islam in the Yemeni Islamist field.

The 1990/1991 Expulsions

The Iraqi Army's invasion of Kuwait in August 1990 had unexpected conse-quences for Yemen's migrants. Less than three months after the unification of North and South, the Yemeni government, then a non-permanent member of the UN Security Council, refused to vote for international sanctions against the government of Saddâm Husayn. Yemen's decision to abstain from voting on a number of resolutions and their official neutrality regarding the conflict were interpreted as support for the Iraqi offensive. Saudi Arabia retaliated, along with other Gulf monarchies, by eliminating the preferential treatment that had been granted until then to Yemeni workers. The expulsion of several hundred thousand of them that followed the Saudi royal decree of 19 Septem-ber, 1990 caused a restructuring and redefinition of the migratory experience in the Saudi kingdom and the other Gulf monarchies that implemented similar measures (while between 700,000 and a million were forced to leave Saudi Arabia, an estimated 45,000 fled Kuwait and 2,000 Qatar, the United Arab Emirates and Bahrain).[22] These decisions formally put an end to the privileges migrants from Yemen had enjoyed.

---

[22] Thomas Stevenson, 'Yemeni Workers Come Home: Reabsorbing one Million Mi-grants', *Middle East Report*, no. 181, 1993, p. 15.

For many, the Gulf War and the modification of the status of Yemeni workers and their families had dramatic effects, but nevertheless such expulsions did not imply a complete break. It actually deepened a basic trend that had begun to appear during the previous decade. The high point of Yemeni immigration in economic and statistical terms had occurred in the mid-1980s, after which a slow decline set in. In fact, from that time onwards Yemenis were gradually replaced by workers, coming from South-East and South Asia, that tended to be more qualified and to speak English, and who were perceived as more docile and less politicised.[23] In addition, even before the Gulf War crisis, the general economic trend in Saudi Arabia had declined, reducing opportunities for foreign workers. The structure of the Saudi population, young as a whole, reduced these opportunities still further as a new generation of Saudis began to enter the job market in larger numbers. In order to meet these challenges, some Yemenis began to move back to the home country even before the Gulf crisis, adapting their transnational practices to the evolving context.

In 1990, the end of privileges linked to the status of Yemeni guest-workers in Saudi Arabia also led to the appearance of strategies for bypassing or coping with the new situation, strategies that essentially involved regional networks of solidarity. These allowed some workers to escape expulsion and to stay in the country despite the diplomatic tension. Saudi entrepreneurs of Yemeni origin 'sponsored' and helped workers from their home regions to maintain legal status. These forms of solidarity explain the particular degree of resistance on the part of Hadramis to the crisis situation: their long-standing tradition of immigration to Saudi Arabia and the success that a number of them had enjoyed made it worthwhile to try to keep up the migratory experience and adapt their strategies. In 1990–1991, workers from the former North Yemen, such as the regions of Ibb, Ta'iz and al-Hudayda paradoxically experienced more violence in the process of the repatriation of workers than did those from the former South Yemen, who before unification had theoretically required a sponsor.[24] Thus they were able in general to anticipate the change in status.

---

[23] The involvement of a number of Yemenis (six from the South and one from the North were executed in January 1980 along with Juhaymân al-'Utaybî) in the Mecca uprising of November 1979 no doubt reinforced the fear of Saudi rulers and businessmen of seeing the foreign population become politicised and turn into a force opposed to the monarchy.

[24] In his work on Hadrami commercial networks, Thomas Pritzkat notes that in the early 1990s, Saudi-Hadrami merchant 'Abd Allâh Buqshân sponsored tens of thousands of fellow Hadramis in Saudi Arabia, giving a sense of the rootedness of re-

During the troubled period of the 1990s, up until the official return of Yemeni expatriates in 1998, transnational relations were sometimes maintained at the regional level with the assistance of para-diplomatic manoeuvres that managed to work around centralised policies affecting bilateral relations.

Other category-related networks, especially those that were religious or political, also made it possible for some Yemenis to remain in Saudi Arabia despite the expulsions. Such was the case with 'Abd al-Majîd al-Zindânî (who did not return to Yemen until the end of 1991 only to become a leader of the newly established al-Islâh party), and various former opponents of the republican regime in the North or the socialist regime in the South who were granted, during the crisis period, the benefit of clemency from certain elements in the Saudi government and treated as political 'refugees' of a sort.

Again, in order to adapt to the new situation, throughout the 1990s and the 2000s, Yemenis as well as Saudis put together underground networks that smuggled many Yemeni workers (but also ones from the Horn of Africa) into Saudi Arabia to work illegally. There are no reliable statistics concerning the minority of workers who entered illegally, and those who remained or who returned after having been expelled the first time. For the most part, they have been forgotten by history, which appears to have retained only the memory of the expulsion, that is, what the states themselves asserted and the mutual understanding intended. The persistence of these flows, either legal or not, was of particular significance.

For that matter, despite the fascinating capacity of actors to maintain transnational exchanges, the success of the governmental decisions still appears to have been validated a priori in academic work as well as in media accounts. Statistics that are compiled are only rarely questioned and the interpenetration of societies is treated as an epiphenomenon. Even today, dispatches and articles announcing the seizure of traffickers, of merchandise (drugs and weapons in particular), and of illegal immigrants by Saudi and Yemeni customs agents contribute to maintaining an illusion of control supposedly exercised by the states of the Arabian Peninsula. The planned construction of a 'security barrier' and the establishment of joint Yemeni-Saudi commissions overseeing the effort to secure the political border defined by the treaty of Jeddah in June 2000, cannot hide the fact that this boundary remains particularly permeable.

---

gional networks of solidarity during that period of crisis. Thomas Pritzkat, 'The Community of Hadramî Migrants in Saudi Arabia and the Rationale of Investing in the Homeland', op. cit., p. 405.

Such emphasis put on the capacity of infra-state actors to bypass states does in no way overlook the reality of the evictions during the Gulf War. Even considering the ways in which the regulations were neutralised by some, for the great majority of the 800,000 or so workers the Saudi decision of September 1990 and that of the other Gulf monarchies led to expulsion, followed by a disaster for many families and for the economy as a whole. The return to Yemen of those who had emigrated was made particularly difficult because it took place in the context of an already complex national unification process. Many studies have emphasised the destabilising effect, on both a micro- and macro-economic level, of the forced return of the workers. Despite the fact that former emigrants brought home their savings (estimated at $1.3 billion) and certain durable goods (especially their cars), things that had a beneficial effect in the short term, in the long run, the cost to the Yemeni economy was enormous. Former emigrants had trouble finding jobs and unemployment was looming.[25] A sign of the seriousness of the economic dislocation was the appearance of 'tent cities' on the outskirts of large cities, especially outside al-Hudayda, the population of which doubled in a few months. The 'rectification of the situation'[26] of the Yemeni workers, that is, the end of their exceptional status among all foreigners in the Gulf area, coincided with the cut of Saudi, Kuwaiti and American development aid. This was a severe retaliation, to the diplomacy of the Yemeni government, supposed to have been pro-Iraqi. Only in the mid-1990s did the resource of foreign aid gradually reappear only to bloom in the context of the 'Global War on Terror'.

A New Migratory Logic

Beyond the concrete suffering of individuals and the dire macroeconomic problems that it caused, the expulsions of 1990–1991 also led to a redeployment (of marginal dimensions) towards new destinations such as China, Europe

---

[25] Concerning the effects of the repatriation of Yemeni workers, see Marc Lucet,'Les rapatriés de la crise du Golfe au Yémen', *Maghreb Machrek*, no. 148, 1995, pp. 28–42 and Nicolas Van Hear 'The Socio-economic Impact of the Involuntary Mass Return to Yemen in 1990', *Journal of Refugee Studies*, vol. 7, no. 1, 1994, pp. 18–38.

[26] *Tashîh wadh'* [Rectification of the situation] is the name of a popular novel published in 2004 by Ahmad Zayn, a Yemeni journalist living in Riyadh, that tells the story of the expulsion of Yemenis (something the author himself lived through) in September 1990, and the difficulties of their return to a country which some barely knew. Ahmad Zayn, *Tashîh wadh'* [Rectification of the situation], Sana'a: Wizârat al-Thaqâfa, 2004.

and North America. In the longer term, the expulsion led to a change in the logic of the migratory experience.[27]

In Saudi Arabia, the new rules applied after the Gulf War forced foreigners, now including Yemenis, to find a *kafîl* to pay for that person's administrative sponsorship, and also to renew their residency cards (*iqâma*) every year. These procedures were expensive, often costing more than a month's salary.[28] In that new system, Yemeni workers were not assured of having their contracts renewed, and were thus liable to expulsion at regular intervals as the *iqâma* could not be obtained by those who were unemployed. Consequently, Yemeni workers found themselves in a more precarious situation than previously and emigration became less attractive. One expatriate living in Jeddah, a native of the former South Yemen who had originally emigrated in the 1980s using a North Yemen passport, had been expelled in 1990 and had only managed to get a new work visa in 1999, described the new situation:

With a salary of 2500 Saudi riyals (about $700), between the *kafîl* who I pay 1200 riyals per year, the various taxes and the renewal of my residency card, there's not much left for me to live on, or to send to my family.[29]

The hardening of conditions on residency for Yemeni immigrants over the course of the 1990s did not only concern Saudi Arabia. For example, something that was no doubt less significant but in some cases just as destabilising for individuals and some localities was a new salary scale that went into effect in the Qatari Army in 1993. As a result, foreign officers, many of whom were Yemeni and originated from Yâfi', saw their pay cut by almost 50 per cent. This change of conditions prompted those who had emigrated to return to Yemen.

The added difficulty in bringing one's family to Saudi Arabia, and the near-impossibility for foreigners of studying at the public universities there[30] made it necessary for migrants to go back and forth more frequently, and thus to do

[27] Engseng Ho, 'Yemenis on Mars: The End of Mahjar (Diaspora)?', *Middle East Report*, no. 211, 1999, pp. 29–31.

[28] Saudi Arabia's entry into the World Trade Organisation at the end of 2005 is eventually supposed to lead to the disappearance of the *kafâla* system, but more than five years onwards the concrete effect for immigrants of that membership remains intangible.

[29] Interview, al-Sûma', February 2005.

[30] In 2005, only 100 places, including 60 for current residents of Saudi Arabia, were reserved in Saudi universities for Yemenis. See: *al-Ayyâm*, June 28, 2005. For its part, the Yemeni government established 100 scholarships for study in local public universities in 2006 that were reserved for expatriates: *26 September*, 13 October, 2006.

more to maintain their connections with the home country. Young Yemeni expatriates, some of whom were born in Saudi Arabia, could either study in private Saudi higher education institutes (an option that was often impossible because of the high tuition fees) or else return to 'their' home country to receive training (often with the objective of returning to their expatriate lives afterwards). Universities and private institutes (particularly the University of Science and Technology (*Jâmi'at al-'ulûm wa al-tiknûlûjiyâ*), or the University of al-Andâlus) were created in the mid-1990s in large Yemeni cities to serve the needs of the important population of Saudi-Yemeni students.

In this already challenging context, the implementation over the period 1990–2000 of a series of 'Saudisation' decrees (*su'wada*) forbidding foreigners from taking jobs in certain specific sectors further reduced possibilities for immigrants in Saudi Arabia.[31] In the view of a Saudi-Yemeni merchant of the Huraybî family, originally from Yâfi' and particularly active in the gold-selling business:

> The need for a *kafîl* since 1990 was not the most significant change in the situation for Yemenis in Saudi Arabia. 'Saudisation' made things more complicated for businesses and reduced the number of opportunities. Because of this many young people went to China or to the United States to do business, and left the Saudi *mahjar* and the Gulf.[32]

In the works since 1975, the 'Saudisation' programme first affected public administration jobs, and then private businesses (grocery stores, the banking sector, fishing industries, taxicabs, women's clothing stores and the gold market). During the 1990s this question emerged as a major issue for public debate and in the Saudi media. The policy's goal was allegedly to solve high unemployment among young Saudis. In Spring 2004 a study commissioned by the Saudi government examined seventy-five businesses and found that the level of Saudisation of workers in the private sector had risen, from an average of 18 per cent in 2000 to 23 per cent in 2004. This figure was still significantly below the announced target of 38 per cent.[33] Even though the Saudisation of the gold

[31] On the 'Saudisation' of labour markets and its shortcomings, see Steffen Hertog, *Prince, Brokers, and Bureaucrats. Oil and the State in Saudi Arabia*, op. cit., pp. 185–222. Hertog writes, on p. 219: 'Given the imbalances of the Saudi labour market, Saudisation would have been a challenge for any government. Nonetheless, it is remarkable how badly co-ordinated and unrealistic many of the Saudi policy measures were'.

[32] Interview, Lab'ûs, January 2005.

[33] Quoted by Pascal Ménoret, 'Chronologie de l'Arabie Saoudite 2004', *Chroniques Yéménites*, no. 12, 2005, p. 230.

market during the first half of the 2000s decade put several thousand foreigners out of work, many of whom were Yemeni, the programme as a whole remained incomplete. Despite statements from the government, many jobs in this specific sector continued to be held by expatriate residents.[34] In addition, this policy had the unexpected effect of pushing part of the gold market to Bahrain and Dubai, where legislation had remained more flexible.

Far from being linear, the Yemeni migratory experience, particularly in Saudi Arabia, constitutes the central point of reference for the transnationalisation of the societies of the Arabian Peninsula. Changes in migratory trajectories are thus an important source of the recomposition of identities, allegiances or group membership. These are more than simply religious relations and it appears that what is essential in transnational relations and in the process of the transplantation of Salafism is related to the normal process of migration. Still, individual migratory experiences are often ambiguous, and consequently cannot be said to be the unambiguous instrument of the so-called 'Saudisation' of Yemeni Islam.

II. Migration as an Ambiguous Experience

The ambiguity of the migratory experience is essentially characterised by a certain disdain, cast in the face of the Saudi model, or at least by a rejection of the international image that Saudi Arabia projects for itself. This biased image, created by the Saudi state since its inception and reinforced through public policies developed since the 1960s as well as in media outlets, ignores a number of episodes of its recent history as well as many of the components of the society, particularly the heritage of the Bedouins, the populations of the Hejaz and the inhabitants of outlying regions.[35] This image also neglects the Shi'ite and Ismaili minorities, and the part played by many foreign populations (Asian, Iranian, Indian, American... and Yemeni) that made important contributions to the construction of Saudi society over the centuries. Such a slanted image leads to the creation of a national mythology, something that has been the object of

---

[34] On the question of the Saudisation of the gold market, see 'Hall mushkilat su'wadat masâni' al-dhahab' [Solution to the problem of the Saudisation of the gold industry], *al-Riyâdh*, 28 August, 2006.

[35] Madawi al-Rasheed, 'The Capture of Riyadh Revisited: Shaping Historical Imagination in Saudi Arabia' in Madawi al-Rasheed and Robert Vitalis (eds.), *Counter-Narratives. History, Contemporary Society, and Politics in Saudi Arabia and Yemen*, op. cit., pp. 183–200.

recent academic studies[36] and even fictionalised, as it was for example by the novelist 'Abd al-Rahmân Munîf in his quintet, *Mudun al-Milh* (Cities of Salt), whose first volume was published in 1984. The overarching narratives constructed by Saudi elites (as well as by foreigners) feature a society that is prosperous, united and even uniform. In religious terms, such an approach grants a special, unchallenged role to a depoliticised Islam that is quietist and subservient to political authority, and that claims direct descent from the teachings of Muhammad Bin 'Abd al-Wahhâb.

In comparison with this static image, Saudi social practices reveal themselves as infinitely more diverse and cosmopolitan. Yet, such diversity is not systematically part of the daily experiences of the immigrants in the Kingdom. The socialisation of Yemeni workers to the ideal-typical Saudi Islam known as 'Wahhabi' or Salafi is even far from automatic. While some immigrants in Saudi Arabia, particularly of Hadrami origin, as in other places in the *mahjar*, prove to have a particularly high capacity for integration, the majority of Yemeni expatriates suffer from social exclusion and even at times misery. They remain separated from their families, who stay behind in Yemen, their purchasing power is very low by Saudi standards, and they are often housed in men's dormitory they call *'uzba*, a term deriving from *a'zab* meaning bachelor, usually with other male workers originating from the same village in Yemen. This kind of life does not lend itself to any participation in society other than work, except for opportunities to practice religious piety. Without leisure activities, without children in school and wives to socialise, without cars for moving around in the sprawling Saudi cities and without disposable income to spend, the great majority of expatriates cannot gain more than a glimpse of the complex Saudi society. As such, the Kingdom is in their eyes no more than a caricature. Nonetheless, in such a peculiar context, skewed and limited, the collective imagination of Yemenis is shaped, and the aspiration to emigrate remains strong, built on the hope for economic success. Considering the frequency of migration, the issues of the image of Saudi Arabia and of experience of work in the Kingdom appear as important to understand in what specific context Salafism emerged. The development of this religious identity, although not a direct result of migratory experiences, took place in a context of intense interpenetration of Saudi and Yemeni societies at the grassroots level.

Ambiguity in relation to the Saudi *mahjar* is not new, and did not only arise as a result of the changes in the status of immigrants that took place in the

---

[36] See Ibid. and Robert Vitalis, *America's Kingdom: Mythmaking on the Saudi Oil Frontier*, Stanford: Stanford University Press, 2007.

1990s. Individual experience seems to have been implicitly linked to tensions and difficulties in bilateral relations and to a deep historical rivalry between the two most populated nations of the Arabian Peninsula. A Yemeni worker in California, interviewed by Ron Kelley in 1983, explained in frank terms why he preferred the United States to Saudi Arabia, although he would have earned more money in Saudi Arabia:

Yes, you can make a lot of money in there [i.e.: Saudi Arabia]. It's true. But life is miserable in Saudi Arabia. I think, first of all, there is disrespect for the Yemeni people. There is something between the two parties—Saudis and Yemenis—which is politics. There is some of the Yemeni land being taken by Saudi and used as oil well right now. Now the government of Saudi paying the government of North Yemen to keep it quiet, let it go as it is. And the people of Yemen don't like that. The people of Yemen very revolutionary. They would go to Saudi but they also like to live free. They don't like to be insult. Now the Saudi people have no respect for nobody other than Saudi.[37]

For a minority of Yemeni immigrants who hold down well-paid jobs or managed to avoid the 1990–1991 expulsions, the Saudi experience is evidently more complete and more diversified. The children of these people, sometimes Saudi-born and educated in the Saudi system, might appear as definitively 'Saudified', and thus by extension allegedly socialised to what many have labelled 'Wahhabism'. Now, unless one thinks that Saudi youth are by essence very pious, and thus able to be categorised in terms of the partial and subjective image that the Saudi state and certain media stereotypes have put forward,[38] the integration into Saudi society of this minority of immigrants does not automatically imply an intensive religious practice, still less an adherence to Salafism such as this was understood by Muqbil al-Wâdi'î or by the dominant Saudi religious establishment. In this regard the population that attends the University of Sciences and Technology in Sana'a (financed from the time of its founding in 1994 by figures close to the Islamist party al-Islâh, especially Târiq Sinân Abû Luhûm) turns out to be an interesting indicator as regards the sociology of the second generation of *mughtaribîn* (migrants) coming from

---

[37] Ron Kelley, 'The Workers Speak' in Jonathan Friedlander (ed.), *Sojourners and Settlers: The Yemeni Immigrant Experience*, op. cit., pp. 104–105.
[38] Concerning the problems of Saudi youth, see especially: Mai Yamani, *Changed Identities. The Challenge of the New Generation in Saudi Arabia*, London: Royal Institute of International affairs, 2000 and Pascal Ménoret, *Racailles et dévots: la politisation de la jeunesse saoudienne 1965–2007*, Doctoral thesis, University Paris-Sorbonne, 2008.

the upper classes. In fact, at this private university, assumed *a priori* to be influenced by the Muslim Brotherhood, nearly half the students (out of 6,000) were, according to a university professor, brought up in the Saudi educational system (a smaller number went through the school systems of other Gulf states).[39] Lacking authorisation to attend Saudi universities, they chose to register at the reputable university, which offers a curriculum that is recognised throughout the Arab world. However, neither the professional orientation nor the dress code of these students reveals anything of the so-called 'Saudisation', largely constructed and imaginary. More often than not dressed in tight jeans, wearing baseball caps, with their hair cut and styled according to modern fashions, and spurning the traditional *thawb* tunic, these Saudi-Yemeni students are certainly products of their socialisation in Saudi society as it is, not as it represents itself (or as it is usually represented). They demonstrate above all the inexactness of the skewed though dominant image of a Saudi Arabia that is essentially pious and resistant to all modernisation. The idea of a single Saudi pattern loses its pertinence from this point. A medical student, originally from Say'ûn in Hadramawt, but actually born in the Saudi capital, admits wishing, after two years at the University of Sciences and Technology in Sana'a, that he could return to Riyadh to look for a job. He claims to know no one from Sana'a, and although his ties to Yemen are tenuous, he has managed to create a network of friends, Hadramis like himself, who have shared his experience of the forced return and hope it is temporary. A foreigner in his own country, decrying the backwardness and poverty of Yemen, he nevertheless recognises the positive qualities of his home country:

Certainly, there is more freedom here than in Saudi Arabia, people are pure-hearted and gentle. But I am simply bored in Sana'a and at this university, my family and all my friends are in Riyadh.[40]

This student's attitude toward his home country recalls the commentary by Engseng Ho concerning expatriate's relations to their countries of origin. He asserts, regarding Hadramis (although his observations can be applied to Yemenis in general, and to other diasporas):

The homeland is poor but pure. Its very Spartan quality is a virtue, for trouble starts not with want but with excess. The homeland is where children are raised, or should be. The outside is where young men venture, mingle their energies with abundant forces

---

[39] Interview, Sana'a, June 2005.
[40] Interview, Sana'a, May 2005.

and resources, and sometimes go astray. It is where piles of money are made, and morals corrupted in equal times.[41]

Elsewhere, Engseng Ho finds the same ambivalence attached to the migratory experience: it allows one to be part of a deeply rooted historical tradition, and it is something that one's ancestors went through, but because of temptations associated with money and because of ill-advised social mixing, it leads to corruption:

The migratory life is a two-way street, one leading to purity of religion and ancestry, the other to contamination. It is brutally simple. Who dares contradict it? Although the geographical destinations vary, the moral one does not.[42]

Far from Yemen, emigrants begin to idealise their homeland. In their minds, it may be economically backward, but at the same time it is thought of as remaining in a state of original Islamic purity as recounted in the prophetic Tradition. Its underdeveloped state is precisely what allows one to think that its society has not changed since the time of the Prophet, and so it has not undergone an excessive Westernisation process that many in Yemen accuse of being behind moral corruption. The notion that the migratory experience is a corrupting influence concerns all Yemenis, including Salafis. Muqbil al-Wâdi'î himself spoke of the unhealthy aspect of being an expatriate, especially in Saudi Arabia. In his opinion, workers and students see the availability of material comfort, and they risk being corrupted by the desire for it, but they also may decide never to return to Yemen because of it. With regard to living outside Yemen or studying outside it, al-Wâdi'î said that he was 'worried that someone might drool over money and tasty *kabsa* (the Saudi national dish, made with rice and mutton) and never come back'.[43] In his eyes, migration certainly involves economic and religious opportunity (it allows people to separate themselves from the alleged theological errors of some in Yemen) but it also implies the sacrifice of good things and the possibility of corruption of the soul, which are processes that must not be encouraged.

---

[41] Engseng Ho, 'Hadhramis Abroad in Hadhramaut: The Muwalladîn' in Ulrike Freitag and William Clarence-Smith (eds.), *Hadhrami Traders, Scholars, and Statesmen in the Indian Ocean*, (1750s–1960s), op. cit. p. 134.

[42] Ibid. p. 137.

[43] Mubqil al-Wâdi'î, sound recording, *As'ila 'an hayât al-shaykh Muqbil al-Wâdi'î wa sîratuhu* [Questions about the life of shaykh Muqbil al-Wâdi'î and about his biography].

Despite these ambiguities, Saudi Arabia represents an unquestionable economic and social opportunity for Yemenis, and this is why so many of them take their chance there, even in violation of the laws regarding immigration. According to World Bank statistics, 35 per cent of the population of Yemen in 2010 is below the poverty line. In addition, annual population growth is running high at 2.9 per cent and unemployment is estimated at 30 per cent, while 51 per cent of the population is below the age of eighteen and serious social problems are persistent (increasing urbanisation, inflation, dwindling water resources).

The desire to emigrate is further stimulated by references to the golden age that extended from the 1960s to the late 1980s. In addition to regular remittances of money, every emigrant seems eager to show that he has achieved success in Saudi Arabia. Gifts are brought back home to one's family, sometimes even a car to show how all the sacrifices in the *mahjar* were not pointless. These gifts also frequently have some connection to Saudi holy places, and allow emigrants to claim that their travels have a religious significance. Dates from Medina, water from the sacred spring of Zam-Zam, prayer rugs (made in China!), religious books or posters depicting the Great Mosque of Mecca give a religious flavour and a special prestige to the migratory experience in Saudi Arabia. These gestures often conceal the harsh working conditions the emigrants experience there.

Despite the difficulties, expatriate status remains quite enviable and success abroad (real or imagined) produces visible effects when emigrants come back to the homeland. Each returning emigrant contributes to the constitution of an idealised image of the *mahjar*. This microsocial process grows as individual reports are aggregated. Despite limitations and difficulties, past and present, the Saudi economic model retains a positive connotation. The ideal migratory experience is one in which an emigrant is able to accumulate some amount of capital in a short time, intending to reinvest it locally. For a student from Yâfi', emigration is supposed to accelerate his becoming an adult. He explains:

Once my studies are completed, I hope I will be able to go meet my brother who is in Najrân [ie: South West Saudi Arabia] working in a clothing store. My priority is to get married and to start a family. Salaries in Saudi Arabia are much higher than here. In Yemen, if I were a teacher getting the salary of a government employee, at best I would earn 25,000 Yemeni riyals a month (about $120). In order to get married, since a wife costs about seven or eight hundred thousand riyals, it would take years. In Saudi Arabia, I can get that in one year, because I can earn up to 100,000 riyals a month.[44]

---

[44] Interview, Lab'ûs, February 2005.

Admiration for the Saudi economic model and the desire to emigrate is nonetheless accompanied by a degree of real rancour and nationalistic rivalry. The contrast between the alleged willingness to work of Yemenis and the supposed laziness of Saudis is one illustration of a widespread anti-Saudi feeling among Yemeni people. For an emigrant vacationing in his native village, Saudi Arabia owes its status to oil and to Yemenis, because 'they built everything they have up there'. Supporting this position, the emigrant's brother observed how badly the exceptional natural resources of the Kingdom are used: 'The Saudis produce 12 million barrels of oil a day, Yemen only 500,000. Believe me, if we had the same resources, we would do better than they do!'[45] The stereotype of pampered and lazy Saudis explains, for others, the reason why the Saudi economy needs foreign workers, especially Yemenis:

Most young Saudis do not want to work, and this is why the Saudisation laws for various jobs that are not well-paid did not succeed. For them the important thing is the car rodeos (*tafhît*),[46] or their cars, or travelling overseas. Only a minority of them really want to work.[47]

For another person, who was forced to return to Yemen and open a small computer store because of the Saudisation laws in the gold market, the situation is as follows:

The laws of *su'wada* allowed the Saudis to keep for themselves all the jobs in which you work sitting down. The jobs where you really work and get tired, they left for the foreigners. [...] The Saudis with their *shmagh*, their *'iqâl* on their heads, their sunglasses and their big cars, they talk big, but when Saddâm Husayn was at their gates in August 1990, they got scared and called for outside help![48]

Unsurprisingly, the stories migrants tell are marked with considerable bitterness, often linked to the trauma of the expulsion of 1990–1991. The feeling of having been 'used' by the Saudi economy and then discarded when political problems arose is frequently mentioned by former emigrants, and this is also the case with the expulsion of older or sick workers who could no longer work,

---

[45] Interview, al-Sûma', February 2005.

[46] Concerning the phenomenon of car rodeos in large Saudi cities, see Awad Al-Otaibi, Pascal Ménoret, 'Rebels Without a Cause? The *tafhit* Groups in Saudi Arabia' in Asef Bayat and Linda Herrera (eds.), *Being Young and Muslim. New Cultural Politics in the Global South and North*, Oxford: Oxford University Press, 2010, pp. 77–94.

[47] Interview, Riyadh, April 2006.

[48] Interview, Lab'ûs, April 2005.

something thought to be unjust and inhumane. The lack of gratitude on the part of the Saudi state and indeed all of Saudi society towards these workers has given rise to a number of the negative stereotypes mentioned above. The Saudis are often considered haughty—and egotistical as well. With regard to a colleague, at one time a teacher of religious sciences in the Saudi school system, who was expelled in 1990, a Yemeni university professor spoke of this ingratitude on the part of the Saudis, declaring:

He lived for more than thirty years up there in Saudi Arabia teaching in their schools for their country. Suddenly they sent him back where he came from. If he had been in the United States they would have made him the President of the country, but they threw him out! [...] I can say that for me, the real servant of the Two Holy Places [*khâdim al-haramayn*—referring to a title claimed by the Saudi King] was him![49]

Such a situation also fosters an ambivalent sentiment towards the religious dimension of the migration in Saudi Arabia. The Senior '*ulamâ*' and religious figures of the Land of the Two Holy Places, and especially the late 'Abd al-'Azîz Bin Bâz, are for the most part respected, but many Yemenis appear to think the Saudis believe in their own superiority in matters of religion. Between the two countries, there is a deep and ancient rivalry for the palm of spiritual purity. Yemenis often criticise the Saudi approach to worship, often thought to be hypocritical. As of consequence, a number of epithets and jokes are frequently passed around by migrants in order to make fun of Saudis, and the inhabitants of the Gulf monarchies. For example, the very word for 'Gulf'—*khalîj*—can easily be transformed into 'scoundrel', *khalî'*, paving way for a number of jokes. With regard to the Saudis in particular, a man who was expelled after thirty years in Jeddah noted angrily that the Saudis 'are the Jews of the Arab world! It's no accident that Su'ûdî rhymes with Yahûdî (Jew, in Arabic)!' Citing rumours about the ancestry of the dynasty of the Âl Su'ûd family, he even claimed that 'certain historians have managed to discover their Jewish ancestors'.[50]

At times, the desire to display one's economic success in the *mahjar* fades into the background because of the harsh reality of the life of a migrant. In repeating certain anecdotes and recollections, former and current migrants show their willingness to speak about the difficulties of their migratory experience. Many of them remember the discrimination they experienced in relation to Saudis, for example in the effort to get a driver's licence, without which jobs are harder to get. Others recall that certain laws seemed only to be enforced

---

[49] Interview, Lab'ûs, April 2006.
[50] Interview, Lab'ûs, April 2005.

against foreigners. Such was the case with the theoretical prohibition, lifted in August 2005, against mobile telephones with cameras included. The law notwithstanding, camera phones were popular with Saudis, but one Yemeni former expatriate told the story of having his phone confiscated by the religious police (*al-mutawwa'*). This man summed his experience there by saying, 'in Saudi Arabia, you work, you pray, and everything is all right. You have to toe the line!'[51]

Migration thus appears in this instance as a chance you take, as much as it is a test of skill. The whole set of stereotyped representations no doubt plays a role in the construction of individual aspirations. Just as with flows of materials, the subjective and ambiguous image of the migratory experience, through criticism, irony, valuation and idealisation contributes to the interpenetration of societies, and plays a part in the transnationalisation of Salafism.

[51] Interview, al-Sûma', February 2006.

4

THE CENTRALITY OF TRANSNATIONAL CONNECTIONS

As will be shown in this fourth chapter, many of the specific social practices of Salafism locate it in a transnational space and associate it with a project of crossing over physical boundaries and fixed identity-images that are constructed by nations and states. In the Yemeni context, such phenomena are evidently shaped by the ambivalent dimensions of Yemeni-Saudi migrations, highlighted in the previous chapter, and by the personal experience of its main founder Muqbil al-Wâdi'î. The Salafi movement, through its doctrine, its history, its roots and the practices of its devotees appears to have a special affinity for transnational interactions. It is in fact marked by a relation of disdain, formulated as a response to political power and states, which are characterised as weak and ineffective by Salafis. Thus there appears to be a kind of predisposition for Salafism (in reality much like other religious movements)[1] to take part in de-territorialised as well as translocal interactions that do not take the nation-state as their main frame of reference, but attempt (although not always successfully) to transcend it completely, or work around it.

The construction of an alternative approach to dominant state-centred narratives is in no way meant to deny the fact that Salafism has 'travelled' or that certain specific practices have only recently appeared in the Yemeni context. The central position of Saudi Arabia (and more marginally of other Gulf states) in the Yemeni Salafi field is as visible in terms of practices as it is in terms of

[1] Thomas Banchoff (ed.), *Religious Pluralism, Globalisation and World Politics*, Oxford: Oxford University Press, 2008.

references. From the clothes worn by its followers to the various theological sources it draws upon, Salafism may appear to some extent as a break with the given Yemeni environment or with what some perceive as Yemeni authenticity. Muqbil al-Wâdi'î, whose central importance has already been evaluated, himself recognised the 'transplanted' nature of his doctrine and referred frequently in his conferences and writings to the opposition and hostility with which he was confronted when he returned to Saudi Arabia in 1979. At the end of his life, when a student asked him about the rapidity of the development of Salafism in Yemen, he said that he was surprised himself:

This has puzzled me. In reality, students came from outside and when they went back home, others met them and came here in their turn. Thanks be to God, the Tradition has been spread among men. The students were Bedouins then, who did not even know the pronunciation of the Arabic language. [...] People chewed qat, and consumed *shamma* [a kind of powdered chewing tobacco], visited the tombs of saints, wore amulets (*hurûz*) and practiced magic. [...] So we hardly knew where to begin in our preaching [because customs that contradicted Islam were commonly practiced]. [...] When I left [Saudi Arabia], I was isolated, I wept when I thought about my situation.[2]

The line of argument that is defended in this chapter states that the Yemeni environment is precisely shaped by transnational phenomena, particularly migrations, and that rather than being exceptional, exchange and travel across borders and through distant localities are commonplace. The development of Salafism in Yemeni society is then much less linked to the direct experience of Saudi society or to the concrete intervention of foreign actors and foreign policy tools than to the indirect effects of migrations and the interpenetration of societies and of religious fields.

I. The 'Transnationalisation' of Salafism in Yemen

The complex relationship of Salafi actors to the state and to society in general favours their insertion into multiple transnational dynamics. Passageways between the Yemeni Salafi political and religious field and other societies of the Arabian Peninsula are various. Over and above simple economic dependence, Salafism is in fact marked by political, cultural and identity-related practices that are more or less formally deployed outside the space of relations

[2] Muqbil al-Wâdi'î, sound recording, *As'ila 'an hayât al-shaykh Muqbil al-Wâdi'î wa sîratuhu* [Questions about the life of shaykh Muqbil al-Wâdi'î and about his biography].

between states. A wide array of the transnational relations seem to be organised in non-institutionalised networks: institutes of higher education, bookstores and Salafi mosques are connected together in external and internal terms. They are linked together by mostly informal ties, often characterised by a certain horizontality and decentralised for the most part. As such, these practices seem to forge what some, building on the famous concept of Pierre Bourdieu, could label a 'transnational habitus'.[3]

The universalist emphasis that is part of Salafi doctrine is represented by the Salafi desire to bypass the state, inasmuch as it is a necessarily limited and truncated expression of nations and territories. Consequently, without being transnational in its essence, Salafi practice is characterised by an affinity for certain forms of social relations and certain strategies of getting around the reality of international borders. For example, an emphasis on *'ibâda* (religious worship and creed) in itself tends towards a decontextualisation of theological references. Whether a particular question is asked in Marseilles, Dammâj, Birmingham, Riyadh or Jakarta makes no difference, because in theory the answer must be the same everywhere. In such a frame of reference, advice and counsel from *'ulamâ'*, published in lists of *fatwâ* or in commentaries on *hadîth*, distributed in the form of audio cassettes or on internet websites, must in principle apply to all believers, whatever school of Muslim law they belong to, whatever their nationality, age or status. As shown earlier, the universalist ambition of Salafism is to be considered one of its central doctrinal features. As such, it places the various Salafi trends in a position of acquaintance with transnational, or translocal, dynamics.

A Variety of Media and Flows

The transnational character of Salafism in Yemen manifests itself in a number of ways and through a wide variety of flows. In terms of its vocation as much as its ambition, this political and religious movement is in fact in every way an actor and an object of the international scene, as regards its dynamics and its structures.

The origin of the religious sources and references used by Yemeni Salafis is in itself a strong indicator of insertion in transnational space. In the Salafi

---

[3] Luis Guarnizo, 'The Emergence of a Transnational Social Formation and the Mirage of Return Migration among Dominican Transmigrants', *Identities*, vol. 4, no. 2, pp. 281–322.

bookstores in Sana'a, Ma'bar, Aden, Tarîm and Ta'iz, the thousands of audio cassettes on sale come from different countries—some from Yemen and Saudi Arabia, others from Egypt, Syria or the United Arab Emirates. Interestingly, the cassettes from each country appear to be associated with specific themes, as if each country had a specialty, or was linked to a specific tendency. The strong presence of the *Surûrî* wing in Kuwait and the interaction with the Muslim Brotherhood in Egypt, for example, seems to explain the fact that the cassettes released by the shaykhs of these countries feature sermons with a strong political connotation. Conversely, conferences on *'ibâda* or recitations of the suras of the Qur'an are often recorded in Saudi Arabia. It is then remarkable that there is no Yemeni preacher renown for reciting the Qur'an (*tajwîd*).

Most often, cassettes of sermons and conferences are copied on demand by the bookshop sellers or as gifts by fellow Salafi 'comrades'. There are no copyrights, and recordings are often of low quality. The sound is muffled, other noises can sometimes be heard and certain tapes of clerics coming from abroad or from distant places are even recorded by holding a telephone up to a microphone. Despite the low quality, these cassettes play a very important role in the diffusion of Salafi doctrine throughout Yemeni territory. The high level of illiteracy (according to the World Bank, 46 per cent in 2010), the low cost of cassettes, the ease of recording and the relative durability of the medium make it an ideal propaganda instrument, effective and simple.[4]

Like the recordings of sung regional poetry studied by Flagg Miller,[5] recorded sermons only rarely are circulated within a pre-established network of outlets. A few 'recording labels', Saudi or Egyptian, do exist and offer higher quality recordings, professionally packaged and embellished with cover art, usually featuring a bucolic landscape, a Qur'an, a parchment or a nib pen (symbols of knowledge). The business of distributing the cassettes is mostly decentralised. Personal relationships linking the staff of various bookstores, the purchase of a cassette by a student or by the imam of a mosque determine much of what is available in the shops. The chain stores Tasjilât al-îmân, densely connected to the movement associated with 'Abd al-Majîd al-Zindânî and the Îmân University he founded are undoubtedly an exception and the most important in Yemen, with branches in all the main cities of the country. The offerings how-

---

[4] For an in-depth analysis of the role played by cassette sermons in Islamist mobilisations, particularly in Egypt: Charles Hirschkind, *The Ethical Soundscape. Cassette Sermons and Islamic Counterpublics*, op. cit.

[5] Flagg Miller, *The Moral Resonance of Arab Media. Audiocassette Poetry and Culture in Yemen*, Cambridge: Harvard Centre for Middle Eastern Studies, 2007.

ever are not identical from one store to another, and the laxity and decentralised character of the ideological control that is practised appear as some even offer cassettes of conferences by Muqbil al-Wâdi'î, who was known for criticising al-Zindânî and the Muslim Brotherhood.[6] The circulation of books is certainly more structured and better organised than that of audio recordings. There are in fact a number of Yemeni Salafi publishing houses, the most important ones being Dâr al-Âthâr and Maktabat al-Athariyya, that have the responsibility for publishing the texts of Muqbil al-Wâdi'î and distributing a number of foreign publications, some written by 'ulamâ' who are close to the Saudi government, especially Sâlih Bin Fawzân al-Fawzân and 'Abd Allâh Bin 'Abd al-Rahmân Bin Jibrîn. These works are published by Dâr al-Imâm Ahmad in Cairo or by other publishing houses based in Riyadh. A bookstore, al-Imâm al-Albânî in Sana'a, specialises in the sale of Salafi works that have been printed in Egypt. Although photocopying such works is theoretically forbidden by Salafi doctrine (it may be considered by some a case of theft), foreign works, pamphlets and tracts are frequently copied and distributed in small bookstores with new adapted covers showing the address and name of the local bookshop. Plaques and small posters are widely distributed and sold at low prices, and constitute a form of *vade mecum* on specific themes (rejection of politics, the *takfîr*, religious psalmodies, and so on). These are often published by Saudi Islamic organisations (especially Dâr al-Watan which distributes the work of a number of 'ulamâ' representing the religious 'establishment') or by organisations in the United Arab Emirates (such as Maktabat al-Furqân, based in the emirate of 'Ajmân). In addition, various local Yemeni magazines (such as *al-Fiqh fî al-dîn*, published by followers of Abû al-Hasan al-Ma'ribî, or *Nida' al-salafiyya*, published by the students' association of the Sharqayn mosque in Sana'a) or transnational publications (*al-Salafiyya* from Riyadh or *al-Bayân* from London and *al-Sunna* published in Birmingham—the latter two being associated to the *Surûrî* wing) play a

---

[6] Muqbil al-Wâdi'î criticised 'Abd al-Majîd al-Zindânî several times: he complained about the poor quality of instruction offered at the Îmân University directed by him, and also about al-Zindânî's call for the foundation of a political and religious assembly that would involve the women of the Islâh party. Al-Wâdi'î also vehemently rejected the initiative of al-Zindânî, calling for Yemenis to invest in a fishing business he was directing. This project, begun during the 1990s in co-operation with other political figures and merchants from the Hadramawt region, turned into a fiasco, and many small investors lost their money. See especially Muqbil al-Wâdi'î, sound recording, *Tanâqudhât al-Zindânî* [The contradictions of al-Zindânî].

part in the diffusion of Salafi doctrine and its integration into a transnational religious field that shares references and practices.

In this regard, and despite being proscribed by Salafi orthodoxy, television is playing an increasingly important role. The new generation of activists, in connection with al-Hikma and Abû al-Hasan al-Ma'ribî, is less reticent in using this medium, although it was criticised by Muqbil al-Wâdi'î even for receiving news and watching sports broadcasts. In this context, privately funded channels from Saudi Arabia or Kuwait (particularly *Iqra* and *al-Majd*) provide satellite broadcasts every day of sermons, or talk shows featuring important religious figures more or less approved by the Gulf monarchies, especially two Saudi former opponents, Salmân al-'Awda and 'Â'idh al-Qarnî.

Much research has focused on the Salafi phenomenon in relation to the virtual space of the internet. Different publications have highlighted the dynamism of ideological debates taking place on the web, and also the role of the internet in the development of Salafi networks and on the internal competition taking place.[7] In the specific Yemeni context, one should probably not overrate the importance of such a media. Although penetration of new technologies is obviously increasing at a fast rate, many in Yemen still do not have access to the web. This being said, the internet has undoubtedly become an active proponent of the transnationalisation of Yemeni Salafism since the mid-2000s. Some foreign websites (the most popular being sahab.net, based in Qatar, where the discussion forums are particularly active) have played a large part in the denunciation of the 'errors' of Abû al-Hasan al-Ma'ribî and as such have favoured a kind of standardisation of the transnational Salafi movement around a set of debates and issues. By way of the internet, internal Yemeni debates, especially those concerning the '*fitna*' of Abû al-Hasan al-Ma'ribî and that of 'Abd al-Rahmân al-'Adanî, have made noticeable waves in other countries.[8] Through Rabî' al-Madkhalî, the rhetoric of condemnation applied to

---

[7] See for example Philip Hallden, 'Salafi in Virtual and Physical Reality', *ISIM Newsletter*, no. 13, 2003, p. 38; Gary Bunt, 'Defining Islamic Interconnectivity' in Miriam Cooke and Bruce Lawrence (eds.), *Muslim Networks from Hajj to Hip Hop*, op. cit., pp. 235–251; Dominique Thomas, 'Le rôle d'internet dans la diffusion de la doctrine salafie' in Bernard Rougier (ed.), *Qu'est ce que le salafisme?*, op. cit., pp. 87–102 and Dominique Thomas, 'Les salafistes et la communication: quand les 'vertueux anciens' s'emparent du net' in Yves Gonzale-Quijano and Tourya Guaaybess (eds.), *Les Arabes parlent aux Arabes. La révolution de l'information dans le monde arabe*, Arles: Actes Sud, 2009, pp. 224–239.

[8] See for example the website 'Salafis du sud' from Montpellier in southern France,

Abû al-Hasan was relayed to all the forums, especially European ones, and thus the warning against the latter's 'dangerous innovations' was passed on beyond the Yemeni space.

As a way of bypassing the limits of the virtual space in Yemen, some columns and pamphlets reacting to national and international news, posted on the websites by their authors are at times later printed out and sold in Yemeni bookstores in order to broadcast them more efficiently. Such short texts, written in a pointed style that is often libellous, frequently stigmatise other religious groups, dissident Salafi or otherwise, while attempting to maintain a position of orthodoxy. In April 2005, for example, in an anonymous text entitled *Unzar mâdhâ qâl al-Qaradhâwî al-khabîth 'an al-bâbâ al-hâlik* [Look what the dirty al-Qaradhâwî has said about the dark Pope], Yûsuf al-Qaradhâwî, an important figure deemed close to the Muslim Brotherhood in Egypt, living in Qatar, was vehemently attacked for having allegedly said positive things about Pope John Paul II, then recently deceased. Part of a wider naming and blaming strategy, this text had earlier been posted on sahab.net by a foreign Salafi cleric and was sold in the spring of 2005 by the Muhammad Bin 'Abd al-Wahhâb Salafi bookstore in Tarîm in the eastern Yemeni province of Hadramawt.

Since the mid-2000s, all the main figures of the Yemeni Salafi movement, even deceased ones like al-Wâdi'î, have their own websites.[9] These usually allow visitors to access some of their publications online, including some older conferences and books, and also to dispatch elements on their biography. Despite this involvement in the virtual world, as mentioned earlier, the importance of the internet in the Yemeni context is bound to be limited. The centre of Muhammad al-Imâm in Ma'bar, for example, had in 2006 no operating workstations for its students, and the town had none available for public access. On top of all that, network access is very slow, and there are intermittent electric power outages, so it is not always easy (if not impossible!) to listen to the sound recordings posted on these sites, and the effect of this medium on local devotees has thus for long been limited. The bad quality of existing equipment goes along with a certain doubt about the legitimacy of the internet as such. It is significant that sahab.net devoted a page to the theological problems raised by

---

particularly the page headed 'La tendance madkhaliste: est-ce que ça existe?' http://salafis-du-sud.over-blog.com/article-3157064.html (accessed on 3 July, 2006).

9 See especially the website of Yahyâ al-Hajûrî: www.sh-yahia.net; for Muqbil al-Wâdi'î: www.muqbel.net; www.olamayemen.com and for al-Hikma association: www.al-hikma-ye.com; and al-Ihsân: www.al-ehsan.org (accessed on 3 August, 2010).

computers and the internet, trying to justify their use. Internet activity undoubtedly counts for more in the external diffusion of Yemeni Salafi communications than in the reception of local preaching.

The participation of Salafism in a transnational space implies a capacity to cross borders, to send and receive across and outside of the controlled space of inter-state interactions. In a more concrete manner than through the World Wide Web, the expansion of Yemeni Salafism takes place by means of flows of people. Since the establishment of Dâr al-Hadîth in the early 1980s and more so since the mid-1990s, significant numbers of foreign students have been travelling to Yemen to stay for more or less long periods of time in Salafi teaching institutes. There are no firm statistics, and it is difficult to establish the number of foreign students in the institutes, but consular estimates consider for example that in the mid-2000s decade, over 100 individuals bearing French nationality were staying in Dammâj simultaneously. They stayed there just for the summer or for years, some of them even planning to settle permanently in Yemen, trying to later open up businesses. The presence of students from the Horn of Africa, Indonesia, America, West Africa and Western Europe has evidently turned Yemen into a noteworthy global centre for Salafism, able to compete with other such centres in Saudi Arabia or Egypt.[10] Some of these students in Yemen are even sent by their families or tutors into centres at a very young age. Such was the case of a Somali boy at al-Khayr mosque in Sana'a, who was fifteen years old when interviewed, and claimed to have arrived four years earlier.[11]

Such positioning of Yemeni Salafism within the wider transnational realm finds other interesting illustrations. Websites based in Europe or in North America list the direct telephone numbers for various Yemeni clerics, along with Saudi ones.[12] These phone numbers are used by activists abroad to ask specific questions and get religious advice from the renowned clerics. On one occasion for instance, and in my presence, in November 2004, Muhammad al-Imâm received a call from one of his sympathisers based in France who was asking what was to be done for a child in his family who had been killed in a car accident.

Another sign of the integration of Yemeni Salafism in the transnational space is that many of the sound recordings made by Muqbil al-Wâdi'î and other

[10] On French Salafis in Egypt, see Romain Caillet, 'Trajectoires de salafis français en Egypte' in Bernard Rougier, *Qu'est ce que le salafisme?*, op. cit., pp. 257–271.

[11] Interview, Sana'a, July 2005.

[12] See for example the list, 'Numéros de téléphone des savants de l'Islam' http://alhaaq. over-blog.net/categorie-175818.html (accessed on 3 July, 2006).

Salafi figures, sold in Yemeni bookstores, contain references to foreign countries: one recorded discourse is entitled *As'ilat shabâb Indûnîsyâ* ['Questions from Indonesian youth']. Others are: *As'ilat ba'dh al-mughtaribîn fî Amrikâ* ['Questions from some expatriates in America']; *Jawâhir al-sunniya fî al-as'ila al-faransiyya* ['Sunni jewels in the French questions']; and finally *As'ilat al-salafiyîn al-brîtâniyîn* ['Questions from British Salafis']. These reach across borders and subsequently constitute an important source of legitimisation for Salafism in internal terms, to the extent that it offers the Salafi elite the prestige of recognition from outside Yemen.

As a result, on several occasions, Muqbil al-Wâdi'î defended the foreign students staying in Dâr al-Hadîth (as they were episodically subject to pressure coming not only from the Yemeni administration but also from the embassies of their home countries). In a variety of publications, he emphasised their role in the diffusion of his doctrine. Making reference to his own traumatic experience in Saudi Arabia from where he was expelled, he said he would prefer that someone bulldoze his house, than to exclude a single foreigner, or see him go to prison. 'Foreign students are an honour for Yemen', he claimed.[13]

The question of the transnational expansion of Salafism and of the specific networks allowing foreigners to come to Yemen is largely taboo and a matter of speculation, as much from the point of view of governments and wider publics both inside and outside of Yemen as for Salafis themselves. The influence of former students from Dâr al-Hadîth in Somalia or Indonesia remains unknown, and is likely to be underestimated. It is quite probable that these former students, who number in the hundreds, have indeed played a part in the conflicts that have occurred in their home countries, sometimes taking religious dimensions.

The international mobility of shaykhs and other entrepreneurs in the Salafi field, which cannot be considered as a novelty, is yet another tangible mark of their participation in transnational space.[14] The academic trajectory of Muqbil al-Wâdi'î is itself an illustration of this tradition: from Mecca, he went to Riyadh, and thence to Medina and probably Cairo, spending several decades of his life outside Yemen. He himself often stressed how his time in Saudi Arabia had literally been a life-changing experience. Similarly, the arrival of

---

[13] Muqbil al-Wâdi'î, sound recording, *Hâdhihi al-surûriyya faihdharuhâ!* [This is the *Surûriyya* so be careful!].

[14] Dale Eickelman and James Piscatori (eds.), *Muslim Travellers. Pilgrimage, Migration, and the Religious Imagination*, Berkeley: University of California Press, 1990.

Abû al-Hasan al-Misrî (later al-Ma'ribî) in Yemen during the 1980s, where he fled to escape repression in his native Egypt, illustrates this mobility within the Muslim world. Outside the Salafi field, repression in socialist South Yemen motivated the flight of many religious figures who would take refuge in North Yemen, and then eventually pass on to Saudi Arabia. Such was the case for a Salafi associated with al-Hikma, Ahmad Hasan al-Mu'allim, and for Sufi figure Abû Bakr al-Mashhûr, who recounted in a work published in 2002 the story of his departure from Aden and his eventual arrival in Jeddah during the 1970s.[15]

Peripheral Yemen

Still, over and above the experience in Saudi Arabia of al-Wâdi'î, and despite the tendency of religious practices in Yemen to spread beyond that country via the internet or through the presence of foreign students, one is obliged to admit that the Salafi elite in Yemen is somewhat isolated, or at any rate not very mobile. Set beside manifestly transnational figures such as Muhammad al-Albânî, Muhammad Surûr, 'Abd al-Rahmân 'Abd al-Khâliq or even the Yemeni Sufis al-Habîb 'Alî al-Jifrî[16] and al-Habîb 'Umar Bin Hafîz,[17] Yemeni Salafi

[15] Abû Bakr al-'Adanî al-Mashhûr, *al-Khurûj min al-dâ'ira al-hamrâ* [Leaving the red circle], Aden: Ribât al-Tarbiyya al-Islâmiyya, 2002.

[16] Born in Jeddah in 1971, al-Habîb 'Alî al-Jifrî is the son of 'Abd al-Rahmân al-Jifrî, founder of the Râbita ibnâ' al-Yaman (League of the sons of Yemen), a secessionist figure in 1994 who has lived in Saudi Arabia as a refugee (he was sentenced to death in 1997, granted amnesty in May 2004 and returned to his native country in September 2006). He is a member of a sayyid family, claiming descent from the Prophet. Al-Habîb 'Alî al-Jifrî is an internationally renowned figure in connection with Sufism ('Alawiyya brotherhood) and participates in an important transnational network that connects Hadramawt, Saudi Arabia, the United Arab Emirates, Syria, Sudan, Indonesia and the United Kingdom. He co-heads the Dâr al-Mustafâ centre in Tarîm that was established in 1996, and which continues to host many foreign students. He presents a weekly television show (*al-Mizân*: the Scale) on Iqra', an Islamic station funded by Saudi money. See his website: http://www.alhabibali.org/ (accessed on 4 August, 2010).

[17] Al-Habîb 'Umar Bin Hafîz was born in 1963. Like al-Habîb 'Alî al-Jifrî, with whom he founded and co-directs the Dâr al-Mustafâ centre, he is also a member of a notable family descended from the Prophet. Born near Tarîm in the former South Yemen, his father was assassinated in 1972, undoubtedly by socialist militants. He took refuge at that time at al-Baydhâ' in North Yemen where he studied in a Sufi centre directed by Muhammad al-Hidâr (for a biography of this important religious figure, see *al-Ayyâm*, 2 June, 2005), and later went to Saudi Arabia before returning

entrepreneurs (apart from Muqbil al-Wâdi'î himself) hardly compare. Furthermore, the new generation of Salafi *'ulamâ'* from the Muqbilian branch never claim explicitly to have studied outside Yemen. Few have ever left, and their unfamiliarity with the outside world is sometimes apparent.[18] In 1999 Abû al-Hasan al-Ma'ribî and Muhammad al-Wisâbî (who runs a Salafi centre in al-Hudayda) were invited to the United States to give conferences, but their visa applications were refused. Muqbil al-Wâdi'î's strained relations with the Saudi government, coupled with apparent poor relations vis-à-vis the Egyptian government, up to his death in 2001, didn't do much to facilitate the mobility of his students and followers.

Yemen from this angle looks like a fallback position, a refuge, kept apart from Western influences and state repression, a country that thinks of itself as at least partially autonomous. For partisans of the Salafi movement, this position is confirmed and legitimised by the hadith that says: 'If things fall into disorder, you still have Yemen' (*Idhâ hâjat al-fitan fa 'alaykum bi-al-Yaman*).[19] This particular image is a valuable asset in terms of the international effect of the Muqbilian Salafi movement, which attracts a certain number of foreigners who admire the 'authenticity' of Yemen. In this situation Yemeni Salafis do express misgivings concerning foreigners. Al-Wâdi'î was asked in the late 1990s about the advisability, for his students, of continuing to study, after Dâr al-Hadîth, at the Islamic University of Medina (arguably the cradle of the quietist transnational Salafi movement where Rabî' al-Madkhalî had directed the faculty of *hadîth* up until the turn of the century, and where he himself had spent time). His answer went as follows:

My advice is to stay in Yemen where there are experienced teachers [...]. But those who claim that I forbid people to go study at the Islamic University are liars. I do not forbid

---

to stay in Yemen after unification. See his website: http://www.alhabibomar.com/ (accessed on 4 August, 2010).

[18] Yahyâ al-Hajûrî published in 2005 a small volume entitled *Mushâhadâtî fî Britânyâ* [My experience of Great Britain] in which he recounted the details of a trip he took to England in 1998. The title of the publication evidently recalled the title of Muqbil al-Wâdi'î's 'testimony' concerning his return to Saudi Arabia (*Mushâhadâtî fî al-Mamlaka al-'Arabiyya al-Su'ûdiyya* [My experience of the Kingdom of Saudi Arabia], see below) but its cover, imagined to be a London street scene, in fact reproduced a drawing of the Arc de Triomphe in Paris!

[19] Cited by Muqbil al-Wâdi'î, sound recording, *al-Zindânî wa majlis al-shaykhât bil-Yaman* [al-Zindânî and the Women's Assembly of Yemen].

it. [...] I can give a written recommendation to someone who is to take charge of a mosque, but I don't do it for people who want to go to the Islamic University.[20]

The Afghan jihad during the 1980s, often made a symbol of the transnationalisation of the Islamist field, did not give rise to any large mobilisation on the part of Yemeni Salafis, who stand in contrast to the Muslim Brotherhood in this respect. This episode illustrated some of the limits of the inclusion of Yemeni Salafis in transnational dynamics. During that period, in Saudi Arabia as elsewhere, Salafis formed socialisation circles and networks that were clearly distinct from those involving the jihadis (*mujâhidîn*) who went to Afghanistan to fight.[21] For Muqbil al-Wâdi'î and his partisans participation in this specific armed conflict proved improper since it implied getting involved in politics, a process they obviously criticised. They also considered that the presence of a socialist regime in the South essentially prevented the Yemeni Salafis from legitimately carrying on a fight against the far-off Soviet enemy. In his book *al-Suyûf al-bâtira li-ilhâd al-shuyû'iyya al-kâfira* [The sharp swords for the unholy communist heresy], published in the mid-1980s, Muqbil al-Wâdi'î did admit that 'the Islamic jihad in Afghanistan is not only the jihad of Afghanis, but also for all Muslims',[22] but he nonetheless still preferred to attack the socialists within the Yemeni context. In this book, he then focused on the problems he considered most important, that of unification of the two Yemens and of the fight against socialist leaders. Transnational politics then only came as second to local ones.

Transnationalisation or 'Saudisation'?

Despite the above mentioned nuances and some limits highlighted previously, the transnationalisation of Salafism since its emergence in the contemporary Yemeni environment is a tangible reality. Flows of people, books and ideas obviously shape the Yemeni quietist movement and place it within a wider and more global trend. The origin as well as the destination of these flows, however, is not to be considered random. It is clear that many of these directly

---

[20] Muqbil al-Wâdi'î, sound recording, *As'ila 'an hayât al-shaykh Muqbil al-Wâdi'î wa sîratuhu* [Questions about the life of shaykh Muqbil al-Wâdi'î and about his biography].

[21] Stéphane Lacroix, *Les islamistes saoudiens*, op. cit., p. 133.

[22] Muqbil al-Wâdi'î, *al-Suyûf al-bâtira li-ilhâd al-shuyû'iyya al-kâfira* [Sharp swords for the unholy communist heresy], op. cit., pp. 71–72.

connect the Yemeni and Saudi environments. If Salafism in general does appear to have a special affinity for transnational interactions, its Yemeni branch seems to have an even greater affinity for connections (although not necessarily one-sided ones) with the Saudi environment. As such, the transnationalisation process appears to many of the Salafis' competitors within Yemen as a kind of 'Saudisation'.

It is a fact that Saudi Arabia has played and continues to play a fundamental role in the development of the Yemeni Salafi field. The centrality of Saudi actors is made tangible by a number of social practices, and by the importance of sources of funding, both private and public, originating from the Kingdom.

The personal trajectory of Muqbil al-Wâdi'î evidently stands as an example of the structuring effect of the Saudi 'big brother' upon things pertaining to Yemen. Other figures in the Salafi political-religious field have also been affected by the Saudi experience. Such is the case with Muhammad Bin Muhammad al-Mahdî, a major figure in al-Hikma association, and Ahmad Hasan al-Mu'allim. The former, in a long interview with the magazine *al-Muntadâ*, told the story of leaving for Mecca at the age of fifteen, and later pursuing religious studies in the Qasîm region, including his meetings with major Saudi '*ulamâ*' and his eventual return to Yemen in 1977 to work in Ibb in an office of the Ministry for Religious Affairs.[23] Ahmad Hasan al-Mu'allim had a number of things in common with Muqbil al-Wâdi'î. A native of Hadramawt, he studied at the Islamic University of Medina during the 1970s and frequently encountered the founder of the Yemeni Salafi movement, as well as Juhaymân al-'Utaybî.[24] Following his implication in the 1979 Meccan uprising (*wâqi'at al-haram*), he was imprisoned for several years before being allowed to move to Kuwait during the 1980s. Kuwait was the locale for a number of debates and the emergence of the political Salafi current ideologically influenced by the Muslim Brotherhood and associated with what was to be labelled the Surûrî Salafi branch.[25] From that point he apparently supported several movements

[23] Interview with Muhammad Bin Muhammad al-Mahdî, *al-Muntadâ*, no. 87–88, October 2004.

[24] Nâsr al-Huzaymî, 'Khatî'a Juhaymân' [Juhayman's sin], *al-Majalla*, 21 November 2009.

[25] Concerning the Islamist field in Kuwait, see Sâmî Nâsir al-Khalidî, *al-Ahzâb al-is-lâmiyya fî al-Kuwayt:al-shî'a, al-ikhwân, al-salaf* [Islamic parties in Kuwait: Shi'ites, the Muslim Brotherhood, Salafis], Kuwait: Dâr al-Niba, 1999; Carine Lahoud, 'Koweït: Salafismes et Rapport au Pouvoir' in Bernard Rougier, *Qu'est ce que le salafisme?*, op. cit., pp. 123–135.

while getting acquainted with the Kuwaiti Organisation for the Renewal of the Islamic Tradition (Jam'iyyat ihya' al-turâth al-islâmî) and took an interest in the criticism of Sufi religious practices in Yemen, particularly the cult of saints in Hadramawt. After unification he returned to Yemen, to his home region, and took over a branch of the dissident Salafi organisation, al-Hikma. During the 2000s, he has been instrumental in a rapprochement between activist Salafism and the currents that came out of the *Sahwa islâmiyya* in Saudi Arabia. He for instance writes for *al-Islam al-yawm* [Islam today] the website of the famous intellectual and Saudi activist Salmân al-'Awda.[26]

The idea of a kind of Saudisation through Salafism is not only based on migratory trajectories. In visual terms the dominant clothing choice among Salafis appears to copy the traditional style from Najd (white *thawb* and red-checked *shmagh* on top of the head), which became dominant in Saudi territory along with the expansion of the Âl Su'ûd monarchy at the beginning of the twentieth century.[27] For women, the spread during the 1980s into North Yemen, and then into the South after unification, of the *'abaya* or the *baltû* (long black tunic) and the *niqâb* (black veil over the face), and the fact that they ceased to wear the more colourful (and traditional) *sitâra* has often been perceived in Yemeni public discourse as the result of a process of 'Saudisation', in which emigrating workers were once and again depicted as the main agents.

The prevalence of Saudi material sold in bookstores and by Islamic audio cassette vendors is quite indisputable. The publications coming from the Kingdom are better quality, binding and printing: subsidies are awarded by Saudi-funded organisations like Dâr al-Watan or the Nadwa al-'Âlamiyya lil-Shabâb al-Islâmî (World Assembly of Muslim Youth) for the publication of religious works (editions of the Qur'an, collections of *hadîth* or a rather odd 'Encyclopedia of religion'[28] that provides a critical analysis of world belief systems such as 'Freudianism' and 'capitalism'). All this represents a clear comparative advantage for the Saudi products, which feature better printing and a larger selection, and are often much cheaper.

[26] See for example: http://www.islamtoday.net/islamion/01.html (accessed on 12 November 2006).

[27] For a 'regionalistic' analysis of Saudi expansion in the Hejaz, see: Mai Yamani, *Cradle of Islam: The Hijaz and the Quest for an Arabian Identity*, London: I.B. Tauris, 2004.

[28] *al-Mawsû'a al-muyasara fî al-adyân wa al-madhâhib al-mu'âsira* [Abridged encyclopaedia of religions and contemporary sects], Riyadh: al-Nadwa al-'âlamiyya lil-shabâb al-islâmî, 1999.

While the conclusions of my research reject the appositeness of the term 'Wahhabism' and of the idea of a mere 'Saudisation', it would be an error to deny the importance of Saudi Arabia in this context, and, for that matter, of the current of thought established by Muhammad Bin 'Abd al-Wahhâb in contemporary Salafi doctrine as it has developed in Yemen. The teaching offered at Dâr al-Hadîth, organised in terms of the study of particular religious texts, shows its Saudi origin (or even to be more precise, its *najdî* origin, since it is associated with the central region of the Arabian Peninsula) clearly, and this relationship is more important than any relationship with any other country, be it Egypt, Syria, Iraq or elsewhere. The current programme at the centre examines the works of Muhammad Bin 'Abd al-Wahhâb, labelled as 'al-Najdî' in studying the *tawhîd* (the doctrine of the oneness of God), Muhammad al-'Uthaymîn (deceased member of the Saudi Committee of Senior '*ulamâ*') and 'Abd al-Rahmân Bin Hasan Âl al-Shaykh (grandson of Muhammad Bin 'Abd al-Wahhâb).

The funding of the teaching centres and for the Salafi movement is without doubt a key element in any attempt to establish the nature of the 'Saudisation' of Yemeni Salafism. It is a recognised fact that various Saudi organisations, most of which are closely linked to the state itself, have played and continue to play an important role in the development of Salafism in Yemen (and also should be mentioned the Kuwaiti-based Organisation for the Renewal of Islamic Tradition). Since the 1970s, although limited in numbers, scholarships granted by the Embassy of Saudi Arabia or by quasi-governmental organisations have allowed Yemeni students to attend institutions of higher learning such as the Islamic University of the Imâm Muhammad Bin Su'ûd in Riyadh (founded in 1953), the Islamic University of Medina (founded in 1961) or the Umm al-Qurâ University in Mecca (founded in 1980). These scholarships (which are not all offered for study at religious schools) accord with the existing structure of the Yemeni political-religious field, at least partially centred around religious figures trained in Saudi Arabia, whether these stand closer to the Muslim Brotherhood or are associated with a quietist Salafism.

Wealthy Saudi '*ulamâ*', especially the late 'Abd al-'Azîz Bin Bâz, as well as the important network of Saudi benevolent associations consistently gave money to fund activities at Salafi centres in Yemen. Mansûr al-Nuqaydân, a former Saudi opposition Islamist figure, explained that Muqbil al-Wâdi'î and Dâr al-Hadîth received from the Saudi government 'every two months, aid in the amount of 15,000 riyals [about $6000] through an intermediary of shaykh 'Abd al-'Azîz Bin Bâz'. This assistance only ceased when in the late 1980s two of the disciples of al-Wâdi'î visited Bin Bâz and raised the question of the legitimacy of the Saudi government in a public gathering.[29] Despite these tensions between both Salafi figures, in the hagiography he published after the death of 'Abd al-'Azîz Bin Bâz in 1999, al-Wâdi'î recalled how helpful he had been with Yemenis: getting them visas to study in Saudi Arabia, and thus 'to go wherever they wanted to go'.[30] In fact, the personal connections between the two scholars played an important role in the continuation of transnational relations, despite diplomatic tensions and even despite criticisms aimed at the Saudi government by Yemeni Salafis. In addition the association Mu'assasat al-haramayn al-khayriyya (Benevolent Foundation of the Two Holy Places), founded in 1988 (or in 1992, sources disagree), under the direct control of the Saudi government, contributed money in the early 1990s for the use of Dâr al-Hadîth in Dammâj. Accused by American authorities of having played a role in the financing of various violent organisations, especially al-Qaeda, this foundation's assets were frozen by the United States Treasury in 2002 (the case never came to trial following a decision in Federal court in September 2005) and the foundation itself was dissolved in June 2004. Muqbil al-Wâdi'î spoke of the role of this organisation on several recordings. The institutional source of this funding caused a debate over the legitimacy of accepting money from a foreign association, in light of the fact that Salafis rejected the creation of associations. Al-Wâdi'î disavowed al-Haramayn in the mid-1990s, when it began to redirect its money towards the dissident associations, al-Hikma and al-Ihsân, considered closer in terms of doctrine. In light of this, al-Wâdi'î accused al-Haramayn and one of its representatives in Yemen (Yahyâ Jughmân) of being implicated in financial corruption and of acting on behalf of Salafi dissidents, even while he was saying that they represented no one but themselves, and had only a handful of followers.[31]

These same Yemeni Salafi associations of the *harakî* or activist generation received assistance from activists from Saudi Arabia or other Gulf States, espe-

[29] Mansûr al-Nuqaydân, 'Géographie des Islamistes en Arabie Saoudite et Affaire du Takfîr. Commenté par Alain Gresh', *Maghreb Machrek*, no. 179, 2004, pp. 117–131. Translation and edition of an article that originally appeared in Arabic in February 2003, posted on a website.

[30] Muqbil al-Wâdi'î, *al-Dîbâj fî marâthât shaykh al-islâm samâhat al-shaykh 'Abd al-'Azîz Bin Bâz* [The silk in the funeral oration of the *shaykh al-islâm*, his excellency shaykh 'Abd al-'Azîz Bin Bâz], op. cit.

[31] Muqbil al-Wâdi'î, sound recording, *As'ilat al-shabâb al-salafî fî hay al-Dâ'irî* [Questions from Salafi youth from the Dâ'irî quarter].

cially Qatar. A young Saudi intellectual, from a family that traced its roots back to Hadramawt, explained that he participated three times in the late 1990s in summer 'tours' of several Yemeni cities in co-operation with the Ihsân association (including Ibb, Sana'a, Bayt al-Faqîh and Aden). He spoke about his role, and about funding sources:

These visits to centres in Yemen allowed us to give conferences but also to monitor their curriculum to the desire of the Saudis who were providing funding in addition to the public funding made available.[32]

The range of these funding sources was loudly criticised by Muqbil al-Wâdi'î, who accused al-Hikma and other dissident associations of preaching a 'da'wa of beggars'. No doubt conscious of the negative effects of their own association with Saudi Arabia and its wealth, Muqbil al-Wâdi'î and his students were always careful to speak of the 'humbleness' of their preaching and of life inside Dâr al-Hadîth. The great Salafi figure said, 'Our da'wa [...] is humble in financial terms, we offer people no more than a few dates and some water'.[33] Questioned by a journalist about the funding sources for Dâr al-Hadîth, al-Wâdi'î denied receiving any government support:

We receive money from generous people in Yemen, from the Land of Two Holy Places, from America, Great Britain and France. Each person pays according to his zakâ, this one 100,000 Yemeni riyals, that one 300,000 or a million riyals. The most important thing is that no government has ever participated. We spread knowledge thanks to money from good people (ahl al-khayr) some of whom are rich and some of whom are poor.[34]

This statement from the main figure in Yemeni Salafism cannot be simply taken for granted. In fact, indirectly or not, governments, particularly the government of Saudi Arabia, did provide some funding for Salafi centres in Yemen, and this is likely to continue today. Still, without forgetting the importance of sources of income in understanding the relationship this book focuses on, this importance should not be overestimated, nor is it central to our evaluation of the phenomenon of Salafism. Money is not everything. The Salafi centres are evidently run on a low budget. Sometimes their facilities are quite dilapidated— at any rate, they have not required much in the way of funding up to now. Their

---

[32] Interview, Jeddah, March 2006.
[33] Muqbil al-Wâdi'î, sound recording, Jawâhir al-sunniya fî al-as'ila al-faransiyya [Sunni jewels in the French questions].
[34] Muqbil al-Wâdi'î, sound recording Liqâ' sahîfat al-bayân al-imâratiyya [Interview with the Emirati paper al-Bayân].

propaganda techniques are limited, and evidently do not concentrate on creating a clientele of donors. In addition, providing funding does not always provide an unambiguous indication as regards the allegiances of the actors involved. As it happens, benefiting from a particular source of funding does not automatically exclude other allegiances (national, regional or political) or even a certain degree of hypocrisy. Non-state actors have a way of linking and mixing various resources and identity-references. Stating that money implies manipulation and control should therefore be reassessed. Those that appear to be the manipulators from the outside can in the end become the manipulated ones as sponsors have in effect little control over the outcomes.

Whether the funding for the *da'wa* comes through the *hawâla*,[35] the *zakâ*, the *awqâf* or from more exotic sources, obscure and even perhaps criminal, it has been the object of many fantasies and conspiracy theories. This question is actually at the centre of rather crudely mechanical narratives concerning the exportation of Salafism to Yemen. In actual fact, Saudi financing appears to come from a wide range of actors, some connected with institutions others close to the Saudi opposition.[36] Through the system of Islamic taxes, the *zakâ* and the *sadaqa*, Saudi philanthropists, some born in Yemen, send money to centres or pay to have a worship centre built in their home village. Once the mosque is built, it usually becomes affiliated to the system of *awqâf*, which allows it to receive a subsidy from the Yemeni government that is used for at least partial compensation for an imam. In this framework any 'Saudisation'

[35] The *hawâla* is a traditional system of money transfer used in a wide range of Muslim societies since the Middle Ages. It rests on the trust established between money-brokers in different cities but also different countries. Due to its largely informal nature, money transfers escape state regulation (and taxation). As such, in the post 9/11 context, the *hawâla* has been accused of being a preferred means of financing terrorist activities, triggering a kind of paranoia. See Nikos Passas, 'Fighting Terror with Error: the Counter-productive Regulation of Informal Value Transfers', *Crime, Law and Social Change*, vol. 45, no. 4–5, 2007, pp. 315–366. In Yemen, such a system is used by many expatriate workers to send their remittances back home and has enabled the emergence of large transnational money transfer agencies, including Bin 'Afîf in Hadramawt or al-Kuraymî all over the country. However, for a long time these companies and the *hawâla* system in general only played marginal roles as most money transfers occurred directly and physically when friends, relatives or colleagues of the expatriates came back to their home village for holidays.

[36] See Thomas Hegghammer and Stéphane Lacroix, 'Rejectionist Islamism in Saudi Arabia: The Story of Juhayman al-'Utaybi Revisited', op. cit. These authors state that during the 1970s, Muqbil al-Wâdi'î and the Saudi group Bayt al-Ikhwân led by Juhaymân al-'Utaybî were given money by a Saudi of Hadrami origin, Yûsuf Bâ Junayd.

is only relative: the state and local institutions and communities retain some right to oversee the new establishments.

Just after the revolution of 26 September 1962, as the republican system was consolidating itself, a lack of qualified teachers from Yemen had motivated a search for foreign teachers, especially Egyptians, Sudanese, Syrians and sometimes Saudis. These teachers were given the nickname of *azhârî* by the Yemenis, a reference to the famous Islamic university in Cairo where some of them had been trained. A more direct example of intervention by the Saudi government in the Yemeni Islamist field, was the Scientific Institutes (*Ma'âhid 'Ilmiyya*) in which many of the foreign teachers would later be employed. These teaching institutions, which were not *per se* associated with the Salafi realm, as they were ontrolled by Muslim Brothers, yet they were for more than twenty years a concrete expression of Saudi intervention in the Yemeni political landscape. In the eyes of their adversaries they were the very image of 'Saudisation' in this context, even of the 'Wahhabisation' of which Salafism is the alleged expression. This para-public educational network was first founded in North Yemen the mid-1970s in order to counter an ideological offensive from the socialist party of South Yemen in border regions. It was financed in the Saudi state budget in the institutional framework of the prior agreement on mutual recognition concluded in 1970 just after the North-Yemeni civil war. This agreement provided for the payment of large subsidies to the Northern government which then distributed the money to various organisations for development or education. The budget for the Scientific Institutes was at first handled through the Ministry of finance of the Yemen Arab Republic, and later through the unified government of Yemen. It was managed in an independent manner by a Directorate of Scientific Institutes, which was led by members of the Muslim Brotherhood, in particular Yahyâ al-Fusayl (who would later become the secretary-general of al-Islâh). More than in public schools, the curriculum of this significant educational network was based on religion. To the extent that the programmes mostly denied the importance of the theological differences between Zaydism and Shafi'ism, these semi-public institutes were accused by their opponents of propagating a 'Wahhabi' version of Islam. In addition, the agreements allowed the best graduates of the institutes to receive grants from the Saudi government to study in the universities of that country, Islamic or not. The sources of funding of the institutes led some academics to describe them as a 'Trojan horse from Saudi Arabia'.[37]

---

[37] Franck Mermier, 'Les héritages d'une histoire morcelée', in Rémy Leveau, Franck Mermier and Udo Steinbach (eds.), *Le Yémen contemporain*, op. cit., p. 27.

According to official figures from the Yemeni government in 1994–1995 1381 Scientific Institutes gave instruction to 326,464 students, or 13 per cent of the total number of children in school.[38] In 2001, a different source estimated that the parallel education system had as many as 600,000 students.[39] Aware of the problems inherent in having a split educational system, the government of the Y.A.R. tried in 1982 to bring the Scientific Institutes back under the control of the Ministry of Education. The law for this purpose that had been approved by Parliament had still to be implemented, because it threatened the fragile political equilibrium and relations with the Islamists. The question of Scientific Institutes was during the 1990s the main source of disagreement between the ruling GPC and al-Islâh, even when the latter was part of the governing coalition between 1993 and 1997. After twenty years of contentious discussions,[40] and the adoption of several different laws, the nationalisation of the Institutes took effect in 2002, putting an end to what had appeared to be a case of Saudi interference in the affairs of another country.

Throughout their existence, the Scientific Institutes have been accused of propagating a political Islam that is benevolent towards Saudi Arabia, but foreign to Yemeni society. During the very long controversy, the defenders of the Institutes claimed that they were intended to 'unify the (religious) under-standing of society and place the differences between sects and schools of jurisprudence at a distance'.[41] As Yemen's population is traditionally divided in religious terms between Zaydis and Shafi'is, the function of the institutes would have been to reduce inter-religious tensions, something Zaydi revivalists denied. At the beginning of the 1990s, at a high point of the controversy, 'Abd al-Wahhâb al-Anisî, future Deputy Prime Minister and member of al-Islâh, declared in regard to the programme followed:

Islam cannot be absorbed by the sectarianism of schools of jurisprudence [...], their method of instruction can only be unified, because the Scientific Institutes are con-

---

[38] Cited by Franck Mermier, 'L'Islam politique au Yémen ou la 'Tradition' contre les traditions?', *Maghreb Machrek*, no. 155, 1997, p. 11.

[39] Fâris al-Saqqâf, *Ilghâ' al-ma'âhid al-'ilmiyya wa tawhîd al-ta'alîm* [The suppression of the Scientific Institutes and the unification of instruction], Sana'a: Markaz dirâsât al-mustaqbal, 2004, p. 7.

[40] See for example Muhammad al-Anisî, sound recording, *al-Harb 'alâ al-ma'âhid* [The war against the Institutes].

[41] Quoted by Fâris al-Saqqâf, *Ilghâ' al-ma'âhid al-'ilmiyya wa tawhîd al-ta'alîm* [The suppression of the Scientific Institutes and the unification of instruction], op. cit., p. 7.

cerned above all with Islam. [...] The instruction is the same at Sa'da as it is at Mukhâ' and there is no tilting in favour of Zaydism, or in favour of Shafi'ism. This method allows us to get rid of confessional differences.[42]

Quite ironically, al-Anisî also refuted the accusation of Saudi financing, and the idea that this financing had caused the educational system to be subservient to the interests of Saudi Arabia:

The Scientific Institutes are the only institution that has never received outside aid, and such aid is not even accepted. Despite all this, some troublemakers have put forth the idea that this institution is financed by Saudi Arabia, but these accusations are incorrect. The institutes' budget is integrated with the state budget, has been from the beginning, and we receive no external aid. Those who say that the Institutes teach 'Wahhabism', I can assure them that this is not true. Of course, the concepts taught are in conformity with Wahhabism and with other methods, not because the instructors are trying as hard as they can to conform to it, but because it is simply valid on these points.[43]

The engagement of the Saudi government in the Yemeni Islamist field, despite various denials, is a reality that fluctuates but still plays a role in the political and religious structure of various movements. Such involvement is a tangible sign of support for Salafism, but also for other Islamist movements, whether these are closer to the Muslim Brotherhood, to Sufi brotherhoods or even to Zaydi groups in a transnational space. The absence of a clear-cut Salafi specificity in this regard as well as the diversity of the Saudi actors involved weakens still further the argument that claims that Salafism in Yemen is nothing more than a foreign policy instrument in the hands of Saudi leaders.

II. Anti-Saudi Salafis?

As mentioned earlier, the existence of financial connections between Yemeni Salafis and Saudi institutions and activists, direct or indirect, is undeniable. However, as regards to the present case study, such connections do not function as predictors of positions taken in support or opposition by Yemeni Salafis relative to the entity that is supposed to be sponsoring them.

---

[42] Cited by Sâlih Bin Muhammad al-Yâfi'î, *al-Mawâqif al-râhina fî al-Yaman min tatbîq kitâb Allâh wa sunnat rasûlihi* [The current positions in Yemen as concerns the application of the book of God and the Tradition of His Prophet], op. cit., pp. 130–131.

[43] Ibid., pp. 131–132.

The dominant mixed feeling of rejection and admiration, influenced by the experience of migration to Saudi Arabia has been expressed in political terms in an interesting way. The fact that Muqbil al-Wâdi'î protested against aspects of Saudi policy during the time he spent there shows the weakness of the association between the doctrine he founded and the Saudi state. The ambiguity of the relationship between al-Wâdi'î and Saudi Arabia discards in a clear manner the idea that Salafism in Yemen is a political export of the central Saudi power (to the benefit of Saudi national interests, and for domination's sake). Consequently, adherence to Salafism in the Yemeni context cannot be taken as a type of 'Saudisation'. In fact that concept is rendered empty by the diversity of political-religious positions even within Saudi society. How are we supposed to characterise this kind of 'Saudisation'? What, specifically, has been transformed in the process into something more 'Saudi-like'? More to the point, 'Saudisation' by means of Salafism makes little sense as soon as the latter's complexity is taken into consideration. The truth is that during the 1980s and 1990s Salafism was the opposite of a Saudi fifth column in Yemen as it was much more a movement developed in opposition to the Saudi monarchy. As such, Salafism in Yemen stands in a particularly ambivalent relation to Saudi state and society. Such a stance can be explained both by nationalistic motives but is also linked to the personal humiliation Muqbil al-Wâdi'î considered himself to have suffered during his migratory experience.

Muqbil al-Wâdi'î's Trauma

It appears that the long experience of Muqbil al-Wâdi'î in Hejaz, in Najrân and in Riyadh during the 1950s, and then from around 1963 to early 1979, played an important part in his political and religious trajectory. In the autobiography he wrote in the mid-1990s,[44] he had much to say about the profound effect the time spent away from Yemen had had on him. As a caretaker of a building in Mecca, he was confronted daily with Sunnism and new interpretations that were then dominant in the Saudi context. Such exposure convinced him that his own Shi'ite Zaydi sect was committing certain theological errors. He decided

---

[44] Muqbil al-Wâdi'î claimed to be opposed to the cult of personality, but he justified the writing of an autobiography by saying that he was responding to requests by various persons, inviting him to answer attacks made against him, and asking him to clarify his thinking on various points. Muqbil al-Wâdi'î (ed.), *Tarjamat Abî 'Abd al-Rahmân Muqbil Bin Hâdî al-Wâdi'î* [Biography of Abî 'Abd al-Rahmân Muqbil Bin Hâdî al-Wâdi'î], op. cit., pp. 16–17.

to turn towards 'the Islam of the *ahl al-sunna*', though at first he allegedly leaned towards the ideology of the Muslim Brotherhood. He set the knowledge of the Saudis, especially as concerns the prophetic Tradition, over against the ignorance of the Yemeni Zaydis of his home region. Direct socialisation into a new religious model that he learned about in the holy Muslim city, plus the experience of a religious diversity he had not known among his tribe, in a Yemeni society rendered stagnant by a system of status groups, initially produced in him a feeling of allegiance to the Saudi 'model' as he had experienced it. The confrontation with religious texts characterised as 'Wahhabi' acted as a trigger. Concerning his youth and his time in Saudi Arabia Muqbil al-Wâdi'î wrote:

I asked to study at the Hâdî mosque [the main Zaydi centre of the city of Sa'da] but I found no help there. After a while, I left the country to go to the Land of the Two Holy Places and to Najd. I listened carefully to the preachers and I admired them. I asked them to tell me which books I should buy. They suggested the *Sahîh* of Bukhârî, *Bulûgh al-marâm*, *Riyâdh al-sâlahîn*, *Fath al-majîd* which is an interpretation of the *Kitâb al-tawhîd* [the principal work by Muhammad Bin 'Abd al-Wahhâb] and they gave me several copies of *Muqararât al-tawhîd*. I was the caretaker of a building in the Hujûn quarter of Mecca and I began to dive into these books, without fully understanding them, because the habits and interpretations in our country do not agree with these readings, especially as concerns the *Fath al-majîd*. After a while I went back [to Yemen], and I disapproved of everything I saw that was in contradiction with those books, such as sacrificing animals, building shrines over gravesites and praying to the dead.[45]

The experience of his first return to Yemen and the attempts by Zaydis in Sa'da (most of them members of the *sâdâ* category) to get him to abandon his new Sunni attitudes only strengthened his resolve to break with the religious environment in which he had been born. His approach was radically revisionist. Returned to the modest condition of a tribal member [*qabîlî*] and as such assumed by many descendents of the Prophet to be incapable of religious knowledge, al-Wâdi'î did not accept the rigid status system and hierarchisation of pre-revolutionary Yemen. His affiliation to Salafism could then appear as a sort of social revenge. He held fast to a Salafism that rejected tribalism and preached the equality of all believers therefore giving him a sense of empowerment.[46]

In 1962–1963, Muqbil al-Wâdi'î fled the civil war that was raging in the far north of North Yemen, a royalist bastion. Then about thirty years old, he left to live in Najrân, on the Saudi side of the border, for two years. At that time

---

[45] Ibid., pp. 19–20.
[46] François Burgat, *L'islamisme à l'heure d'al-Qaida*, op. cit., p. 34.

he realised how much Saudi society was marked by the presence of different religious groups, not much in agreement with his own conception of Islam or for that matter with the conceptions favoured by the dominant Saudi religious institutions. After having confronted the Zaydis of Sa'da, he now came to grips with the important Ismaili minority in Najrân (of the Sulaymânî branch). He identified their alleged errors as well, and would eventually say that he considered them 'worse than the Jews and the Christians'.[47]

Any account of Muqbil al-Wâdi'î's migratory experience is limited by the state of available sources. These are almost all hagiographical, monitored and commented on by al-Wâdi'î himself or by his heirs and many details remain unknown. However his political path of development can be retraced. During the 1970s he directly participated to the movement of the *ahl al-hadîth* inspired by the teachings of Muhammad al-Albânî and the *Jamâ'a salafiyya muhtasiba* that would eventually give rise to the dissident movement of Juhaymân al-'Utaybî. Despite self-censorship and his recantation of anti-Saudi positions just before death, the timeline of the documents allows the stages of al-Wâdi'î's relationship with Saudi Arabia to be determined with some accuracy.

Once close to the Muslim Brotherhood, he appears to have at least partially broken away from their political thought (he was critical of the fact that they seemed 'more interested in newspapers than in religious books')[48] before going to study in Medina in the early 1970s. Reacting to the emergence of the *Sahwa islâmiyya* movement, and to official religious institutions whose learned quality he appreciated but which he considered too close to the monarchy, he became part of the Islamist tendency which Stéphane Lacroix and Thomas Hegghammer have called 'rejectionist'.[49] In the Saudi context this trend is characterized by a complex position with regard to the state: the monarchy is not legitimate in religious terms because the Âl Su'ûd family does not belong to the Quraysh tribe (that is, the same tribe as the Prophet). However, it is appropriate to respect the political decisions made by the government. Al-Wâdi'î's own use of the more religious expression *ardh al-haramayn wa Najd* [Land of the Two Holy Places and the Najd] instead of the usual formula *al-Su'ûdiyya*, which refers to the Âl Su'ûd ruling family, expressed a certain unease which was con-

---

[47] Muqbil al-Wâdi'î (ed.), *Tarjamat Abî 'Abd al-Rahmân Muqbil Bin Hâdî al-Wâdi'î* [Biography of Abî 'Abd al-Rahmân Muqbil Bin Hâdî al-Wâdi'î], op. cit., p. 62.

[48] Muqbil al-Wâdi'î, *al-Makhraj min al-fitna* [Leaving dissension behind], op. cit., p. 127.

[49] Thomas Hegghammer and Stephane Lacroix 'Rejectionist Islamism in Saudi Arabia: The Story of Juhayman al-'Utaybi Revisited', op. cit.

sistent with the 'rejectionist' trend. In a recording dating from the 1990s, al-Wâdi'î referred to his intention and his hesitations with regard to this country's name, declaring that he used 'the term *Su'ûdî* in the sense in which it is commonly used, but for all that this nationality was never revealed by God'.[50] In the context of the Salafi doctrine endorsed by al-Wâdi'î, a government can be corrupt without having to be declared unholy (*kâfir*), and the same can be true of an entire society. This nuanced position helps explain the complex relationship that Muqbil al-Wâdi'î and the whole Salafi movement in his country had with both Saudi and Yemeni states.

Caught up in the issues and internal struggles of the Muslim political-religious field, al-Wâdi'î in the mid-1970s entered a phase of radicalisation that landed him in prison several times in Saudi Arabia and once for a short time (eleven days during a Ramadan holiday) in Yemen under the presidency of Ibrâhîm al-Hamdî, that is between 1973 and 1977. Few writings or other information remain from that period of political unrest, during which a large segment of the range of Islamist groups on the Arabian Peninsula took shape. Al-Wâdi'î never mentioned his own brief visit to Cairo, and his probable expulsion from Egypt, although this incident was corroborated by one of his former disciples at the time of his death. His role in the development of the opposition movement led by Juhaymân al-'Utaybî led to his being imprisoned, and eventually permanently expelled from Saudi Arabia, to return only in his last months of life. He was accused of having written certain texts criticising the monarchy that were distributed by Juhaymân al-'Utaybî beginning in August 1978. He never repudiated their content as such, but he denied having written them.[51] These texts, particularly *al-Imâra wa al-bay'a wa al-tâ'a* [*The state, allegiance and obedience*], describe among other things the conditions that a legitimate Muslim leader (*imâm*) must satisfy in order to obtain the allegiance of believers. In this text, the 'imposed king' (*al-malik al-jabrî*) who leads Saudi Arabia is accused of 'not being of the Quraysh tribe', of 'not applying religious precepts', indeed of 'destroying religion and fighting its supporters' and of demanding obedience instead of meriting loyalty.[52] The millenarian option that the movement of the *Ikhwân* and al-'Utaybî chose a few months later in the seizure of

---

[50] Muqbil al-Wâdi'î, sound recording, *Nasihatî lil-shabâb al-su'ûdî* [My advice to Saudi youth].

[51] Muqbil al-Wâdi'î (ed.), *Tarjamat Abî 'Abd al-Rahmân Muqbil Bin Hâdî al-Wâdi'î* [Biography of Abî 'Abd al-Rahmân Muqbil Bin Hâdî al-Wâdi'î], op. cit., p. 27.

[52] Rifa'a Sayyid Ahmad, *Rasâ'il Juhaymân al-'Utaybî* [The Letters of Juhaymân al-'Utaybî], op. cit., p. 67.

the Grand Mosque of Mecca on the first day of the fifteenth century of the Islamic calendar, and the hailing of the coming of the *mahdî* in the person of Muhammad al-Qahtânî seem not to have been shared by al-Wâdi'î and appeared as rather opportunistic coming from a movement that had reached an ideological deadend. He criticised the resort to violence and the brandishing of weapons within the holy sanctuary of Mecca. He rejected the idea of *khurûj* (revolt) against a government that in the final analysis remained a Muslim government. In *al-Makhraj min al-fitna* he stated about the *Ikhwân*:

> They did not fight against God or the Prophet, they did not spread corruption over the Earth; they thought they were in the truth but they made a mistake. We have considered that they were wrong to enter the Holy Shrine as they did. Still we ask God to give them victory because their faults are nothing in comparison to those committed by the governments of Muslims. This I believe, and I am a witness before God of this. I know that the government [of Saudi Arabia] does not like for me to write this.[53]

As shown by his participation to Juhaymân al-'Utaybî's movement prior to the seizure of the Holy Meccan Shrine, Muqbil al-Wâdi'î was clearly an opponent of the monarchy when he was in Saudi Arabia. His traumatic expulsion and return to Yemen only seem to have reinforced such a stance. Such a relationship to the Saudi government is to a certain degree ideological but can also be compared to the mixed feelings that 800,000 Yemeni workers, expelled from Saudi Arabia and other Gulf states would have a decade later. As a matter of fact, ideology and individual inclination are indistinguishable. The anti-Saudism of Muqbil al-Wâdi'î's publications also appears as a result of the ambiguity of his migratory experience. In this respect he symbolises the complexity of the connections between transnational relations and the development of Salafism in Yemen, and his story stands in contradiction to any hypothesis of a mechanical process of importation of Salafism.

The injustice that al-Wâdi'î felt he suffered when he was expelled justified in his opinion the criticisms he levelled at the Saudi government. He referred to a verse from the Qur'an, (*al-Nisâ'* 4–148: 'God does not like the utterance of bad language, unless one is treated with gross injustice'.) in order to legitimise his own interpretation of the concept of *jarh wa ta'dîl* (refutation and rectification) and justify his opposition to the monarchy.[54] In this context the arguments between *'ulamâ'* and leaders, and also those between entrepreneurs in the religious field, can be made public without this action constituting revolt or

[53] Muqbil al-Wâdi'î, *al-Makhraj min al-fitna* [Leaving dissension behind], op. cit., p. 144.
[54] Ibid., p. 14.

dissidence. This element of al-Wâdiî's doctrine (which appears to contradict the otherwise quietist stance), explains the vehemence of his speeches and attacks, but it also explains his marginalisation and his specific place in the transnational political-religious field. In the Yemeni environment, availing himself of a freedom of expression that he judged to be non-existent in Saudi Arabia because of the oppressive power exercised by the monarchy, he produced sermons, essays and recordings that were remarkable for their vehemence and their energy, and thus created a reputation for speaking his mind. Doctrinal and theological disagreements, even minor ones, gave rise to sharp critiques and polarisation in respect of fierce debates (concerning for example whether or not it was licit to have a *majlis shaykhât*, a council for women, whether a benevolent association should be created, or even the quality of the chain of transmission of certain *hadîth*).

Opponents of the Saudi Regime

All during the 1980s and the early 1990s, Saudi policies gave Muqbil al-Wâdiî and his partisans many occasions to show that affiliation with Salafi doctrine did not imply an allegiance to the monarchy or to its interests, real or imagined. Despite their declared apolitical stance, Yemeni Salafis criticised the government that was so often touted as their 'godfather' or their 'sponsor'.

Apart from the matter of his own expulsion, and the difficulties he had in reclaiming his precious library, Saudi diplomacy (in Yemen, Palestine, Sudan, towards Russia, towards the United States and during the first Gulf War) continued to draw sharp critiques from the Yemeni Salafi movement. In various sermons Muqbil al-Wâdiî went as far as insulting King Fahd (who died in August 2005) whom he accused of being 'stupid' (*safîh*) as well as other princes of the Âl Suûd family who sought to 'create conflict between Yemen and Saudi Arabia' and thus to take for themselves the riches of his country.[55] Responding to a question from a young Yemeni about King Fahd, al-Wâdiî responded by saying, '...he is a man who does not love religion but he is not an unbeliever (*kâfir*) [...] even if he helps the enemies of Islam and hates '*ulamâ*".[56] More generally, following violence in Mecca in 1987 between pro-Iranian demon-

[55] Muqbil al-Wâdiî, sound recording, *Nasihatî lil-shaabayn al-yamanî al-suûdî* [My advice to the people of Yemen and Saudi Arabia].
[56] Muqbil al-Wâdiî, sound recording, *Ihdharû fitnat al-suûdiyya* [Beware of the dissension from Saudi Arabia].

strators and Saudi police,[57] al-Wâdi'î stated that the Âl Su'ûd family had fallen into 'disgrace' (*khizî*) and that it was 'now known that they are agents of America and Russia.'[58] He invited them to abdicate in favour of an imam from the Quraysh tribe and the *ahl al-sunna*.

Written in the mid-1980s, *al-Suyûf al-bâtira li-ilhâd al-shuyû'iyya al-kâfira* [Sharp swords for the unholy communist heresy] is a publication that inveighed against socialist ideology both in Afghanistan and in South Yemen. Muqbil al-Wâdi'î in this essay emphasised the importance of the struggle against those he labelled 'communists' of South Yemen. According to him, it was not so much a matter of fighting the regime in Aden, but of realising that Saudi Arabia was supporting it. He stated that the latter was under the control of the United States, whose objective was only to corrupt both peoples. According to him, it was then 'preferable to be poor and keep one's honour' rather than become 'rich and humiliated (ie. by becoming a client of the Kingdom)'. He also did not hesitate to attack implicitly the blind allegiance of Saudi '*ulamâ*', who seemed incapable of addressing the internal problems of their country:

We hear the senior '*ulamâ*' of the Land of the Two Holy Places speak of Islam, may God reward them. But I do not know if they are aware of the corruption present in Najd and in their country. Their silence on this matter, can it be explained by the fact that they are unable to do anything, or are they really unaware of the situation?[59]

For al-Wâdi'î, the struggle against distant communists in Afghanistan was certainly a duty for all Muslims, but it had the effect of causing the people and their '*ulamâ*' to turn their attention away from internal problems, such as the corruption of the leaders. He observed that 'the communists jealously hate Saudi Arabia because God has blessed it financially', but they do not fear the Saudi army. According to him the Saudi government was then guilty of not using its money properly to defend God and religion as it should. He criticised the fact that the Saudi state allegedly encouraged communism in Aden, and

---

[57] Concerning the events that officially caused 402 deaths at a pro-Iranian demonstration in Mecca on 31 July, 1987, see the pro-Shi'ite narrative: Fahd al-Qahtânî, *Majzarat Makka: qissat al-madhbaha al-su'ûdiyya lil-hujjâj* [The butchery of Mecca: the story of the Saudi massacre of pilgrims], London: al-Safâ, 1988.

[58] Muqbil al-Wâdi'î, sound recording, *al-Ilhâd al-Khumaynî fî ardh al-haramayn* [The blasphemy of Khomeini against the Land of the Two Holy Places]. Al-Wâdi'î also published a more general work on Shi'ism under the same title.

[59] Muqbil al-Wâdi'î, *al-Suyûf al-bâtira li-ilhâd al-shuyû'iyya al-kâfira* [Sharp swords for the unholy communist heresy], op. cit., p. 255.

that it had, according to him, given the People's Democratic Republic of Yemen 'ten million riyals'. In his opinion, this situation was the reason why Saudi Arabia is 'not respected in the hearts of the people'. In the course of bitter criticisms he however conceded that the rise of the socialist regime in the South could not be said to be the work of the Kingdom. To say that it was created by the Saudis would, in his view, be 'absurd' (*bâtil*). But his rancour and hostility against Saudi Arabia soon reappeared, as he wrote:

We hate the royal family and we continue even today to tell people about their great misdeeds in regard to religion, many atrocities committed in the Land of the Two Holy Places, the Najd and the Hejaz, and financing given to infidels. We speak also of '*ulamâ*' who, for fear of their government, cannot speak openly and spread the truth, and of the fact that certain preachers of the faith are not allowed to go into mosques.[60]

Still in other texts he stated how much he respected the Saudi people, despite the blunders and errors of the royal family. He made a clear distinction between the two: 'When I speak of Saudi Arabia, my brothers, I mean King Fahd and those who follow him. The Saudi people understand religion better than the Yemeni people.'[61]

At the time of the Gulf War of 1990–1991, Muqbil al-Wâdi'î vividly denounced the position of the Yemeni government and rejected that of the Muslim Brotherhood, which was staging demonstrations in Yemeni cities in support of Saddâm Husayn, whose ideology he judged heretical. At the same time he attacked the Saudi state, which instead of being able to defend itself against Iraq through use of its great wealth and the enormous quantity of weapons it had purchased, felt obliged to call in the United States and its allies to defend it. As in Afghanistan, as in the conflict with the communists of South Yemen, this supposed lack of courage on the part of the Saudis led them to try to buy their way out of fights instead of actually fighting for themselves. The Saudi army seemed to be poorly trained, unable to stand up to the enemy that threatened the country.[62] Still, no doubt because Muqbil al-Wâdi'î and the Salafis were caught out to some extent by a Yemeni population that massively supported Iraq, the Gulf War had fewer lasting effects within the Islamist field in Yemen than in Saudi Arabia. Indirectly this event did however provoke a schism within the Salafi movement, leading to the creation of the Hikma

---

[60] Ibid., p. 59.

[61] Muqbil al-Wâdi'î, sound recording, *Ihdharû fitnat al-su'ûdiyya* [Beware of the dissension from Saudi Arabia].

[62] Ibid.

association, which followed the leaders of the Saudi *Sahwa* movement into a more political version of Salafism. At the time, Muqbil al-Wâdi'î held that the legal opinion issued on 13 August, 1990 by Abd al-'Azîz Bin Bâz and the Committee of Senior *'ulamâ'*, authorising the presence of 'infidel' allied forces on Saudi territory was unfounded. He judged the action 'very dangerous' because American President George Bush and the allies had stated that their objective was to install democracy—an unholy form of government—in Saudi Arabia and Kuwait.[63]

During the Yemeni civil war of 1994 and during the months of tension that preceded it, the Salafi political-religious field was filled with pointed critiques of the Saudi state and its policies. The Saudis were accused of not applying their own anti-communist policies by actually supporting socialist secessionists. Worse, this hypocrisy was in the quietist Salafis' view linked to an ancient habit of sowing discord in Yemen and in the entire region, even in the smaller Kuwaiti and Qatari emirates.

In Yemen, al-Wâdi'î repeatedly accused the Saudi government of simultaneously financing the tribes, the Shi'ites and the communists, thus attempting to provoke *fitna*, that is, dissension or chaos, in order to benefit from the allegedly great natural resources of Yemen. Utterly lacking in principle or morality, Saudi foreign policy was accused of being guided only by material and financial interests, such that the government could not even reveal its actual diplomatic aims. In a conference recorded in 1993, the Yemeni Salafi leader attacked this hypocrisy and inconsistency as something that affected directly the population of Yemen:

I say to Saudi Arabia, Palestine is close to you, why don't you attack the Jews? One could also ask them: why are you helping [John] Garang [ie: leader of a south Sudanese rebel movement] against the Sudanese Muslims? Why did you help the communists when they were in Aden? If you listen to Saudi radio you think you are listening to angels who never disobey God, but if you look at their requirements and their actions you see that they are unworthy. Yes, one who aids a communist against a Muslim is unworthy! So we demand that the respected *'ulamâ'* in Saudi Arabia force their government to apply the Book and the Tradition.[64]

---

[63] Muqbil al-Wâdi'î, *Tuhfat al-mujîb 'alâ as'ilat al-hâdhar wa al-gharîb* [Precious responses to questions from one who is present and one who is absent], op. cit., pp. 315–316.

[64] Muqbil al-Wâdi'î, sound recording, *Ihdharû fitnat al-su'ûdiyya* [Beware of the dissension from Saudi Arabia].

Saudi support for the Southern secession of April 1994 was interpreted by various actors in the Yemeni and international Islamist field, including the Salafis, as aid offered to 'infidel' socialists. In fact, this analysis ignores the complexity of the secessionist coalition. It was indeed not reducible to an ideological dimension since it included many different groups, some of whom were ferociously opposed to the Marxist leaders of the P.D.R.Y.: military elites, Hadrami merchants, bureaucrats, descendants of the Prophet and Sufis, for example.

However the fact that the Saudi government recognised the ephemeral Democratic Republic of Yemen on 21 May, 1994, and the fact that the Saudis most probably funded those who would eventually lose the war, all illustrated for Muqbil al-Wâdi'î and his supporters the faults of the Saudi monarchy. Al-Wâdi'î likened the alleged Saudi spies sent into Yemen to 'ants' and explained that the recurrent tensions between the two countries were a mark of the Saudis' desire to destabilise Yemen:

As you know, Saudi Arabia wants to spread the *fitna* in our country. I say, if all the Yemenis were in an oven, they would not hesitate to light the fire![65]

In the eyes of Muqbi al-Wâdi'î, the Saudi government was not the only power seeking to destabilise Yemen. He thought that some Yemenis, who were in fact 'agents of Saudi Arabia, representatives of Saudi *'ulamâ'* or people who are acting on behalf of religion but who are ignorant'[66] were calling for a holy war (*jihâd*) against the communists in Yemen that would 'turn this country into Lebanon',[67] that is, start up a civil war. This statement was made before the war of 1994, and it coincided with the end of fighting in Afghanistan, a time when numerous *mujâhidîn* were returning home, some in search of new battles to wage. Yemen, then newly unified and including socialists in its government, was thus described as a potential target for them. A number of narratives mention the operations of Saudi Islamist militants, Usâma Bin Lâdin in particular, who was allegedly in Najrân for several months in 1991, recruiting and organising fighters against 'the communists' with the approval of some elements of the Yemeni security services.[68] Rather than attack Yemen in an effort to allegedly gain control of lands that were potentially rich in natural resources, al-

[65] Ibid.
[66] Ibid.
[67] Muqbil al-Wâdi'î, sound recording, *Nasihatî lil-shabâb al-su'ûdî* [My advice to Saudi youth].
[68] Interview with tribal leader, Sana'a, November 2004.

Wâdi'î advised young Saudis to fight the corruption that existed in their own society. He said that they had no right to meddle in internal Yemeni affairs, and declared, 'You have Shi'ites and socialists and Ba'athists in your country—[deal with them,] or look toward Israel!'[69] In saying this, al-Wâdi'î explicitly separated himself from the Saudi state (which had supported the P.D.R.Y. and which a few years later supported the secession movement) but also from opposition groups in Yemen or in Saudi Arabia that called for an armed struggle against the regime and the socialists.

In 1994 al-Wâdi'î implicitly criticised the position of the Yemeni affiliates of the Muslim Brotherhood, some of whom, including Abd al-Wahhâb al-Daylamî, future Minister of Justice (1994–1997) and later head of al-Îmân University, had approved attacks against civilians in Aden during an offensive against secessionist forces. Al-Wâdi'î rejected their version of the conditions necessary for a proper proclamation of jihad. In order to be legitimate, he stated that holy war had to be commanded by '*ulamâ*', and must not involve fighting between Muslims. In a conference that analysed Saudi interference in Yemeni affairs, particularly during the 1994 war, Muqbil al-Wâdi'î made this clear:

Yemen will never manage to fix what is wrong with it through jihad but only through the *da'wa* (preaching) or the assassination of communists [...], Ba'athists and Nasserists. Yemen may also solve its problems by making the people understand that these people are evildoers. [...] If the jihad is targeted at the communists it is acceptable, on the condition that no Muslim is attacked.[70]

The point of view defended by the Yemeni quietist Salafis during this period illustrates the subtlety of the activists' and entrepreneurs' positioning within the wider Islamist political-religious field. The severe criticisms made by the Salafis against the Saudi kingdom prevented them from being considered the stalking horses of the Saudis. But it was also impossible to classify them with the religiously-inspired violent groups that sprang up on the Arabian Peninsula at that time, and which eventually were drawn towards the movement represented by al-Qaeda. Despite external funding and despite the importance of migratory experiences in Saudi Arabia in the elaboration of the doctrine, the emergence of Muqbilian Salafism occurred in a relatively autonomous manner. This movement was never a branch or pawn of any Saudi movement, regardless of the fact that some of these were opposed to the Saudi monarchy. With regard

---

[69] Ibid.

[70] Muqbil al-Wâdi'î, sound recording, *Ihdharû fitnat al-su'ûdiyya* [Beware of the dissension from Saudi Arabia].

to the partisans of the *Surûriyya*, the Muslim Brotherhood, the *Sahwa islâmiyya*, partisans of armed action, *"ulamâ'* of the palace' or of government policy, the dominant Salafi trend in Yemen maintained its independence along with its doctrinal originality. The connections established during the 1960s and 1970s with a number of Saudi figures, especially with the movement of Juhaymân al-'Utaybî and with Rabî' al-Madkhalî, appear to have been affected by al-Wâdi'î's expulsion and by his desire to take full advantage of the potentialities of the Yemeni environment that appeared as less repressive than the Saudi one.

For 'Abd al-Fattâh al-Hakîmî, a Yemeni journalist specialising in Islamist movements, 'Muqbil was certainly a student of Saudi thought but he founded his own doctrine'.[71] In fact, the writings and conferences that al-Wâdi'î published during the 1980s, up until the mid-1990s, only rarely referred to Saudi figures, notwithstanding the fact that he was doctrinally close to some of them and had known them for a long time. In 1993, when 'Abd al-'Azîz Bin Bâz declared that the Yemeni legislative elections were licit because they would help defeat socialism, al-Wâdi'î did not alter his critique of *hizbiyya* and of elections. In this very context he published his most violent attacks of the democratic electoral system and of Saudi Arabia. As regards Rabî' al-Madkhalî, he only gained prominence in Yemen after al-Wâdi'î's death, taking sides with Yahyâ al-Hajurî during the succession crisis that shook up the Salafi field after 2002. Quite clearly and despite the aforementioned affinity for transnational flows, the development of the Muqbilian branch of Salafism took place in relation to local issues, and there was even reliance upon nationalist rhetoric, something Yemenis were expected to identify with. The traumatic experience of a brutal expulsion, shared by Muqbil al-Wâdi'î and the Yemeni workers, no doubt reinforced the popular anti-Saudi feeling that al-Wâdi'î exploited during the 1980s and 1990s.

Final Re-Evaluation of the Relationship with Saudi Arabia

Without any immediately apparent explanation, the manifest opposition of the Muqbilian Salafi branch to Saudi Arabia was toned down early in the new century. This re-evaluation of the position of the Salafis appeared to mark a new phase in the Yemeni field, shaped by increased interest and involvement on the part of Saudi religious and governmental figures. In this manner the Yemeni Salafi movement, distinguished by the strong personality of Muqbil al-Wâdi'î and his criticism of the Saudi monarchy, was normalised to some extent and abandoned some of the features that had set it apart.

[71] Interview, Aden, May 2005.

Once again, it was the individual trajectory of Muqbil al-Wâdi'î that would symbolise and even represent this alteration. While the medical treatments he had received at a hospital in Jeddah, where he returned in 2000, were unsuccessful, the founder of the Yemeni Salafi current made an unusual request to his partisans and his editor: he wanted to withdraw from circulation the writings and recordings he had published or released that criticised Saudi Arabia. He stated the request in these terms: 'I say this, and no one has paid me or forced me to. To the contrary, what I see in my soul and my conscience makes me do it'. He went even further, inviting all Muslims to 'co-operate with the Saudi government, if only through respectful speech, for its enemies are as numerous within as without.[72]

This final reversal, accomplished a few weeks before his death, constitutes for some an inexplicable action, which was added to by the medical treatment he received in early 2001 in Germany and in the United States, a place he had been so critical of. Shortly before his death in July 2001, he released a final cassette entitled *Mushâhadâtî fî al-Mamlaka al-'Arabiyya al-Su'ûdiyya* [*My experience of the Kingdom of Saudi Arabia*], in which he praised the generosity of the Saudi regime, the quality of the welcome he received (luxury hotels, a delegation on the tarmac at the airport, a chauffeur at his disposal) and spoke of his interview with the Saudi Minister of the Interior, Prince Nayif Bin 'Abd al-'Azîz. By this, he formally reconciled with Saudi Arabia, judging that the hospitality he received cancelled out to some extent the injustice he had suffered when he was expelled in 1979. A manager at the large Salafi bookstore, Dâr al-Âthâr, put it this way:

It is only right that you don't see the old cassettes of shaykh Muqbil, dealing with Saudi Arabia, because we must respect his last words, which were correct. That was his will, and so we don't sell the older sermons anymore.[73]

Many of his adversaries, Zaydis and Muslim Brotherhood, considered for their part that al-Wâdi'î had finally revealed his true face and in the end lent credence to the accusations of hypocrisy that had been directed at him since his return to Yemen. At another time, they thought, al-Wâdi'î himself would have denounced so harshly such an attitude of weakness in relation to a regime in power. In fact, in 1995, in a conference where he refuted the *Surûrî* doctrine, he had expressed intolerance towards those who changed their positions in an

---

[72] Muqbil al-Wâdi'î, sound recording, *Mushâhadâtî fî al-Mamlaka al-'Arabiyya al-Su'ûdiyya* [My experience of the Kingdom of Saudi Arabia].
[73] Interview, Sana'a, June 2005.

effort to adapt to new political situations by camouflaging (*talawwun*) themselves and abandoning former principles. He declared then:

In truth, I don't like those who practice camouflage. If I liked that practice, I would be able to come and go in Saudi Arabia. But this is a matter of religion, and it is only religion that prevents me [from returning there].[74]

In 2003, Yahyâ al-Hajûrî, in collaboration with Umm Salama al-Salafiyya, the wife of Muqbil al-Wâdi'î, published a narrative giving details about his last months, thereby trying to justify the final reversal of his positions.[75] In their eyes, his four-month stay in Los Angeles under medical treatment was made legitimate by attacks on United States policy, even while al-Wâdi'î was in the country. He described the United States as a 'pit of disbelief and corruption' (*wakr al-kufr wa al-fasâd*). Despite the medical care he received, Muqbil al-Wâdi'î increased the pace of his activities, publishing 220 *fatâwâ*, showing that he had not given up preaching, criticising the United States and calling for its destruction. So the 'reversal' never appeared as total to him and his sympathisers. In order to make his mentor's return to the Land of the Two Holy Places acceptable, Yahyâ al-Hajûrî insisted on the exceptional quality of the hospitality he and his entourage had received. He pointed out that his master had been treated as an equal to the Saudi senior '*ulamâ*'—that he had been received by the grand *muftî* of the Kingdom, 'Abd al-'Azîz Bin 'Abd Allâh Âl al-Shaykh, by Muhammad al-'Uthaymîn, by Rabî' al-Madkhalî and by several princes of the royal family of Âl Su'ûd.

Al-Wâdi'î's change of attitude was even symbolised by his burial. He was buried in Mecca in al-'Adl cemetery beside the senior Saudi shaykhs Bin Bâz and al-'Uthaymîn, who had died a short time before. Umm Salama remarked in her narrative that 'no one from the Embassy of Yemen was there' for the ceremony.[76] He received honours from the Kingdom he had denounced and hated, and at the end was slighted by a republic that had managed to instrumentalise him, one with which he had always tried to maintain cordial relations.

Actions that appear at first glance to be explained in terms of the immediate interest of Muqbil al-Wâdi'î himself, perhaps solely with regard to the necessity of obtaining necessary medical treatment, can also be understood by a shifting

---

[74] Muqbil al-Wâdi'î, sound recording, *Hâdhihi al-surûriyya faihdharuhâ!* [This is the *Surûriyya* so be careful!].

[75] Umm Salama al-Salafiyya (ed.), *al-Rihla al-akhîra li-imâm al-Jazîra* [The last journey of the imam of the Peninsula], op. cit.

[76] Ibid, p. 46.

political context. It is evident that the final re-evaluation of the relationship between the Yemeni Salafi leader and the Saudi government is partly obscure, and cannot be solely reduced to a strategy or to particular processes. The determining factors identified here highlight to what extent the rapprochement with the Saudi government was gradual, ambiguous and fragile. At any rate, they do not counter the argument that is being made throughout the book regarding the assumption of the low level of Salafi indebtedness or allegiance with regard to Saudi Arabia.

Before this reconciliation, the fact that Muqbil al-Wâdi'î's violent criticisms of the Kingdom were published while the centre at Dammâj was receiving funds from para-public organisations, personalities or merchants close to the Saudi regime, illustrates the ambivalence of the connections between the monarchy and the Salafi movement. As explained above, the Salafi rejection of politics was only an illusion. From the beginning of the 1980s the quietist Salafis in Yemen were characterised by their overall rejection of the power of the Âl Su'ûd family. The apparent contradiction involved in having a state finance and support its own opponents only highlights the diversity of the state actors and the shortcomings of their rationality and policies. The royal family, like religious elites, is not a unitary bloc. The ambiguity of relationships maintained by various protagonists illustrates the impossibility of identifying fixed 'national interests'. Different actors at every level of the decision-making process are capable of inflecting public policy and of producing outputs that turn out to be unexpected and involuntary. In the present case study the amplitude of interpersonal transnational relations and the great prevalence of migratory experiences both tend to increase the diversity of policies and the number of points of contact between the two societies. For this reason, the unintelligible or contradictory nature of certain policies regarding the funding of political-religious actors is connected to the plurality of actors that make and carry out apparently rational decisions. While he was very critical, Muqbil al-Wâdi'î never broke completely with certain elements of the Saudi government or with the official religious institutions, which had undergone an internal shake-up that placed them from time to time in the forefront during the decade following the Gulf War. Thus the reversal of 2000 was not just something that Muqbil al-Wâdi'î did, but it was also the result of struggles and recompositions within the structures of Saudi power. In fact, in order to counter the expansion of the protest movement of the *Sahwa islâmiyya* and that of violent movements known as jihadi the Saudi government tended to co-opt quietist Salafis or the *Jâmiyya* movement, particularly Rabî' al-Madkhalî and

Sâlih al-Fawzân. This policy ended up promoting an apolitical tendency that was close to al-Wâdi'î's theological position, one based on opposition to politicised groups as such, opposition to democratic reform and opposition to violent actions directed against governments, something attributed to a deranged minority (*al-aqâliyya al-hâla*).[77]

In addition to these considerations concerning the plurality of state actors and various alliances made with actors in the religious field, other factors shed light on the reconciliation between Muqbil al-Wâdi'î and most of the quietist Salafi movement along with him in Yemen and the Saudi monarchy. The late 1990s were marked by an easing of tension in diplomatic relations between Saudi Arabia and Yemen, and this arguably played a role in the Yemeni Salafi leader's change of heart. After the trying episode of the war of 1994, and despite occasional problems that arose in certain areas, the settling of the conflict over the border mobilised the agendas of both governments. The Yemenis began to receive more Saudi development aid after parts had been cut off at the time of the Gulf War and a first agreement on the border question was signed in February 1995. The Yemeni President 'Alî 'Abd Allâh Sâlih was welcomed on an official state visit by King Fahd in June 1995 and an agreement for co-operation on security matters was concluded in July 1996. During this time, emigration to Saudi Arabia increased significantly, although visas and work permits were not delivered officially by the Embassy.

A few weeks after al-Wâdi'î left for Jeddah for medical treatment, the Saudi and Yemeni governments signed a border treaty putting an end to more than sixty-five years of simmering conflict. In such a context many of the ill shaykh's critiques became unnecessary, and to this extent the rapprochement was legitimate. This is no mean feat when one considers the relationship between the Yemeni government and the Salafis. Thus al-Wâdi'î's final about-face appeard as consistent with certain observed changes and a general improvement in bilateral relations.

Consequently, the final reversal by al-Wâdi'î was part of a complex process marked by the plurality of non-state actors, the improvement in bilateral diplomatic relations and finally by co-optation of currents close to Rabî' al-Madkhalî by the Saudi monarchy. In fact, the return of Muqbil al-Wâdi'î to Saudi Arabia after twenty years, and even the recantation of bitter critiques hurled at the Saudi government, appear more as a culmination than as a sudden break.

It remains true that this reversal—like so many of the contradictions that appear in the intellectual production of Salafism—appears to reveal something

---

[77] Sâlih al-Fawzân, sound recording, *al-Irhâb* [Terrorism].

not only concerning the complex personality of Muqbil al-Wâdi'î, but also concerning the nature of transnational religious relations. It highlights the limits of an analysis of political or religious ideology outside its local, international or transnational context. The relationship with Saudi Arabia then appears to be more closely linked to a personal experience than to an allegiance or aversion with an ideological basis. Consequently these relations are multifaceted. Salafism in Yemen influenced by the charismatic force of Muqbil al-Wâdi'î was built upon the same ambiguity as that which marked the migratory relations between Yemen and Saudi Arabia.

The study of the relationship between Muqbil al-Wâdi'î and the Saudi government, and the relationship between him and religiously-legitimised opposition movements in the Kingdom, both demonstrate the weakness of the dominant narratives that concentrate on processes of importation and exportation of Salafism in regard to Yemen. The argument citing supposed allegiance to the Saudi monarchy and domination through Salafism quickly runs out of speed as soon as one apprehends this political-religious movement in its proper context, taking into account its history since the mid-1970s.

In fact, the direct and personal confrontation with Saudi Arabia that many actors of the Salafi political-religious field have encountered, sharing this experience with hundreds of thousands of Yemeni migrants, cannot be systematised. Saudi domination, the migratory experience and the discovery of a different form of religion during a period spent living in Saudi Arabia have produced among religious leaders, activists and non-politicised workers as much adherence as rejection, as much admiration as mockery, as much pride as nostalgia and as much enthusiasm as frustration. This plurality of feelings is the very source of 'everyday' transnational relations and constitutes a structure in the imagination that is fertile soil for the development of Salafism. The ambivalence of the migratory experience reveals the flexibility of transnationalism and the fundamental character of an individual trajectory. Essentially it is for this reason that policies of control established by states fail so often, and are all the more likely to do so when one considers that representations and structures of the imagination themselves are constructed, and travel from place to place. The hypothesis, according to which the migratory experience, like 'membership' in Salafism, implies a transfer of allegiance, cannot be verified. Through the double example of the ambiguity of the individual trajectories of emigrants and the difficulties of the relationship between Muqbil al-Wâdi'î and the Saudi regime, we understand how little mechanical 'Saudisation' is involved by Salafism. Transnational flows are not Trojan horses for states, they have no power to shape or determine the loyalties of actors.

THE CENTRALITY OF TRANSNATIONAL CONNECTIONS

The relatively autonomous development of Yemeni Salafism from the 1980s onwards does not imply that such a process was separate from other aspects of the interpenetration of societies within the Arabian Peninsula. The daily importance of transnational relations remains a central variable throughout this research. As will become apparent in more concrete terms in the following chapter that focuses on a case study in the region of Yâfi', emigrants are only the indirect importers of new religious practices. Neither manipulated by the states, nor acting from any intention to change things, they do not have control over Salafism's transplantation. Often things happen despite them, in a fortuitous and temporary manner, and so Salafism has become part of a Yemeni context shaped by many recompositions and by the everyday presence of transnational links. Financial relations, exchanges of audio cassettes and religious books, and scholarships for study, all represent expressions of transnational religious relations that are the main object of these chapters.

5

YÂFIʿ: SALAFISM BEYOND THE BORDER

The idea of a disconnection between the proselytising practices of the Saudi state and institutions and the development of the Salafi movement in Yemen is not only validated by the attitude of Yemeni religious entrepreneurs and their often critical approach to the political regime of the Âl Suʿûd. An attentive study at the grassroots level tends to also support the alternative narrative that is at the heart of this monograph.

From an approach essentially centred on Salafi leaders, this chapter will now switch to a level of analysis that focuses primarily on anonymous individuals, sometimes activist Salafis or just sympathisers and actors with daily involvement in contemporary transnational relations. Through the study of migratory trajectories towards the Gulf monarchies and the development of Salafism among a limited population, I come to draw attention not only to the variety and the significance, but also the ordinary character of transnational connections.

Far from the common border with Saudi Arabia, the region of Yâfiʿ is characterised by the intensity of its relations with abroad, and by a significant implantation of Salafism. In conducting research inside the Faculty of Education (*kulliyyat al-tarbiyya*) of the village of Labʿûs, employing about thirty teachers to supervise the higher education of some 350 students, my intention was to grasp in a concrete way the phenomenon of diffusion and adaptation of Salafism at the local level. How can one link transnational relations with transformations in religious practice on the part of certain individuals identified as Salafis? What dynamics and recompositions explain at the local level the development of this new identity?

This inquiry is the result of seven trips of different length to Lab'ûs and to other villages in Yâfi' in 2002, 2004, 2005 and briefly in 2006. A direct encounter with the object of my research was my goal, and I hoped to gain a more intimate knowledge of Salafism. At the same time, I was in effect taking part in an effort to demystify Salafism. Instead of attempting to grasp this movement exclusively through texts, through an abstract intellectual history or in terms of broad theological concepts, I allowed ordinary social processes, not motivated or deliberately constructed, to shed light on the political and religious transformations undergone among the students and teachers of the small faculty in Lab'ûs. In this context, I defend the idea that the entire set of these social processes is strongly marked by the transnational, particularly the migratory experience and the ambition of emigrating to Saudi Arabia and elsewhere in the Gulf monarchies. Religious transnational relations occur in this interaction and in connection with the daily presence of the other societies of the Arabian Peninsula. Local recompositions are fully integrated into global dynamics that go beyond the national framework and the space limited by territories and borders.

I. Regional and Transnational Identity of Yâfi'

I first travelled to the Yâfi' region in the spring of 2002. In many ways, this encounter, with what would years later become my principal area for research, even then revealed many of the dynamics that are focused on in the present work.

At that time there was no asphalt road leading to the small town of Lab'ûs, where I was travelling for a period of linguistic immersion. I was expecting to find a place that had been preserved from Western influence, a sort of autarky in pristine purity. No doubt I imagined I would find what the anthropologists Najwa Adra, Steven Caton, Joseph Chelhod, Paul Dresch, Shelagh Weir and Robert Serjeant had had the luck to find in their visits to other regions of rural or tribal Southern Arabia. But instead of the end of the earth, instead of a lost world of Yemeni authenticity of which I had dreamed, I found a vast extent of mixed rural/urban landscape, the home of several thousand people, with large fields planted in terraces, some impressive stone buildings and everywhere the traces of migration and globalisation.

When I went back again to Lab'ûs in January 2005, a road had been built, climbing through steep mountains and deep valleys. But the village was still lacking in modern infrastructure, almost unaffected by development policies initiated by the state or financed by international institutions. It only had limited access to electricity (from 4 p.m. until 1 a.m.) thanks to a generator that had been given to the town at the beginning of the 1990s by a merchant who had taken up residence in Saudi Arabia. Yâfi', which for centuries had had close relations with distant lands, had by then only began to be linked most closely to its immediate national environment. Despite recent transformations and a proactive policy on the part of the Yemeni government that aimed at reducing the isolation of this former southern region, Jeddah, Riyadh and Doha seemed closer in people's minds and in their daily lives than the town of al-Baydhâ', which was only 40 kilometres away. However, up until the unification of 1990, al-Baydhâ' had been on the other side of the border between the two Yemens. Measuring the progress made in the process of ending the isolation of Lab'ûs and its region, an inhabitant from Yâfi', one who had once emigrated to London, recalled that at the beginning of the 1960s, when he was a student in Aden, he had to walk ten days to get back to his home village during summer vacation, a trip that now took less than three hours. The paradox of relative distances, and differences in the meaning of what is near and what is distant are not necessarily part of modernisation or the contemporary process of globalisation. Far from the border, the space of 'the Frontier' at any given time, and of translocality, is a reality at once ancient and immediate.

Situating Yâfi'

Yâfi' is a region of high mountains in the former P.D.R.Y.. Lab'ûs is its largest town, sitting at an altitude of 1,900 metres about 150 kilometres north-east of Aden. It is bordered by the Dhâla' plains to the west and by those of Abyan to the south. This region of approximately 5,000 square kilometres is historically divided into two distinct entities, governed until 1967 by two families of sultans: the Âl Harhara in Upper Yâfi' (Yâfi' al-'Uliyâ or Yâfi' Banî Mâlik) and the Âl al-'Afîf for Lower Yâfi' (Yâfi' al-Suflâ or Yâfi' Banî Qâsid). This division is still pertinent and is continued in the local allegiances of different urban centres, in various districts and with regard to tribal groups, still well established.

Yâfi'î identity is based upon a particularly rich history. In ancient times, the region was one of the main sources of incense production, and for this reason had extensive commercial and political relations with the Himyarite kingdoms. As a symbol of the region's reputation and its ancient roots, popular belief has it that the legend of the Seven Sleepers (*ahl al-kahf*), mentioned throughout a Qur'anic sura, actually took place in the area around Sa'adî in Lower Yâfi'.

Much later, in the seventeenth century, Yâfi'î armies played a leading part in the struggle against Zaydi expansion under the Qasimid imam, something that remains a source of local pride, and that goes along with a claimed reputation of refusal to submit to the power of a central state, whether it be the central Yemeni state in Sana'a or a British or socialist one in Aden. Robert Serjeant, linking the characteristics of remoteness and independence, has said: 'So inaccessible is Yâfi'î country that it rarely comes under a centralising power and then not for long'.[1] Still an illustration of this reputation, during the 1960s the sultan of Upper Yâfi' refused to allow his region to become part of the federation of emirates proposed by the colonial administration in Aden. As punishment, the region was bombed. This gave rise to one of the most active resistance movements in Southern Arabia, the Yâfi'î Reform Front.[2]

A number of anecdotes emphasise the independent spirit of the region during the contemporary period, and the fact that it is always at loggerheads with the central state. The mythology of rebelliousness has been reactivated, and now feeds on a lively regionalist feeling that has become since 2007 a means of political expression. As a consequence, the secessionist movements of the South have gained tremendous popularity in Yâfi'. In Lab'ûs, during the *ziyârat al-Mihdhâr* (important tribal festival) of January 2005, some participants in the tribal dance of the *bara'* carried jerrycans and storm lanterns as a protest against an expected hike in the price of fuel that had been announced by the government. Because of these symbols, not threatening in themselves, the festival got out of hand with regard to the authorities who had hoped to turn the reunion into a ceremony of declaration of allegiance to Yemen's long-time ruler, 'Alî 'Abd Allâh Sâlih. The representative of the Yemeni government, who

---

[1] Robert Serjeant, 'Yâfi', Zaydîs, Al bû Bakr b. Sâlim and Others: Tribes and Sayyids', in Robert Serjeant, *Arabian Studies*, Cambridge: Cambridge University Press, 1990, p. 83. Paul Dresch also insists on this specific nature of the Yâfi' and says: 'Much of Yâfi's territory is extremely rugged and there is little feudal there at all: families each have small terraced holdings of their own. Upper Yâfi' and Lower Yâfi' subdivide extensively. Each had a sultan (apart from the plethora of section shaykhs) whose family was called the dawlah locally and claimed vague precedence, though various of the shaykhs themselves had treaties independently, with Aden and none obeyed the others, while the Lower Yâfi' Sultan was associated primarily with a sacred drum and the ability to make rain. To describe the importance of these persons in British terms of sovereignty was not possible'. Paul Dresch, *A History of Modern Yemen*, op. cit., p. 38.

[2] Sâlim 'Abd Rabbuh, Munda'î Dayân, *Jabhat al-islâh al-yâfi'iyya* [The Yâfi'î Reform Front], place and publisher unknown, 1992.

had just been named to his post, was infuriated by this public defiance, and privately promised to make changes in the situation, uttering a threat expressed in terms of the region's history: 'Yâfiʿ cannot remain in opposition forever!' One indication that the region's independent streak remains a reality was provided by the presidential vote in September 2006. The candidate of the united opposition, Faysal Bin Shamlân, received almost 46 per cent of the vote in Upper Yâfiʿ, and 58 per cent in Lower Yâfiʿ, as against only 22 per cent nationally. In October 2008, one of the leaders of the protest movement in the South, a native of Hadramawt named Hasan Ahmad Bâʿûm, took refuge among the tribes of Yâfiʿ, who refused to give him up to representatives of the army who had come to arrest him.[3] The gunfight and the tensions that ensued were further testimonies to a tradition of defiance with regard to central power. In administrative terms, the fact that the region straddles two governorates (Lahj and Abyan), although its population, the 'coherence' of its identity and its historical importance would justify its occupying a single governorate by itself, is proof to many Yâfiʿîs that one government after another seeks only to divide the region in order to control it more easily.

The tribal structure of the region, somewhat weakened over the course of the socialist period, remains a reality. The ziyârat al-Mihdhâr celebrated in Labʿûs by a number of towns, villages and tribes in Upper Yâfiʿ is an opportunity to reactivate such identity. Each year this festival, which originally featured visits to the tomb of a local saint, brings together a crowd of around 30,000 people. Beyond its contemporary political function, that of a council of local tribes which is attended by a representative of the central government, it provides an occasion for popular culture to celebrate the local traditions of poetry and dancing (qasîda, zâmil and barʿa). There are also 'verbal jousting' contests in which members of different tribes challenge each other in terms of quick-wittedness and respond to one another along with what is called bidʿ wa jiwâb (initiation and response) qasâʾid.[4]

The central state, over the 1990s, was unable to provide public services for more remote areas, particularly roads and electricity, and this incapacity led to a sort of reaction in the form of 'retribalisation' in society. Actually, certain traditional religious and tribal structures (especially the maktab)[5] were revived

---

[3] al-Ayyâm, 18 October 2008.
[4] On the specific issue of Yâfiʿî oral poetry and the dynamism of oral poetry in that region, see Flagg Miller, The Moral Resonance of Arab Media. Audiocassette Poetry and Culture in Yemen, op. cit.
[5] Ibid.

after unity, and transformed. They remain a central mechanism of conflict resolution.

The Yâfi'î identity is not as deeply engraved or formalised as that of Hadramawt, but in many ways it could be compared to the one that has developed in this eastern province of the former South Yemen. The two regions are 400 kilometres apart, but their relationship is ancient and both populations are notable for migrating in significant numbers. Many Yâfi'îs found employment as mercenaries from the sixteenth century onwards in Hadrami armies. The Qu'aîtî sultanate in Hadramawt, its capital situated in al-Mukallâ, was established in the nineteenth century by descendants of emigrants from Yâfi' who had been living in India.[6]

The efforts to value regional identities are not uniform at the level of the entire country of Yemen, and are still an emerging phenomenon in Yâfi'. The enchanting grey stone architecture, tribal poetry, popular proverbs and the political movements that fought British colonialism in the 1960s have, since Yemeni unification, all been studied by scholars and researchers native to the area. This attention to the construction of identities interestingly appears to be related to transnational space. As with Hadramawt, an encounter with the 'Other' and with foreign lands via migration encouraged a conscious search for the origins and traditions of the ancient motherland. Flagg Miller analyses the complex relationship between the inside and the outside in Yâfi'î culture.[7] The traditional poetry he studies is strongly marked by the transnational or translocal, if only in the system of circulation of cassette recordings of poems. Many of these are written in Yâfi' but recorded abroad, and many speak of longing for Yemen, and contain a direct link with things that happen there—a poem may commemorate a death, a wedding, a feud, and so on. In their production, poets appear to be fully aware of this translocal dimension of their scattered audience.

Apart from traditional poetry, a migrant's connection with home has since the mid-2000s passed occasionally by way of the internet. Of course, the network is rarely accessible within the country and even if computers were available, electricity and phone lines often are not. However, there are a large number

---

[6] Paul Dresch, *A History of Modern Yemen*, op. cit., p. 21. For a more completely developed approach to the connection between Hadrami sultanates and the diaspora, see Linda Boxberger, *On the Edge of Empire: Hadhramawt, Emigration and the Indian Ocean (1880s-1930s)*, op. cit.

[7] Flagg Miller, *Inscribing the Muse: Political Poetry and the Discourse of Circulation in the Yemeni Cassette Industry*, Doctoral dissertation, University of Michigan, 2001, p. 24.

of internet forums (*muntadâ*) dedicated to Yâfiʿî matters.[8] Posters are for the most part young expatriates living in Saudi Arabia, Qatar, the United States or even China. Internet forums appear as modern incarnations of translocal phenomena. These are intended to celebrate the popular culture of Yâfiʿ and discuss general issues about religion, families or recent events in the country. Active mobilisation with a secessionist edge in the former governorates of the P.D.R.Y. evidently gives discussions a political dimension, and in the end they become efficient spaces of mobilisation against the Yemeni regime.

The geographical isolation of Yâfiʿ and its status as an enclave have not prevented its insertion in transnational dynamics. In connection with Hadramawt or otherwise, migratory flows very early on allowed peoples from the high mountains of Yâfiʿ to establish contact with the outside world. For centuries, Yâfiʿîs had to leave their country in order to survive unfavourable climatic conditions, poor soils and warfare. They fled poverty as well as political and tribal instability. They migrated to the interior of Yemen or its shores or even left South Arabia or the Peninsula. Since the nineteenth century, they contributed a great deal to the economic development of Aden and to that of the Abyan fertile plain. In that region, which is irrigated by the Wâdî Banâ', the post-unity reprivatisation of agricultural land following socialist nationalisation in the 1970s returned profit to a few great families in Upper Yâfiʿ, many of whom live in Saudi Arabia. The mercenary tradition, its eye ever turned beyond Yemen, which attained its highest development in the eighteenth century when the Yâfiʿîs had a monopoly over the guard of the sultan of Hyderabad in India,[9] continues today in the smaller Gulf states where Yâfiʿîs are often employed in police forces or in the army. At the beginning of the nineteenth century, Wahhâbî incursions from the Najd region into Hadramawt were supported by certain tribes from Yâfiʿ that had been living for a long time in the eastern province.[10]

In the contemporary period, the workers coming from Yâfiʿ are present throughout the Arabian Peninsula, the United States, the United Kingdom and more recently in East Asia. They are active in commerce but also occupy unskilled jobs. Despite the absence of precise figures concerning the destinations of these migrants, Saudi Arabia is for the Yâfiʿîs, as for all Yemenis, the

[8] Among the most popular internet forums concerning Yâfiʿ see Shabâb Yâfiʿ [Youth of Yâfiʿ]; www.shababyaf3.com; Nâdî Yâfiʿ [The club of Yâfiʿ]; www.yafea1.com or Multaqâ abnâ' Yâfiʿ [Forum of the sons of Yâfiʿ]; www.alyazedi.com (accessed on 4 December, 2006).

[9] Linda Boxberger, *On the Edge of Empire: Hadhramawt, Emigration and the Indian Ocean (1880s–1930s)*, op. cit., pp. 49–50.

[10] Ibid., pp. 150–151.

main host country. Yâfi'î migration to this country is massive, and it is likely that over 100,000 workers were settled there in the mid-2000s decade. After the crisis of 1990–1991, migratory flows reorganised quickly and resumed. In the city of Jeddah, merchants who had over the previous decades gained Saudi citizenship handled the economic integration of Yemeni guest-workers by selling (or exceptionally by granting) them the services of a *kafîl* and then by employing them in their different businesses.

Everyday Transnational Experiences

As a result of the massive migration flows, in Yâfi' itself, direct experience of migration, whether to Saudi Arabia or to the other Gulf countries is something that is massively shared by families and social groups. One frequently hears that current or former expatriates are more numerous than the people who have stayed in Yâfi' all their lives. Networks have also spawned a vast community that relates to the same place of origin. The interaction between internal and external phenomena is complex, and distances and borders alike are variable things. As Flagg Miller says, 'The Yâfi' identity is to a large extent contingent on the identities of those living outside the Yâfi'.[11] The region is deeply shaped by transnational relations, and this also affects what one sees. Each year during the summer, or in the holidays, when emigrants return, cars with Saudi plates, and to a lesser extent cars from Qatar or the United Arab Emirates, furnish a concrete illustration of migratory links and of insertion into translocal space.

The interpenetration of societies, largely independent of states, affects the daily lives of actors. Speaking of the transformations of his native region over several decades, a teacher of Lab'ûs explained:

During the 1960s, before independence, Lab'ûs was a very poor village. Emigration to Saudi Arabia, and also to America during the 1970s and 1980s changed everything. The *mughtaribîn* built big, fine houses here. You see, all these buildings, these nice houses, Gulf money bought all that! The recent development of the region may lead to Yâfi' being transformed into a governorate. This has not been decided but the government is thinking about it.[12]

---

[11] Flagg Miller, 'Yafi' Has Only One Name: Shared Histories and Cultural Linkages Between Yafi' and Hadramawt' in Mikhail N. Souvorov and Mikhail A. Rodionov (eds.), *Cultural Anthropology of Southern Arabia: Hadramawt Revisited*, St Petersburg: Museum of Anthropology and Ethnography Peter the Great, 1999, p. 65.

[12] Interview, Lab'ûs, April 2005.

Thus, in terms of economic development but also in terms of institutions and of the visual appearance of the area, the pervasive effect of migratory relationships has transformed Yâfi'î society in the most profound ways. The transnational thus appears in a very concrete manner within the local. During the first decade of the twenty-first century the government of Qatar financed a road connecting Rusud, the administrative capital of Lower Yâfi', and the coastal plain of Abyan. The example indicates ways in which a sort of para-diplomacy pulls Yâfi' away from Yemen, and how much this region is identified by its insertion into transnational exchanges, even more than by its location within definite borders. For a young man, a native of Rusud, this gesture by the Qatari government did not necessarily indicate that the relations between Qatar and Yemen were particularly good. He referred implicitly to the impor-tance and the long history of the relations between Yâfi' and the Gulf emirate, and observed, 'It is perhaps the relations between Rusud and Qatar that are good, rather than the relations between Yemen and Qatar!'[13] The fact that this small town and its region once supplied Qatar with a significant portion of its soldiers and policemen (during the 1970s and 1980s) helps understand the establishment of networks for solidarity that do not pass directly by way of diplomacy between states.

Through emigration, positions of domination that are political, economic and religious are at the same time created and maintained. Merchants (*tujjâr*), through investments in businesses in Yemen and by constructing expensive and luxurious homes in their own villages (homes that combine traditional Yâfi'i architecture with a certain modernity, such as elevators or indoor pools) announce ostentatiously their success outside Yemen. In such a context, it is unimportant that the house is only occupied during the holidays, a few weeks a year or even that the links have only become symbolic. The success of one is the success of a whole family, a clan, a tribe; it is shared by all those in the vil-lage who never left or who have come back, some against their will. Interestingly, since the 1980s this mechanism has also functioned in connection with resi-dents who have left in order to pursue jihad in Afghanistan or in other areas of conflict and through these means young villagers have become respected, creating a political and also a religious resource. The aura they have gained on the distant battlefield has spilled over and is shared by all.

In 2003, in the last nationwide legislative elections, at least two deputies elected from Yâfi' came from rich merchant families whose members live both

[13] Interview, Lab'ûs, March 2005.

in Saudi Arabia and in this region. From the district of Muflahî, 'Abd al-Khâliq Bin Shayhûn, member of al-Islâh, was elected, and from Lab'ûs, Muhammad 'Abd al-Hâfiz al-'Isâ'î, a member of the ruling GPC party. For both of these men, it was not their tribal membership or their genealogy *per se* that justified their notability in a society where the contemporary political leadership is usually made up of members of traditional elites. It was quite clearly the success of their clan in transnational relations and their economic success as *tujjâr* that produced their social ascension in their home country, then becoming a political resource.

In Lab'ûs as in the Saudi *mahjar*, the 'Isâ'î family, especially 'Umar Qâsim (died 2008) and his cousin 'Alî 'Abd Allâh, have occupied pre-eminent places since the 1980s. Based on their financial success in Jeddah in the agri-food business (Canada Dry beverages), appliances and electronics (Has, Panasonic), real estate and, above all, automobiles (they own the Japanese concession for Mitsubishi in both Saudi Arabia and Yemen), they represent a point of reference as well as an opportunity for Yemenis that work in their numerous Saudi businesses. As a sign of the deference shown him, 'Umar Qâsim al-'Isâ'î was commonly called 'the *shaykh*' by the inhabitants of Lab'ûs and his portrait was hung beside that of President Sâlih in the local assembly hall (*al-majlis al-mahâlî*) of the directorate (*mudîriyya*) of Lab'ûs—a building he himself had paid to have repaired following the decentralisation law of 2000 that established these local assemblies. In Saudi Arabia, his money also went to finance an ongoing relief effort for Yemeni expatriates, offering them medical care and assistance in navigating the Saudi bureaucracy.[14] In its home region, after unification and the fall of the despised socialist regime, the 'Isâ'î family started reinvesting money earned in Saudi Arabia. The family bought up farmland on the fertile Abyan plains, created specialised businesses in the transportation sector, invested in agri-food and bought the Mövenpick Hotel in Aden at the end of the 1990s.

In 1997 and 1998, 'Umar Qâsim al-'Isâ'î financed the creation of the Faculty of Education in Lab'ûs. In co-operation with the University of Aden, and thanks also to financial support from the Kuwaiti state, the former headquarters of the Yemeni socialist party in the small Yâfi'î town was remodelled to make housing for the teachers, classrooms and a student centre. In addition, computer

---

[14] Regarding the charity activities of the 'Isâ'î family, see: '*Khadamât jalîla iqaddamahâ maktab al-'Isâ'î lil-mughtaribîn al-yamaniyîn*' [Considerable services offered by the 'Isâ'î bureau to Yemeni expatriates], *26 September*, 4 March, 2003.

equipment and a library were purchased. The initial contribution promised by the Yemeni-Saudi benefactor was 70 million Yemeni riyals (corresponding to about $600,000 at that time). Since then the same donor has continued to contribute to the faculty each year (in 2005 he gave 9 million Yemeni riyals, or $50,000). Each student was also offered a daily stipend of 200 Yemeni riyals (something around one dollar but still a valuable if not decisive help for many). This direct aid to students was unique in the area, and explained the relatively widespread reputation the university had acquired both within and outside of Yâfi'. Some students were from distant regions, for example Ta'iz or Dhamâr, towns lying more than 200 kilometres away. The financing was however not complete at all times for at the inauguration of the university branch in 1998, according to the assistant Dean, 'classes began without chairs because the promised funding had not arrived!'[15] In 2005, students' stipends were not paid on time, which caused some difficulties for those who depended on these to buy food or books. Nonetheless the system of student aid places the 'Isâ'î family as well as transnationalism at the centre of the lives of students and teachers. At their homes (where their father and their brothers were often expatriates) as at the university, their lives are largely dependent on things that happen outside of Yemen: on fortunes made, on economic hardships or on administrative restrictions.

As a consequence, those who remain in Yâfi' are often aware of the distinctive qualities of their region. Thus, the fragile status of Yemeni workers in Saudi Arabia has more effect on the society and the economy than decisions made by the Yemeni central government, so close in geographical terms and yet seemingly so far away in political ones. Because of this, the interdependence of the local and Saudi economies is often emphasised. For a grocer in Lab'ûs who has two brothers that work in the Saudi city of Dammâm, on the coast of the Arab-Persian Gulf, the situation is such that:

Saudisation in the job market and unemployment prevent some of the *mughtaribîn* from renewing their residence permits and creates problems with regard to finding a *kafîl*. As a reaction, the difficulties of emigrants affect the economy of our region directly, and even my own business is not going as well as formerly.[16]

In this particular context, pride in belonging to the same family, the same tribe or the same region as a merchant who made a fortune as an emigrant,

[15] Interview, Lab'ûs, April 2005.
[16] Interview Lab'ûs, May 2005.

contributes to the positive image Yâfi'îs have of migrating, and consequently creates a strong desire to travel away from the homeland. Despite diplomatic problems, change of status of Yemeni workers in Saudi Arabia (previously mentioned as having less of an effect on workers from the former South Yemen) as well as economic difficulties, migration remains frequent, although not always a satisfactory experience. Many expatriates return to Yâfi' because they fail to find a job or a *kafil* or because they are expelled while others return because they want to go to school, or because they miss their country and their family.

A flippant remark from a young teacher in the education faculty of Lab'ûs, and member of the ruling GPC, exhibits what are thought of as shared expectations and references in Yâfi'î society, as well as signs of political, economic and religious success. Speaking of the fact that many young people are emigrating from the region, including two of his own brothers, he jokes:

I want to have fifteen sons—five will go fight in Iraq or Palestine and will become martyrs, five will become famous '*ulamâ*', and five will go work in Saudi Arabia or in the Gulf and will become rich merchants (*tujjâr*).[17]

In discussions, the overwhelming popularity of the desire to emigrate comes up again and again. A schoolboy from a town near Lab'ûs was asked what he intended to do when he received his diploma. He answered, saying that he wanted 'to go study at the university *bunchar*'. The term comes from the English word 'puncture', which refers to tyre repairers.[18] Such a joke was a rather clever way of expressing his desire to abandon further studies and go work in a Gulf city where Yâfi'îs are famous for being employed in car garages as low-skilled workers. It also expressed the importance of such an experience which for many was almost to be considered a rite of passage as the *mahjar* was also considered a life-making experience. Another young man, who worked in a garage in Lab'ûs because he had not been able to find a *kafil* in Saudi Arabia, had had to cope with the idea of working in his own country because his attempt to work illegally in Saudi Arabia had been unsuccessful and he had been deported.

At the same time, those who are expatriates are conscious of the sacrifices their situation compels them to make, especially with regard to their families. On the issue of the emotional price paid by Yemeni workers abroad, Fred Halliday wrote:

It is not difficult to read on the faces of Yemeni workers a deep sadness born of years of emotional restriction and harshness: if one could see the faces of the women and

---

[17] Interview, Banî Bakr, May 2005.
[18] Interview, Banî Bakr, May 2005.

children left behind in the villages [...] there would no doubt be the same melancholy. The pain of emigration, and the sadness it occasions at home, are a recurring theme in Yemeni poetry.[19]

Answering a friend who had said that the great difference in age between him and his brother was due to the fact that his father only rarely returned from Saudi Arabia, a young Yâfi'î who had recently emigrated said: 'This attitude is illicit in religious terms (*harâm*); one does not have the right to abandon one's family in this way'.[20] This same man, interviewed in Saudi Arabia, declared:

Here, it is like a prison, I feel much happier in Yemen where I feel freer [...]. Here, you have to pay for everything, for the residence permit, for the *kafîl*, for other permits and for rent. [...] I live in Saudi Arabia only because I need to improve my financial situation for a few years, especially to get enough money to get married. I have a diploma from the Faculty of Education in Lab'ûs and I hope I will be able to get a job working for the government of Yemen in two or three years. I don't want to stay here too long!

Young people's desire to emigrate is viewed in an ambivalent manner by members of older generations, or by those who have not undergone the expatriate experience. These people are certainly aware of the limited nature of opportunities in Yâfi', and in Yemen in general: rapid population growth and the entry into the job market of a large cohort of people born during the 1980s have considerably reduced the number of available jobs. Despite the important place migration holds in Yâfi'î identity, the intrusion of the transnational and the reference to Saudi Arabia, whether in an economic, political or religious context, is not always seen as positive. For those educated under a socialist regime, over and above any desire to emigrate and undergo the migratory experience, it is quite often thought that the daily presence of Saudi Arabia is responsible for a retrograde development of society, particularly represented by Salafism itself, and a supposed loss of traditional values, ones that the socialist period, with its authoritarian policies and its forced march toward modernism, did not manage to get rid of. In a more general sense, with a polemical edge, a teacher of the Lab'ûs faculty remarks:

The effects of emigration by Yemenis toward the Gulf upon society are clear. In economic terms they are positive. People are making money and there is investment. In return, the effects on the educational system are negative. The fact that young people want to emigrate affects their desire to continue their studies. 95 per cent of the young

---

[19] Fred Halliday, *Britain's First Muslims. Portrait of an Arab Community*, op. cit., p. 15.
[20] Interview, Riyadh, April 2006.

189

people of Yâfi' want to leave, and that means they don't intend to pursue higher education beyond secondary level. Even people with diplomas leave, and in the host country they take jobs that don't match their qualifications.[21]

In the reality of individual experiences, in the aspirations of each person and in the investments made locally by the *mughtaribîn* and more so by the *tujjâr*, the society of Yâfi' finds itself affected by important transnational dynamics. It is also marked by its privileged relationship with the Saudi neighbour and the monarchies of the Gulf, however distant. In the final analysis this profound but often neglected context can be seen to be just as significant in regard to the identity of today's Yemenis and the things that they claim membership of, as are diplomatic relations, institutional financing and strictly religious relationships. The transnational dimension of Yâfi' is based on a cumulative effect that has been stimulated by state actors, but which for the most part escapes their influence.

II. Bin Bâz and the French Chicken

The implantation of Salafism into the Faculty of Education of Lab'ûs, nothing in itself unique or specific, takes place in a particular context whose principal characteristics have been discussed above. The development of Salafism thus cannot be separated from multiple recompositions both local and transnational. From this point, changes in the situation of Yemeni workers in Saudi Arabia, the desire of Yemenis to emigrate, the image-construction of translocal personalities, the reaction to the fall of the socialist regime in the early 1990s and the individualisation of religious identities are among the wide number of variables that must be taken into account when grasping the reality of Salafism in the Yâfi'î context and more specifically in the Faculty of Education of Lab'ûs.

As observed throughout the previous chapters, adherence to Salafism, at the level of anonymous sympathisers or of religious entrepreneurs, is flexible and ambivalent, and cannot be considered as a result of mechanical processes that connect up abstract actors. Uncovering or denouncing a unilateral intervention on the part of Saudi Arabia to the benefit of the development of Salafism in Yemen is an obvious short-cut for analysis. What remains to be understood here is the resonance and the effect of Salafism in the environment of Yâfi'. How can the success of this political-religious movement in the eyes of students and some professors be linked to the phenomenon of interpenetration between Saudi and Yemeni societies?

[21] Interview, Lab'ûs, May 2005.

The Faculty of Education in Lab'ûs

By 2006, the Faculty of Education in Lab'ûs, which opened in 1998, was handling about 350 students in five different sections: Arabic/Islamic, English, mathematics/physics, biology/chemistry, and social sciences. The first two were immediately popular, but the latter was closed down in 2006 for lack of students. Administratively, the faculty is a branch of the public university of Aden, and its primary function is to train teachers. In the beginning, the college only offered students a two-year course, at the end of which a sort of 'thinned-out' diploma (called *diblum*) was awarded. It theoretically allowed graduates to qualify to teach in rural primary schools but the number of job opportunities was meagre. For city schools and secondary schools, four years of higher education were imperative and so the course in Lab'ûs was extended in 2004 to offer students a bachelor's degree called *bakaluriûs*. The college's efforts met with success for in 2002, they had only 184 students, a figure that would double over the next few years. Still, the short course, unique in the region, constituted an advantage for students from poor families who could not afford longer programmes. The same was true for the housing offered to students, and above all as concerns the daily stipend of 200 Yemeni riyals offered to each student by the merchant 'Umar Qâsim al-'Isâ'î. The almost total lack of female students was, for some of the most conservative students who objected to cross-gender interactions, an advantage in comparison with other schools in the region (particularly those of neighbouring Radfân or Lahj) or the University of Aden where coeducation was the rule. The faculty at Lab'ûs had only one female student in 2002, and two in 2005.

Admission of students was selective, but took place over a vast geographical area: less than 10 per cent of students were originally from Lab'ûs. The poor quality of roads in the area and the high cost of transportation forced students to stay in the small town for long periods without returning to their villages or seeing their families. Students stayed in their dormitories over the weekends and had few, if any, leisure opportunities outside of the faculty. As such, the college in Lab'ûs was rather a closed system, and constituted a fascinating case study in which a number of issues and transformations became particularly salient. Such a 'confined' environment therefore allowed an observer to study certain internal social relationships, particularly phenomena of religious emulation and the appearance of charismatic figures.

Being admitted to the faculty and even studying hard does not necessarily mean that students will find a satisfactory job at the end of two- or four-year curricula in Lab'ûs. Many students' hopes are not fulfilled. Hiring through the Ministry of Education is slow, and students usually have to wait two or three years before getting a job, which will be badly paid in any event (around 20,000 Yemeni riyals per month, $100). The educational system also mandates a year-long waiting period after graduation from secondary school before beginning university studies. Such a period was once reserved for compulsory military service, but that obligation came to an end in 2001. Thus a student's trajectory is interrupted by periods of inactivity, which in the particular environment of Yâfi' are incentives to emigrate to work, or to take classes in one of the many private centres for religious education.

Many students leave Yemen or want to do so once they get their diplomas. In the spring of 2006, in Jeddah, I happened to meet by chance a young gradu-ate I had first encountered in 2002 in Lab'ûs. He had got a job in a clothing store that belonged to the 'Isâ'î family. Another student, who had graduated in June 2005 from the mathematics/physics section of the teachers' college in Lab'ûs, had left Yemen soon after to work in Riyadh in a ready-to-wear store belonging to other prominent merchants from Yâfi', the Huraybî family. Upon leaving secondary school in the late 1990s, he had already spent a year working for the same *kafîl* in Jeddah.

My own level of interest with regard to the Salafi phenomenon at the college in Lab'ûs arose during my first stay in Yâfi' during the spring of 2002. Apart from the immediate visual impression produced by 'minor behaviours' and other 'distinctive practices' described above, the presence of Salafism in that small student population became visible during student elections organised in April 2002. These elections were held to choose three student representatives in each of the five college sections. The ballot was largely partisan to begin with. There were candidates from the ruling GPC, from al-Islâh, others running as independent (who, rumour had it, would switch to support for the GPC in exchange for financial stipends) and also a few candidates, considered marginal, from the Yemeni Socialist Party, none of whom gained election. At the time, over a third of potential voters ended up abstaining from voting. In general, the abstainers justified their choice with reference to their rejection on religious grounds of a partisan system, and their rejection of political partisanship (*hiz-biyya*) as such. The elections were scheduled to be held every two years, but the elections for 2004 were postponed repeatedly, mainly due to a succession of teacher strikes. In April 2006, they still had not taken place. A student explained that this was simply because 'no one here will participate!' Despite the fact that voting was by secret ballot, the majority of the students who refused to vote on religious grounds were identified and singled out as a specific group (not always in a negative way) by their fellow students and by a number of teachers who were consistently using a number of labels to designate them: *abû lihiya* (literally 'bearded father'), *mutawwa', Wahhabî, ahl al-sunna* or *Salafî*. The use of the term Salafi to refer to that specific group of students and also of teachers appeared as immediately relevant to me. Obviously, as mentioned earlier, being 'a Salafi', either in the specific context of the faculty or outside, does not imply exclusive allegiance to a particular set of teachings, or the possession of a 'membership card' and it certainly does not indicate a fixed religious or political stance. As is emphasised throughout this monograph, Salafi doctrinal canons, defined by foreign *'ulamâ'* and by Yemeni ones, particularly by Muqbil al-Wâdi'î, do function as a frame of reference, but there are many ways of putting them into effect. My use of the term Salafi acknowledges the multiple character of sources and influences that may be upheld or respected by individual actors. However, such a term does help frame a specific group inside the faculty of Lab'ûs as it does outside.

In the college as elsewhere, membership in Salafism is essentially a matter of following certain objective distinctive practices, among which the dress code and a number of theological and political reference points. These allow Salafis to self-identify as a specific category and to be perceived as such by others. A refusal to wear trousers, leaving the beard uncut and wearing the *'imâma* on one's head are signs that make the category immediately visible at the college. Among students, the presence of these signs allows people to identify a group in objective terms, whose numbers can then be estimated relative to the size of the student body. During my successive stays in Yâfi', I steadily evaluated that proportion to around one-third.

By all means, in Yemen as a whole, such a high degree of adherence to Salafism is not common. It is obvious that the specific Yâfi'î environment as well as that of the faculty itself favour a number of mechanisms that explain such occurence. In this respect the conclusions drawn from the case study at this point are merely illustrations, not necessarily a judgement about proportions. This data can still be used to analyse elsewhere a few mechanisms that connect religious transformations to transnational relations and translocal recompositions.

During a visit to the region in February 1999, Muqbil al-Wâdi'î himself had noticed that the people of Yâfi' seemed particularly receptive to the Salafi message. They had given him a warm welcome, shooting bullets in the air to greet him and his delegation. In a conference recording he told a story about the time he visited Upper Yâfi', when because of a lack of room in the scheduled meeting place at a mosque, he had been obliged to hold a conference outdoors. He said of this occasion:

> The road leading to Yâfiʿ is difficult by car, it takes five hours to go up the mountain, although it only takes two hours on foot! [...] But when we saw the warm welcome people were giving us, their desire and their love for the *daʿwa*, both old and young, the fatigue of the trip disappeared. Their fervour was astonishing![22]

In another recording he cited as evidence of the vitality of Salafism in Yemen, the example of Yâfiʿ. He pointed out the contrast between the geographical isolation of the region, and its openness to the Islamic preaching of the *ahl al-sunna*:

> A person of Yâfiʿ told me he had carried the *daʿwa* even to the tops of mountains where only three people lived. Arriving at the top, he realised that the sunna had already come to them, that it had been there before him.[23]

Within the faculty of Education in Labʿûs, the significance of Salafism led to a kind of polarisation. Through their distinctive activities the Salafis often appeared as outsiders, or perhaps as people who willingly excluded themselves. Students were housed in groups of eight, and the dormitory rooms were often constituted based on geographical origin and also on religious orientation. As was customary for religious individuals, in dormitory space occupied by Salafi students, a bench or board was placed across the entrance in order to mark a boundary (much like in a mosque) beyond which all persons were expected to take off their shoes. The majority of students spent the afternoon and even the evening chewing qat, and many considered this a necessity in order to study or do homework. But Salafis forbade qat consumption. In doing so they separated themselves from the primary form of socialising, and were thus obliged to find other things to do. They would read, listen to sermons and go to one of the mosques surrounding the college.

In the same way, the Salafis' refusal to watch television created a spatial boundary of sorts. On campus, the two available cafeterias and student stores (where things like soap, student supplies and food could be purchased) showed they recognised these differences: one cafeteria was run by a young man who had studied for two years at Dammâj in Muqbil al-Wâdiʿîs time, and he made sure that Salafi doctrine was respected in his cafeteria. The other manager put

---

[22] Muqbil al-Wâdiʿî, sound recording, *Rihlat Yâfiʿ* [Journey to Yâfiʿ].

[23] Muqbil al-Wâdiʿî, sound recording, *Liqâʾ sahîfat al-bayân al-imâratiyya* [Interview with Emirati paper *al-Bayân*].

a television set in his own cafeteria, and when there was electricity he would show football matches and American or Egyptian movies. No rule existed but there was a strong correlation regarding one's political and religious tendencies and one's choice of cafeteria.

Food preparation was another issue that set Salafis apart from the majority of students and teachers. For a number of years, imported frozen chickens have formed a staple of the Yemeni diet because they are cheaper than local poultry (*al-dajâj al-baladî*). Many of the frozen chickens are imported from France, particularly from the Doux company of Brittany, which sells hundreds of thousands worlwide each day. At the college, French chicken (*al-dajâj al-faransî*) with rice is served in the teacher's cafeteria and also offered to students (for financial reasons as well as religious ones a number of students cook for themselves in their rooms). However, in the 'Salafi' cafeteria, French chicken was declared banned because it was claimed that the chickens had not been slaughtered in the accepted Islamic way, by having their throats cut, and therefore the chickens were not *halâl* (licit). The main replacement item was then cans of tuna produced in Yemen. The students in this case referred themselves to a *fatwâ* supposedly pronounced by the Saudi senior cleric, 'Abd al-'Azîz Bin Bâz. This declaration stated that a representative of the *'ulamâ'* had seen for himself that the French slaughterhouses did not observe the sanitary rules of the Muslim faith. This matter led me, as a French national, being repeatedly questioned by Salafis about the manner in which chickens were slaughtered. One said to me:

I have a question for you. Is the French chicken killed by having its throat cut, or by electrocution? We have seen several articles showing that the chickens are not killed by having their throats cut, and so they are not *halâl* even if it says they are, on the package. Once in the newspaper, *al-Ayyâm* they even showed a photo of a chicken that still had its head on![24]

Along with the refusal to chew qat, the rejection of French chicken, a powerful and visible symbol of local adherence to Salafism within the faculty, became a manifest symbol of distinction and was regarded as such by all. These norms illustrated not only the group's focus on questions that appeared to some as formalities, but also the influence of a transnational political and religious movement on individual practices that seemed far removed. The *fatwâ* of Bin Bâz, whether real or imaginary (I have found no record of it) came to symbolise what was perceived as a process of 'Saudisation' of Yemeni Islam. At least, these things represented a reference that took hold and acquired a meaning, not in

[24] Interview, Lab'ûs, April 2005.

relation to a mechanical process of importation but in the particular context at the Faculty of Education. The refusal to eat French chicken gave rise to debates and to identification by third parties, but it also produced social solidarity among Salafis. It is primarily this local dimension, that also happens to be shaped by transnationalism, that explains the success of Salafism as a political and religious practice.

Quite surprisingly, the choice of a mosque was not a significantly important factor in terms of intrafaculty relations. Most of the students who practised their religion usually went to the nearest mosque—although accused by a small minority of being favourable towards *hizbiyya*. In 2002, this particular worship centre was being managed by a second-year student in the Arabic/Islamic section. For Friday prayers, students and teachers would go to a mosque (masjid al-ʿAbâdî) that was larger but further from the school, one built in 2004 with funds donated by Yâfiʿî *mughtaribîn* living in various Saudi and Gulf cities. This mosque was visited in March 2005 by Yahyâ al-Hajûrî, who arrived from Dammâj to host a conference. In a small town where distraction is a rare thing, this was an important event, attracting the attention of many people outside strictly Salafi circles. As a religious frame of reference, Salafism was locally esteemed, but not everyone was willing to put up with all the restrictions it involved.

Contrary to what might have been expected, the faculty's polarisation did not cause serious tension or conflict within the group of students and teachers. Salafis had in effect become valued by most in performing the role they had chosen for themselves. The fact that their mosque might be attended by others, or that they might lead group prayers for professors inside the faculty premises showed that in some ways they had made religion their province. They had acquired a degree of monopoly within the religious field at the microsocial level.

Occasionally, the new norm they were trying to enforce for everyone was perceived as intolerant, and thus gave rise to criticism and a degree of apprehension. In the Arabic literature course, for example, the study of pre-Islamic poets was criticised by a few hardliners, which irritated a number of teachers who were loath to have their programme of study dictated by Salafis, or called in question as such. In their households and between family members, the Salafis' intransigent doctrine was likely to create tensions as young sympathisers were aiming to impose on others their religious practices and morality. Patronising of sisters and female relatives clashed with the practices of women in the countryside who were used to working in fields with their face unveiled and had been raised in the relatively liberal era of socialist South Yemen.

However, inside the faculty, the polarisation between those who were nick-named *abû lihiya* and other students and teachers was less a matter of serious conflict than of jokes and symbolic actions, which illustrate the competition between different membership groups in the political-religious field. One evening while the call to prayer for the *maghrib* was still echoing, at a moment when a bunch of students were relaxing in a room chewing qat and talking, two young Salafis arrived and asked everyone to go to the mosque with them: 'Come with us, it is time for prayer!' The other students waved their qat branches and replied that for them, it was the hour of *takhzîna*, a time to 'load up' with a little qat, a reaction that in its own way was rather shocking by Salafi standards. Failure to attend prayers is indeed regarded by them as a serious offence. Responding indirectly to the weakness of the religious practice of his peers in the faculty, one Salafi student had written a *fatwâ* from Bin Bâz on the wall next to his bed, in which the Saudi scholar said that those who fail to attend the *fajr* prayers at about 5 a.m. because they stay up late and don't wake up that early, have committed an act of impiety (*kufr*) without themselves being declared *kufâr*, impious, on that account. The student explained:

This text is for those who visit the room, who skip prayers because of qat or because they are lazy. When they read it, they know they are doing something wrong. [...] There are different levels of *kufr*. The devil can make you commit an act of impiety, but since you had no desire to leave your religion, you are still not a *kâfir!*[25]

Such a moral discourse, inspired by the Islamic principle commanding each one to promote virtue and prevent vice, was even supported by some teachers, members of the faculty. In May 2005, in a course on the *tafsîr* (interpretation of the Qur'an) in the Arabic/Islamic section, one teacher mocked those who miss certain prayers, ironically observing, 'Why pray the prayers of the *'ashâ* (last prayer of the day, around 8 o'clock)? Is that not the moment at which the effect of the qat is at its strongest?' This teacher also said to his students:

Even if you chew qat, you must still pray! Take the qat out of your mouth and put it aside. Prayers take fifteen minutes, you need five minutes for the ablution ritual (*wudhû'*) and ten minutes for the prayer itself. Prayer is the foundation of religion. How can someone who does not pray call himself a Muslim?

Another element of interest in this situation was a certain amount of 'peace-ful co-existence' of Salafi students and teachers with socialists, a group that included a good many teachers who had been trained under the P.D.R.Y.. Such

[25] Interview, Lab'ûs, May 2005.

co-existence did not appear as a given but highlighted the gap between an apparently aggressive Salafi doctrine and milder and more tolerant practices. The faculty's Dean, ostracised within his own central administration because of his political orientation, was a leading member of the Yemen Socialist Party yet still highly respected by the students.[26] Also, 'Aydarûs Nasr al-Naqîb, a former professor of social sciences of the faculty, had been elected as member of Parliament from the Rusud district in the legislative elections of 2003. He had left his teaching post in order to devote his time to political activity and assume the leadership of the socialist faction in the Yemeni parliament. These men, like other teachers, were pure products of the socialist regime of Aden, and many of them had been educated during the 1970s and 1980s in Eastern Europe (Bulgaria or Russia) or even in Cuba. Their world vision, influenced in their own manner by another type of transnational relations—which had long disappeared—seemed worlds apart from that of the new generation of students and of younger teachers, yet did not foster violence and visible intolerance.

When one considers the sharp intransigence of sermons preached by leading Salafi figures, and the accusations of impiety they hurl at socialist leaders and activists, the fact that the two corresponding segments of a small university community can coexist and even have some respect for each other seems coun-ter-intuitive. Actually, the chaff that goes on between qat-chewers and Salafis, or between piety-conscious students and socialists, including occasional moments of tension, stands in contrast to the violent nature of certain speeches and prejudices that are mentioned elsewhere in this monograph. This capacity to live and let live at the local level and to work around mere doctrine once again shows that the study of Salafism should not be limited to an analysis of the ideological output of its leaders. To say, in this context, is not to do, and Salafism in concrete terms is quite different from the requirements and prohibi-tions listed in theological treatises or in the fiery sermons preached by Salafi entrepreneurs. Practices only become intelligible when the context of their adoption is taken into account. The gap between the doctrine preached by the entrepreneurs and its application on the ground is not the result of faulty interpretation or by imperfect 'importation'. It is simply part of every process of adaptation. Salafi political-religious practice may appear as no more than a fashion, that is, a means of setting oneself apart, of taking up a dissenting stance

---

[26] After leaving his post in the faculty at the Lab'ûs branch, his participation in the Southern movement in Aden since 2007 caused him to be arrested and thrown into jail various times.

with respect to one's own society, considered as corrupt, while at the same time becoming part of a closely-knit group.

Determinant Factors in the Local Development of Salafism

The causes of the development of Salafism among students and the Faculty of Education in Lab'ûs are not immediately clear. The factors usually mentioned by the proponents of a state-centred analysis, involving processes of importation and exportation, are in reality only marginal. A number of elements speak to the limited scope of such an analysis. The region of Yâfi' is not characterised by a high level of Saudi state funding, nor by a high level of institutionalisation of religious instruction (such was the case in the former North Yemen's Scientific Institutes), nor by any structured network of Salafi centres, not even by physical proximity to the border. Thus the recent emergence of these new political-religious practices seems to be for the most part spontaneous, that is, not connected to institutional action or to some plan that could be uncovered or hypothesised. In fact, Salafism is not a response to a stimulus from higher up, but is above all the result of many complex recompositions within a local context that is deeply influenced by transnational links.

The immediate environment of the teachers and the institutional structure undoubtedly played a role in the diffusion of Salafi practice in Lab'ûs. I mentioned above the establishment of a sort of monopoly on religious questions on the part of the Salafi group. Its members led group prayers and determined what debates were legitimate (qat, 'French chicken', *hizbiyya*) among the faculty. Through numbers, the charisma of certain individuals, and the social and cultural importance of religion, the Salafis managed to impose norms that structured and polarised the entire university community. The school system actually favoured the most 'pious' students (without this being the result of any apparent intentional arrangement), and this created a certain momentum: the best of these students would end up teaching in public schools, or in some cases be added to the university faculty itself. Without ever having studied in private Salafi institutes, the students were placed in contact with the main historical figures claimed by the Salafi tendency: Bin Bâz, al-'Uthaymîn, al-Albânî, Ibn 'Abd al-Wahhâb, Ibn Taymiyya and the Yemenis al-Wâdi'î and his eighteenth-century predecessor al-Shawkânî. The oldest and most respected instructor, who taught a course in Islamic law (*fiqh*) had worked in Saudi schools for more than twenty-five years before being expelled in 1990. Through his knowledge and the respect he commanded, he represented a reference point for students that allowed them to associate Saudi Arabia and religion directly. As already explained earlier with regard to the 'Isâ'î family, this instructor's history, that is, his long absence from Yâfi', made him into an indirect symbol of the positive (although ambivalent) image that is connected to the Saudi *mahjar*.

In the absence of centralised programmes and university-approved books, teachers have considerable freedom to teach as they see fit, and a certain number of them in the faculty did openly profess allegiance to the heritage of the Salafism of Muqbil al-Wâdi'î, while also associating themselves with Saudi references. For students in the Arabic/Islamic section, courses in the science ('*ilm*) of the *hadîth* were mainly based on questions about procedures and creed. Students were invited to ask questions according to a system similar to the one popularised through conferences given by '*ulamâ*' which are recorded and later distributed in cassette form in Salafi bookstores. The plurality of sources of jurisprudence, particularly Zaydi ones and others diverging from the Shâfi'î school, were only rarely mentioned. Claimed 'errors' committed by other Muslim sects were sometimes criticised. In a course on ritual ablutions in May 2005, a teacher suggested that his students 'observe the errors' (*shubuhât*) of the Zaydis (whom he referred to as Shi'ites) when visiting Sana'a. This reference to the 'Shi'ites' of North Yemen was exemplary of Salafi doctrine, but also had to do with the development of regionalism since unification in Yâfi', something that had taken place in all the governorates of the former South Yemen.

In their own manner, the local society and the university community endorsed Salafism—but without there appearing to be any unified or external motivation to do so. Salafism developed without any overt dissension, other than that which concerns symbolic matters such as the refusal to chew qat. Apart from the teacher of Islamic law (*fiqh*), the former expatriate mentioned above, all the teachers that could be identified as Salafis had been trained in Islamic sections at Yemeni public universities (at Aden or Sana'a), and had only occasionally visited the major Salafi centres of Dammâj or Ma'bar. The same went for the *abû lihiya* students who were for the most part direct products of the Yemeni public education system.

As elsewhere in the former South Yemen, the fall of the socialist regime had led throughout the 1990s to a manifest religious revival of which the emergence of Salafism was one among the many manifestations. The regime of the P.D.R.Y. in Aden, during its time in power, had promoted a kind of acculturation (whose success should probably not be over-rated) that a contemporary re-Islamisation process was intended to correct. It had banned the headscarf from universities, nationalised religious property and *awqâf*, repressed the traditional elites, either religious or tribal, and imposed an ideology many arguably considered as alien to Yemeni history and culture. As a sign of the post-socialist backlash, in Lab'ûs, the grand mausoleum dedicated to the glory of the socialist martyrs and to those who fought against colonialism had been abandoned in the re-Islamisation process. A new mosque sat across the street from it, symbolising the shift in dominant political and cultural references.

In the story he told about his trip to Yâfi' in the late 1990s, Muqbil al-Wâdi'î implicitly linked the development of his movement to the reaction against socialism. After having visited the villages of Muflahî, al-Had and Banî Bakr, he observed that he had met 'young people, free from all *hizbiyya*', who told him that there was no need to talk to them about communism and the short-comings of politics, they already knew about them.[27] Thus al-Wâdi'î's view, shared by many others both in and out of the Salafi realm, was that socialism had in the end led to a rejection of partisan systems that only reinforced the relevance of his own doctrine.

The socialist experience also instituted a particularly marked generation gap. This has affected the global process of the individualisation of religious practices: faced with increased awareness of possible choices and trajectories because of political and religious movements, television, books, and various personal encounters and experiences, many individuals consider themselves capable of creating their own religious identities, or putting these together through '*bricolage*'.[28] Salafism bloomed because of such a process. It claimed to renew the heritage of the first Muslims, and thus found itself involved in a double separation. It set itself apart from popular Islam, but also separated itself, in the Yâfi'î context, from 'loose' Islamic practices and from the positions of older generations who had been educated under the P.D.R.Y.. Thinking back fifteen years to the regime he had known during his youth, a civil servant from a village near Lab'ûs recalled:

During the socialist period, we forgot about religion. The classes in school focused mainly on philosophy, literature and Marxist history. [...] During Ramadan, the teachers did not fast. They smoked and drank and ate during the day.[29]

---

[27] Muqbil al-Wâdi'î, sound recording, *Rihlat Yâfi'* [Journey to Yâfi'].

[28] Ample literature has been published on the issue of the individualisation and the hybridisation of religious identities, see for example André Mary, 'Métissage and Bricolage in the Making of African Christian Identities', *Social Compass*, vol. 52, no. 3, 2005, pp. 281–294 and Danièle Hervieu-Léger, *La religion en mouvement: le pèlerin et le converti*, Paris: Flammarion, 2000.

[29] Interview, Lab'ûs, May 2005.

The eventual fall of the socialists, accomplished with the help of armed Islamist militias during the 1994 war, played an important role locally in the redefinition of political and religious allegiances. Salafism among the teachers and students of the Faculty of Education was thus part of a wider process of reaction that affected many, including other movements such as Sufism and traditional elites that had been disempowered by the leftist revolution of the 1960s.

Quite obviously, the particular importance of the transnational phenomenon in Yâfi'î society plays a part in the development of Salafism, itself a movement characterised by an affinity for a wide array of transnational interactions. Such transnationalisation is probably the most significant variable if one wants to understand the Salafi phenomenon at the local level. The physical absence produced by migration can be understood as a powerful factor in social change. Irrespective of physical distance, it creates an indirect presence of the foreign, something that is immaterial and not quantifiable, but which is quite real in its effects. This instance of the dialectic of the present and the absent, although largely ignored by the international relations theory literature, is of central importance in this case study. Consequently, adherence to Salafism among students and teachers in the Faculty of Education in Lab'ûs is not only the result of a general 're-Islamisation' reaction but also that of the particular translocal context of Yâfi'.

The success of the *mughtaribîn* and the *tujjâr* is widely depicted as the only perspective for young people who often hope to attain the 'Saudi dream' or more generally the 'Gulf dream'. So-called 'Saudisation', relative to Yemeni Islam, or to be more precise the transplantation of Salafism, is linked to the interpenetration of societies rather than to the physical presence of Saudi Arabia, in the person of its government or its elites through religious, economic, educational or political initiatives that might be seen as Trojan horses by some. Transplantation of Salafism takes place from the bottom up, in the everyday lives of families, among students, through television, through relatives returning from Saudi Arabia or the Gulf monarchies on holiday, just as much as through the informal diffusion of the thoughts of charismatic religious figures. In this way, what Steven Verdovec has called 'everyday transnationalism'[30] accomplishes its effect, slowly but surely. In reality, Salafism 'travels' in the form of an inchoate aspiration. In the construction of such an aspiration, the ambiguity of migratory experience turns out to be fundamental.

[30] Steven Verdovec, *Transnationalism*, op. cit., p. 61.

Any attraction that exists for Saudi Arabia and the other Gulf monarchies is economic above all. As highlighted previously, migration frequently seems to produce the rejection of the Saudi social and religious image, mostly constructed by migrants but also by the Saudi state itself and by media and academic narratives. Direct confrontation rarely gains adherents for Salafism. In fact, only a few people who have had real commercial success in the *mahjar* and who are fully integrated into Saudi society economically, or even naturalised in an administrative sense, are even in a position to act as the indirect agents of a positive kind of 'Saudisation'. In order to take advantage of their wealth and new status in their home region in Yemen the *tujjâr* begin to act as they are expected to do in common opinion, and exhibit what they themselves think of as the proper signs of their new identity, and at times of their hard-won Saudi nationality. Religion, clothing and sometimes the use of a different Arabic dialect all serve as symbols of distinction. For their part, the majority of Yemeni migrants, who form a sort of lumpen proletariat, seldom have time or the opportunity to display their status once back in their home country other than through a few limited symbols.

Thus, in Lab'ûs as in the aforementioned Sana'a-based University of Science and Technology, the students who have travelled to Saudi Arabia or to other Gulf monarchies usually do not profess Salafism, nor do they display the distinctive markers of Saudi or '*Khalîjî*' identities. Actual migratory experience does not seem to lead to the development of Salafi activism. In Lab'ûs, a student born in Qatar and educated there (his father worked in the Qatari national army) registered for classes in 2001 in the English section at the college. Although his family was originally from Yâfi', he had only visited the region during summer holidays. His aspirations, his way of life and his religious practice could in no way qualify him among the *abû lihiya*. Upon receiving his diploma in 2003, he wished to return to Qatar but could not get the visa. His low grades also prevented him from getting a job in the Yemeni Ministry of Education. He therefore began to work as a vendor of qat in Hadramawt and continued to hope that he could leave Yemen again.[31]

By contrast, Salafi students appeared to be the direct products of the Yemeni context, with all its contradictions and recompositions. None of those encountered in the faculty had had a direct experience of migration. Their religious inclination was consequently not to be perceived as a 'Saudisation' but as shaped by their daily experiences, many marked by ordinary transnational encounters.

[31] Interview, Lab'ûs, January 2005.

To a certain extent, their Salafi affiliation was a symptom of their embeddedness in the Yemeni environment.

By its ambivalent character, the indirect presence of Saudi Arabia restructures many identities in the local space. Since the change in status of Yemeni workers (through the decree of September 1990 and the 'Saudisation' laws in the job market), and because of the economic difficulties that the Kingdom has experienced transnationalism is handled more and more through intermediaries. Although these relations are hampered, they continue, changing their form and managing to work around the strategies of control that are implemented by states. In this framework, individuals who do not benefit directly from emigration are still actors in the change brought about by global phenomena.

In Yemen, and in Yâfi' in particular, migratory experiences and anecdotes, besides items on television and in other media, make the presence of Saudi Arabia a daily reality. For each person, this presence both attracts and repels. Since the 1980s but especially since unification, bilateral and transnational relations have been topics of great debates, and have undergone significant transformation. Physically, the experience of the *mahjar* has become ever more fragile and difficult to attain, leaving Engseng Ho to question the persistence of the *mahjar* itself.[32] The normalisation of bilateral relations through the signing of a border treaty in June 2000 did not prevent a tightening of conditions for entering and staying in Saudi Arabia, particularly in the framework of the 'Global War on Terror'. However there remains a 'Frontier', an immaterial space that exists in people's imaginations and informal interactions and is made more tangible through globalisation. The impossibility for many young people of becoming economically successful in the way that once was possible, makes them all the more desirous of attaining the 'Saudi way of life' in terms of the image that Saudi society and the Saudi state promote for themselves, especially as concerns religion. The particular capacity of religion to play a role in transnational space, and the universalist claims of Salafism, both work in favour of the transplantation of Salafism and of cultural and religious references connected to Saudi society.

As a consequence, students at college who are identified as Salafis have a symbolic relationship with Saudi Arabia that is one of admiration, but they remain conscious of the difficulties of emigration and the limits of piety in a society of which they have only the most approximate knowledge. As one of them observed:

[32] Engseng Ho, 'Yemenis on Mars: The End of Mahjar (Diaspora)', op. cit.

The path taken by the leaders of Saudi Arabia is just, but unfortunately people don't follow it. The people are often hypocritical. I think it is better to have a system like in Yemen where people are free and things are not required by laws.[33]

Others acknowledge that since Saudi Arabia is the 'centre of Islam' it is impossible not to love it. Although they explicitly claim to be followers of Muqbil al-Wâdi'î, the sharp criticisms he voiced with regard to Saudi Arabia until the late-1990s are not brought forward in the discourse of the young Salafis at the college. The 'reluctant' political dimension of Salafism and its development as a tendency opposed to the rule of the Âl Su'ûd are thus forgotten. The role of the Saudi government is generally approved by these students, particularly as concerns that government's role in 'promoting virtue and preventing vice', that is, in defending public morality, prohibiting cross-gender interactions and alcohol, and in the carrying out of physical punishments. One young Salafi put it this way:

It is the role of states like Saudi Arabia to make Islamic precepts respected. First it is necessary to say what is Evil, and then it becomes licit to use batons, for example, to punish people who drink alcohol or who do not attend prayers.[34]

Restrictions on personal freedoms are thus perceived as a necessity, and in this framework the Saudi system appears to be preferable to the Yemeni republican system. But this position is not free from contradictions. Despite their evident refusal to participate in elections and their principled rejection of democracy based on theology, *abû lihiya* students generally have a positive perception of the democratic form of political organisation. Democracy, however critical in its foundations, is supposed to guarantee certain public freedoms, which they cannot manage to label as negative, although Muqbil al-Wâdi'î and other prominent *'ulamâ'* did so consider them. Such is the case with street demonstrations, prohibited under Salafi doctrine in the name of one's allegiance to the *walî al-amr*. According to a young Salafi student, Saudi Arabia is not a perfect regime but the Yemeni government is no better. In order to support his argument he affirms this contention without perceiving the contradiction that underlies his position:

The difference between Yemen and Saudi Arabia is that here we have a republic, and they have a kingdom. A kingdom, by definition, cannot be free! [...] At the last dem-

[33] Interview, Lab'ûs, May 2005.
[34] Interview, Lab'ûs, May 2005.

205

onstration by doctors in Sana'a, when they demanded more jobs, the government sent in the army. At another demonstration the army killed three children. Frankly, is that democracy? I think that all countries have their problems![35]

In the course of another discussion with the same group of Salafi students, one of them, insisting upon the corruption in his country, joked that 'if we applied the physical punishments (*hudûd*) in Yemen that they use in Saudi Arabia, the President of Yemen would be lacking a hand!'

This ability to defend the Saudi model of piety as opposed to an allegedly liberal Yemeni system is not only contradictory but also limited in scope. While these students or teachers do exercise a certain pressure, even symbolic violence against other groups, because they represent a new Islamic norm, such polarisation and the constitution of a monopoly can function in a limited and closed space such as that of the college, but such things prove to be less effective outside that 'confined' environment, and at all events poorly structured. In addition, the concrete implications of such allegiances are quite meagre, in the end leaving Salafism to be no more than a marginal movement unable to significantly transform the social structures.

III. Activists Without Structures?

The Local Salafi Field

The idea of Salafism as mostly spontaneous cannot conceal the properly ideological and institutional dynamics at work in Yâfi'. Although only weakly structured, the local Salafi political-religious field is deployed in the region and gets external actors involved, directly and indirectly, through transnational flows.

In Yâfi', the large number of Salafis at the college does not appear to be linked to the existence of a regional network of institutes or mosques in which Salafi students might be trained and socialised. As such, its mostly spontaneous character is manifest, as is its poor institutionalisation. In fact, the main Salafi centres are all located in the former North Yemen. In Aden, no prominent Salafi figure has emerged and it is the activist branch or *salafiyya munazzama*, represented by al-Hikma and al-Ihsân associations, that is better established in the second largest city of the country. 'Abd al-Rahmân al-'Adanî's project in the late 2000s to establish his own institute in the outskirts of Aden faced strong criticism by Yahyâ al-Hajûrî who accused him of supporting *hizbiyya*

---

[35] Interview, Lab'ûs, May 2005.

and of siding with the dissident Salafis. A religious institute near Lahj in the village of Sabr had opened during the 1990s by a former student of al-Wâdi'î, Sâlih al-Bakrî, originally from Banî Bakr in Yâfi', but this initiative was limited and also faced accusations from the orthodox Salafis in Dammâj, Ma'bar and Sana'a of supporting Abû al-Hasan al-Ma'ribî and his political doctrine. Another Yâfi'i who studied at Dammâj, 'Abd Allâh Bin Ahmad al-Marfadî, managed a Salafi mosque in Aden, close to the local headquarters of al-Hikma association in al-Mansûra quarter. Despite their relative geographical proximity, such worship and teaching centres did not appear to be attended by the young people at the college in Lab'ûs. When they claimed direct participation in a national Salafi network, they more often than not referred to Dammâj and Ma'bar, centres that by all accounts were far from Yâfi'. Some students had, often during the year between high-school graduation and the beginning of their university curriculum, spent brief periods at some of these institutes, or had visited less august centres for a few days, especially one that was founded in the nearby Radfân region, right on the road to Aden. One Salafi student in Lab'ûs claimed:

> Here in Yâfi' there are no important religious centres. On the other hand during the summer, special classes (*dawrât*) can be organised in village mosques. People from Ma'bar in particular come to give series of conferences.[36]

Another student, in the English section, began in 2001 to take training at Dammâj, although he was still in high school at the time. He spoke of his admiration for the Dâr al-Hadîth centre:

> It's paradise there, the climate is excellent, the centre is surrounded by fields in which raisin grapes are being grown, and apples and pomegranates. It's really a beautiful environment! [...] I had a free room for five months in a dormitory. But if you have the money and you want to live quietly you can rent an individual room. The dormitory is located underneath the mosque and the library. [...] When I was at Dammâj, shaykh Muqbil was getting medical treatment in Germany and in Saudi Arabia, so unfortunately I never got the chance to meet him or attend one of his conferences.[37]

Out of these individual experiences and others, in Yâfi', a local Salafi field gradually grew up but by the mid-2000s it nevertheless still appeared to be lacking proper institutionalisation. Fragile and tangible as it was, the political or doctrinal orientation of the dozen or so mosques in Lab'ûs remained difficult

---

[36] Interview, Lab'ûs, May 2005.
[37] Interview, Lab'ûs, May 2005.

to define with certainty. In addition, it varied greatly depending on who was defining it. Mosques did not always appear to be affiliated with a determinate tendency and for this reason, both inside and outside the faculty, attendance at one or another did not directly constitute a discriminating factor in belonging to Salafism. In this rural-urban environment, religious 'offer' was in effect more limited than in cities. To the extent that the region is not subject to the same level of religious pluralism as on the highlands of the north, where groups of Zaydis, Shafi'is, Sufis, Ismailis and Salafis may be in competition, identities were less marked and less exclusive. However, despite being limited, religious and political plurality was a reality. If within the faculty a certain polarisation opposed two groups (Salafis and those loosely affiliated with the ruling GPC party, whose local head claimed to have 150 members in the student community),[38] the town of Lab'ûs and the region of Yâfi' apparently escaped such binary confrontation. The Islâh party and the Yemeni Socialist party were still active and well represented. The Sufis had been implanted there for a long time, being linked to the centre of Husayn Muhammad al-Hidâr in al-Baydhâ' and to Dâr al-Mustafâ in Tarîm. This religious group also had a bookstore and operated a worship centre in Lab'ûs.

Despite this diversity the local political-religious field was marked by a degree of mutual acceptance that contrasts with the debates that at the national and international level pit different Salafi movements, the Muslim Brotherhood, Sufis and socialists against each other. In Lab'ûs (but several kilometres from the university) the main Salafi mosque (al-Sîra) hosted Muhammad al-Imâm in early 2005 for a conference on cross-gender interactions and women (*Fitnat al-nissâ*). Two Salafi bookstores were located in Sûq Uktûbar (the name comes from the anti-colonial uprising of 14 October, 1963 in the neighbouring region of Radfân), the main shopping quarter of Lab'ûs. The first was affiliated with al-Ihsân association, and the second (bearing the explicit name of Maktabat al-Salafiyya) was smaller and aligned with Muqbilian orthodoxy. Both bookstores were nonetheless rather informal and not well stocked, another indication of the lack of institutionalisation of this tendency. They sold a few books and a few cassettes, sometimes very old, and seemed to be rather poorly informed on the current debates that affected the national or transnational Salafi movement.

In the Yâfi'î environment, the loose structure of the local Salafi field and the absence of any formal institution meant that students in the faculty as well as

[38] Interview, Lab'ûs, April 2005.

sympathisers outside were only weakly socialised into the doctrine they claimed to follow. If the internet had the potential to raise the awareness of the activists it still only had a marginal role due to the sluggishness of connections and the limited access to electricity. For these individuals, as for the general population, access to Salafi documentation, publications and knowledge remained limited and so the nature of adherence to Salafism could not systematically be characterised as profound or based on a deep understanding of the issues at stake. However the intrinsic passion of the discourses uttered by the Salafis was real, especially in the eyes of younger people looking for alternatives to the loose or otherwise localised and seemingly conservative Islam of their parents.

In many respects adherence to Salafism seemed to be merely formal and attached to nothing more than a few 'minor behaviours'. Some students and teachers had been to Dammâj or to another institute but most of them have only an imprecise notion of what Salafism actually implied. During a visit to Yâfi' in 1997, Muqbil al-Wâdi'î himself had been dismayed at the questions asked by those in attendance. He was expecting questions concerning profound theological issues, but the mostly young Yâfi'îs present only asked him about internal Salafi controversies and about his opinion concerning different foreign *'ulamâ'* ('Abd al-Rahmân 'Abd al-Khâliq, Salmân al-'Awda and Muhammad Surûr). Rather irritated, al-Wâdi'î then told them that all such questions were pointless, and he invited the young *ahl al-sunna* in his audience to 'seek useful knowledge' rather than focusing on pointless issues.

Much like in this telling anecdote, the students in the faculty had a taste for the debates and controversies that affected the Salafi field, but they did not always associate these with their local implications. Certainly, they listened to cassettes and shared them, and read books about internal schisms, made references to the major transnational figures, Yemeni and Saudi of quietist Salafism, heavily criticised the Muslim Brotherhood and the Sufis. But their concrete activation of quietists Salafi injunctions, requirements and prohibitions remained relative. Although some labelled the mosque nearest to the faculty 'partisan' and accused it of aligning with al-Islâh, Salafi students continued to pray there. At the individual level, their practices were in no way limited to injunctions, recommendations and prohibitions enunciated in sermons, books and anthologies of the prominent figures of quietist Salafis. As in the case of the Tablîghî activists analysed by Mohammad Talib, Salafis were referring to a variety of sources and were constantly reinterpreting what they had read or heard, confronting it in the environment in which they were fully embedded. Mohammad Talib writes:

A Tablîghî exists in a state of constant interaction with realities which enjoin different theories and practices. Other reality-defining agencies as well as constructions of the 'world' compete with each other for Tablîghî attentions. When a Tablîghî endeavours to walk straight, the researcher must depict the various undulations of the pathway. Similarly, when a Tablîghî appears to listen to a 'single drummer' the researcher should adequately portray the polyphony in the ideological voices with which he engages. We should work to portray a process, and not a product.[39]

It is specifically such a portrait and process that the Yâfi'î case studies draws. What characterises the Salafis' procedure is a desire, sometimes unconscious, to adapt to the local context and to local issues. Flexibility in practice can coexist quite well next to rigidity in theory. For one teacher of Islamic studies, being registered to vote does not contradict his adherence to Muqbilian Salafism, including its harsh critique of *hizbiyya*, of elections and of the *fitna* of Abû al-Hasan. Although he does follow the Salafi rule of not belonging to a political party, he still insists:

I can vote in the legislative elections if a good candidate appears. It doesn't matter if he is part of *al-Islâh*, the GPC, socialist or independent, the important thing is that he is honest.[40]

At a level that is less political but significant all the same, a certain plasticity accounts for a kind of normalisation of Salafism. Another young Salafi, working far from his family, relieves boredom by watching television—something explicitly prohibited by the doctrine to which he claims allegiance. Confronted with this contradiction, he admits that what he is doing is prohibited, but he says he only watches 'soccer matches and certain American action films'![41]

Consequently, somewhat in the manner of practices of adolescent rebellion or deviance that appear from time to time in European and American societies (hippies, punks, grunge, goths, and straight-edge), Salafism can be adopted in the form of a fashion or subculture, that is, as a simple social and generational marker whose meaning is adapted to its context.[42] In such a case it does not always fulfil a political function that might be determined *a priori*. In the specific

---

[39] Mohammad Talib, 'Construction and Reconstruction of the World in Tablîghî Ideology' in Muhammad Khalid Masud (ed.), *Travellers in Faith. Studies of the Tablîghî Jamâat as a Transnational Islamic Movement for Faith Renewal*, op. cit., p. 78.

[40] Interview, Lab'ûs, April 2005.

[41] Interview, Lab'ûs, February 2005.

[42] Dick Hebdige, *Subculture: The Meaning of Style*, London: Routledge, 1979.

environment of Yâfi' and of the Faculty of Education, the Salafi subculture functions through the appropriation of signs (beards, a style of clothing, 'minor behaviours') that bring with them a kind of dissociation and a symbolic rejection of other parts of society, but these may turn out to be simple 'fashion statements' that express self-exclusion, while in other cases they may become actual 'menaces to public order' when engaging in violence, stigmatisation and intolerance.

Still, such a portrait is a long way from the dominant image of Salafis as criminals linked to networks and groups that are part of international terrorism, expressions of a major 'menace to society' that justifies the occasional excesses of security forces. The adaptation and reappropriation of clothing-related markers and other distinctive practices according to the context explains why Salafism does not have the same meaning in the majority Zaydi environment of Dammâj that it has in Lab'ûs or even in Riyadh, Birmingham, Paris or Buffalo. Despite certain proselytising policies, the Saudi government is incapable of controlling the trajectories of Salafis because they are involved with an environment that is beyond that government's power.

Salafi Trajectories

The flexibility of individual practices observed among students and teachers of the college at Lab'ûs once again highlights the limits of any understanding of the Salafi phenomenon based solely on its ideological production. Such production, in the form of cassettes, books and pamphlets was instructive to analyse the issues that shape the Salafi political-religious field, and regarding the weakness of theories that associate Salafism with Saudi Arabia, but it is not of much help for understanding the scope of individual trajectories of Salafi activists.

As stated above, the identification and designation of Salafi students and professors at the college does not imply that such allegiances are fixed once and for all. Such identifications are based on objective indicators that have been described previously, but they are also flexible and far from definitive. The study of factors that lead some people to 'enter' Salafism has turned out to be interesting: the same is true for the analysis of processes that lead to people leaving the movement. Why do some become ex-Salafis? How does one handle one's departure from the group? These questions, often neglected in the study of activist trajectories, nonetheless allow us to understand that spiritual, as political, careers are fluid things.[43] Individual trajectories are not records of

[43] Danièle Hervieu-Léger, *La religion en mouvement: le pèlerin et le converti*, op. cit., p. 98.

unalloyed progress, but include changes of direction, phenomena of 'burnout' and retreat.[44]

In fact, to the extent that Salafism at the Faculty of Education represented a type of subculture that was not organised around formal institutions, it never established highly structured political-religious identities. Consequently, once its followers are removed from the particular environment that had motivated their act of political-religious affiliation at a particular moment, they may gradually abandon some of the more restrictive injunctions of the Salafi doctrine. This retreat from previous positions is not necessarily rational, and perhaps not brutal, either, or even permanent. Due to the more or less deviant character of Salafi practice, such a retreat becomes necessary for those who seek a level of social integration that Salafism only rarely allows in the long run.

In the closed environment of the college, shaped by transnational relations, the fall of socialism and the greater individualisation of religious identities, Salafism ties individuals together and can be understood as a resource for actors. Various behaviours function as social markers that allow them to be recognised within the peer group, and to distinguish themselves from others. Salafism is a simple and efficient way of creating a sort of strongly bound community that functions according to its own norms, without requiring a definite break from society. Within the group, having studied in a Salafi institute in Yemen can lead to the recognition of a certain notability that has some value in dormitory society, in the classroom, in the mosque or in handling relations with third parties (including intruders like myself). Socialisation by renowned clerics does grant individuals a quantum of legitimacy. Along these lines, charismatic figures may emerge among the students and teachers who are able to guide the others, leading them for a moment or for a longer period of time to adhere to the Salafi doctrine.

In Lab'ûs, the alleged menaces to society that qat, partisan *fitna* and urbanisation represent, provide reasons for the Salafis to stick together. The desire to preserve the unity of believers through the refusal of *hizbiyya* is itself a political act and statement, and creates cleavages. The microcosm of the college

---

[44] On the issue of retreat, role exit and careers, Howard Becker writes: 'Obviously, everyone caught in one deviant act and labelled a deviant does not move inevitably toward greater deviance [...]. The prophecies do not always confirm themselves, the mechanisms do not always work'. Howard Becker, *Outsiders: Studies in the Sociology of Deviance*, op. cit., p. 36. See also Olivier Fillieule (ed.), *Le désengagement militant*, Paris: Belin, 2005 and the seminal research on 'role exit' by Helen Rose Fuchs Ebaugh, *Becoming an Ex: The Process of Role Exit*, Chicago: Chicago University Press, 1988.

is not immune from debates, rivalries and internal conflict. The universalist vocation of Salafi doctrine, along with the emphasis on religious procedures and the fight against religious innovations reinforces a feeling of superiority, relative to the corruption of ordinary society. In this context the individualisation of religious identities paradoxically promotes a certain uniformity through the appearance of stereotyped practices that are factors of social cohesion. To the extent that Salafism is a fashion statement or subculture, each student tends to conform through practices and signs that are immediately identifiable. In this regard, belonging to the group is a powerful means of integration for individuals who often feel marginalised because of unemployment in their home societies, or because the 'Saudi way of life' to which they aspire has become more and more inaccessible.

This immediate capacity for social integration is in turn linked to the structure of the educational process. As mentioned earlier in this chapter, this system has a general tendency to value the Islamic norms that Salafis try to impose on society in general and at the college in particular. The cultural capital and the theological knowledge they bear are often recognised and appreciated by the teachers, particularly within the Islamic section. In the environment of the university, Salafis are implicitly encouraged by the institution on which they depend. The Arabic/Islamic section had about 140 students in 2005, mostly because it had the reputation of being the easiest. In this section not all students were Salafis, but they were most certainly a majority. Their seriousness and their intensity in class, their willingness to work and the fact that the teachers themselves generally subscribed more or less to the quietist Salafi doctrine they claimed to apply, made it possible for them to get good grades, which strengthened the stability of the group. Salafis were thus outsiders and moral reformers at the same time, and as such they were simultaneously stigmatised and valued highly.

Salafism was an integrating factor within the college and within the student community, but with regard to things that happened outside the school, its value was often reversed. Certainly, some Salafis with diplomas managed to get teaching jobs, to continue studying elsewhere or to help run a mosque, a bookstore or some other kind of activity that maintained a link to the 'Salafi economy'. Those who found a sort of 'Salafi niche' job of this kind could usually sustain their political and religious identity. But most students at some point had to re-evaluate their positions in regard to society as a whole. Such an observation also appears as relevant as regards to graduates from the leading Salafi institutes such as Dâr al-Hadîth. In fact, diplomas in religion are not worth much, even if one is trying to find work in Saudi Arabia or elsewhere. Students are well aware of the limitations of religious curricula. One student who had spent five months at Dammâj, and then a year at the university in Sana'a in the 'Science of the Qur'an' section explained the necessity of getting a diploma that would make getting a job possible later:

I quit my studies in Sana'a after a year because it was too far from my home [i.e.: in Radfân] and my family. So I registered for classes in Lab'ûs. I didn't want to continue at the school established by *shaykh* Muqbil because it does not grant a recognised diploma. [...] The *ahl al-sunna* centres like the one at Dammâj or Ma'bar do not actually help much in finding a job. The instruction is only religious and not broadly-based... it is important to get a diploma.[45]

In the same manner, a young professor in the Islamic section, trained for four years at the University of Aden but who wished to continue his studies elsewhere, decided that it was necessary to adapt to the requirements of his employer, that is, the Yemeni state that sought to monitor religious education. Despite his admitted closeness to the instructions given by quietist Salafis, he said that he did not want to study in their network of institutes, preferring to register at al-Îmân University, despite the fact that it was run by clerics close to the Muslim Brotherhood, a group he strongly criticised. But that school offered college credit equivalence, and the possibility of earning a diploma that would be recognised by the government, among others. In order to justify his choice he recalled that it is important to acknowledge the difference between the content of instruction and 'the partisan work that is going on there', thus between Abd al-Majîd al-Zindânî and other professors.[46] Faced with mundane and material imperatives, the intransigence expressed in the discourses of Salafi *'ulamâ'* was then only partially applied.

Another sign of the need for integration and recognition outside Salafi circles is the apparent unease of certain activists towards a number of their distinctive practices. The desire to set oneself apart from a corrupt society thus has limits. A significant anecdote exhibits this lack of assurance. In April 2006, the college was visited by 'Abd al-Wahhâb Râwah, former Minister of Education and new President of the University of Aden and as such the head of the Lab'ûs branch. Such a visit was a rare opportunity for both teachers and students, who wished to draw the visitor's attention to the dilapidated state of their dormitories, the lack of funds in general and the delay in payment of the funds granted by primary

---

[45] Interview, Lab'ûs, May 2005.
[46] Interview Lab'ûs, April 2005.

donor 'Umar Qâsim al-'Isâ'î. Because of all of this, it appeared important for everyone to project a favourable image of the student community, and each individual wished to do the same. The campus was cleaned up, and a large banquet was planned for all. The day of the visit, although classes were supposed to occur as scheduled while the President of the university was conducted on a tour of classrooms in the company of the local Dean and several local dignitaries, one third-year student in the Arabic/Islamic section appeared to become uncomfortable while attending his Islamic law class. As usual, he wore a *ma'waz* (a kind of skirt) that, accordingly to the Salafi doctrine he claimed to support, only stopped at mid-calf. But that day, in the face of an august visitor to Lab'ûs, and realising that his mode of dress might not meet with the approval of the visitors, he carefully covered his legs with his *'imâma*, thus attempting to hide what normally would be an intentionally distinctive practice. At that specific moment, a sign of his allegiance to Salafism seemed to have become something shameful. Without much doubt, other such reversals laid in store for him and for his fellow Salafi students, and they would all feel the need, at times, to adapt or to conceal certain practices.

Quite clearly, adherence to Salafism implies a number of constraints in daily life that few manage to stick to indefinitely. Avoiding all political discussion, all qat-chewing or all television (to mention two of the dominant modes of socialisation) is not easy over the long run. Salafis, deviant as they may appear, are symbolically in a state of revolt against their families, and as such are often subject to social pressure which sooner or later wears them down. For example, still on the occasion of the visit of the President of the University of Aden to Lab'ûs in April 2006, a Salafi teacher in his mid-thirties, who was in charge of student social activities, agreed to chew qat for the first time in his life. Sitting among his friends, he was rather carried away by the occasion, saying, 'If my father could see me I think he would throw a huge party! I'll have to call him up and tell him!' He insisted that his participation in this socialisation ritual was a one-time thing, and he was careful not to let his own students see him do it, lest they be disappointed in someone who normally set an example for them. One of his Salafi colleagues mockingly saw in this symbolic act the 'tightening of the devil's hold' on his friend.

These anecdotes indirectly recall the case of a Lab'ûs student named Sâlim. On his own, he exemplified a number of the dynamics described above. In fact, his 'career', his personality and his apparent motivations illustrate the relationship between Salafi political-religious practice and its environment, and also the relationships to transnational and migratory questions. I am part of this

narrative, since the relationship I formed with this student in the Arabic/
Islamic section was itself an interesting variable.

During my first stay in Lab'ûs in April and May of 2002 I met Sâlim. Through
his charisma, he represented real authority among students, and his expertise
in religious matters was recognised by all. His fidelity to the principles of quietist Salafism was the mainspring of his dominant position at the college. He was
particularly zealous, spending his afternoons listening to recordings of the suras
of the Qur'an, or of conferences given by Yemeni or Saudi Salafi *'ulamâ'*, especially Muqbil al-Wâdi'î. His sister was at that time the only female student at
the college. To the extent that he believed that the feminine voice should not
be heard in public, as also the face and hands of a woman should remain hidden, he acted as an intermediary for his sister to help her communicate with
teachers. He would sit with her in the back of a class and ask out loud the
questions that she would eventually whisper to him. In conformity with the
principles of Salafism which he sought to put into effect, when student elections were held he urged his friends not to participate. He denounced the
hizbiyya and the disorder that even such an election might create at the college.
He had briefly visited a Salafi institute, but he had rarely lived away from Yâfi',
where he was born. By any account, Sâlim had never left Yemen. During my
stay, he was initially particularly suspicious of me. My presence at the college
was condemned by him. He accused me of being a spy, tried to stir up other
students against me, refused to greet me and criticised the fact that I was not
susceptible to religious proselytising. Involuntarily, I probably weakened his
dominant position in the micro-environment of the college. Our exchanges
were limited to his attempts to make me convert to Islam, and these exchanges
were somewhat strained.

Three years later, I happened to come across Sâlim in the Sûq al-Salâm
quarter of Lab'ûs. Unexpectedly, he was happy to see me, and welcomed me
with warm words. He did not ask me if I had converted to Islam, but about
my family, and my marriage and whether I thought that Yâfi' had changed
since the last time we had met. As we went on talking, the subject of religion
did not come up directly. He told me what he had been doing, even speaking
of his private life (something that was rather unusual by local standards). In
June 2003 he had received his diploma with excellent grades. Nonetheless he
had remained unemployed but he married and decided to try his luck in Saudi
Arabia. In 2004 he used a pilgrimage visa (*'umra*) to go and look for work in
Jeddah. During that Ramadan he obtained a month-long contract in a clothing
store, but then became unemployed again. He also claimed that being away

from his family was hard for him as his first child had been born in his absence. He said that life in Saudi Arabia was good, but not for all the world would he have left his family in Yâfiʿ.[47] His attempt to live the expatriate life had failed. In a way, this failure represented his inability to convert his theological knowledge and his dominant position at the college into success in the job market. During his time in Saudi Arabia, he found out that the Yemeni Ministry of Education was willing to hire him, and he was later assigned to a primary school in a small village of the Dhî Nâkhab wâdî in Upper-Yâfiʿ region. He recalled:

The day my father called me to say that I had finally obtained a teaching position in a school, I was in Mecca. I had just finished praying near the Kaʿba, asking God to help me find a job! I was really happy, I went straight back to Yemen and started working in January 2005.

This brief account of Sâlim's story is nothing exceptional. It is however a vivid illustration of numerous processes that have already been presented, concerning the significance of migratory trajectories, and their often structuring character.

In terms of political-religious allegiances, the confrontation with the contingencies, responsibilities and difficulties of the world outside the college has its effects. Within the framework of my study, social, familial and professional integration, generally different from that which is produced inside the college, often appears to lead to development beyond the stage of intransigent Salafism. In the process, the restrictive distinctive practices end up being applied in a more flexible manner. However, this kind of normalisation is still no more automatic a thing than deviance itself and observance to the strict Salafi doctrine. The identification of mechanisms for a gradual or negotiated end to outsider status cannot mask other processes, more marginal, of increasing affirmation of deviance, especially through a passage to violence.

In May 2005 Sâlim, who had been an intransigent Salafi when I had left him three years earlier, appeared to have undergone a particular process. In fact, he no longer considered himself an adherent of the orthodox Salafism of Muqbil al-Wâdiʿî; he had joined the Hikma association. He said that he regularly read *al-Muntadâ*, the monthly publication of the association, which had been created in the early 1990s following internal disagreements within the Salafi current in Yemen. This young teacher evidently approved of the work of the association, both charitable and political, and he accepted the principle of institutionalisation of the Salafi movement. Without abandoning his distinctive clothing habits or his beard, he claimed to follow a movement that was severely criticised by Muqbil al-Wâdi'î and his partisans. Through al-Hikma, Sâlim started belonging to a political-religious movement that more explicitly and willingly claimed adaptation to the Yemeni context than Muqbilian Salafism. Nothing in Sâlim's statements or actions indicated that this form of normalisation was exclusive, or that it implied a rejection of his earlier practices. Nonetheless, his increased flexibility towards society and politics probably made it easier for Sâlim to participate in the activities, concerns and discussions of those around him. A sign of conforming to such norms established by third parties: as Sâlim was going to Aden to visit his relatives who were taking a holiday there, he took care to purchase for his father in Lab'ûs a quantity of the highest grade of qat—even though he continued to severely criticise qat-chewing. No doubt his old self would have perceived such an action as a symbol of his own weakness towards the moral and religious corruption of Yemeni society.

It is certainly difficult to establish an automatic cause and effect connection between the disappointing Saudi experience of Sâlim and the process of normalisation or to a certain extent of politicisation presented above. As claimed earlier, the issue of the necessity for social integration once outside the college appears as a powerful incentive to soften one's intransigence. Owing to the specific Yâfi'î context and to the importance of transnational connections, the Saudi variable should probably not be dismissed too quickly. The daily presence of the transnational in connection with migrations, investment and financing by the *mughtaribîn* structures individual aspirations and for a significant part explains the particular development of Salafism at the college in Lab'ûs. Religious identities are subjected to processes of individualisation: activist trajectories appear more flexible, more dependent on individuals' prior experiences and aspirations. Thus, leaving for a Saudi or Gulf city, being far from home and ending up unemployed are all experiences that are capable of producing disappointment and a rejection of the idealised Saudi model. Some, like Sâlim, probably thought they would be up to the task of reaching the 'Saudi dream' thanks to their religious practice or their diplomas. Still, in the *mahjar* as in Yemen, Salafism is only rarely a resource that can be mobilised to earn a revenue and a sufficient status. Despite the image attached to it, the Land of the Two Holy Places, which is subject to the laws of market economics and to the harsh realities of capitalism, generally places a higher value on the hard work of its immigrants than on the knowledge of apprentice *'ulamâ'* who move to that country. In addition, for the *mughtaribîn* and for those who were expelled in 1990, Salafism has little attraction. The ambiguous character of the migratory experience therefore only indirectly favours the diffusion of Salafism. In this framework, this political and religious practice appears to the students at the college as a kind of 'Saudisation' by default, or an *ersatz* form of the same. For Sâlim and for many others, in terms of economics, the 'Saudi way of life' remains illusory and inaccessible: only its 'scraps' in the form of a zealous and quietist interpretation of the religious texts can become a reality but then again only for a limited period of time.

The Yâfi'î case-study, specific as it is but not unique, helps draw a number of conclusions that are valuable in clarifying other contexts and other phenomena of religious transplantation. This field study did not base itself on abstract concepts or large-scale narratives, but approached Salafism by way of concrete examples, microsocial anecdotes and direct experience. This ethnographic research was necessary, because it is complementary to an analysis of ideological production via cassette recordings, biographies of outstanding individuals and other publications. Such an account has highlighted the necessity of distinguishing between the entrepreneurs in the political-religious field, the *'ulamâ'*, from the anonymous 'activists' or simply the 'sympathisers', more or less motivated, informed and organised, who try as best they can to apply Salafi doctrine. These people do not form a rigid, monolithic bloc, but are characterised by a set of practices that are infinitely varied, which actors appropriate for their own use with flexibility, as they use them to construct their identities. At another level, this study reveals the ordinary, everyday reality of transnational relations, and the way in which they affect Yemeni society, constructing a space that can properly be described as transnational or translocal. Dynamics of different levels become involved in this process, and phenomena of cultural hybridisation, the reduction of distances and the overlapping of spaces appear, affecting the whole. Yâfi'î Salafism is concretely involved in transnational flows and constitutes a tangible mark of the interpenetration of societies. The pluralism of allegiances, the transplantation of identities and the variety of connections beyond borders are all structuring components of globalisation.

A 'grassroots' approach also helps challenge once again the mechanical discourses that reduce changes in political and religious allegiance in Yemen to a simple 'imported' phenomenon supposedly arranged by the Saudi government for its 'self-interest rightly understood'. The expansion of Salafism proves in fact to be linked to the intensity of transnational relations, but at the same time depends on many complex processes that are largely unpredictable, but which cannot be neglected, since they often reveal the deep dynamics that underlie events that affect the Arabian Peninsula. Obviously, state diplomacy has an effect on these transformations and recompositions. As happened in 1990, when Yemeni workers were expelled, and in connection with the 'Saudisation' of certain jobs, it can disturb transnational relations. But state policy is neither central nor even univocal in this connection, and obviously it is not always successful in achieving its aims. At any rate, states are unable to interrupt the interpenetration of societies.

Because of this, any future congruence between state policy and the concrete development of social or religious practices does not necessarily imply a cause and effect relationship. If one takes into account, in analysis, the closed environment of the Faculty of Education in Lab'ûs, the wide range of social processes—phenomena of individualisation of religious identities, the unintentional aggregation of instances of behaviour and the construction of an ambiguous imaginary concept concerning migration to Saudi Arabia—sketch Salafism as something flexible, even autonomous or spontaneous. This observation, added to the analysis of the strained relations between the Yemeni Salafi movement and the Saudi government, is the basis for alternative narratives of the 'voyage' undertaken by Salafism. These narratives put individual experiences at the centre of the analysis and make it clear that Salafis are not some kind of puppet manipulated by an invisible Saudi hand, exercising its influence beyond its own borders.

PART 3

AN INTEGRATED SALAFISM

6

A 'YEMENISATION' PROCESS?

THE QUEST FOR ORIGINS

In the context of his 'travelling theory', developed to analyse intellectual and literary movements of the nineteenth and twentieth centuries, Edward Said invited his readers to distinguish between different steps of the process of transplantation or relocation of such movements. Although this approach was developed in order to analyse objects that are generally very different from Salafism, it turns out to be quite relevant for the study of transnational relations and social innovations. Over and above the question of transplantation itself, Said emphasised the phenomena of resistance to change and adaptation to context that are generated by the emergence of a social practice that is perceived as imported or exogenous. In this way he explained the extent to which movement from one environment to another could bring about a transformation and re-evaluation of practices. Taking account of the voyage of Salafism in translocal space, and studying the 'conditions of its acceptance' and the resistances that confronted it are the objects of this third section. With regard to this matter, Edward Said noted:

The specific problem of what happens to a theory when it moves from one place to another proposes itself as an interesting topic of investigation. [...] What happens to it when, in different circumstances and for new reasons, it is used again and, in still more different circumstances, again?[1]

---

[1] Edward Said, *The World, the Text and the Critic*, op. cit., p. 230.

Further on in his book, after exploring the necessity for a literary critic (and thus a political scientist, sociologist or anthropologist as well) to take into consideration the malleable nature of theories (and by extension, social practices), and the fact that they should never be elevated to the status of dogmas, Edward Said explained:

To measure the distance between theory then and now, there and here, to record the encounter of theory with resistances to it [...], to map the territory covered by all the techniques of dissemination, communication, and interpretation [...]: if these are not imperatives, they do at least seem to be attractive alternatives. And what is critical consciousness at bottom if not an unstoppable predilection for alternatives?[2]

It is precisely this active search for alternatives that has been at the centre of my approach throughout this monograph. The large-scale mechanical narrative of the transplantation of Salafism has thus been given a sort of counter-field, in the effort to take into consideration the ambiguity of migratory trajectories and the difficult relations Yemeni Salafi entrepreneurs have had with Saudi society and the state that governs it. The force and the meaningful nature of transnational religious relations directly blur the notion of a point of origin. Quietist Salafism is as much the product of a successful process of transplantation as it is a matter of recomposition within Yemeni society, and it cannot from that point be considered exogenous. Building on the idea of its embeddedness in the translocal Yemeni context I assert in this section that, more than by some process of 'Saudisation', contemporary Salafism is really characterised by a certain 'Yemenisation', that is, a capacity to adapt to local issues and practices. Transplantation forces a re-orientation of repertoires of action, as much as it causes changes with regard to the opportunities and constraints that affect actors. The malleability of practices, the necessity of not limiting the analysis of the Salafi phenomenon to a matter of what '*ulamā*' and high-profile individuals produce, as well as the process of adaptation, all put into question the concrete content of the Salafi identity in the Yemeni context. Neither allegiance to Saudi Arabia, nor strict adherence to the doctrine established by Muqbil al-Wâdi'î and his heirs, quietist Salafism appears to be definable only through certain distinctive practices. In the end, all this demonstrates this political and religious identity's ordinariness, and illustrates the limits of all efforts to conceptualise something like a Salafi essence.

[2] Ibid., p. 247.

I. How can one be Yemeni?

One of the most tangible signs of the embeddedness of Salafism in the Yemeni environment undoubtedly has to do with the capacity of its partisans, activists and entrepreneurs to compete locally with other identities and allegiances, either religious, political or geographic. Zaydis, Sufis and the Muslim Brotherhood are examples of competitors, but affiliation to Salafism also contends with other individual or group identities whether tribal, social, national or historic. Such a situation brings naming and blaming arguments but it also favours self-justifications and strategies through which each group emphasises its own legitimacy through authenticity. The issues linked to origins become important stakes in these fierce competitions. While the alleged Saudi origin of the Salafis is often highlighted, Sufis are accused by the Salafis of practicing associationism (*shirk*) when they practice the worship of saints and when they visit the tombs of saints. Twelver Shi'ites and Zaydis are said to be guilty of insulting the companions of Prophet Muhammad (*subb al-sahâba*) and the Caliphs 'Umar and 'Uthmân because they hold in particular reverence the fourth Caliph 'Alî Bin Abî Tâlib. The partisans of the Jamâ'at al-Tablîgh, a missionary group that originated in India which is marginally present in Yemen, are criticised because they consider certain *hadîth* as authentic, while the Salafis consider them to be false or weak (*dha'îf*), and because they take as a point of reference the Hanafi school of jurisprudence. As stated earlier, tribal affiliations are deemed pre-Islamic and considered with suspicion as they are built on a restrictive allegiance and a principle of inequality between Muslim believers.

The forms that these inter-faith and inter-identity competitions and mutual resistances take within the Yemeni political and religious field are indicative of many things concerning Salafism itself. More so than elsewhere, the central nature of the critique of *hizbiyya* is a main characteristic of the Salafi movement in Yemen. This adaptation is an indication on the one hand of the limitation of Salafism's supposed apolitical nature, and on the other, of its opposition to the tribal divisions and multiparty politics, which are part of the dominant context. Refusal and stigmatisation of political participation as well as an allegiance to the *walî al-amr* are a direct response to the principle of *khurûj* (revolt) which for long remained associated in the Yemeni environment to the Zaydi concept of *khurûj 'alâ al-hâkim al-zâlim*. In this regard, the fact that Muqbil al-Wâdi'î's original religious allegiance and his early socialisation occurred within Zaydism are likely to have played a role in his rejection of such a concept and of political participation, just as they were instrumental during his encounter with the very different religious context in Saudi Arabia. The social innovation of Yemeni Salafism thus incorporates a break with the Zaydi environment into which it developed from the late 1970s. In Saudi Arabia, but also in the pre-and post-revolutionary Yemeni context that Muqbil al-Wâdi'î witnessed in Sa'da, affiliates to the Muslim Brotherhood emerged as the main alternative to the power of the monarchy and to republican regimes that were not religiously inspired. Although they were often instrumentalised and co-opted, the main forces of opposition in Saudi Arabia were to a large extent influenced by the political project of the Muslim Brothers.[3] Social and educational actions carried out by their activists within the societies of the Arabian Peninsula established them as a new Islamic reference. Faced with this movement and with Zaydism, both of which encouraged political participation in some way or another, Salafism as formulated by Muqbil al-Wâdi'î and his partisans took shape as a third, essentially reactive, movement which aimed to preserve Muslim believers from involvement in political matters. Zaydism in the north, the Muslim Brotherhood across Yemen and indeed the entire Arab world, and the Sufis in a variety of regions became the competitors and the opponents which Salafism had to stigmatise, and from which it had to distinguish itself.

Competition Over Origins

Forced to deal with competition within the political and religious fields, Salafi entrepreneurs and activists are in a way compelled to demonstrate the endogenous character of their movement, and their autonomy with regard to Saudi matters. Quietist Salafi doctrine as formulated in the 1980s by Muqbil al-Wâdi'î claims universality and rejects political engagement, a statement contested by its opponents. In the Yemeni environment, Salafism cannot allow itself to be described as simply imported, but is inclined to further prove its embeddedness in local culture. The transplantation of this political and religious identity metaphorically reaches a stage corresponding to what could be termed a 'Yemenisation' phase. This transformation, like the voyage described by Edward Said, in its entirety, is not necessarily a chronological one, but involves distinct dynamics that sometimes operate together or may even contradict one another. It also involves the debate about homogenisation and the cultural effects of globalisation. Do these processes bring about a global, uniform culture, shared by all, of which Salafism would be a component? Or are phenomena of cultural exchange and transplantation characterised by processes of fragmentation, hybridisation and reappropriation of practices and identities?

[3] See Madawi Al-Rasheed, *Contesting the Saudi State*, op. cit., pp. 59–101.

It is understood that the concept of 'Yemenisation', like that of 'Saudisation', cannot be considered as natural, or as hermetically sealed. The concrete integration of Salafism within transnational dynamics, like the interpenetration of societies, prevents us from thinking that relocalisation is exclusive, or that it can call off other processes such as transnationalism. Like 'Saudisation', 'Yemenisation' is expressed through certain symbolic practices, and in the recourse to particular references considered by most to be 'authentically' Yemeni. 'Yemenisation' constitutes first and foremost a metaphor or an aspiration, that is, a desire to match up with a dominant image (sometimes stereotypical) that society holds up to itself, especially in connection with forms of tribalism or with Islamic purity. In general, this process (not necessarily centralised or self-conscious on the part of the actors involved) challenges the idea according to which practices tend to become more uniform as they are subject to transplantation processes.

In Yemeni politics, the question of the authenticity of various actors is the object of heated debates and symbolic struggles. In one way or another, everyone's authenticity is challenged, even that of the actors who appear *a priori* to epitomise the 'Yemeni identity'. In an implicit fashion, each movement and each actor tends to offer a different definition of the characteristics that are allegedly intrinsic to the Yemeni history and society. As highlighted previously, the Salafis are nonetheless the preferred target of this argument. Their relationship with Saudi Arabia and with 'Wahhabism' points at their supposed imported character, and they can find themselves delegitimised on this count. Such narratives only intend to characterise the Salafis as feudal bondservants of Saudi Arabia, and so to conclude that they are enemies who have infiltrated Yemen and who are thus completely illegitimate.

However, Arab genealogy and the mythical distinction between the descendents of 'Adnân and Qahtân, equivalent to a distinction between Arabs of the north and Arabs of the south, plays in favour of the Salafis and allows them to strike back at the attacks aimed at them in the religious and political fields. Accused of being a political and religious movement alien to Yemen, the Salafis can claim in turn a certain national authenticity. Both the Sufis and Zaydis, the principal foils and opponents of the Salafis in Yemen, see their supposedly authentic Yemeni identity called into question. Indeed both grant Hashemites, descendents of Prophet Muhammad, a natural leadership over their community or group. However these Hashemites claim descent from 'Adnân and are thus to be characterised as Northern Arabs. Popular mythology has it that Hashemites came from Mecca to Yemen after the coming of Islam. In such a narrative, the Qahtânî tribes (sociologically the main 'clients' of Salafism in Yemen) appear to be the only 'real' Yemenis. Such affiliation allows Salafis, despite their acknowledged novelty, to highlight their own legitimacy and to portray their competitors as the true aliens.

The terms of the debate over origins are evidently more complex than that. Zaydism certainly represents many of the features of Yemeni society, particularly since it was the doctrine of the imams, but it did not originate from the Arabian Peninsula as such. In fact, Zaydism as a distinct religious identity emerged in the eighth century in Mesopotamia and Central Asia, and is thus also an importation in its way, something its opponents never miss a chance to point out. Legends tell that the Zaydi state was established in the southern part of the Arabian Peninsula at the end of the ninth century following a call for mediation issued by two tribes that had been at war. These Yemeni, Qahtânî, tribes were incapable of settling the conflict by themselves, and so they turned to external actors—Hashemite clans, who enjoyed a high degree of religious legitimacy. Following this mediation, the Zaydi Imamate was founded, and this institution would continue to exist until 1962. The peacemaking role of Zaydi leaders and elites, represented up to the present day in the *hijra* (territory designated as sanctuary, in which conflicts and commercial disputes may be settled),[4] is supposed to confer upon the *sâda* or Hashemites the ability to maintain calm, faced with the 'chaos' that the warlike world of tribes represents. By all accounts, such a representation of the role of Hashemites on the highlands of Yemen is a distortion of reality,[5] but it remains strongly rooted in people's minds, and lends itself easily to the symbolic struggle being carried on in the political and religious fields. Consequently, the historical externality of the Hashemites is

[4] Ismâ'îl Bin 'Alî al-Akwa', *Les hijra et les forteresses du savoir au Yémen*, Sana'a: CFEY, 1996.

[5] In his *Yemen Chronicle*, Steven Caton gives an interesting and detailed account of a conflict that took place in the early 1980s in Khawlân al-Tiyal and whose structure directly put into question the opposition between a tribal world ruled through violence and a specific *hijra* ruled by the *sâda*. Steven Caton explains that his Hashemite interlocutors were used to designating their *hijra* world as exterior to chaos and anarchy (*fawdhâ*) and to portraying the tribes as uncivil. Yet while the author (who was then studying tribal poetry) was residing in a *hijra*, an event disrupted such a representation and triggered a war that would last for years: two young daughters of a neighbouring tribe had been abducted and a member of the *sâda* was soon designated as the culprit, thus highlighting the ineffectiveness of the Manichean representation of the two main Yemeni social strata. Steven Caton, *Yemen Chronicle: An Anthropology of War and Mediation*, New York: Hill and Wang, 2005.

an advantage for them, but also makes them suspect in the eyes of society. Building on such a paradox, Muqbil al-Wâdi'î maliciously pointed out in a text on Zaydism the fact that this sect arrived rather late in Yemen, in the 'third century of the Hijra', by contrast with the *ahl al-sunna* he claimed descend from who were born during the first years of Islam.[6]

In addition, although the long-lived regime of the Zaydi Imamate was of central importance in the struggle against foreign invasions (especially against the Ayyoubid dynasty in the twelfth century and the Ottomans in the sixteenth and nineteenth centuries), the nationalist reputation of Zaydism lost some of its relevance in recent history. In fact, during the Civil War that followed the republican revolution of 26 September, 1962 in North Yemen, the defence of the ousted Zaydi regime was handled by troops armed and financed by Saudi Arabia. Republicans for their part received support from Saudi Arabia's regional rival, Egypt, which sent as many as 70,000 troops. Much later, especially at the time of the Sa'da war, the revival that Zaydism had experienced since the 1990s was taken by many Yemenis as connected to the Iranian revolution and thus to Twelver Shi'ism. Consequently, despite its historical position, and the fact that it perfectly represents many things that are specific to Yemen, and was actually adopted by Qahtâni tribes, Zaydism like Salafism cannot completely escape being accused of being foreign.

Salafis in Competition with Sufis in Tarîm

The same holds true of the Sufis as they also grant privileged status to Hashemites. As with the Zaydis, the leaders of the Sufi brotherhoods have a very ambiguous relationship with the Yemeni identity. Despite a history of 'transplantation' similar to that of Zaydism, they put themselves forward as the emblem of local authenticity, and attribute their renewed popularity since the 1990s to a return to traditional Islam and to popular beliefs. This claim and this particular type of connection to regional, 'autochthonous' history led Alexander Knysh in his study on a Sufi revival in Hadramawt to opine that the Sufis had a comparative advantage over the Salafis and over other inheritors of Muslim reformism.[7] In this region, the Hashemites, once allies of the British

---

[6] Muqbil al-Wâdi'î, *Maqtal al-shaykh Jamîl al-Rahmân al-Afghânî* [The assassination of shaykh Jamîl al-Rahmân al-Afghânî], op. cit., p. 3.

[7] On the issue of competition over origins, Alexander Knysh writes: 'I would argue that, unlike the salafi (reformist) master discourse, which is perceived by many Yemenis as a foreign importation (either from Egypt or Saudi Arabia), the 'Sufi' movement of

Empire, now aspire, after a brief and destructive socialist episode, to form once more the intellectual, religious and political elite of the region. The high value they claim to place upon local identity should in theory prevent them from being accused of being an exogenous movement.

But the manner in which they would represent the national identity appears to most Yemenis and to the country's rulers as a little flawed. Since the 1960s, in the North and in the South, Yemen has undergone profound changes, characterised especially by the rejection, at least symbolically, of traditional Hashemite elites by republican ideology. The Zaydi *sâda* and the Sufis have been the principal victims of this movement. In fact, for their Salafi opponents, the many saints worshipped by the Sufis are commonly considered foreigners because most came from the northern part of the Arabian Peninsula. During the war of 1994 many of the Sufis took sides with the secessionists, something interpreted by their detractors as a sign of their allegiance to foreign powers (particularly Saudi Arabia, connected to them through rich merchants of Hadrami origin). In this context the defeat of the secessionists appears to be part of a profound movement in favour of the eviction of the Hashemites, a levelling of social categories and a rewriting of history at the expense of this group, which for centuries had claimed both material and spiritual power. For Engseng Ho, in the aftermath of the war, the destruction of Sufi tombs by the Salafis further

Habib 'Umar [ie: Bin Hafiz] and his followers (as well as other Sufi-based movements in contemporary Yemen) cast themselves as resuscitators and protectors of the 'native' spiritual tradition'. Alexander Knysh, 'The Tariqa on a Landcruiser: The Resurgence of Sufism in Yemen', *Middle East Journal*, vol. 55, no. 3, 2001, p. 412. Further in the same article he asserts: 'To counter their perceived lack of local roots, the Salafis have to demonstrate the relevance of their discourse to the problems faced by their homeland. To this end, they are compelled to couch their views in a pan-Islamic, universalist rhetoric, which for many Yemenis, still rings hollow. This does not mean that the 'nativist' movement is necessarily parochial and anti-global, as the international ramifications of Habib 'Umar's educational and missionary project finely demonstrate. On the other hand, despite the purported international character of the Salafi movement in Yemen, it sometimes can be appropriated by tribal leaders seeking to assert their independence (or distinct identity) *vis-à-vis* the government or their tribal rivals who adhere to a more patriarchal (local) version of the Islamic tradition. As a result, somewhat paradoxically, the pan-Islamic, transnational discourse of the *salafiyya* becomes 'localised' through its integration into the parochial politics of Yemeni provinces'. Ibid., p. 414. See also, Alexander Knysh, 'Contextualizing the Salafi-Sufi Conflict (from the Northern Caucasus to Hadramawt)', op. cit.

placed the heritage of the Prophet's descendants—as well as their once political and religious pre-eminence—at a distance:[8]

Even ancestors and saints were evicted from their graves. Digging deeper still, those with very long memories thought of southern Yemen as now caught up with its northern compatriots, republicans who three decades earlier had evicted their own sayyids [i.e., *sâda*], the Zaydi imams. All sayyids as offspring of the Prophet from Mecca, were really northern Arabs, descendants of 'Adnân; true Yemenis, in contrast, were southern Arabs, sprung from the loins of Qahtân, in the reckoning of really ancient genealogy.[9]

Despite the fact that they are not established in very many locations in Yemen, Sufis nonetheless constitute a local alternative to Salafism. The presence of Sufi centres in Tarîm, al-Baydhâ', Aden, al-Hudayda and in the region of the Hujariyya, a certain editorial dynamism and the international charisma of some figures allows Sufism to oppose the new Salafi entrepreneurs with a religious practice that does not break so sharply with local traditions due to its strong association with the Hashemite elites, but still appears to be involved with modernity through its transnational connections.

In the specific Hadrami context, the alleged automatic link between Salafism and 'Wahhabism' (and thus involving a relationship with the successive Saudi states) is nothing new. This association dates from the early nineteenth century, at which time the inheritors of Muhammad Bin 'Abd al-Wahhâb, allies of the first Saudi state (1744–1818), conducted a campaign to destroy the tombs of 'Alawî saints revered by Sufis in Hadramawt.[10] During the contemporary period, the most significant and most widely publicised expression of the competition between Sufis and Salafis in that region occurred during the episodes of violence in 1994–1995. This violence had religious roots: the rejection of *shirk* (association with divine attributes) and of the notion of intercession on the part of Muslim saints. Muqbil al-Wâdi'î himself asserted that it was not permitted to pray alongside those he termed the *qubûriyûn*, that is, Sufis who worship tombs.[11] The episodes of violence took place as the result of a heated debate that had

---

[8] The privileged place given by the Yemeni government since the turn of the twenty-first century to Hadrami Sufi brotherhoods should somehow nuance this reading of history, according to which the destruction of tombs is the endpoint of a vast anti-Hashemite historical process carried on by the republican state.

[9] Engseng Ho, *The Graves of Tarim: Genealogy and Mobility across the Indian Ocean*, op. cit., p. 328.

[10] Ibid., p. 315.

[11] Muqbil al-Wâdi'î, sound recording, *Shaykh Muqbil ibn Haadee answering questions in Birmingham*, 1997.

emerged in the early twentieth century.[12] In the case of the anti-Sufi raids of the mid-1990s, religious motivation was only part of the issue. The political context of that period as well as a certain category-based animosity build on rejection of the Hashemites, explained the violence of Salafis (along with that of other Islamist groups) towards the Sufis. Hashemite members of Sufi elites, among which ʿAbd al-Rahmân al-Jifrî, head of the League of the Sons of Yemen (*Râbita abna al-Yaman*), as well as non-sufi Hashemites, ʿAlî Sâlim al-Bîdh and Haydar Abû Bakr al-ʿAttâs, had taken the lead in the southern secession of 1994.

Since these violent episodes, competitive relations within the religious and political fields in Yemen have somewhat cooled off. This reduction in tension has accompanied the social and political integration of Sufis. Beginning with the legislative elections of 1997, following which al-Islâh ceased its participation in the government, the Sufis began gradually to move closer to the GPC ruling party, before becoming an important ally in Hadramawt. As a consequence, the late 1990s and 2000s witnessed a significant revival of Sufism in the fore-front of the political scene.[13] In a system largely based on clientelist politics and patronage, the new alliance of Sufism with the government has most likely enhanced the attractiveness of that religious identity. A member of the Islâh party, who at one time had been close to the Salafis in al-Hudayda explained that students who received a diploma from the *Kulliyyat al-ʿulûm al-sharʿiyya* (a private school run by Muhammad ʿAlî al-Murʿî, a local Sufi figure and a GPC member of Parliament) 'could get a post in the administration without diffi-culty'. According to this man, this was a sign that the Sufis 'supported the government, and that the government supported them!'[14] In the town of Tarîm, the establishment of an important Sufi teaching centre, Dâr al-Mustafâ, in 1996 around the figures of al-Habîb ʿAlî Zayn al-ʿAbidîn al-Jifrî (son of aforemen-tioned ʿAbd al-Rahmân al-Jifrî) and al-Habîb ʿUmar Bin Muhammad Bin Hafiz undoubtedly redynamised this religious identity by lending it transnational prestige. In such a fast-evolving context, the description given by David Buch-man in 1997, of a Sufism that was persistently under pressure and obliged to conceal itself, appeared a little dated.[15] Among the signs of the rapprochement

---

[12] On this subject, see Alexander Knysh, 'The Cult of Saints and Islamic Reformism in Early Twentieth Century Hadramawt', *New Arabian Studies*, no. 4, 1997, p. 139–167.

[13] Alexander Knysh, 'The Tariqa on a Landcruiser: The Resurgence of Sufism in Yemen', op. cit.

[14] Interview, Sanaʿa, June 2005.

[15] David Buchman, 'The Underground Friends of God and their Adversaries: a Case

with the government were the multiple visits to Dâr al-Mustafâ by President Sâlih since 2002, and active Sufi participation in the election campaign of GPC candidates in Hadramawt during the legislative elections of April 2003.[16] Since 2002, despite the limited representativeness of Sufism, which by all standards remains rather marginal among the wider public, al-Habîb 'Umar Bin Hafîz has hosted the religious television programme presented by the state TV channel during the month of Ramadan. Such a position was a clear indication of the government's will to promote his religious movement.

In a way, the co-opting of the Sufis of Hadramawt also allowed the government to benefit from Sufi connections to important networks outside Yemen. To an even greater degree than the Salafis, the Sufi brotherhoods are part of dynamic transnational connections. While being persecuted by the socialist government during the 1970s and 1980s, Sufi elites found refuge in cities like Jeddah and Dubai, making use of a number of economic or political networks that spawned well beyond the Arabian Peninsula. Much like Zaydism, these were essentially structured around inter-Hashemite connections. Despite its recent establishment, the Dâr al-Mustafâ centre in Tarîm quickly became part of a large international network that extended from the United Kingdom to India, passing through the Sudan, the United Arab Emirates, Egypt and Saudi Arabia: al-Habîb 'Alî al-Jifrî was born in Jeddah, lives part of the year in Abu Dhabi and ranks among the most popular transnational clerics being affiliated to a variety of foundations and institutes across the globe. Many of Dâr al-Mustafâ students are themselves Saudi and appear to be playing an increasing role in the religious field. Interestingly these links highlight the fact that religious transnational relations between Saudi Arabia and Yemen are not all one way, and are not all limited to Salafism. They also highlight the great diversity of social, political and religious identities in Saudi Arabia, a country that is far from a monolith. The Hadrami, or more generally Yemeni, origin of many Saudis appears to encourage the continuation of, or return to, social practices associated with the 'homeland'.

In Tarîm in the mid-2000s, the division of public space also indicated how much the status of Sufism had changed. Such identity no longer had to conceal itself: relations in the local religious and political field appeared to have become

Study and Survey of Sufism in Contemporary Yemen', *Yemen Update*, no. 39, 1997, pp. 21–24.

[16] Amira Kotb, *La tariqa Ba'Alawiyya et le développement d'un réseau soufi transnational*, MA dissertation, IEP d'Aix-en-Provence, 2004, p. 75.

more peaceful and Sufis in a way had the upper hand. Still the presence of competition between antagonistic identities was immediately visible in the religious capital of Hadramawt.

For centuries, the town of Tarîm, located in the Hadrami valley has been a renowned centre of learning and spirituality. In the mid-2000s, it appeared as a kind of open religious market, built upon tradition but open to the world through the Hadrami diaspora, and because of the many foreign students who came there. In such a small space, experiences and transnational exchanges with Indonesia, Saudi Arabia, the Comoros Islands and the United States mixed and identities collided and competed with one another. Numerous mosques, associations and bookstores that support different movements faced one another.

Probably more so than elsewhere in Yemen, resistance to Salafism was fully and openly expressed as it was then the Sufis who dominated the 'religious market' in Tarîm. Despite the trading of insults leading to occasional clashes, there apparently was a baseline level of mutual respect or just benign indifference. Each Monday night the Muhammad Bin 'Abd al-Wahhâb bookstore (whose name expresses allegiance to the Salafi movement and hostility to Sufi practices quite precisely) on the central plaza of Tarîm turned off its speakers and shut shop early for a weekly conference of Sufi masters of Dâr al-Mustafâ, located a couple of kilometres outside town. Sufis settled in the middle of the plaza, gathered their sympathisers while the Salafis were silenced and had to find temporary 'refuge' elsewhere.

In Tarîm, the Sufis drew on foreign sources in order to strengthen their anti-Salafi pitch. A store affiliated with the Sufi networks of that holy town offered a number of works that put into question the legitimacy of Salafi doctrine. One of these, published in Singapore by a cleric originating from the Hadrami diaspora, entitled *Contemporary Salafism: origins and methods*[17] tried to link Salafism to violence and the practice of *takfîr*. Another, *Wahhabism in Contradiction to the Qur'an and the Sunna*[18] was intended to show that pilgrimages to tombs, including the tomb of the Prophet, are not proscribed by Islam.

Confronted with such competition and Sufi revival, the Salafis seemed a bit obsolete in Tarîm. The main Salafi mosque (al-Sunna) hardly compared to the Sufi worship centres sitting alongside imposing bookstores, whose international

---

[17] Mustafâ 'Abd al-Rahmân al-'Attâs, *al-Salafiyya al-mu'âsira: usûluhâ wa asâlîbuhâ*, [Contemporary Salafism: origins and methods], Singapore: Karjây al-mahdûda, 1992.

[18] 'Umar 'Abd al-Salâm, *Mukhâlafat al-wahhâbiyya lil-qur'ân wa al-sunna* [Wahhabism in contradiction to the Qur'an and the sunna], Beirut: Dâr al-Hidâya, 1995.

appeal was evidenced by the number of foreign customers. In order to give their preaching a makeover, the local Salafis tried to go on the offensive. Their modest centre, run by Abû Sa'îd al-Hadhramî, had in early 2005 invited a trainer from Dammâj to advise them and to reorganise their course offerings.

In this part of Yemen, Muqbilian Salafism appeared as only marginal, although the region is the most tightly linked to Saudi Arabia. The nearest significant teaching institute established by former students of Dâr al-Hadîth was 300 kilometres away from Tarîm, located in al-Shihr on the Indian Ocean coast, near al-Mukallâ . It was until the mid-2000s headed by 'Abd al-Rahmân al-'Adanî (al-Mar'î), who would later come at odds with the Salafi leadership in Dammâj. Apart from a few bookstores (particularly the one already mentioned, which sold cassettes and printed tracts by Muqbil al-Wâdi'î, Yahyâ al-Hajûrî, Rabî' al-Madkhalî and so on against the Sufis, the Muslim Brotherhood, or still other 'ulamâ', Yemeni or foreign, including Abû al-Hasan al-Ma'ribî) that showed that there was some demand for the Salafi doctrine, the dominant trend of Yemeni Salafism was poorly established, and had apparently fallen victim to the internal schisms that have opposed the direct heirs of Muqbil al-Wâdi'î, the partisans of Abû al-Hasan al-Ma'ribî and the members of the Ihsân and Hikma associations. Locally, the latter gained a broader base of social support thanks to the charisma of its local leader, Ahmad Hasan al-Mu'allim, who carried out significant charitable work.[19] In addition, together with al-Ihsân, thanks to its local networks, its flexible doctrine and its connections with merchants operating in Saudi Arabia or Qatar, the Hikma association appeared to be considered somehow more endogenous than Muqbilian Salafism which historically as well as institutionally was too closely associated to former North Yemen. Regional tensions and the rise of a popular secessionist stance in the former governorates of P.D.R.Y. since the late 2000s decade are likely to have only confirmed such a trend.

The Salafi Perspective

In the Salafis' point of view, the transnationalisation of Sufism in Hadramawt appears as the sign of its exogenous nature. As such, transnational connections

---

[19] The implications of this charitable work, especially in the area of instruction and professional training, are frequently denounced by liberal opponents of the *salafiyya munazzama*: '*Taghalghal al-mashrû' al-wahhâbî fî Hadhramawt* [Penetration of the Wahhabi project in Hadramawt]', *al-Nidâ'*, 24 August, 2005.

are another sign of deviance that can sometimes delegitimise actors. The prestigious connections between Sufis and foreigners, and their alliance with the government of 'Alî 'Abd Allâh Sâlîh do not manage, in the opinion of Salafis, to hide their alleged weak base of support in the society. For the Salafis, if Sufis can attract students from far away, have access to substantial funding and build a local bastion as in Tarîm, their past actions and present theological errors should discredit them. For their Islamist perpetrators, the campaign to 'expose' the Sufis, including the destruction of tombs in 1994–1995 had been a success. Such was the analysis of a Salafi activist from Tarîm, who asserted that any revival of Sufism was bound to fail, and that his own religious doctrine was guaranteed to be authentically Hadrami and Yemeni. He stated:

The people who follow Sufism come from outside, from foreign lands: Indonesia, America, France—but they are following a wrong path and everyone knows it. That's why the people here, from Yemen, are instead affiliated to the *ahl al-sunna*.[20]

The claim of an endogenous character for Salafism is clearly a response to accusations of importation. The entrepreneurs of the Salafi movement are compelled to demonstrate that their doctrine is authentically Yemeni not only in historical terms, but in terms of a theological heritage as well. The revealed nature of the Qur'an and the sanctity of the Tradition, the filial connection to the *salaf al-sâlih*, the first generations of Muslims, allow them to claim that popular traditions, including so-called innovations (*bid'a*) corrupted the original Islam, and that such a process cannot be imputed to the *ahl al-sunna*. In their own narrative, the apparent disappearance of the latter from Southern Arabia for centuries, or at least their political weakening, was an anomaly that reformism and the emergence of the Muqbilian Salafi trend are supposed to have corrected, in varying degrees. From this point it is the Zaydis, the Sufis, the Muslim Brotherhood and the division into *madhhab* that have broken away from the rich history of Yemen, and thus have separated from Muslim heritage as well. In fact, when asked why his doctrine had developed so quickly in Yemen, Muqbil al-Wâdi'î answered:

The diffusion of the movement of the *ahl al-sunna* in Yemen is linked to two things. First, it originated in Yemen: the Prophet sent Mu'âdh, Abû Mûsa, 'Alî Bin Abî Tâlib and Khâlid Bin al-Walîd [i.e., the companions of the Prophet Muhammad] and they were at the head of the *salaf*. So it is a kind of return to the sources. The second reason is that Yemenis are ready today to receive the Book and the Tradition.[21]

[20] Interview, Tarîm, March 2005.
[21] Muqbil al-Wâdi'î, sound recording, *Liqâ' sahifat al-bayân al-imâratiyya* [Interview with the Emirati paper *al-Bayân*].

A 'YEMENISATION' PROCESS? THE QUEST FOR ORIGINS

In a conference on the theme of the Salafi presence in Yemen, 'Abd al-'Azîz al-Bura'î made exactly the same argument several years later, after the death of al-Wâdi'î. He recalled that the founder of the centre at Dammâj had played an important role in the spread of Salafi doctrine in Yemen, but that Salafism had actually been present there since the beginning of Islam. Much more than a simple importation, it was something that was being reborn. He declared:

> The preaching of the *ahl al-sunna* in Yemen is not limited to this or that individual. It represents Yemeni society as a whole [...] You will find the *ahl al-sunna* working as grocers, construction workers, soldiers, officers, school directors, teachers, mechanics, etc.[22]

Finally, the arguments about origins put the very idea of importation in question, a statement that Muhammad al-Imâm has likened to 'a hostile formula put forward by the Shi'ites and the Sufis.'[23] Salafi entrepreneurs maintain that the implantation of their movement took place in a land that was historically and culturally favourable to it. It is even held to have preceded the Saudi state by being based on local Yemeni traditions. Consequently its development was allegedly independent, not connected to transnational processes. In this context, it is being held as intrinsic to Yemeni society in some way. Such an approach to the Salafi phenomenon substitutes endogenous development and local auto-production for the dominant narrative involving mechanical importation. What is of particular interest here is not to determine if Salafism 'really is' authentically Yemeni, but only to identify the claims and strategies of actors that intend, whether formally or not, to dissociate themselves from any 'Saudisation' process.

II. Nationalism, Syncretism, Tribalism and Adaptation: 'Yemenisation' in Practice

Situating Oneself in History and Society

Beyond the claim of a Yemeni origin that was, as they assert, for a long time disguised by Zaydi power and practices of popular Islam (grave worship in

---

[22] 'Abd al-Azîz al-Bura'î, sound recording, *Nubdha 'an marâkiz ahl al-sunna fî al-Yaman* [Statement concerning the ahl al-sunna centres in Yemen].

[23] Interview with Muhammad al-Imâm in Yemeni independent weekly, *al-Taghiyîr*, March 20, 2009. In the same interview, when asked about when Salafism developed in Yemen, he goes on to say: 'It emerged when the Prophet sent Mu'âdh, Abû Musâ, 'Alî and Khâlid Ibn al-Walîd and others. The Prophet said that God sends someone every new century to renew its religion... and this is what happened to shaykh Muqbil after the events in 1400 of the Hijra [al-Imâm appears to be referring to the seizure of the Mecca mosque in 1979, on the first day of the new century, by Juhaymân al-'Utaybî and the *Ikhwân*]'.

particular), the Salafis have demonstrated a great ability to adapt to the Yemeni context. Since its emergence in connection with Muqbil al-Wâdi'î, Salafism has been characterised by a process of developing autonomy. As highlighted in the previous chapters its internal dynamics are in fact relatively isolated from the Saudi state, and from many of the issues that forge transnational Islamism. Instead of a jihad waged against the Soviet occupier in Afghanistan, instead of a struggle against impious governments, instead of supporting the various parties and movements that in Palestine, Lebanon, Algeria or elsewhere fought (and, in some instances, still fight) different enemies, and instead of elaborating a political platform for change, Yemeni Salafis claimed to prefer to focus on *da'wa* activites and on the study of the *hadîth*. At the same time, they stated that the struggle against the socialists of Aden had to take priority over distant combats. In a publication relating to the Afghan jihad published in the early 1990s (thus after the departure of the Red Army), al-Wâdi'î, maintaining his nationalistic and parochial stance, claimed that the battle against the Soviets was not a duty for every Muslim, contrary to what the Muslim Brotherhood had maintained, along with many Saudi *'ulamâ'*:

> The capacity of the Ruined Brothers [i.e., *Ikhwân al-muflisîn*, a sarcastic reference to the Muslim Brotherhood] to involve numerous *'ulamâ'* in their scheme is so great that these *'ulamâ'* have said: 'The Afghan jihad is an individual obligation (*fardh 'ayn*)!' But I tell you that these words and this *fatwâ* have been produced by ignorant men! The fact that they assert that the jihad in Afghanistan is an individual obligation means that Muslims, whatever country they come from, should all go to Afghanistan and stay there until it has been purified and rid of its communists. But the Muslim countries are infiltrated by communists, Ba'athists and Nasserists. The Afghans have not done anything about that, even after Muslims went to their country. This *fatwâ* [i.e., the position taken by the Muslim Brotherhood] is a joke (*mahzala*).[24]

The 'Yemenisation' of Salafism takes concrete form especially in the reappropriation of the tribal system, the increasing politicisation of Salafi entrepreneurs and in the appropriation of historical figures deemed authentically Yemeni. More subtly, they are also returning to the use of some popular beliefs that in other connections are considered to be pre-Islamic.

The particular importance that is given to traditional pharmacopoeia and to varieties of honey indicates to what extent local traditions are complied with by Salafis, despite the fact that they may be theoretically objectionable. Such

---

[24] Muqbil al-Wâdi'î, *Maqtal al-shaykh Jamîl al-Rahmân al-Afghânî* [The assassination of shaykh Jamîl al-Rahmân al-Afghânî], op. cit., p. 13.

is also the case with practices that involve breaking magical spells through prayer. One young Salafi coming from Yâfiʿ claimed to have spent significant time at the Maʿbar institute a few years before in order to straighten out his problems with his wife, thanks to the recitation of the Qurʾan. According to him, a magician had cast a spell on him that had been carried out by *djinn*.[25] Another man, originally from al-Baydhâʾ, said that he had gone to the same centre with his wife, who was seriously ill, in order to try to have her cured.[26] Although such supernatural practices are allowed by the sacred texts, they appear to run counter to the rationalism that is supposed to typify Salafi doctrine. They seem to express a need for Salafis to avoid being seen as outsiders, disconnected from their cultural environment. They also highlight the fact that the Salafis themselves are fully integrated into society and as such, are not in need to establish roots. This form of syncretism no doubt allows Salafi institutes to attract an audience beyond the groups of students they already have, and by this means to integrate themselves even more explicitly at the local level, in villages and towns, performing a social function that is generally valued by the population in general.

In the context of a broader process of legitimisation in the political sphere, the Salafis sometimes allow themselves to function as a conduit for decisions made by the government. In January 2006, Muhammad al-Imâm came to the rescue on behalf of the Yemeni Ministry of Public Health, which was unable to get the population to accept being vaccinated against polio. A persistent rumour, passed on by a number of religious authorities, had insinuated that the Ministry's vaccination campaign was in reality a plan to sterilise children. In this context, the Salafi leader, going against a dominant popular feeling, guaranteed that vaccinations were good and necessary, and called on each person to co-operate with the authorities.[27] In the same way as al-Imâm's position taken against the supposed duty of armed jihad in Iraq in 2003, this episode reveals a stance that often willingly supports the policies of the state. Although the Salafis are supposed to be indifferent to the activities of governments, they appear more and more interested in gaining respectability on that side, emerging as responsible actors capable of providing support for public policies, not those ordered from Riyadh, but those defined in Sanaʾa.

The alleged rejection of tribalism that is part of Salafi doctrine does not at all exclude the possibility of occasional support being provided for the mecha-

---

[25] Interview, Labʿûs, May 2005.
[26] Interview, Maʿbar, April 2006.
[27] *Almotamar net*, 31 January 2006.

nisms or the principles of tribalism. Muqbil al-Wâdiʻî, when confronted during the 1980s with opposition from Zaydi elites in the region of Saʻda, received the protection of his own tribe. On a number of occasions, he admitted how much the shaykhs of various tribes had helped him, not only logistically (for example by buying vehicles for him) but also morally. As a sign of the particular importance he placed upon his own clan, in his autobiography he listed the members of his Wâdiʻa tribe who had studied at Dammâj. In a way, such a list implied that membership of the same tribe with Muqbil al-Wâdiʻî was in, and of itself, a remarkable quality. His tribal list was presented following another list containing the names of the best students to study at Dâr al-Hadîth since the creation of that institute. In general, despite his criticism of tribalism, al-Wâdiʻî admitted that in the face of communism,[28] and in opposition to Saudi meddling,[29] the tribes of Yemen constituted a necessary and effective defence. Consequently, despite its various claims, Yemeni Salafism basically accommodates the state of the society within which it develops, in a manner similar to that which takes place in the Saudi religious field, in which tribal and social considerations are never absent.

The universalist claim of the doctrine of the Yemeni *ahl al-sunna* should not lead us to ignore certain nationalist positions which they also defend. In the name of supporting one's country, Salafi entrepreneurs attacked the World Bank, for example, which they accused of imposing reforms that favour an accumulation of national debt and higher inflation.[30] They also attacked the United States, which they judged to be guilty of having 'stolen Yemeni oil, leaving people to die of hunger'.[31]

The 1994 war gave the Salafis—and particularly al-Wâdiʻî—the opportunity to express openly nationalistic positions more clearly. In that context the Salafi founder took offence at Saudi support for the 'socialist' secession movement. The criticism delivered at that time made an issue not only of the *hadîth* that mentions the special position of Yemen in regard to the Muslim religion, but also of the breadth of anti-Saudi sentiment among the people at large. Along

---

[28] Muqbil al-Wâdiʻî, *al-Suyûf al-bâtira li-ilhâd al-shuyûʻiyya al-kâfira* [Sharp swords for the impious communist heresy], op. cit., p. 35.

[29] Muqbil al-Wâdiʻî, sound recording, *Nasîhatî lil-shabâb al-suʻûdî* [My advice to Saudi youth].

[30] Muhammad al-Imâm, sound recording, *'Awâqib al-zulm* [The consequences of oppression].

[31] Muqbil al-Wâdiʻî, sound recording, *Jawâhir al-sunniya fî al-as'ila al-faransiyya* [Sunni jewels in the French questions].

the same lines, Muhammad al-Imâm recalled the saying of the Prophet referring to the piety of the Yemenis (and of the people of the Levant—*al-Shâm*) as opposed to the corruption of the Najd, whence cometh the 'horn of the devil' [*qarn al-shaytân*]. He explained then that the spirit of the inhabitants of Yemen was superior to that of all the other Muslim peoples:

> No other society possesses the virtues proclaimed by the Prophet and by Islamic law to the extent that the people (*ahl*) of Yemen do [...] In the beginning people converted to Islam one by one, but the people of Yemen came to Islam as a group in order to receive the religion of God.[32]

The frequent recourse by Salafi figures to arguments with a nationalist slant, like their capacity to keep from breaking completely with popular practices, shows that neither they nor their adepts are 'outlandish men' who are disconnected from the reality of the culture around them.[33] As highlighted previously, the struggle they carry on in the political and religious fields sometimes symbolises, as if in miniature, the larger historical rivalry between the *sâda* and the *qabâ'il* who are a majority in the Yemeni highlands. In addition, Salafism's inclusion in the matter of tribal issues shows that it perceives itself as an integral part of Yemeni society and that it considers it to be an embodiment of its national identity.[34]

Appropriating National Sources

The process of the 'endogenisation' of Salafism also passes by way of the appropriation of local historical and religious references. While their adversaries

---

[32] Muhammad al-Imâm, sound recording, *Fadhâ'il ahl al-Yaman* [The virtues of the people of Yemen].

[33] Samir Amghar and Patrick Haenni, 'Au sortir du mythe impossible de l'outlandish man ... l'universel positif de l'islam post-salafiste' in Jocelyne Dakhlia (ed.), *Créations artistiques contemporaines en pays d'islam: des arts en tension*, Paris, Kimé editions, 2006, p. 2.

[34] In reality the portrayal of Yemeni society as tribal by essence raises different problems. In fact, the fascination that this form of social organisation exercises over Western researchers and journalists, the historical domination over non-tribal regions and the persistence of a patronage system including the government, the army and the large tribal confederations of the highlands should not prevent one from nuancing to some extent the influence of tribalism in contemporary Yemen. Such a form of social organisation does not concern the entire territory of the country, and it is not clear whether even the majority of the population perceives itself as tribal. See Paul Dresch, *Tribes, Government and History in Yemen*, op. cit., pp. 387–396.

emphasise the alleged foreign character of their sources, Salafi entrepreneurs react by promoting the values of figures that are deemed Yemeni in essence. Furthermore, in contrast to the heirs of Muhammad Bin 'Abd al-Wahhâb, Salafis in Yemen never appear to claim allegiance to the Hanbali *madhhab*, the dominant theological school in Saudi Arabia.

Quoting 'Aqîl al-Maqtarî, the local head of al-Hikma in Ta'iz, Bernard Haykel rightly recalls that the connection established between the various branches of Salafism and the reformist thought of judge Muhammad al-Shawkânî highlights a process of 'Yemenisation' of that movement.[35] Historically, al-Shawkânî promoted a reassertion of the importance of the sunna in his writings, something of a departure from his original Zaydi identity. Working under the authority of three successive Zaydi imams at the end of the eighteenth century and at the beginning of the nineteenth he introduced a re-evaluation of the importance of the *hadîth*. His innovative doctrine essentially bypassed sectarian differences, all the while establishing itself as an intimately authentic part of the history and general context of Yemen. It is quite clear that Muhammad al-Shawkânî shared many of the positions of his reformist predecessor Muhammad Bin 'Abd al-Wahhâb, and because of this has been held in high regard in Saudi religious universities and among the country's main scholars. Bernard Haykel has described what he sees as a certain 'concordance of views' held by the two reformists. On some topics, the resemblance is so great that some of al-Shawkânî's writings, republished in Saudi Arabia in the twentieth century, were even wrongly attributed to the Najdî scholar.[36] Still, differences between the two clerics do exist, especially as concerns the excommunication of other Muslims, something al-Shawkânî refused to do. At any rate his doctrine, belonging to a current referred to by Bernard Haykel as '*Traditionist*',[37] cannot be assimilated to Wahhabism. Moreover, al-Shawkânî, while serving as supreme judge (*qâdhî al-qudhâ*), was asked by the Zaydi imamate to refute on both political and theological grounds the Wahhabi doctrine, whose partisans were at that time mounting an offensive in Hadramawt.[38] This characteristic lends the figure of al-Shawkânî a nationalistic image that actors in the Yemeni political field can arguably exploit. His ability to transcend differences in a country where two religious identities—Zaydism and Shafi'ism—have for

[35] Bernard Haykel, 'The Salafis in Yemen at the Crossroads', op. cit.
[36] Bernard Haykel, *Revival and Reform in Islam. The Legacy of Muhammad al-Shawkânî*, op. cit., p. 225.
[37] Ibid., p. 109.
[38] Ibid., p. 129.

a very long time faced one another, and his indisputably 'Yemeni image' make it desirable for the republican regime and others to use him as a symbol. As a sign of this value, when the new republic in the North was still under the pressure of the royalists, the government in 1966 arranged for al-Shawkânî's tomb (who had died in 1834) to be moved to the symbolically important location of the Zaydi Great Mosque in the old city of Sana'a.

Even today, the figure of al-Shawkânî remains generally valued, because people from various political or religious orientations find different reasons to approve of him. From Yemeni public universities (including the Faculty of Education of Lab'ûs where professors in the Islamic section frequently mentionned his name and used his writings) to the primary schools, and from the Scientific Institutes to Dâr al-Hadîth, al-Shawkânî is the very emblem of the religious identity of Yemen and of the progressive merger of both Zaydi and Shafi'i identities. Only some isolated segments of the Zaydi population, most belonging to the category of descendants of the Prophet, are openly critical of this theologian, saying that he broke completely with Zaydi doctrine and ended up nothing but a 'pale copy' of Muhammad Bin 'Abd al-Wahhâb.[39]

The teachings of al-Shawkânî and his particular positions on certain issues have made him a figure particularly prized by Salafi *'ulamâ'* in Yemen. Equal to the Saudi scholars Bin Bâz, al-'Uthaymîn or the scholar from the Levant, al-Albânî, he is undoubtedly a fundamental theological reference in the modern and contemporary period for this current, which shares with him the desire to separate from traditional schools of jurisprudence. His unwavering allegiance to the three successive Zaydi imams makes him a model of respect for government on the part of the *walî al-amr*, and a model for the role of counsellor to princes and *'ulamâ'*. Rather than oppose a regime that was considered unjust by common opinion, and rather than inviting people to the *khurûj* as provided for in Zaydi doctrine, al-Shawkânî opted to remain loyal. The parallel with the careers of the Saudi senior *'ulamâ'*, particularly Bin Bâz at the time of the Gulf War of 1990–1991, is striking. The latter, in order to preserve the monarchy, did not hesitate as *muftî* of the Kingdom to approve in religious terms certain unpopular decisions that seemed to contradict religious doctrine. This national orientation is one of the specific characteristics of the Yemeni current, and undoubtedly sheds light on a part of its original position in the transnational Salafi field.

While few *'ulamâ'* did find approval from Muqbil al-Wâdi'i, Muhammad al-Shawkânî was only criticised on a minor point: the authorisation under

---

[39] Samy Dorlian, *Les filières islamistes zaydites au Yémen: La construction endogène d'un universel politique*, op. cit., p. 57.

certain conditions of masturbation by men. His works of *fiqh* (especially *al-Durar al-bahiyya* [*The sublime pearls*]) are taught at the Dâr al-Hadîth centre alongside classical medieval treatises. It is also significant that in order to legitimise the destruction of Sufi shrines in the mid-1990s, al-Wâdi'î made reference to the writings of al-Shawkânî rather than to those of Muhammad Bin 'Abd al-Wahhâb, who had just the same maintained similar positions on the matter.[40] In this way he implicitly showed that the opposition to the *shirk* as practised by the Sufis was not a recent importation from Saudi Arabia as some of its adversaries stated, but was to be considered part of the history and the identity of Yemen.

Similarly, when Abû al-Hasan al-Ma'ribî laid claim to the heritage of Muhammad al-Shawkânî in a publication entitled *al-Imâm al-Shawkânî wa manhajuhu fî al-takfîr* [The imam al-Shawkânî and his method, as concerns the *takfîr*], the choice could not be seen as entirely fortuitous. His attempt to align himself with the great Yemeni theologian with respect to a major issue was most likely a way of neutralising his own foreign origin.

The reappropriation of the heritage of Yemeni historical figures by the Salafis does not only concern al-Shawkânî. His reformist predecessor Muhammad Bin Ismâ'îl al-Amîr, also known as Ibn al-Amîr al-San'ânî (died 1769), also of Zaydi origin but unlike the *qâdhî* al-Shawkânî, belonging to the category of the *sâda*, is like him invoked as part of the process of endogenisation undertaken by Salafi leaders.[41] The Hikma association, through its al-Kalima al-Tayyiba research centre, published in 2005 a commentary on the Qur'an (*tafsîr*) by Ibn al-Amîr in a luxury edition. According to one of the directors of the association, it was the first time that Ibn al-Amîr's complete writings had been published in Yemen.[42] A connection between contemporary Yemeni Salafi movements and this theologian, who in his time praised the reforms introduced by Muhammad Bin 'Abd al-Wahhâb in the Najd before criticising him, shows

---

[40] Muqbil al-Wâdi'î, sound recording, *Ahdâth 'Adan al-akhîra* [The latest events in Aden].

[41] Interestingly, Paul Dresch recalls that the first book published in the North Yemeni Republic in 1964 was a biography of Ibn al-Amîr. Its author, Qâsim Ghâlib Ahmad, a religious man from Aden and thus a Shafi'i, insisted upon the fact that Ibn al-Amîr had drawn on both Sunnism and Shi'ism. Thus, like al-Shawkânî (to whom the author devoted another work four years later), he symbolised the transcendence of primary religious allegiances in favour of a republican identity. Paul Dresch, *A History of Modern Yemen*, op. cit., p. 102.

[42] Interview, Sana'a, February 2006.

once again the lack of significance of the association between contemporary Salafism and 'Wahhabism'.

In an even more explicit manner, in a conference recording of the early 1990s entitled *Hawl kalimat wahhâbî* [*Concerning the term 'Wahhabi'*] that was later published in print form,[43] Muqbil al-Wâdi'î expressed his discomfort with the term 'Wahhabi' as applied to his own group. According to him, this term was being used as a 'malicious' (*khabîtha*) label by his enemies 'in order to turn people away from the Tradition'. He did point out that the political alliance approved by the Najdî scholar with the Âl Su'ûd in 1744 (and the worldly interests that explained it) did not prevent him from considering the preaching of Muhammad Bin 'Abd al-Wahhâb as 'blessed' (*mubâraka*). Al-Wâdi'î also asserted that the Najdî scholar's legitimisation of rebellion (*khurûj*) against the Muslim Ottomans was not to be seen as an error, to the extent that it was the 'immoral' Turks who had attacked Najd. In this context, and in al-Wâdi'î's view, 'Wahhabis' had only acted in legitimate self-defence. Despite all this, al-Wâdi'î did express reservations with regard to a number of actions and positions taken by the founder of 'Wahhabism', and declared that he preferred the teachings of Yemeni reformist '*ulamâ*':

It is necessary to realise that shaykh Muhammad Bin 'Abd al-Wahhâb (may God have mercy on him) was a wise man from the 12th century of the Hijra. Like any man, he was right sometimes and wrong sometimes, and he was sometimes as ignorant as he was wise at other times. If we were imitators, we would practice the imitation [*taqlîd*] of our Yemeni jurist Muhammad Bin Isma'îl al-Amîr al-San'ânî who lived at the same time. He was even wiser than Muhammad Bin 'Abd al-Wahhâb, but the latter was able with God's help to make an alliance with the government, and thus disseminate his knowledge.[44]

It appears that in the eyes of al-Wâdi'î, it was essentially because of his political alliance with the Âl Su'ûd dinasty and their first state that the doctrine founded by Muhammad Bin 'Abd al-Wahhâb has importance today. In strictly theological terms, it was not particularly innovative, and was even inferior to the teachings of other Yemeni jurists who however did not have the opportunity to participate in significant political events mainly because of Zaydi domination at the time.

The promotion of the value of local references is one of the major issues involved in the schisms that have rocked the Salafi political and religious field

[43] Muqbil al-Wâdi'î, *Maqtal al-shaykh Jamîl al-Rahmân al-Afghânî* [The assassination of shaykh Jamîl al-Rahmân al-Afghânî], op. cit., pp. 32–42.
[44] Ibid., p. 32.

since the beginning of the 1990s. The politicisation of the Hikma and Ihsân associations, followed by the re-evaluation of the objectives of the supporters of Abû al-Hasan al-Ma'ribî, can be interpreted as a measure of their increasing involvement in the Yemeni context, marked by multiparty politics and by election contests. The same is true as concerns the rejection by quietist Salafis of *hizbiyya*. Whatever position a group defends regarding this matter, the very fact that this specific debate is able to structure the movement and create tensions inside it is in itself a clear indication of the Salafis' capacity to insert—or embed—themselves durably in the Yemeni context.

Since the beginning of the twenty-first century, the important controversy between Abû al-Hasan al-Ma'ribî and the 'orthodox' Salafis who claim to be the true successors to Muqbil al-Wâdi'î is to be seen as evidence of a divergent interpretation with regard to the subjects of institutionalisation and political participation (rather than as a mere dispute between competing heirs). At an even deeper level, there is an evident disagreement about the ability of *'ulamâ'* to actually transcend national and historical contexts. In this theological and political confrontation, the question of 'Yemenisation' seems to be at issue, as an opposition between a claim to universalist discourse and another discourse that adheres to a national or local space, takes on social and charity work, if it does not actually ally itself with an existing government or fight political battles openly. The debate that emerged around the Syrian national Muhammad Surûr in the 1980s continues indirectly to divide the Salafis within the Muslim world and, of course, to have its own repercussions in Yemen. In effect, this controversy leads actors to ask questions about the scope of interpretations, their supposed infallible character or the actual relative status of what the scholars might say. In these ways they address the sensitive issue of adaptation to context.

More specifically, in Yemen, for the activist Salafis aligned with various dissident strains, and particularly for Abû al-Hasan al-Ma'ribî, the use of ancient and foreign (particularly Saudi) references is only justified to the extent that the references possess exceptional (and thus rare) theological knowledge. Consequently, Abû al-Hasan, while continuing to claim descent from Muqbil al-Wâdi'î, considers that the changing situation since the turn of the century calls for a re-evaluation of doctrine. In fact, between 1999 and 2001, a rapid succession of deaths took away a number of renowned scholars that had emerged throughout the second half of the twentieth century as the founding fathers of contemporary Salafism: al-Albânî, Bin Bâz, al-'Uthaymîn, al-Jazâ'irî and al-Wâdi'î. In al-Ma'ribî's view, this loss was critical as it left the *ahl al-sunna* in the position of orphans, lacking major figures upon whom they could depend.

For him, their 'successors'—Rabî' al-Madkhalî, Sâlih al-Fawzân, 'Abd al-'Azîz Âl al-Shaykh, 'Abd Allâh Bin Jibrîn or in Yemen, Yahyâ al-Hajûrî and Muhammad al-Imâm—lacked not only charisma and independence but also knowledge. Their lack of capacity to actually be recognised by all as legitimate figures confronted them with competition from a new generation influenced by Muhammad Surûr's relativist approach. Thus, according to one of his followers, in typical form, Abû al-Hasan refused, at Muqbil al-Wâdi'î's death, to accept Rabî' al-Madkhalî or the other Yemeni or Saudi religious leaders as legitimate authorities. He argued that because they claimed to exercise leadership, they were, as he asserted, actually blindly competing for the approval of existing regimes.[45] In the view of the scholar from Egypt who adopted Yemen as his home, they were guilty of preaching a de-contextualised Islam—and without, according to him, the requisite skills or credentials. He then rejected the me-tooism practised by his former associates, who seemed to think 'if Rabî' [al-Madkhalî] said it, it's true!', and who reminded him, when he saw them, 'of qat vendors and shepherds guarding donkeys'.[46] Much like Muhammad Surûr's doctrine, Abû al-Hasan ended up thinking that only 'ulamâ' that are in touch with the national situation and, to consider his own case, 'those who know Yemen' are able to deliver opinions that are really relevant to contemporary issues in that country. The fact that the independence of religious men in relation to the government is far from assured, makes this all the more true. Instead of universalism, Abû al-Hasan opts for a less audacious relativism, which according to him is better adapted to the level of competence of the contemporary 'ulamâ'. Taking a humorous and critical attitude towards this approach, one Muqbilian Salafi of Hadramawt said, 'For Abû al-Hasan, Yemen has no 'ulamâ', neither does Saudi Arabia! He must go looking for his references I don't know where, perhaps in China!'[47]

In the framework of this internal controversy, the adversaries of Abû al-Hasan have been inclined to see the schism of 2002 as a calculated, underhanded strategy intended to discredit the Salafi movement as a whole, rather than as a step in the process of independence and of taking a position at a distance from Saudi references (both processes that, in effect, remain quite

---

[45] Interview, Sana'a, April 2008.

[46] Abû al-Hasan al-Ma'ribî, sound recording, *Murshid al-hayrân* [The guide for the embarrassed].

[47] Interview, Say'ûn, April 2005. This quip refers indirectly to the prophetic command to seek religious knowledge 'even in China'.

incomplete). A Salafi close to Yahyâ al-Hajûrî claimed to expose the true projects of the Salafi dissident of Egyptian origin:

Intelligent people should know that those who are spreading the idea according to which Yemen does not have any *'ulamâ'* in it since our shaykh [i.e.: Muqbil al-Wâdi'î] died, who was a learned man in the matter of the *hadîth* and a man who renewed our religion, those people are speaking in order to make people suspicious of the centres of the *ahl al-sunna*, the centres of Dâr al-Hadîth, and the people who founded them. [...] Behind this idea, there is no other intention than to provoke disorder (*fitna*) and cause strife.[48]

The violence of the internal struggles between different Salafi tendencies highlights the degree to which questions about adaptation and autonomisation touch on sensitive points. For its part, the process of reappropriation of references and local issues stresses integration of Salafi actors at all levels in Yemeni history and society. The debate over Yemeni authenticity and endogeneity, by fostering confrontation between various religious and political movements, marks a reversal of the Salafi claim to be apolitical and of the universalist project around which Salafism is originally structured. Along these lines, Salafism is beginning to be normalised as an element in the Yemeni political and religious landscape. It continues to constitute a touchstone of opposition for many actors and groups, but at the same time, it is being instrumentalised by the state, used as a resource by actors and has been gradually politicised. Its doctrine, which is far more flexible than its adversaries believe and more compromising than the dominant analyses tend to suggest, resonates with many of the issues that are specific to Yemeni society, including with ones that are shaped by transnational dynamics. The 'Yemenisation' of Salafism demonstrates, finally, to what extent globalisation is a complex and broadly ambivalent process that produces at least as much cultural, political and religious fragmentation as it does uniformisation. In fact, through the adaptation of practices and the 'vernacularisation' of references and norms, Salafis draw attention to the increasingly complex and fragmented character of identities as well as practices.

---

[48] Sa'îd al-Mashûshî al-Yâfi'î, *Anbâ' al-fudhalâ'* [News of noble people], Sana'a: Maktabat al-Athariyya, 2002, p. 5.

7

POLITICS AS USUAL

THE NORMALISATION OF SALAFISM

Following Edward Said's concept of 'travelling', the final stage of this current account of Salafism (but surely not the end of Salafism in Yemen itself!) appears to be this movement's normalisation within Yemeni politics. Such a process of inclusion or adaptation is by no means necessarily strategic, or the product of an intentionally constructed centralised project imagined by the Salafi entrepreneurs. It again appears as a largely spontaneous and unconscious phenomenon that is actually concomitant with the other phenomena highlighted previously. As such, the 'Yemenisation' of Salafism is not sequential: the various processes of competition with other political and religious groups and the normalisation of Salafism take place simultaneously.

Embedded as they are, and because they just cannot be the 'outlandish men' they claim to be, Salafis don't need to blend into Yemeni Society; they are themselves the products of its recompositions at the local, national and transnational levels. This normalisation of Salafism occurs through their emergence as incongruous political actors, as the object of political issues and as instruments in the hands of others.

Such normalisation is manifest in the way the quietist Salafis in Yemen have, willingly or not, participated in the 'Global War on Terror' since late 2001, and have also participated in the ideological struggle against the 'Hûthî' rebels within the framework of the Sa'da war. In doing so, they have emphasised their position as allies of the Yemeni government. Such developments appear to have occurred simultaneously with a complex reorganisation of the Yemeni Salafi movement. While some entrepreneurs have realigned themselves with the broader international Salafi field and its Saudi figures, others have sought to reassert the specificity and independence of the Yemeni branch.

I. The Politics of the 'Global War on Terror'

Reappropriation by the State of the International Agenda

Despite its frequent inability to provide, across the whole of its territory, effective public services, and despite the fact that its authority was increasingly challenged by clan-based, tribal, political and regional protests even prior to the 2011 uprising, the government of Yemen, and the domestic and institutional structures that it commands should not be ignored. They are not *per se* a touchstone of opposition for the Salafis, nor a competitor in the first instance, but the relationship between the two has been far from straightforward. The Salafis' oft-proclaimed disdain for politics and patronage jobs did not actually prevent them from being the instruments of the political, tribal and military elites who control Yemen's government.

In the aftermath of September 11, 2001, observers, including Yemenis, wondered for a while where Yemen would be situated in the 'Global War on Terror'—as target or as partner. A number of elements tipped the scales towards the former. First, a large number of Yemenis were acting as combatants in Afghanistan and Pakistan (a total of 112 Yemeni nationals have been imprisoned at Guantanamo and 89 still were in mid-2011), and second, the alleged number two man in the preparation of the attacks on New York and Washington, Ramzî Bin al-Shayba, was a Yemeni. He was arrested in Karachi in 2002 and is still awaiting trial almost a decade later. Third, Yemen's leaders for long appeared to somehow deny the relevance of the issue of jihadi militancy, often asserting that religious extremism did not exist in Yemen and that it was only propaganda by 'socialist secessionists' that suggested otherwise. In a 1999 speech to students from the religious al-Îmân University, 'Alî 'Abd Allâh Sâlih stated it was not acceptable to label any of those who had fought in Afghanistan as terrorists.[1] Another sign of the government's eagerness to minimise the presence of transnational jihadi groups in the country was Prime Minister 'Abd al-Qâdir Bâ Jammâl's assertion that 'al-Qaeda does not have an organisation in Yemen'.[2]

---

[1] Anwâr Qâsim al-Khadrî, *al-'Unf fî al-Yaman* [Violence in Yemen], Sana'a: Markaz al-Jazîra al-'Arabiyya lil-Dirâsât wal-Buhûth, 2008, pp. 48–57.
[2] AFP, 23 May 2002.

In this context, Yemen has frequently been mentioned in sulphurous terms, often being described in the media as the 'country of origin of Bin Lâdin' (a fact that appears to have little if no political or social relevance, but that stigmatises the country, in a way making it ontologically responsible for Bin Lâdin's deeds) or being compared to Somalia or Afghanistan. Public opinion and the media in Western countries and the Gulf monarchies echo the notions that Yemen is unstable, corrupt, underdeveloped and peopled by bearded tribesmen with rifles, whose actions have deprived the government of Yemen of all authority. That government is supposed to be not only weak, but also tolerant of terrorist-connected activities on its territory. A succession of assassination attempts, some failed, and the low credibility of the government's stated anti-terrorist policy have helped perpetuate this over-simplistic image of Yemen in the international media and among Western and regional decision-makers.

On 12 October, 2000, the attack on the American warship *USS Cole* while in port at Aden had identified Yemen as a danger zone for terrorist attacks. Seventeen American sailors had been killed in the operation. Usâma Bin Lâdin apparently claimed responsibility on numerous occasions, including his son's wedding in early 2001, at which he recited a poem on the subject. Immediately after the attack, the FBI launched an investigation in coordination with Yemeni authorities. Some members of the Yemeni government were eventually suspected of having known about the preparations for the anti-American attack at Aden, or of later obstructing the Federal agents' inquiry. These accusations were later given substance in April 2005 through declarations by a former naval commander and Yemeni ambassador in Damascus, Ahmad 'Abd Allâh al-Hasanî during an interview for *al-'Arabiyya* news station.[3] However, no concrete proof, direct or indirect, of the complicity of Yemeni officials in this sort of dry run to September 11 has ever been provided.

Anxious not to repeat the errors that in 1990–1991, during the Gulf War, caused it to be sanctioned by Western and neighbouring nations, the Yemeni government declared in favour of co-operating with the 'fight against terror', and of redefining its policies and its internal political alliances.[4] In a sign of this new stance, 'Alî 'Abd Allâh Sâlih travelled to Washington in November 2001 to meet President George Bush. During the following years, co-operation

---

[3] *al-Ayyâm*, April 30, 2005.
[4] Ludmila Du Bouchet, 'La politique étrangère américaine au Yémen', *Chroniques Yéménites*, no. 11, 2004, pp. 101–121 and Robert Burrowes, 'Yemen: Its Political Economy and the Effort Against Terrorism' in Robert Rotberg (ed.), *Battling Terrorism in the Horn of Africa*, Cambridge: World Peace Foundation, 2005, pp. 141–172.

took specific forms. An FBI office was opened in Sana'a, American patrol boats for the surveillance of coastlines were delivered and France also started up a number of training programmes for security service personnel. As an official ally, the Yemeni President was invited by President Bush to take part in the G8 summit in Georgia in June 2004.

From that point Yemen appeared to be compelled to juggle the expectations of a population that was not completely unfavourable to anti-imperialist rhetoric, even when voiced by al-Qaeda, against the demands of the United States and its allies, who indiscriminately criminalised any expression of opposition or protest that came from a religious source. The government of 'Ali 'Abd Allâh Sâlih for a while extended a sort of minimum form of co-operation on security—the FBI office, a few American soldiers as trainers for Yemeni armed forces, some militants arrested or extradited (including the famous Dr Fadhl, an Egyptian jihadi ideologue, who practiced medicine from 1994 to 2001 in the public hospital of Ibb and was imprisoned for three years in Sana'a before being secretly deported to Cairo in 2004). After the assassination in the Ma'rib desert of Abû 'Alî al-Hârithî, thought to be the local leader of al-Qaeda, by means of a US Army drone in November 2002, official protests were only formal as the government in Sana'a had obviously been informed of the operation on its territory. In 2003, Muhammad al-Mu'ayyad, an official of al-Islâh (along with his assistant Muhammad Zâyid), was arrested in Germany in a sting organised by the German and American secret services. Al-Mu'ayyad was accused of being a financial conduit for Hamâs and al-Qaeda, and was extradited to the United States where in 2005 he was sentenced to seventy-five years in prison. He was found guilty by a jury only of the accusation involving Hamâs. Yemeni officials protested, and allowed popular demonstrations in support of al-Mu'ayyad to take place but never put into question the relevance of their co-operation with the United States and its allies. At the end of 2008, a legal agreement was reached between the prosecutors and the defence and al-Mu'ayyad and Zâyid returned to a hero's welcome in Yemen in the summer of 2009.

In order to compensate the price of concessions to the Western policy environment, the government tried to maintain its line of integrating possible sources of resistance—tribes, religious actors and, to a lesser extent, political parties—into state structures. However, the regime lost partners in the process, but tried to hold on to the essential ones. It refused to order the closure of the private university al-Îmân, which the United States had accused of training men for jihad. American demands to freeze the assets of the school's founder,

'Abd al-Majîd al-Zindânî, were also rejected. The government did admit that foreign students at Islamic institutes should be more strictly managed and by the end of 2001 the government asserted that more than 600 had been expelled from Yemen. In June 2008, Vice-President 'Abd Rabuh Mansûr Hâdî said that the government had during the three previous years expelled 16,000 foreigners (the figure was no doubt inflated) suspected of having ties to terrorist activities.[5]

Still, many accused the government of leniency: arrested militants from Yemen or other countries usually got short sentences or were released. In 2007, Jamâl al-Badawî, thought to have been the main organiser of the attack on the *USS Cole*, was placed under house arrest after escaping from prison in February 2006 and after having first been sentenced to death in 2004. Such a move, along with others, symbolised for many the lax attitude of the Yemeni government and what was frequently denounced as a double-game.

The Yemeni government maintained a discourse that was critical of American foreign policy (especially concerning Palestine and Iraq), trying to preserve some symbols of its independence, but it bowed, more or less proactively, to demands from the outside in security matters. From time to time various Yemeni institutions divided up available roles in order to maintain a semblance of sovereignty, and to prove that the government could keep up nationalist rhetoric despite the alliance with the United States in the 'Global War on Terror'. In 2002, for example, the Consultative Council (*majlis al-shûra*), the upper chamber of Parliament made up of members named by the President, voted to approve a resolution calling on Arab countries to cease all co-operation with the United States as long as that country maintained its pro-Israeli policy.

In the same manner, thanks to the resources of 'state fundamentalism', the government affirmed its own legitimacy and tried to reduce the space for manoeuvring available to the Islamist opposition. During the winter of 2006, like other Arab governments, it stuck its oar in with regard to the Danish cartoon affair involving drawings that ridiculed the Prophet, claiming to defend Islam by supporting a boycott of Danish products, and by organising large 'spontaneous' demonstrations in the country's largest cities. In return, it broke new ground and was in a singular position when it announced strong support for the Hamâs Palestinian party the day after its victory in elections in January 2006, and also during its consequent struggle with the Palestinian Authority and Fatah. In 2008 a lively debate occurred in the Yemeni media and in society

---

[5] *Mareb Press*, 16 June 2008.

and parliament concerning a government-supported initiative that called for the setting up of a so-called Virtue committee (*hay'at al-fadhîla*), a type of religious police inspired by the Saudi model that would enforce religious morals and fight social corruption.[6] Such a move illustrated how elements in the government did not wish to be outflanked by their religious opposition and by Salafis of various trends. Figures of the Islâh party were directly involved in this operation, particularly 'Abd al-Majîd al-Zindânî, but also Sâdiq al-Ahmar, succeeding to the position of his late father 'Abd Allâh at the head of a tribal confederation, Hâshid.

In order to demonstrate that its refusal to engage in direct confrontation with Islamist groups was reasonable, the Yemeni government also worked out a strategy of communication allowing it to conciliate certain antagonistic demands. Accordingly, during the first few years after 2001, the government was often eager to show that dialogue was more effective than repression. In 2002, for example, Yemen was the first to create a committee to promote dialogue in an effort to 'de-radicalise' militants.[7] Such an initiative received broad coverage in the international media and was later copied and significantly improved by other governments, particularly Saudi Arabia, which devoted massive amounts of money to the project and worked out a consistent strategy.[8] The head of the Commission of Intellectual Dialogue (*Lajnat al-hiwâr al-fikrî*), Hamûd al-Hitâr (who would subsequently be named Minister of Religious Affairs in 2007, at which time the dialogue committee had ceased to function) frequently highlighted the success of his own initiative. According to Judge al-Hitâr, it was because of the 'dialogue committee' headed by himself, not because of any repression, that Yemeni society had not been plagued by terrorist attacks during the years after 2001.[9] It was more likely because of a series of compromises, sometimes elaborated at the highest levels of state consultation, that militants were partly deflected from the path of violence against the state or from anti-Western violence on Yemeni territory. Much like during the 1990s, some militants were still

---

[6] Anahi Alviso-Marino, 'Contentious Dynamics for Sociopolitical Change? The Case of the Islah Party in the Republic of Yemen', *Chroniques Yéménites*, no. 16, 2010, pp. 57–90.

[7] Christopher Boucek, Shazadi Beg and John Horgan 'Opening up the Jihadi Debate: Yemen's Committee for Dialogue' in Tore Bjorgo and John Horgan (eds.), *Leaving Terrorism Behind: Disengagement from Political Violence*, New York: Routledge, 2008, pp. 181–192.

[8] Christopher Boucek, 'Saudi Arabia's 'Soft' Counterterrorism Strategy: Prevention, Rehabilitation and After care', *Carnegie Middle East Programme*, no. 97, 2008.

[9] *al-Sharq al-Awsat*, 6 March, 2004.

apparently co-opted into economic structures or even military ones. This political formula, made up of compromise and moves towards integration was successful in the sense that it spared for some time (up until the second half of the 2000s decade) the country a high level of political violence, and kept the Yemeni authorities from being a target for armed militants.

From the point of view of the Western allies of Yemen, the presence of many Yemenis in Iraq after 2003, including some who were supposed to have been 'de-radicalised' by Judge al-Hitâr, pointed to the insufficiency of the anti-terrorist policy of its government. In December 2005, the choice of 'Alî 'Abd Allâh Sâlih, to be accompanied by 'Abd al-Majîd al-Zindânî, to the summit held by the Organisation of the Islamic Conference in Mecca, followed by the official visit to Sana'a in February 2006 made by leaders of the Palestinian Hamâs, angered the United States. In the same month, the dramatic and surprising escape of twenty-three militants accused of belonging to al-Qaeda also made decision-makers and analysts doubt the sincerity of Yemen's allegiance. The twenty-three men had been imprisoned in a high-security prison in Sana'a, but managed (most likely with some degree of insider support) to dig a tunnel that allowed them to escape through a neighbouring mosque. Nineteen were recaptured, killed or surrendered in the following months (including Jamâl al-Badawî), but the four who remained at large managed to create new cells. Around these four figures, especially Nâsir al-Wihayshî, militants reorganised to establish the Brigades of Soldiers of Yemen (*Katâ'ib jund al-Yaman*) and al-Qaeda Organisation of Jihad in the Arabian Peninsula (*Tanzîm qâ'idat al-jihâd fî jazîrat al-'arab*).

Maintaining Relations with the Salafis

In January 2009, following the release of the seventh issue of al-Qaeda Organisation of Jihad in the Arabian Peninsula's online journal *Sadâ al-Malâhim* (The Echo of Battles), the group announced its merger with the Saudi branch of al-Qaeda and the subsequent establishment of al-Qaeda in the Arabian Peninsula (AQAP). This development was primarily seen as the result of the success of counter-terrorism policies in Saudi Arabia. Indeed, militants from that country had been forced to find shelter in Yemen. It was also considered a worrying sign of the emergence of Yemen as a safe haven for violent groups and as a possible launching pad for operations outside of the country, particularly in Saudi Arabia. As such, it came to be seen as a symptom of Yemen's growing instability.

Bleak prospects appeared to be confirmed by the attack in August 2009 on the Deputy Minister of the Interior of Saudi Arabia, Muhammad Bin Nayif (though a failure, extremely sophisticated), and by the (also unsuccessful) attack on the Amsterdam–Detroit flight at Christmas 2009 by Nigerian student Umar Farouk Abdulmutallab, who had been trained in Yemen. Targets of AQAP militants were not only foreign as inside of Yemen, operations focused on security officials, groups of tourists and economic and diplomatic facilities. Among these, the attack in September 2008 on the American Embassy and in April 2010 the assassination attempt against the British ambassador, made international headlines. Other events went largely unnoticed abroad as they targeted local officials but nevertheless illustrated both the growing organisational capacity of AQAP and its transnational dimension.

The regional—or even international[10]—implications of the emergence of AQAP legitimately raised the anxiety of many, particularly the government of the United States and the international media. It also forced the Yemeni authorities to claim to take visible action: in late 2009 and early 2010, airstrikes (that were actually carried out by the Americans although the Yemeni government publicly took responsability) targeting alleged al-Qaeda camps in Shabwa, Ma'rib, Abyan and Sana'a governorates illustrated a new proactive approach to counter-terrorism.[11] The announcement in June 2010 by the Yemeni Ministry of Interior of the arrest of some fifty foreign students, originating from Australia, the United States, Europe and South East Asia, all allegedly linked to al-Qaeda, was also meant to prove that Yemen was on board, and to illustrate how serious the Yemeni government had become when it came to fighting violent Islamist groups. Years before that, Western and regional pressures had already encouraged the Yemeni government to prove its involvement in the 'Global War on Terror' through repression. In doing that and then in turning a blind eye towards the conflict, the international community had undoubtedly played a role in triggering in June 2004 (a few days after President Sâlih's participation to the Georgia G8 summit) the Sa'da war opposing the Yemeni army to the Zaydi revivalist 'Hûthî' rebels. The international context along with other internal dynamics, has significantly transformed the relations between the Yemeni state and society, fostering direct repression and an attack on civil liberties instrumental in the 2011 uprising.

Contrary to other political and religious groups, the quietist Salafis do not appear to have paid a high price as a result of the government's gradual acceptance

---

[10] Gregory Johnsen, 'The Expansion Strategy of al-Qaeda in the Arabian Peninsula', *CTC Sentinel*, vol. 2, no. 9, 2009, pp. 8–11.

[11] Gregory Johnsen, 'AQAP in Yemen and the Christmas Day Terrorist Attack', *CTC Sentinel Yemen Special Issue*, January 2010, pp. 1–4.

of a struggle against terrorism. Although they were easy to label as criminals in international discussions because of their doctrinal intransigence and the ambiguities of their position, the Salafis appear to have been spared overt repression. Interestingly, the various data that led people to think that a visit to Dammâj was a stage in the development of a radical militant in league with al-Qaeda did not generate a marked reaction on the part of the Yemeni government with regard to Salafi institutes, nor was surveillance significantly increased. Long after the Yemeni authorities claimed to control the religious institutes, the many foreigners who were living illegally in Yemen without residence visas appeared to continue to benefit from benign neglect on the part of both national and local authorities. In this way, external pressures were reappropriated and transformed by the government and members of the elite who responded to them according to their own interests, allowing certain figures to appear as criminal and minimising the role played by other groups or movements.[12] The presence of several hundred foreign students in various Salafi centres, particularly at Dammâj, continued to worry the diplomats from their home countries.

Despite international pressure, the signs of a continuing alliance of convenience between quietist Salafis and the Yemeni government were many. From the point of view of the government, the Salafis played several functional roles, just as in Saudi Arabia. Not only did they allow religious opposition to be offered against the Islamists connected to the Muslim Brotherhood as well as those coming from the ranks of the Zaydi revival, but they also helped delegitimise in theological terms the recourse to violence on the part of groups linked to al-Qaeda. Thus in 2005, when the government announced that it was closing down 1,300 illegal religious institutes that had been operating without an official licence[13] (out of an estimated total of 4,615 institutes attended by 320,232 students),[14] no Salafi institute was closed down or even forced to change its curriculum or course offerings.

On the contrary, after long years of debate, in 2002 the Scientific Institutes that historically had been managed by the Muslim Brotherhood were reinte-

---

[12] Ludmila Du Bouchet, 'The State, Political Islam and Violence: The Reconfiguration of Yemeni Politics since 9/11' in Amélie Blom, Laetitia Bucaille and Luis Martinez (eds.), *The Enigma of Islamist Violence*, London: Hurst, 2007, pp. 137–164.

[13] On this subject, see '*al-Shatât al-ta'limî* [Disorder in education]', *al-Thawra*, 7 April, 2005.

[14] '*al-Ta'lîm al-madhhabî al-sirî ... al-ishkâlât wa al-hulûl* [Secret sectarian instruction... difficulties and solutions]', *al-Nâs*, 25 April, 2005. On this subject, see also 'Yemen Deports Indonesian Students', *Yemen Times*, 5 September, 2005.

grated into the public system. This action represented in symbolic and concrete terms the new state's policy. The attempt at a partial marginalisation of the Muslim Brotherhood involved various manipulations, all aimed at associating the Brotherhood with violent movements and terrorists. The assassination of Jâr Allâh 'Umar, vice secretary-general of the Yemeni Socialist Party and principal architect of the bridging between the socialists and some Islamists during the congress of the Islâh party in December 2002 gave the official government media an opportunity to criticise the Islamist party and therefore legitimise repression. For Nâsir Yahyâ, an intellectual and member of al-Islâh, this manoeuvre was a direct attempt to discredit his party while preserving relations with the Salafis, that is, according to him, the groups that are really violent, those which 'declared that the Yemeni constitution is impious [...] and who are known to the state'.[15]

In early 2008 and again in 2010, a number of foreign students from the Muhammad al-Imâm centre were accused of possession of weapons while others participated in combat between Salafi militants and 'Hûthî' rebels near Dammâj, but still this did not appear to trigger any significant shift in state policies. In the eyes of decision makers, the contradiction between a doctrine that made a point of rejecting violence, and actions taken by individuals who were less scrupulous about refusing armed action, did not appear to justify open repression against Muqbilian Salafis.

Such a lax strategy was not necessarily counter-productive, since Salafism offered the government ideological resources and a set of Islamist allies who could still reject and oppose the violence of groups affiliated with al-Qaeda. Instead of being proscribed, the quietist Salafis with Yahya al-Hajûrî at their head remained on the same side as the government, which could make use of their call for loyalty to the *walî al-amr* something that would obviously prove useful in the framework of the 2011 revolutionary movement.

The ability of the Yemeni government to preserve intact its relations with the Salafis after the 9/11 attacks was not a new thing. The development of the Muqbilian movement since the early 1980s generally had been treated favourably by the Yemeni leadership, and also by some members of the security services. The stated apolitical attitude of the Salafis, their loud opposition to the doctrine of the Muslim Brotherhood (the most manifest opponents of regimes in the region) and their equally fervid rejection of socialism had made them allies of government long before the issue of terrorism started to structure world politics.

---

[15] Nâsir Ahmad Yahyâ, *al-Tatarruf wa al-takfîr fî al-Yaman* [Extremism and excommunication in Yemen], Sana'a: Dâr al-Kutub al-Wataniyya, 2003, p. 15.

Until the late 1990s, the anti-Saudi bias shown by Yemeni Salafis complemented the policy of 'Alî 'Abd Allâh Sâlih, then involved in a boundary dispute with its big Saudi neighbour Interestingly, al-Wâdi'î's reversal on Saudi issues coincided with the signature of the Treaty of Jeddah in June 2000.

In the meantime, local authorities, as Muqbil al-Wâdi'î frequently recounted in his autobiography, would in individual cases raise opposition to a Salafi mosque or centre, or restrict the mobility of him and his companions but this remained rather marginal. In the mid-1990s, the support of the governing party for the Zaydi revival, particularly by means of the Believing Youth group (*al-Shabâb al-mu'min*) which never hid its opposition to Salafi doctrine, symbolised a concomitant strategy of encouraging rivalries in the political and religious field in order to divide the Islamists and let them focus on others than the government.

Despite the sometimes contradictory aspects of the Yemeni government's policy, it is remarkable to note that at no time were repressive actions clearly favoured against the quietist Salafis. In 1994–1995, following the destruction of some Sufi and Ismaili shrines in Aden, Harâz and Hadramawt, a number of Salafi militants were jailed. Muqbil al-Wâdi'î argued that they had only done their duty as Muslims in fighting against what he labelled *shirk*. He was then able to obtain their release when he went to the authorities to plead their case. When Muqbil al-Wâdi'î was receiving treatment in al-Thawra public hospital in Sana'a in the spring of 2000, he received a visit from many Yemeni dignitaries, including Ghâlib al-Qâmish, director of Political security, the main agency of the intelligence services, and Muhammad 'Abd Allâh Sâlih, brother of the President, a general in the Army and director of Central security (*amn al-markazî*). Such visits created rumours as to what the exact relations between the founder of the Yemeni Salafi movement and Yemeni intelligence were. When Muhammad 'Abd Allâh Sâlih died in May 2001, Muqbil al-Wâdi'î, who seldom complimented people, declared that he was 'an honest man, not a disloyal, lying politician'.[16] Several times during the 1990s, Muqbil al-Wâdi'î mentioned that he knew he was under constant surveillance by the Yemeni intelligence services. He would say that he had nothing to hide, and that he took responsibility for any criticism of the government he might make. However, although he was particularly critical of other nationalist Arab leaders, he never directly attacked the Yemeni government, still less its principal figure since 1978: 'Alî 'Abd Allâh Sâlih. Whether through helping repatriate the

---

[16] Muqbil al-Wâdi'î, sound recording, *Mushâhadâtî fî al-Mamlaka al-'Arabiyya al-Su'ûdiyya* [My experience of the Kingdom of Saudi Arabia].

library of Muqbil al-Wâdi'î, issuing visas to foreign students wishing to go to Dammâj, turning a blind eye to violations of visa rules by these same foreigners or welcoming opponents coming from abroad like Abû al-Hasan al-Ma'ribî and ensuring their security, the Yemeni government collaborated with the Salafis and fostered their development. This alleged co-operation has brought many opponents to consider that the Yemeni government, as much as Saudi Arabia, was in fact mainly responsible for the transplantation of Salafism. Even worse, a socialist activist from the Abyan region, criticising the new importance of Salafis in his little home town, al-Husn (that would in 2011 become a battle-field between alleged al-Qaeda militants and the security forces), described what he saw finally as a defeat for his government, which could no longer control that which it had mostly created while trying to use religious identities as policy tools:

The government favoured the installation of the Salafis in the north at Dammâj in order to counter the Zaydis of al-Hûthî. In the beginning the partisans of Muqbil were there to provide that counterweight, but then they spread out across the country, and the government couldn't do anything about it.[17]

As such, the Salafis, supposedly apolitical, played a role for the government that was essentially political, contributing to the weakening of the various oppositions' mobilisation capacities. Already in electoral terms, as was demonstrated at the faculty in Lab'ûs, Salafi abstention from voting on religious grounds benefited candidates of the ruling GPC party. By staying out of the electoral equation and by stigmatising the Islâh party, Salafism also broke up the dynamics of the opposition.[18] In theological terms, they de-legitimised the political ploy of 'resorting to Muslim vocabulary', holding that this was a worldly, profane and materialistic perversion that ignored the global character of Islam. Thus in September 2006, during the campaign for the presidential election, Abû al-Hasan al-Ma'ribî, contradicting his previous position, gave implicit support to the President running for re-election, 'Alî 'Abd Allâh Sâlih, appearing with him

---

[17] Interview, Ju'âr, April 2005. On this subject, 'Alî 'Abd Allâh Sâlih delivered a speech in May 2007 before the *'ulamâ'* in which he attempted to show that the state he was the leader of had never engaged in repression against Zaydi identity, and that all forms of religious allegiance were being respected. He assured them of the government's neutrality in religious matters, even denying that Salafism had ever been encouraged in the past as a means of controlling Zaydism. See *al-Thawra*, 15 May, 2007.

[18] François Burgat, 'Salafistes contre Frères Musulmans', *Le Monde Diplomatique*, June 2010, p. 7.

at a meeting in the city of Ma'rib. Without abandoning the idea that the Salafis were opposed to party politics, he declared that it was forbidden to contest the power of the *walî al-amr* by standing as a candidate or by voting against the President. In this context, the opposition candidate Faysal Bin Shamlân, deemed a technocrat but rallying under the banner of the Joint Meeting Parties (*al-Liqâ' al-Mushtarak*), with the support of the affiliates of the Muslim Brotherhood of the Islâh party,[19] was considered illegitimate from a religious point of view. At the same time, Yahyâ al-Hajûrî released a cassette roundly criticising the leaders of the Muslim Brotherhood in Yemen who had published recommendations (*tazkiya*) in favour of 'the socialist Faysal Bin Shamlân'.[20]

The quest for respectability of Abû al-Hasan al-Ma'ribî thus contrasted with the suspicions that were directed towards him at the end of 2001. At that time he was accused, without ever being questioned directly on the point, of having connections to al-Qaeda. His centre in Ma'rib was placed under close surveillance by the Yemeni security services, and a number of his foreign students were expelled.[21] This temporary repression did not last long, and Abû al-Hasan quickly clarified his position concerning violence against the state and against 'Western interests' through a number of publications.

At the beginning of 2009, an intense debate was raging in various Salafi currents, especially the activists in the Hikma association. The approach of legislative elections, scheduled for April 2009 (and eventually first put off for two years following an agreement between the government and the opposition before being cancelled due to the 2011 uprising), once again gave rise to speculation about the attitude of the Salafis and the possibility of their making endorsements of candidates or political parties. Abû al-Hasan al-Ma'ribî denied that there were any plans to enter an open alliance with the governing party, and he went on to explain that he considered the elections illegitimate since

[19] On the 2006 presidential election and the coalition of opposition parties, see: Marine Poirier, 'Yémen nouveau, futur meilleur? Retour sur l'élection présidentielle de 2006', *Chroniques Yéménites*, no. 15, 2008, pp. 129–159; Sarah Philips, *Yemen's Democracy Experience in a Regional Perspective: Patronage and Pluralized Authoritarianism*, London: Palgrave Macmillan, 2008; and Michaelle Browers, 'Origins and Architects of Yemen's Joint Meeting Parties', *International Journal of Middle Eastern Studies*, vol. 39, no. 4, 2007, pp. 565–586.

[20] Yahyâ al-Hajûrî, sound recording, *Wudhûh al-butlân fî tazkiyât shuyûkh al-ikhwân al-muslimîn lil-ishtirâkî Faysal Bin Shamlân* [Clarification of the futility of recommendations by the shaykhs of the Muslim Brotherhood in favour of the socialist Faysal Bin Shamlân].

[21] *al-Quds al-'Arabî*, 29 December, 2001.

it appeared that they were being organised in a chaotic manner. He further explained that under certain conditions, it might be necessary to vote for a candidate who would 'serve Islam and the Muslims, or fight against evil and corruption, whether that candidate was standing as a member of the GPC or al-Islâh'.[22] For their part the partisans of al-Hikma, after aligning themselves with al-Islâh, appeared to be continuing their rapprochement with the GPC, begun in 2006 during the presidential campaign. Such a move was however brutally put to end in early 2011 because of the popular uprising and the subsequent recomposition of the political landscape. Salafis of al-Hikma then announced their plan to actually establish an independent political party.

Until 2011, the politicisation of the Salafi movement, with many still claiming to be apolitical, appeared to depend much on the Yemeni government. Islamist actors (Salafis, but also the radical wing of the Muslim Brotherhood, as is seen in the case of 'Abd al-Majîd al-Zindânî), threatened by repression, were pushed to silence some of their criticism and move closer to the existing rulers. But this rapprochement was not without a degree of ambiguity on the part of the government, which kept these allies at arm's length, in order not to suffer a backlash from its Western partners. As shown during the debate surrounding the establishment of the Virtue Committee in 2008 and during the campaign denouncing the Israeli war on Gaza in January 2009 when huge demonstrations were organised, the partnership between the Yemeni rulers and its not very commendable Islamist allies was kept discrete and served primarily to mobilise internal support.

Interestingly, the Sufis of Hadramawt had since the late 1990s played a role similar to that of their Salafi adversaries. In fact, the Sufis—like the Salafis—legitimised an approach to religion that was not directly politicised or oppositional. Personalities such as al-Habîb 'Alî al-Jifrî and al-Habîb 'Umar Bin Hafîz, who were figures of international stature, also constituted an alternative to figures within the Muslim Brotherhood, especially 'Abd al-Majîd al-Zindânî, who in the context of the fight against terrorism could no longer play the front man, or who like Muhammad al-Yadûmî and the leaders of the unified opposition participating in the Joint Meeting Parties, adopted a less conciliatory attitude towards the government.

In a similar manner, in 2005, the Yemeni government encouraged the first visit to Yemen of the popular Egyptian preacher, 'Amr Khâlid, yet another example of the instrumentisation of so-called apolitical religious groups.[23] 'Amr

---

[22] Interview of Abû al-Hasan al-Ma'ribî, *Abwâb*, March 2009, p. 35.

[23] On the trajectory and teachings of 'Amr Khâlid, see especially Patrick Haenni and

Khâlid was granted a private meeting by President Sâlih, and in 2009 and 2010 launched a number of development projects in coordination with the Sâlih Charitable Foundation created in 2005 by the Yemeni President with the objective of competing with the Islâh Charitable Association established in 1990, and closely related to the political party of the same name. 'Amr Khâlid had gained transnational recognition through the work of his association, Life Makers (*Sunnâ'a al-hayâ*). Through a variety of cassettes and television programmes, 'Amr Khâlid contributed in the emergence of that which Patrick Haenni has dubbed 'market Islam',[24] that is, an approach to religion that is primarily individualistic and depoliticised, which tries to rise above local specificities and provides an opportunity to 'work around Islamism' by specifically putting forward Muslim ethics. 'Amr Khâlid asserts, in fact, that reform as such (*islâh*) is individual before being social, and he proposes economic and social development based on faith, thereby leaving the state only a minimal role. The promotion of such concepts in religion, encouraged by the majority of governments in the Middle East, is based on the notion of a depoliticisation of religion, and as such is not completely antagonistic to the worldview of quietist Salafis. By showcasing these figures and these tendencies within Islam, the Yemeni government could aptly erode the support for the Muslim Brotherhood. State fundamentalism then turns out to be an effective defence. Symbolically, in the Yemeni political equation, it becomes legitimately possible to be a pious Muslim without signing on to an Islamic political project and without being an opponent of the existing government. Although doing it in a manner that is without doubt less evident than that of the Sufis and the 'market Islam' represented especially by 'Amr Khâlid, all of whom they oppose, the Salafis participate in their own way in this movement and in the move away from the heritage of the reformists and the Muslim Brotherhood.

The strategy by the Yemeni leadership after September 11, 2001 to preserve its relations with quietist Salafis appears in retrospect as a practical one. The preservation of relations kept the Salafis fixed in a mainly supportive position *vis-à-vis* the government, even though it was carrying out more and more manifest acts of repression, harder and harder to ignore, against large segments

---

Tjitske Holtrop, 'Mondaines spiritualités, Amr Khâlid, shaykh branché de la jeunesse dorée cairote', *Politique Africaine*, no. 87, 2002, pp. 45–68.

[24] With regard to these 'new religious entrepreneurs, independent and seldom interested in great political schemes [...], preferring the personal quest for salvation, self-realisation and the effort toward economic success' (pp. 7–8), see Patrick Haenni, *L'islam de marché*, Paris: Seuil, 2005.

of the political spectrum. Consequently, the supposedly apolitical Salafis did not pay a price in direct terms for the government's reappropriation of the international anti-terrorist agenda. However, such was not the case with certain members of the Muslim Brotherhood, partisans of the Zaydi revival and militants affiliated with al-Qaeda, all of whom during the first decade of the twenty-first century were increasingly at odds with the Yemeni state, then precipitating the country into massive protest in 2011.

II. Salafis as Allies of the Government in the War in Saʻda

The alliance of convenience between the various heirs of Muqbil al-Wâdi'î and the Yemeni government after the 9/11 attacks took on a palpably political dimension in their struggle, ideological but also apparently armed, against the movement known as the 'Hûthîs' in the war of Saʻda. This war, in terms of its duration, its fierceness and regional breadth certainly deserves specific attention. Since June 2004, the governorate of Saʻda, in the north of Yemen, has been the locus of violent clashes opposing the Yemeni national army to a movement or rebellion that is commonly called the 'Hûthîs', after the family name of its successive leaders, Husayn al-Hûthî and his younger brother 'Abd al-Malik.[25]

Each of the six periods of combat that succeeded each other between 2004 and the beginning of 2010 were characterised by an escalation of the violence, despite repeated efforts at mediation and attempts at reconstruction.[26] Aerial bombardment became more and more frequent, refugee numbers exploded and the areas involved in the fighting grew larger and larger. The intervention of the Saudi army in November 2009 was clear evidence of the tendency of this war to expand. Because access to the region was frequently cut off even for humanitarian workers, and because journalists and researchers were also forbid-

---

[25] The term 'rebellion' as used to refer to the actions of the 'Hûthîs' may appear loaded, to the extent that the initiative in the offensive against Saʻda in June 2004 was not carried out by them directly. The 'Hûthî' movement nonetheless changed in several important ways since its development: their discourse has evolved significantly from taking a position that was only defensive or reactive, towards a more and more intransigent approach with regard to the government. The label 'Hûthîs' (*hûthiyûn*) is a subject of controversy, since the actors so referred to do not all accept the term, preferring to refer to themselves as the *ashâb al-shi'âr* (adepts of the slogan) or *Shabâb al-mu'min*, Believing Youth. But 'Hûthî' gradually caught on with the media and in Yemeni politics, even outside the group of the government's allies, and is now the accepted term.

[26] On the series of phases of the conflict, see International Crisis Group, *Yemen: Defusing the Saada Time Bomb*, Middle East Report, no. 86, 27 May, 2009.

den to go there, reliable independent information has been rather scarce. No reliable estimate of the number of victims has been made, but it appears possible that more than 10,000 people have been killed, while the number of displaced persons approaches 200,000.

Zaydi Revivalists vs Emerging Salafis

In part, the Saʿda war had to do with the framework of the rivalries involving the Zaydi revival movement and the emergence of Salafism. For reasons that are as much historical as they are doctrinal, Zaydism, more than any other form of religious allegiance, has functioned as a touchstone of opposition to Salafism during its development in the Yemeni context. In the environment of Dammâj, where Muqbil al-Wâdiʿî originated from and chose to settle when he returned from Saudi Arabia, he ran up against serious opposition, coming essentially from conservative Zaydi elements. Already, at the end of the 1950s, after returning for the first time to study at the Hâdî mosque of Saʿda, he had been confronted by the hostility of the Zaydis, a group that at that time dominated the politics of northern Yemen. Almost twenty years later, when Muqbil al-Wâdiʿî had just been expelled from Hejaz, traditional Zaydi 'ulamâ', part of the still powerful Hashemite aristocracy, and a number of tribes, even including some elements of his own tribe (al-Wâdiʿa), offered resistance, sometimes violent, against the implantation of his Dâr al-Hadîth institute and against the religious doctrine he was establishing, which they considered a spin-off from Saudi Islam. Al-Wâdiʿî stated that he was threatened with death several times after his permanent return. In this context, he was unable to stand apart from the society in which he found himself, and he had to seek protection from the members of his tribe.

When religious identities are mentioned, most would easily assert that the vast majority of the population of Yemen is divided into two schools of Islam: Shi'ite Zaydism, which represents about a third of the population, and Sunni Shafi'ism, to which the majority of the country belongs, but whose members are in the minority in the highlands of the north. Building on such alleged division, it would be logical to say that the opposition between these two identities is a structural element in the political and social landscape of contemporary Yemen. However, over the course of the second half of the twentieth century, the confrontation between these religious identities has gradually given way to a process of convergence, which can in no way be reduced to a 'Sunnification' of Zaydism.[27]

---

[27] For analysis of the transformations induced by this religious convergence, see Gabri-

Describing the Yemeni state as a Sunni regime is problematic to the extent that a large percentage of the political, economic and military elite population—beginning with President 'Alî 'Abd Allâh Sâlih—are of Zaydi origin although they do not refer to this heritage in an overt way. In fact, Zaydism has mostly been absorbed within a larger identity (one which certainly is dominated by Sunnism), although a certain number of its particular practices were preserved (a specific call to prayer in Zaydi mosques, the consistent Zaydi origin of the *muftî* of the Republic, the rehabilitation of certain royalist elites in public institutions, and so on). At the same time, the automatic negative perception of Zaydism as an intrinsically Shi'ite identity has been largely abandoned, even among Islamists. At present, the divide between Shafi'i Sunnism and Zaydi Shi'ism only marginally determines political allegiances and identities and is not *per se* a relevant variable in the analysis of Yemeni society. Only at both ends of the religious spectrum, that is for Salafis and Zaydi revivalists, does the divide remain significant, giving way to mutual stigmatisation with the Salafis even putting into question the Islamic character of Zaydism. Nevertheless, the historical process of convergence which began in the eighteenth century by the reformist Muhammad al-Shawkânî, was reinforced during the post-revolutionary period in the public education system, and finally became the common notion in the age of the mobility of populations, inside and outside the country. Such a process has arguably been instrumental in legitimising the Republic that came out of the 1962 revolution, in the eyes of the royalists who had during the entire 1960s fought from their bastion of Sa'da, to re-establish the old regime of the Zaydi imamate.

As stated, this convergence of religious identities is not admitted by everyone: the Salafis reject it as they see a direct and essential association between Zaydism and Twelver Shi'ism. For their part, a small minority of the Zaydis initiated a movement for revival over the course of the 1980s that too contested the idea of a convergence and that intended to reassert the specific characteristics of Zaydism. These Zaydi revivalists were influenced by Hashemites Badr al-Dîn al-Hûthî (died 2010) and Majd al-Dîn al-Mu'ayyadî (died 2007), and decided to promote traditional Zaydi sources (Zayd Bin 'Alî, al-Imâm al-Qâsim

ele Vom Bruck, 'Regimes of Piety Revisited: Zaydî Political Moralities in the Republic of Yemen', *Die Welts des Islams*, no. 50, 2010, pp. 185–223, and Laurent Bonnefoy, 'Les identités religieuses contemporaines au Yémen: convergence, résistances et instrumentalisations', op. cit.

Bin Muhammad or Muhammad al-Samâwî, for example) through a variety of publications or activities targeting younger people (night and summer classes, cultural and sporting events) in Sanaʾa, Dhamâr, Hajja and Saʿda.

By placing great value upon theological and historical references of Zaydism, confronted with a republican Muslim identity and with what it perceived as a Saudi-style Salafism, a minority worked out an essentially symbolic relationship with Twelver Shi'ism and its political expressions, especially Hizbollah in Lebanon and the Islamic Republic of Iran. Such was the case during the 1980s with the Nahrayn mosque in Sanaʾa directed by Hamûd ʿAbbâs al-Muʾayyad. In the streets of the capital, well into the 2000s decade, vendors sold reprints from the writings of Muhammad al-Shîrâzî, a prominent Iraqi ayatollah, and others. The bookstores nearby the Zaydi Great Mosque in the old city of Sanaʾa also stocked books and cassettes of Shi'ite clerics produced in Iran, Iraq or Lebanon. In this context, it was not surprising to see in 2004 a portrait of the Ayatollah Khomeini in the living room of a Zaydi household in a village of the governorate of Hajja, where the principal source of news was the cable channel *al-Manâr*, broadcast by the Lebanese Hizbollah.

Beyond this essentially symbolic shift in the direction of the practices of the Twelver Shi'ites,[28] the Zaydi revival manifested itself in a still more meaningful way in what might be characterised as a quest to construct a Zaydism without the doctrine of the Imamate. For many Zaydi revivalists, the specific reverence for scientific knowledge and university education, and thus for rationality as well, appeared as a means of re-legitimising their identity in a republican context.[29] In consequence, for these intellectual, religious and political actors it was no longer a matter of insisting upon the power of the imam or the supposed pre-eminence of the descendents of the Prophet (something that leading Zaydi clerics had collectively approved to abandon in 1990),[30] but upon the modernising character

---

[28] On the issue of the links between Zaydi revivalism and Twelver Shi'ites, see Abdullah Lux, 'Yemen's Last Zaydi Imam: The Shabab al-Muʾmin, the Malazim, and Hizb Allah in the Thought of Husayn Badr al-Din al-Huthi', *Contemporary Arab Affairs*, vol. 2, no. 3, 2009, pp. 369–434.

[29] Gabriele Vom Bruck, *Islam, Memory, and Morality in Yemen: Ruling Families in Transition*, op. cit.

[30] In November 1990, the main *'ulamâ'* of the newly created al-Haqq party published a manifesto asserting that the restoration of the imamate was no longer an obligation of their creed and that they recognised the legitimacy of the republican system. This founding act put a symbolic end to the quarrels linked to the civil war of the 1960s, but did not bring about unanimity (Badr al-Dîn al-Hûthî for example did not sign

of Zaydism. Faced with a Sunnism they considered sclerotic, Zaydis presented themselves as intrinsically favourable to *ijtihâd* (theological reform through the reinterpretation of texts).[31] This trend, represented by different institutes, media outlets or minor political parties asserted the alleged rationality of Zaydism in accordance with the founding motto: *al-'aql qabl al-naql* ('reason before the letter'), implying that the prophetic *hadîth* could only be approved on condition of conforming to reason such as it is revealed in the Qur'an. Such an approach was evidently at odds with the literalist Salafi doctrine. Despite their dynamism among urban elites, these Zaydi revivalists seldom mobilised outside of limited Hashemite circles, and thus for long remained the affair of a minority.

In this context the struggle these Zaydi groups undertook against the 'Wah-habisation' of Yemeni Islam became a credo that offered them new vitality. For them the alleged transplantation of exogenous Saudi practices was represented not only by Muqbilian Salafism directly implanted in the region of Sa'da, but more broadly through the heritage of the Muslim Brotherhood and in the network of the aforementioned Scientific Institutes financed by the Saudi government.

Gradually within the Zaydi revivalist realm the reaction to Salafism became institutionalised, particularly through various religious centres like the Shahîd al-Samâwî Institute in Sa'da or the Badr Centre in Sana'a. The 1990s were marked by intense editorialising: the great classical works were republished, re-commented and printed (some for the first time) in Yemen. A new political and religious movement emerged whose main figures, born after the revolution of 1962, made a sharp distinction between Zaydism in general and the power of the imamate. Of this new generation, Bernard Haykel wrote:

Zaydism for these men is an inherited identity and persecuted religio-cultural tradition, one that is embedded in manuscripts that they now seek to bring to the light of day. They see themselves as defending a tradition that is very much on the defensive and one that has suffered serious reversals at the hands of the opponents, mainly Salafis, who are funded or patronised by the governments of Saudi Arabia and Yemen, each for its own reasons.[32]

---

it). Bernard Haykel, 'Hizb al-Haqq and the Doctrine of the Imamate', unpublished, presented at the annual conference of the Middle East Studies Association in 1996.

[31] James Robin King, 'Zaydis in a Post-Zaydi Yemen: 'Ulama Reactions to Zaydism's Marginalisation in the Republic of Yemen', *Shi'a Affairs Journal*, vol. 1, 2008, pp. 53–84.

[32] Bernard Haykel, 'Recent Publishing Activity by the Zaydis in Yemen: a Select Bibliography', *Chroniques Yéménites*, no. 9, 2002, p. 226.

Thus contemporary Zaydism has been restructured in a number of ways. Once dominant, Zaydism now conceives of itself as dominated, confronted with a general threat. Thus to identify oneself as a Zaydi in the absence of the reign of an imam, that is, in the absence of that which once constituted the central characteristic of that form of religious allegiance, necessarily involves the promotion of new elements.

The Zaydi revival took a political term with the creation of the Haqq (Truth) party in 1990 and the reactivation of another political formation, the Union of Popular Forces (*Ittihâd al-quwa al-shaʿabiyya*). Both appeared as unable to develop as anything more than elitist movements. They nonetheless asserted their acceptance of the republican regime and officialy abandonned the principle of the political pre-eminence of the class of the descendants of Prophet Muhammad. Nonetheless, these two parties, particularly al-Haqq, sometimes remained ambiguous about their position with regard to the imamate: their leaders did not call for it to be restored, but their support was drawn above all from clans or individuals who were associated with the royalists during the civil war of the 1960s. These two marginal political formations aimed both at representing the Zaydi populations of the highlands but most of all perceived themselves fighting against the development of the Salafi movement. Badr al-Dîn al-Hûthî, associated with al-Haqq party, had for instance authored in the early 1990s several collections of *fatâwâ* in which he contested the legal opinions formulated by the Saudi *ʿalim* ʿAbd al-ʿAzîz Bin Bâz.

The struggle against what Zaydi revivalists label 'Wahhabi Salafism' also mobilised foreign books and recordings in order to criticise this doctrine and to point out its 'theological errors'.[33] Many Zaydi intellectuals derived support for their position from a narrative, supposedly written by a British spy named Hempher, who claimed to have been posted to Basra in the eighteenth century. However, this narrative has widely been described as a fake. In his text titled 'Memoirs of a British Spy' (available in different Zaydi bookstores and also on the internet), Hempher explained how he had allegedly instrumentalised Muhammad Bin ʿAbd al-Wahhâb so that he would help dismantle the Ottoman Empire and weaken the Muslims. Building on such narratives denouncing the connections between Muhammad Bin ʿAbd al-Wahhâb and British imperialism in the eighteenth century,[34] Zaydi critiques claimed that Saudi Islam, repre-

---

[33] See, for example, the recorded sermon by Iraqi Twelver Shi'ite cleric, Fâdhil al-Mâlikî, *Nazarat al-islâm fî al-salafiyya* [Opinion of Islam concerning Salafism].

[34] See also Muhsin al-Amîn, *Kashf al-irtyâb fî attbâʿ Muhammad Bin ʿAbd al-Wahhâb*

sented as they claimed in Yemen by the contemporary Salafi movement, was not only a theological impostor but also a product of an anti-Muslim plot orchestrated by the Western colonial powers. In a manner similar to these publications, the lives of historical 'Wahhabis' who repent their errors were often used as illustrations of the moral superiority of Shi'ism, whether this is the Twelver branch or the Zaydi one. In a book entitled *Rihlatî min al-wahhâbiyya ilâ al-ithnî 'ashariyya* ['My journey from Wahhabism to Twelver Shi'ism'], 'Isâm al-'Imâd, a Yemeni scholar based in Qom in Iran, told the story of how, after having attended religious courses in Saudi Arabia under 'Abd al-'Azîz Bin Bâz and at the Islamic University of the Imâm Muhammad Bin Su'ûd in Riyadh, he discovered Shi'ism and decided finally to convert to the allegedly 'authentic' Islam. However, the veracity of this story and this conversion were not accepted by all, especially not an anti-Shi'ite website that proclaimed that "Isâm al-'Imâd was never a Sunni, still less a "Wahhabi". His family is in effect Zaydi and his father was one of the founders of the conservative party, al-Haqq'.[35] Competition between the various identities appeared to give the various actors the right to twist the truth to a considerable extent, but at least they were all on a level playing field.

In 1993 on the occasion of the first ever multiparty general elections, the newly established Haqq party gained two seats in the Yemeni Parliament, both in Sa'da constituencies. One of them was held by Husayn, son of prominent Zaydi revivalist cleric Badr al-Dîn al-Hûthî. In the mid-1990s, while it was vacillating between opposition and support for the government (its secretary-general, Ahmad al-Shâmî, briefly held the post of Minister of Religious Affairs in 1997), the Haqq party underwent a broad internal reconfiguration:[36] personal rivalries and conflicts over strategic aims, such as the relationship with the government brought about a secession on the part of a movement that had appeared in the early 1990s, the Believing Youth (*al-Shabâb al-mu'min*). This group was headed by Husayn al-Hûthî along with others such as his brother Yahyâ and 'Abd al-Karîm Jadbân, both of whom who would later be elected in Parliament and join the ruling GPC.

[Clarification regarding suspicion against the partisans of Muhammad Bin 'Abd al-Wahhâb], place and publisher unknown, 1991.

[35] Regarding the challenge to the veracity of the narrative of 'Isâm al-'Imâd, see http://www.ansar.org/arabic/al3mad.htm (accessed on 22 September, 2010).

[36] Samy Dorlian, 'Les Reformulations Identitaires du Zaydisme dans leur Contexte Sociopolitique Contemporain', *Chroniques Yéménites*, no. 15, 2008, p. 164.

Initially, the Believing Youth had been established to act at the local level to counter the increasing influence of the Salafi movement in the area around Saʿda. This association mobilised its militants not only for the defence of Zaydism, but also as part of a criticism of American foreign policy and of the regional power imbalances. Such a critique was expressed from 2002 on through the slogan, 'God is great, death to America, death to Israel, curse upon the Jews, victory for Islam (*Allâhu akbâr, al-mawt li-amrikâ, al-mawt li-isrâ'îl, al-laʿna ʿalâ al-yahûd, al-nasr lil-islâm*)' its partisans shouted on numerous occasions.[37] Such a claim was indisputably an echo of Iranian revolutionary slogans, but the action initially remained only symbolic. It did not lead to armed action against the United States or its allies, nor even against the government in Sanaʾa. Despite persistent accusations by the Yemeni government, nowhere was there any tangible sign of organisational connections with the Iranian government nor with Twelver Shi'ism as a political and religious doctrine.[38] Consequently, the specific history and the rhetoric of the group did not make the Believing Youth an exponent of transnational Shi'ism, comparable to Shi'ite minority groups in other Gulf states.[39] As such, the Believing Youth stood in a religious and political field that was both larger (since opposition to the international and regional power imbalances at the global level is not something Iran has a monopoly on)[40] and more local, since it could only be understood within the specific Yemeni context and that of Zaydism. Its slogan assured it of a certain level of popularity in a Yemeni environment strongly marked by anti-Americanism and anti-Zionism,[41] particularly since after 9/11, following the government's demand, many of the other Islamist groups, including al-Islâh and the

---

[37] On the slogan and its origin, see *al-Balagh*, 10 March 2009.

[38] Abdullah Lux writes: 'The thought, world-view, theology, and assumptions of Husayn Badr al-Dîn [al-Hûthî] as well as much of the course of action he undertook are purely Jarudi Zaydi—and to fail to appreciate this is to misread him entirely. What he attempted, however, at the level of method was a remote, but express, borrowing from Khomeini and Hizballah—gleaned from his readings and observations at a distance [...]', Abdullah Lux, 'Yemen's Last Zaydi Imam: The Shabab al-Mu'min, the Malazim, and Hizb Allah in the Thought of Husayn Badr al-Din al-Huthi', op. cit., p. 393.

[39] Laurence Louër, *Transnational Shia Politics: Political and Religious Networks in the Gulf*, London: Hurst, 2008.

[40] Thus Husayn al-Hûthî did not go to study in Iran after his term in the legislature ended in 1997, but to the Sudan (a centre of Islamist contestation in its own right), where he obtained a Master's degree in Islamic law at the University of Khartoum in 2000.

[41] Khaled Fattah, 'Yemen: A Slogan and Six Wars', *Conflicts Forum*, 28 October, 2009.

Salafis, had silenced or at least toned down their criticism of the United States' foreign policy in order not to be confronted with state repression. A few days after the attacks on New York and Washington, President Sâlih had indeed called all political forces together at a military post to demand that they mute their anti-Americanism and support the new alliance of the government in the 'Global War on Terror'.[42] In that context, the Believing Youth appeared as one of the only independent forces capable of refusing such a demand. In January 2003, the famous slogan was shouted in the presence of President Sâlih in the Mosque of the Imâm al-Hâdî in Sa'da, and repeated at will by partisans of the Believing Youth even in the Great Mosque in the old city of Sana'a. The failure of a number of attempts at mediation between the government and the association led the governor of Sa'da to attempt on 18 June, 2004, to arrest Husayn al-Hûthî. The police operation quickly escalated into a full-scale battle involving significant military resources.

From that point on, the conflict structure evolved from one phase of the combat to another. On 10 September, 2004, Husayn al-Hûthî, who had taken refuge in a cave, was killed during a military offensive. The government announced the end of the war, but tensions continued and fighting broke out again in March 2005. Badr al-Dîn al-Hûthî, past his eightieth year, and 'Abd Allâh al-Rizâmî, the second al-Haqq party MP elected in 1993, were brought forward as the new leaders of the rebellion. During 2006, 'Abd al-Malik al-Hûthî, the younger brother of Husayn, born circa 1980, emerged at the head of the movement. Since the beginning of the war, government referred to them under the name of 'Hûthîs' and accused them of having flown the yellow flag of the Hizbollah, as well as being in favour of the re-establishment of the Zaydi Imamate. Gradually, the rebellion went beyond the phenomena of the Zaydi revival *per se* and its ideological dimension only appeared as marginal.

The manner in which political repression was carried out by the national army and certain tribal militias (most of which were affiliated to the loose Hâshid tribal confederation) and the brutality of certain rebels with regard to citizens who had supported the government, and whose houses were sacked, and the sometimes clumsy conduct of military operations in the field all favoured the expansion of the war, as mechanisms of solidarity began to draw more and more people in, pushing it further and further away from its Zaydi revivalist core.

---

[42] François Burgat, 'Le Yémen après le 11 septembre 2001: entre construction de l'Etat et rétrecissement du champ politique', *Critique Internationale*, no. 32, 2006, pp. 11–21.

Salafis at War

The context of the war in Sa'da since 2004 has given the Salafis an opportunity to put their alliance with the Yemeni government into practice and of playing a directly political role. By allying themselves in a more or less concrete fashion to the government of President Sâlih against the rebels, the Salafis appear to have acted pragmatically in applying their doctrinal disapproval of the Zaydis, in a manner similar to what they had already been able to do in 1994–1995 against the socialists and the Sufis. This time, they took the government's propaganda and played an instrumental role.

In the framework of war, struggles internal to the Yemeni Salafi realm appeared to be somewhat forgotten. From Dammâj to Ma'rib, and passing by Ma'bar, the main Salafi entrepreneurs stigmatised Shi'ism and Zaydism in an identical fashion. Outside Yemen, the monthly journal *al-Sunna*, edited in London by allies of Muhammad Surûr, published an article likening the Zaydi reaction to Twelver Shi'ism, and to a form of Hashemite extremism.[43] In the first few weeks of fighting in 2004, Abû al-Hasan al-Ma'ribî published a short booklet entitled *al-Fatâwâ al-shar'iyya fî ahdâth Sa'da* ['Legal opinions concerning the events in Sa'da'] in which he clearly condemned the rebellion, comparing it directly to the Twelver Shi'a *râfidha*. He admitted that there was certainly 'a great difference between the *rawâfidh* and the Zaydis' but he asserted that the partisans of al-Hûthî were responsible for a 'religious *fitna* that was more serious than anything else'. According to Abû al-Hasan, 'it was unanimous, the people of the east, the west, the north and the south have come together to support the President of the Republic of Yemen'. Still, he maintained that the anti-American and anti-Israeli slogan of the Believing Youth could not by itself justify the repression with which the group was then confronted. In fact, while continuing to reject the recourse to violence, Abû al-Hasan did not express any fundamental disagreement with this slogan adopted by al-Hûthî. For him, the military campaign conducted against the Believing Youth group was justified on religious grounds, particularly with reference to the ancient schism between Shi'ites and Sunnis. Abû al-Hasan declared:

Should we believe that the only reason the government is fighting the partisans of al-Hûthî is because of their slogans? Many mosques in Yemen criticise and denounce the actions of America and Israel against the Muslim world, especially in Palestine and in

[43] Hikmat al-Harîrî, '*Zâhirat al-Hûthî fî al-Yaman* [The Hûthî Phenomenon in Yemen]', *al-Sunna*, no. 138, 2004, pp. 85–98.

Iraq. Despite all this the government of Yemen does not fight against them. To the contrary, the radio, the press and the political leaders of Yemen take an even harder line than the mosques! Beware of empty slogans that are just decoration, and do not forget what the *rawâfidh* have done to harm the *ahl al-sunna* throughout history.[44]

Thus, for the Salafi entrepreneurs, the Sa'da war was an opportunity to denigrate Twelver Shi'ism and Zaydism even further. In an international context affected by the war in Iraq where the United States was being accused of implementing a pro-Shi'ite policy, tensions and recriminations were many. These were expressed in various tracts or pamphlets, through sermons or websites and fed on a fertile terrain: Salafis alleged that Shi'ism itself was a Jewish plot to divide Muslims.[45] In such a climate of mistrust and accusations, *al-Muntadâ* magazine (published by al-Hikma) carried a number of articles that were particularly severe in criticising the movement of al-Hûthî: the rebellion was said to be connected with 'a secret plan for spreading the Iranian revolution', or simply referred to as 'a cancer'. In an issue of that magazine published in 2005, 'Abd al-'Azîz al-Duba'î declared that 'the Armed Forces have an important role to play in eradicating this *fitna*, and the intellectual forces must eradicate its roots'.[46] In 2008, the Kalima al-Tayyiba Centre published a slim volume written by Muhammad al-Mahdî and entitled *al-Zaydiyya fî al-Yaman: hiwâr maftûh* ['Zaydism in Yemen: an open discussion'] In this publication, the leading figure of al-Hikma emphasised the theological errors of Zaydism (especially as concerns the relationship to the prophetic Tradition, and the *hadîth*) and its intellectual and historical relationship with Twelver Shi'ism. Outside of Salafism, other Islamists once affiliated with the Muslim Brotherhood and later allied with the government, such as 'Abd al-Fatâh al-Batûl and the Nashwan

---

[44] Abû al-Hasan al-Ma'ribî, *al-Fatâwâ al-shar'iyya fî ahdâth Sa'da* [Legal opinions concerning the events in Sa'da], Ma'rib: Dâr al-Hadîth, 2004, p. 15.

[45] See Muhammad al-Imâm, sound recording, *Khatar al-tahazzub* [The danger of party politics]. In this sermon from the mid-1990s the director of the Ma'bar institute speaks of the figure of 'Abd Allâh Bin Saba', a Yemeni Jew, who soon after the death of the Prophet Muhammad was accused of spreading certain lies about the early caliphs (*al-khulâfa al-râshidîn*). These lies were later used as a pretext by Shi'ites to justify their allegiance to 'Alî, the son-in-law of the Prophet.

[46] See for example '*al-Fasl al-thânî min fitnat tanzîm al-shabâb al-mu'min* [The second period of the *fitna* by the organisation of the Believing Youth]'; '*al-Judhûr al-fikriyya lil-fitna al-hûthiyya* [The intellectual roots of the fitna of al-Hûthî and also '*Adhwâ' 'alâ al-khat al-siriyya li-tasdîr al-thawra al-irâniyya* [Clarification regarding the secret plan for spreading the Iranian revolution]' published in the magazine *al-Muntadâ*, no. 92–93, 2005.

Bin Sa'îd al-Himiyarî Centre, also played an important part in the stigmatisation of Zaydism.

Among the heirs of Muqbil al-Wâdi'î, in Dammâj, that is, in a region directly affected by the fighting, the alliance with the government appeared to have taken a more concrete form. Yahyâ al-Hâjûrî gave an increased number of conferences, especially during the sixth round of fighting in late 2009, in which he described the 'Hûthîs' as a spin-off of the Lebanese Hizbollah. Demonstrating even greater attachment to Yemeni government policy, he criticised the opposition parties, particularly al-Islâh and the Muslim Brotherhood, accusing them of complacency with regard to the rebellion. He accused them of wanting to weaken the government, while characterising the position of the Salafis as 'respectful of the state and its efforts against disorder' (*fitna*).[47] One of his former students, now also a teacher in Dammâj, 'Abd al-Hamîd Bin Zayd al-Hajûrî, in a short book published in January 2010, alleged a connection between the 'Hûthîs' and the militants of al-Qaeda.[48] He suggested that both of these groups shared a common objective: to spread corruption among Muslims and to destroy the nation. He even credited certain groups inside the Yemeni security apparatus with discovering this connection.

Beyond this co-operation in terms of propaganda, the alliance between Salafis and the government as regards the war in Sa'da appears to have taken other forms. In March 2007, the death of two foreign students from Dâr al-Hadîth in Dammâj (one French and one British), both apparently killed in clashes with 'Hûthî' fighters, confirmed the rumours stating that some Salafis were participating in the war alongside the government's forces, illustrating the increasing closeness of the relationship. In 2009, during the sixth round of fighting, more extensive engagements around Dammâj left several dozen fighters dead (about twenty in August, and seventeen the following month).[49] Details concerning the dead combatants were sketchy, but these engagements generated stories in the Yemeni and international media suggesting that the Dâr al-Hadîth centre was training armed militants or jihadis.[50] There were

---

[47] Yahyâ al-Hajûrî, sound recording, *al-Kalima al-wâdhaha 'amâ yadûr fî Dammâj min fitnat al-râfidha* [The clear word on what is happening in Dammâj with the disorder of the râfidha].

[48] 'Abd al-Hamîd Bin Zayd al-Hajûrî, *Tawjîh al-muslimîn ilâ al-tarîq al-shar'iyya fî al-ta'âmul ma'a al-khawârij min ashâb tanzîm al-qâ'ida wa al-hûthiyin* [Guidance for the Muslims towards the legitimate path for dealing with the khawârij of al-Qaeda organisation and the Hûthîs], place and publisher unknown, 2010.

[49] *News Yemen*, 23 September, 2009.

[50] *al-Quds al-'Arabî*, 26 August, 2009.

claims that the fighting had involved mainly Salafi militants against 'Hûthî' fighters. Reacting to such accusations, Salafis generally stated that those fighting were tribesmen from Dammâj and not Dâr al-Hadîth students *per se*. Yahyâ al-Hajûrî denied that there was any programme to arm students from Dammâj to fight alongside government troops. He maintained rather that all the tribes of Yemen were engaged in a battle against the 'Hûthîs'. In his words, any Salafi involved had only joined a broad movement against what he called the *râfidha*, and Dammâj had played no particular role.[51] Surprisingly, 'Abd al-Malik al-Hûthî, whose opposition to the Salafi movement was well known, also denied that his partisans had engaged in combat against the students of Dammâj as such. His position was that portraying the war as a religious opposition was a propaganda ploy to divide the population of Sa'da over sectarian issues.[52]

In November 2009, three and a half months after the beginning of the sixth phase of armed combat in the war in Sa'da, military intervention from Saudi Arabia took place, opening a broader regional chapter of the conflict and giving it a new dimension. The acceptance of military assistance from outside Yemen, like the earlier calls for support from tribal militias, seemed tantamount to a government's admission of failure of its military strategy, something that could further weaken its legitimacy. The reasons for the Saudi decision to help the Yemeni army remain unclear, and were likely to be the result of certain internal changes affecting the monarchy.[53] On 5 November, 2009, Saudi jets bombed rebel positions inside Yemen, while Saudi Army units attempted without much success to push certain 'Hûthî' groups out of positions within Saudi territory (around Jabal Dukhân). The Saudi government affirmed that it had acted in legitimate self-defence, in the interest of its own sovereignty and after a 'Hûthî' attack had killed a customs official. The 'Hûthîs' claimed that the Yemeni Army had tried to trap them by attacking from inside Saudi territory before being

---

[51] Yahyâ al-Hajûrî, sound recording, *al-Kalima al-wâdhaha 'amâ yadûr fî Dammâj min fitnat al-râfidha* [The clear word on what is happening in Dammâj with the disorder of the râfidha].

[52] Official declaration of 'Abd al-Malik al-Hûthî: http://www.almenpar.net/news.php?action=view&id=1493, 26 August, 2009.

[53] Since the 1960s, Prince Sultân Bin 'Abd al-'Azîz Âl Su'ûd, Minister of Defence and first in line to succeed to the Saudi throne, has been considered the authority within the Saudi royal family on Yemeni matters. It appears that his failing health during 2009 may have left a certain vacuum, in addition to tensions between his own heirs and between various actors in the Ministry of Defence and those in the Ministry of the Interior in charge of the fight against terrorism.

forced to fall back under rebel pressure, leaving 'Hûthî' combattants inside Saudi territory and forced to protect themselves from Saudi attacks.

For a long time, the official position of the Saudi government with regard to the war in Sa'da had been to criticise any foreign interference. This position allowed Saudi diplomats to denounce the alleged involvement of Iran.[54] Such a stance did not apparently prevent certain Saudi actors, particularly some from the Ministry of Defence, from intervening covertly, especially with money, in support of the Yemeni Army, or from mobilising certain tribes (particularly in an effort in June 2008 to form a 'popular army (*jaysh sha'bî*)' around the figure of Husayn al-Ahmar and men from the Hâshid tribal confederation).

Early on, the military intervention of Saudi Arabia launched in November 2009 was described by religious actors as part of a sectarian battle against Shi'ism. The grand *muftî* of the Kingdom, 'Abd al-'Azîz Âl al-Shaykh, conferred religious legitimacy on the war, saying that the Saudi soldiers participating in the operation were to be described as 'mujahideen' fighting on the side of God.[55] This position was held by the entire Saudi Sunni religious field. Zayd al-Madkhalî, a figure in the quietist Salafi movement in Saudi Arabia, described the soldiers as guarantors of the unicity of God (*tawhîd*) and of religious dogma (*'aqîda*). For his part, Rabî' al-Madkhalî sent a message of support to the students of Dammâj, who were according to him engaged in 'the purest jihad'[56] against the partisans of al-Hûthî. The solid front presented by Saudi *'ulamâ'* in condemning the Hûthî rebellion no doubt promoted an even more ideological reading of the war by Yemeni Salafis, who continued to give conferences and make declarations in support of the Yemeni and Saudi Armies.

Such a commitment to the war in Sa'da, and the similar stance taken in regard to the 'Global War on Terror', illustrates once again the limits of the claim made by Salafis to be apolitical. Local and international contingencies have turned the Salafis into political actors who are then in the process of being normalised embedded as they are in the Yemeni national and regional scene.

III. Salafis Struggling Between the Local and the Global

The 'Yemenisation' of Salafism that is expressed in its politicisation and its normalisation as part of the political and religious landscape turns out to be particularly complex and ambivalent. The reappropriation of symbols by activ-

---

[54] Interview, Sana'a, 14 January 2009.
[55] *al-Hayât*, 11 November 2009.
[56] *al-'Ulûm*, http://aloloom.net/vb/showthread.php?p=24058.

ists, acceptance of nationalistic logics of action, and opposition to Saudi power and instrumentalisation by the Yemeni government do not conceal other processes that are occurring simultaneously. Yemeni Salafi activists and scholars find themselves caught up in contradictory dynamics that sometimes push them in favour of an alignment with positions defended by Saudi actors, and at other times push them in the direction of the assertion of local specificities.

In fact, the processes of adaptation to the Yemeni context reveal a paradox: their involvement in local issues, that is, their internal normalisation, occurs at the same time as normalisation within the transnational Salafi field. It is particularly because the Salafis have been integrated into the Yemeni political system (at the price of being instrumentalised by the government) that they have abandoned part of that which was specific to them. Their involvement in the struggle against terrorism produced a realignment with regard to the positions defended by Saudi 'ulamâ' affiliated to the religious institution.

Saudi References Back in the Game

The symbolic break with the 'Saudi godfather' that was supposed to imply increased sensitivity to local contexts on the part of Yemeni Salafis, has only been partial. As such, the roads leading to 'Yemenisation', like those leading to 'Saudisation', have turned out to be particularly contorted.

The emergence of the issue of 'terrorism' on international agendas appears to have prepared the way for the global normalisation of the Yemeni Salafi movement, just as much as the death of Muqbil al-Wâdi'î. In order to avoid stigmatisation as well as state repression, Salafi actors gradually became involved in an effort, self-conscious or not and not necessarily centralised, to attain respectability. Interestingly, such an effort took the shape of a realignment with regard to positions defended by Saudi 'ulamâ' close to the monarchy. This process was speeded up after September 11, 2001, and soon favoured a restructuring of the Salafi field alongside debates linked to violence and the nature of allegiance to governments. The main issue for Salafi entrepreneurs was to assert their difference from groups accused of being jihadi, and to prove their good faith by participating in the struggle against armed militant groups. In Yemen, among the heirs of Muqbil al-Wâdi'î, criticism of the Saudi regime was replaced by criticism of violent groups, the partisans of Sayyid Qutb, those of Usâma Bin Lâdin and all the adepts of the Saudi *Sahwa islâmiyya* movement who adopted an oppositional stance. Those who carried out assassination attempts, who excommunicated members of the government or who called for violent actions were to be considered as lost souls, and they became, in Yemen, in Saudi Arabia and elsewhere, the primary target of a uniform transnational Salafi rhetoric.

Thus in Yemen the context of the 'Global War on Terror' (as well as a marked improvement in bilateral Saudi-Yemeni relations with the signature of the June 2000 Jeddah border treaty) ended up favouring a re-emergence of Saudi sources. An entire body of literature published in Riyadh by the new guarantors of official Islam was intended to exculpate the governments, society, the 'ulamâ' and religion with regard to responsibility for the violent options taken by some. Works by 'Abd al-'Azîz Âl al-Shaykh, grand muftî of the Kingdom, Sâlih al-Fawzân, member of the Committee of Senior 'ulamâ',[57] Sultân al-'Îd, head of the Khâlid Bin al-Walîd mosque in Riyadh,[58] Zayd Bin Muhammad al-Madkhalî,[59] and 'Abd Allâh al-Ghâmidî[60] appeared in Yemeni Salafi bookstores more so than in the past. Beyond allegiance to the Saudi government, all these authors shared an opposition to the inheritors of the Muslim Brotherhood, and to violent action. In addition to theological arguments that they provided, these texts and conferences often constituted a legitimisation of the Saudi government's policy choices, including those related to the alliance with the United States.

Such productions evidently stood in sharp contrast to the offensive character of some recordings and books published by Muqbil al-Wâdi'î and other Yemeni Salafi entrepreneurs during the 1980s and 1990s. This reversal and the incoherence it represented symbolised all the ambiguity of the changes that the Salafi political and religious field had undergone. As these changes had played out, they showed the correlation of the nominally-opposed phases of 'Yemenisation' and 'Saudisation'.

In the post 9/11 and post-Muqbilian context, al-Hikma, al-Ihsân and the partisans of Abû al-Hasan al-Ma'ribî also continued to take part in transnational flows and to benefit from the ambivalent attraction which the Saudi reference exercised. Thus, the position defended by Abû al-Hasan al-Ma'ribî on the issue of the incapacity of contemporary 'ulamâ' to transcend national contexts did

---

[57] Sâlih al-Fawzân, al-Jihâd: anwâ'ihi wa ahkâmihi [The jihad: its forms and modalities], Riyadh: Dâr al-Imâm Ahmad, 2005.

[58] Sultân al-'Îd, al-Irhâb bayn al-tadmîr wa al-tabrîr [Terrorism, between destruction and justification], Riyadh: Dâr al-Imâm Ahmad, 2005.

[59] Zayd Bin Muhammad Al-Madkhalî, al-Irhâb wa âthâruhu al-sayyi' 'alâ al-afrâd wa al-umam [Terrorism and its negative impact upon individuals and nations], op. cit.

[60] 'Abd Allâh al-Ghâmidî, sound recording, Jarîmat al-irhâb wa awhâj al-irhâbiyyn [The crime of terrorism and the agitation of terrorists].

not prevent him from continuing to seek support outside Yemen. Hoping no doubt to expand his audience, he published his works in Riyadh, where he had a resident visa that he renewed each year. The Hikma association in 2004 had invited popular Saudi preacher, 'Â'idh al-Qarnî (once a leading figure of the *Sahwa*, he had been co-opted by Saudi officials in the early 2000s decade), for a series of conferences, while al-Ihsân in 2006 welcomed Salmân al-'Awda, also a former opponent of the monarchy, as well as a number of potential financial contributors from Gulf emirates. The emergence of these associations in the specific Yemeni context appeared as a delayed echo of the transformations that have occurred since 1980 in the transnational Salafi field, particularly in Saudi Arabia, Jordan and Kuwait.

Between the early 1980s and early 2000s, built up around Muqbil al-Wâdi'î, the Yemeni Salafi movement, in its great diversity, proved to be one of the most original departures seen in the Arabian Peninsula, or in the Muslim world in general. Yemeni Salafis put forward a principle of allegiance to the *walî al-amr* and refused direct political participation, and for a long time possessed a real independence with regard to various political groups and governments. In periods of crisis, they did not hesitate to condemn these, but they never broke completely with these movements or institutions, never crossing the red line of overt criticism of the Sâlih regime for example. They benefited from a favourable context in which the fall of socialism occurred, religious identities became more individualised and the interpenetration of societies increased. The charismatic figure of al-Wâdi'î allowed the movement to expand over virtually all of Yemen in less than twenty years and made him a revered figure both inside and outside of the country.

Undoubtedly it was the particular stance of the Yemeni cleric, blending doctrinal intransigence and criticism of the Saudi regime, which made Salafism successful. Unlike the senior *'ulamâ'* of the Land of the Two Holy Places, who like him also happened to pass away at the turn of the century, Muqbil al-Wâdi'î appeared never to have made concessions (at least until his return to the Saudi kingdom in 2000). His reluctance to return to Saudi Arabia—or even to make a pilgrimage—was for a long time a measure of his integrity. He built a reputation for speaking frankly and for honesty, which the simplicity and austerity of the Dâr al-Hadîth centre symbolised. Unlike Saudi preachers, the Yemeni scholar cultivated an image of humility, projecting himself as a man of the people, a man of knowledge and a man of the tribes. In such a manner this movement made use of the latitude the political system offered, a generally non-repressive system as it existed at the time in North Yemen and then in united Yemen. The freedom of expression that this movement enjoyed helped it avoid the trap of violence against the state. Even though the Muqbilian branch was considered exogenous by many both inside and outside of Yemen, it turned out to be highly autonomous in terms of the issues it focused on in its ideological production, and also in terms of organisation. Its rhetoric was often tinged with nationalism, and its involvement in tribal issues was evidence of a gradual but spontaneous process of integration, along with a voluntary process of Yemenisation.

However, the latter did not prevent rapprochement with Saudi Arabia, symbolised by the return to good graces of Muqbil al-Wâdi'î in 2000. As a consequence, from the early 2000s decade to the present, a gradual if fragile rapprochement between Salafi entrepreneurs in Yemen and Saudi Arabia has grown to stand as a symbol of another type of normalisation of Yemeni Salafism, occurring at a global level. Indeed, without the critique of the Saudi regime, part of its distinction was lost, and it seemed to get caught up in the kind of compromises it had until recently avoided. Positions with regard to violence against states were clarified, and the debate increasingly focused on issues related to the internal schism created by Abû al-Hasan al-Ma'ribî or on the endorsement of state policies whether against al-Qaeda, tenants of the *Sahwa* or Shi'ite movements. In the absence of charismatic, uncontested local references, actors were led to search outside of Yemen for their references, as a means of supporting their positions. As a result, the Yemeni Salafi field restructured itself around foreign figures and debates.

Holding on to Distinctive Qualities?

Much like other processes highlighted in the previous chapters, the reinstating of Saudi references is by no means one-sided or permanent. The global normalisation of Yemeni Salafism and its near dissolution in a wider standardised quietist Salafi movement headed by figures of the Saudi religious establishment may well be reversed. At the end of the first decade of the twenty-first century, a new controversy, this time opposing Yahyâ al-Hâjûrî and a former student at Dâr al-Hadîth, 'Abd al-Rahmân al-'Adanî (cf. Chapter 2), provided the opportunity for the branch now led by Yahyâ al-Hajûrî to distinguish itself, and perhaps even to marginalise itself globally, by letting the issue of the specificity of the Yemeni Salafi movement return to centre stage

The controversy (labelled *fitna* by the partisans of Yahyâ al-Hajûrî) had its roots partly in a personality clash between al-Hajûrî and al-'Adanî but also in a financial dispute. In 2008, following the creation of a religious institute by

al-'Adanî on the outskirts of Aden, al-Hâjûrî accused al-'Adanî of having devi-
ated from Salafi orthodoxy, of having engaged in partisan activity and of having
sought to enrich himself. The arguments about this, some carried on via websites, became heated enough that a transnational effort at conciliation was
launched. This involved a number of Saudi '*ulamâ*', notably Rabî' al-Madkhalî
and 'Ubayd al-Jâbirî (both connected with the Islamic University of Medina),
both of whom refused to take sides. Muhammad al-Imâm himself maintained
a kind of neutrality. Yahyâ al-Hajûrî made his objections clear, and finding
himself isolated, he began to openly criticise the Saudi '*ulamâ*' in retaliation,
reasserting the claim to Yemeni independence and specificity. He claimed to
be the only one who had seen through the mask worn by al-'Adanî, not only
with regard to the particular controversy, but because he knew him for a long
time at Dammâj. As an illustration of his own shift, in 2009, Yahyâ al-Hajûrî
claimed that he no longer considered the Islamic University to be a legitimate
Salafi institution, since partisans of political action (*hizbiyûn*) had dominated
it for several years.[61] Such an iconoclastic position illustrated the tensions that
persisted between local matters and global ones, between the parochial and
the universal within the Yemeni Salafi movement. Not surprisingly, al-Hajûrî's
position echoed a statement al-Wâdi'î had made in the early 1990s regarding
the same university. In fact this controversy symbolised the desire of certain
entrepreneurs, Yahyâ al-Hajûrî among them (a man who has never seemed able
to exercise leadership on his own account), to preserve their influence in Yemen
and internationally by appearing as independent actors.

'Saudisation', 'Yemenisation', 'autonomisation' and 'normalisation' are concepts and complex mechanisms that appear to operate simultaneously. In fact,
in the process of the transplantation that has been analysed, it seems more
accurate to describe the stages as coinciding rather than as a succession. Rather
than a mechanically imported Salafism disconnected from any real context,
this monograph presents a multiform political and religious movement that
has adapted to local issues at all levels, becoming a standard component in the
social and political landscape of Yemen. As such, quietist Salafism is also the
object of much opposition, and it is often instrumentalised and/or reappropriated by actors. Throughout these processes, it never loses any of its transnational
character, or its connection with various recompositions of the Salafi field in

---

[61] Yahyâ al-Hajûrî, *al-Tawdhîh lamâ jâ' fî al-taqrîrât al-'ilmiyya wa al-naqd al-sahîh*
[The clarification concerning scientific declarations and the authentic criticism],
place and publisher unknown, 2009.

Saudi Arabia or the Middle East in general, nor even its relationship to the migratory experience. Such an alternative approach to the Salafi phenomenon does justice to the non-linear character of the dynamics and the importance of individual trajectories, first among them that of Muqbil al-Wâdi'î. It also demonstrates the ambivalent effects of the transplantation of ideas, doctrines and practices. The hybridising phenomena largely prevail over homogenisation, although the results of these processes cannot be predicted in advance with any certainty. Actors' reappropriation of 'religious products' that are apparently 'standardised' (as is, perhaps, Salafism) prevents one from considering the normalisation of Salafism as an end in itself. On the contrary, Salafism is a social, political and religious practice that is ever changing. Therefore, the revolutionary process launched in February 2011 all over Yemen is likely to produce yet other recompositions and to directly affect the Salafi movement and its relations both with Saudi Arabia and politics in general.

CONCLUSION

The trajectory of the Salafi object, from its Saudi origin, constructed and 'myth-ified', up to its eventual integration within the Yemeni political and religious fields, is without doubt an instructive one. It helps highlight a wider range of transnational processes and the transformation of religious identities in the Muslim world. Building on a concrete case study, it also underlines the limits of state control over transnational religious movements, even ones they finance and believe to inspire. Such a conclusion has clear theoretical and policy relevance and adds up to existing research in other areas of the world or on other groups and sects.

This book's novelty resides in its ambition to focus on a specific movement, Salafism, whose emergence, while perceived by many as a threat, had, until recently, been surprisingly overlooked by academics. Focus on connections between Salafism and Saudi Arabia (which is undoubtedly one of the most consistent bogeymen of contemporary international relations), also challenged the idea that a religious doctrine can be made appealing to a wider public through flows of money and, in the process, can trigger new and sustainable political allegiances and identities.

In order to look into such phenomena, this book purposely broke with the narrative of the mechanical Saudisation of Yemeni Islam, and proposed an alternative approach to the emergence of Salafism. It drew on different academic traditions: political science, the sociology of international relations and anthro-pology. This multidisciplinary procedure was required to account for the plu-rality of spaces and levels in play, as well as for the web of local and transnational problematics, both individual and collective. As such, this research fostered reflection on issues of domination and imperialism, be it cultural or political, and on the shortcomings of an approach to international politics which sees power as the only variable. The Salafi movement in Yemen shows how much social change can be triggered by phenomena of domination. However, and most of all, it also highlights how much change in social and religious practices cannot be analysed as part of a grand design. Its meaning and implications can never be determined *a priori*. In its Yemeni environment, although connected to Saudi Arabia and to transnational flows, Salafism then becomes what the different actors make of it.

In the course of such a demonstration, an important preliminary step was to define and analyse the largely constructed, fictive, even imaginary characteristics of 'Saudi Arabia' as the point of origin of Salafism. From that representation stemmed the large-scale political and historical narratives of importation and exportation that link the development of Salafism in Yemen to Saudi domination. These flawed and imprecise narratives are still put forward by a broad range of actors, particularly ones of Zaydi origin, as well as by various analysts. In doing so, consciously or not, they place the Saudi state at the centre of social processes and assign meaning and purpose to the latter.

Building on a 'predilection for alternatives', my research further attempted (without ever claiming to assume the whole group of determinant variables) to account for the diversity of explanatory factors of the expansion of Salafism. Such a multi-level approach, oscillating between prominent Salafi entrepreneurs and anonymous activists, and focusing on the gaps and Fontiers of world politics, helped understand the main social recompositions that clarify the emergence of Salafi practice in a contemporary Yemeni context: interpenetration of societies on the Arabian Peninsula, individualisation of the relationship to religion, but also, for instance, the fall of socialism in South Yemen. Obviously, the variable linking the development of Salafism to Saudi domination was never absent and, in the end, appeared to be more efficient in the form of interactions 'from below' and in migratory phenomena, than in voluntary policies implemented by the state or by political, economic and religious elites.

Throughout the chapters, a peculiar quietist version of Salafism emerged, one that is not rigid or beholden to the Saudis, but one that is an unconscious political and religious movement affected by complex and contradictory dynamics. The figure of Muqbil al-Wâdi'î, commonly perceived as a 'Trojan horse' financed by the Saudi government, turned out to be a passionate critic of the monarchy, calling into question even the religious legitimacy of the Âl Su'ûd. As a matter of fact, if such had ever been the purpose of Saudi funding to the Salafi institutes, the Yemeni Salafis have turned out to be pretty incompetent agents working for the interests of their Saudi sponsors, especially during periods of crisis. Their apolitical and quietist doctrine has had a certain tendency to evolve into nationalism, regionalism or even tribalism. In such a framework the capacity of religious actors to control the orthodoxy and the allegiance of actors has also proven limited.

Beyond a simplistic picture that declares that anonymous Yemeni migrants brought 'Wahhabism' passively home in their suitcases, the ambiguous character of the migratory experience was stressed. Admiration for an apparently successful economy is generally coupled with a severe critique of Saudis and their government. Through the case study of the Faculty of Education in Lab'ûs in Yâfi' region, translocal relations were examined. Processes through which some young Yemenis, often incapable of attaining the 'Saudi way of life' through economic success, tried to attain it through religion, that is, rituals and mimetic conduct were highlighted. Consistent attempts by the Saudi government since the mid-twentieth century to portray itself as the 'Servant of the Two Holy Places' and to fund certain groups have undoubtedly played a role in the process of the development of Salafism in the Yemeni context, yet they do not appear to have triggered significant shifts in allegiances. They do not either appear to have been able to substantially affect bilateral relations or to improve Saudi Arabia's image among the wider public. As such, they cannot be seen as globally successful.

Despite Salafism's 'tropism' towards Saudi Arabia, it is involved in many processes of adaptation that add up to a 'Yemenisation'. In this framework, Salafi practice at the grassroots is characterised on one side by flexibility and on the other by the fluidity of individual trajectories, in relation to the dogmas elaborated by the 'ulamâ'-entrepreneurs. Salafism ends up being integrated with regard to local issues, that is, it is used, competed with and attacked, and in the process of these challenges becomes part of the Yemeni political landscape.

The formulation of an alternative narrative of the emergence of Salafism was tantamount to an attempt to rescue part of history, in its social and political transformations, from the exclusive influence and control of the state and its meta-discourse. In order to do just that, it was necessary to banish the mechanical and self-serving narratives of nations, history and their interests, replacing it with an approach focused on social recompositions and aggregations of individual practices.

The rebuttal of so-called mechanical processes of importation helped go beyond what are to be seen as rhetorical questions: Without the Saudis, would Salafism have developed in Yemen? Could this political and religious movement be disconnected from its relations with Saudi Arabia? Is Salafism what the Yemeni Salafis claim: a return to source texts intended to finish off centuries of misrepresentations by Zaydis, Ottomans, Sufis, Nasserites and socialists? Supported upon the *hadîth*, claiming the heritage of Yemeni Traditionist theologians, Salafis assert to be authentically Yemeni. Not unlike the argument about the chicken and the egg, debate over the Salafi 'cosmogony' appears as flawed. It comes down to asking whether Salafism in Yemen appeared because the cultural ground was favourable (based on the alleged essential piety of the Yemeni people and the precedent of Muhammad al-Shawkânî) or because of its ability to transform the environment it moved into, gaining the allegiance of some thanks to financing or to a process of acculturation that operated through teaching centres, the Scientific Institutes or through corruption of tribal culture. The identification of an actual point of origin (not a mythical one like that identified in actors' narratives—Saudi or Yemeni) would imply that Salafism would be frozen in time, an unchanging essence. In the event, Salafism turns out to be an ever-changing practice and, as such, the search for a physical origin becomes a pointless operation.

At the same time, the idea of transplantation could not be completely rejected as this notion underlines the recent emergence of Salafism into the contemporary political and religious field as well as its deep involvement in transnational space and the 'Frontier' of Saudi-Yemeni relations. This notion illuminates the fact that the doctrine worked out by Salafi entrepreneurs partly breaks with their environment and insists on its own novelty within Yemen. It is significant that it was over the course of his long experience as a migrant to Saudi Arabia that Muqbil al-Wâdi'î managed to discover what he saw as the theological 'errors' of his Zaydi upbringing. The acculturation that uprooting implies was undoubtedly able to exercise a significant role in shaping the individual trajectory of the founder of the Yemeni Salafi movement. Muqbilian Salafism did not claim allegiance to the Hanbali school of jurisprudence, but found some of its roots in valued sources which were linked to the Saudi environment. By this inclination as much as through Saudi financing, Yemeni Salafism found itself tied to Saudi Arabia, its state and society, in a number of ways. However, relations proved more than ambivalent and adaptation to the local environment influenced new practices and let the doctrine evolve.

In a new context, Salafism fulfils new functions. In fact, for anonymous actors—much like for the renowned entrepreneurs of the religious realm—it doesn't have the same meaning in Yemen that it had in Saudi Arabia, or that it has elsewhere. The weight of context, political, institutional, historical and social structures must be recognised. The effects of transplantation are felt at all levels, and Salafism in the specific Yemeni space receives a new meaning, which it might have lost to some extent in Saudi Arabia because of the proximity of the royal family and the state. As exemplified by reactions to the 2011 popular uprising, change in local context favours important evolutions and recompositions. As demonstrations in Sana'a and elsewhere were gaining momentum in the Spring of 2011, figures from al-Hikma were starting a new phase in their politicisation, promising to establish a political party and calling for the departure of 'Alî 'Abd Allâh Sâlih. At the other end of the Salafi spectrum, Yahyâ al-Hajûrî and other core members of the *salafiyya da'wiyya* were denying the legitimacy of the revolutionary process.

The metaphor of the transplantation helps underline the double nature of the Yemeni Salafi movement. It is partly the result of an endogenous development, but also the output of the interpenetration of societies of the Arabian Peninsula, of the encounter of persons, of different trajectories and different influences, particular individual careers and charismatic personalities. Its rapid and notable emergence since the early 1980s is part of the history of the Arabian Peninsula—in fact part of the Muslim world as a whole. It cannot be disconnected from of the old fascination Saudi Arabia holds for the people of Yemen because of its wealth and its vocation as a model of Islamic piety in the Muslim world. In this framework the development of the political and religious movement is only secondarily and indirectly linked to a proselytising policy engineered by Saudi Arabia. Transnational relations (migration, private development aid, financing of centres, media, commerce, and so on) are at the heart of the recompositions that explain the success of Salafism in the Yemeni environment. Focusing on the double nature of the Yemeni Salafi movement allows us to ultimately reach beyond the opposition of an endogenous practice made from internal recompositions and a disconnected imported practice. Although localised and adapted, Salafism is most of all transnational and involved in a complex voyage that is still continuing.

ABRIDGED BIBLIOGRAPHY

As most sources used in the process of this research have already been presented in detail in the numerous footnotes, this bibliography is only a selection of books and articles in Arabic, English and French. Some might have been already quoted or referred to in the core of the text while others may appear here for the first time. This selection deals directly with issues related to Salafism, Islam, Yemeni and Middle East politics and not with theory, international relations and sociology of religion. I have also added a selection of primary written sources published by Islamic scholars.

Paul Aarts and Gerd Nonneman (eds.), *Saudi Arabia in the Balance: Political Economy, Society, Foreign Affairs*, London: Hurst, 2005, p. xvi–462.

Rifaʿa Sayyid Ahmad, *Rasâʾil Juhaymân al-ʿUtaybî* [The letters of Juhaymân al-ʿUtaybî], Cairo: Maktabat Madbûlî, 2004, p. 438.

Ismâʿîl Bin ʿAlî al-Akwaʿ, *al-Zaydiyya: nashâtuhâ wa muʿtaqidâtuhâ* [Zaydism: its dynamism and beliefs], publisher unknown, 2000, p. 126.

Hamid Algar, *Wahhabism: A Critical Essay*, Oneonta: Islamic Publications International, 2002, p. 96.

Anahi Alviso-Marino, 'Contentious Dynamics for Sociopolitical Change? The Case of the Islah Party in the Republic of Yemen', *Chroniques Yéménites*, no. 16, 2010, pp. 57–90.

Samir Amghar and Patrick Haenni, 'Au sortir du mythe impossible de l'outlandish man... l'universel positif de l'islam post-salafiste' in Jocelyne Dakhlia (ed.), *Créations artistiques contemporaines en pays d'islam: des arts en tension*, Paris: Kimé éditions, 2006, pp. 1–17.

Samir Amghar, 'Les salafistes français: une nouvelle aristocratie religieuse?', *Maghreb Machrek*, no. 183, 2005, pp. 13–32.

Masʿûd ʿAmshûsh, *al-Hadhârim fî al-arkhibîl al-hindî* [Hadramis in the Indonesian Archipelgo], Aden: Dâr Jâmiʿat ʿAdan, 2006, p. 173.

Saeed M. Badeeb, *The Saudi-Egyptian Conflict over North Yemen, 1962–1970*, Boulder: Westview Press, 1986, p. 148.

ʿAbd Allâh Saʿîd Bâ Hâjj, *al-Yamaniyûn fî al-Suʿûdiyya khilâl rubuʿ qarn (1965–1990)* [Yemenis in Saudi Arabia during a quarter of a century (1965–1990)], Sharjah: Dâr al-Thaqâfa al-ʿArabiyya, 2002, p. 53.

Amîn Sa'îd Bâ Wazîr, *Halqât al-qur'ân al-karîm wa majâlis al-'ilm fî masâjid 'Adan* [The Qur'anic circles and the scientific assemblies in the mosques of Aden], Sana'a: Markaz al-'Ubâdî, 2005, p. 206.

Asef Bayat, *Street Politics: Poor People's Movements in Iran*, New York: Columbia University Press, p. 232.

Claire Beaugrand, 'Émergence de la nationalité dans le Golfe: vers la monopolisation étatique du contrôle des mouvements de biens et de personnes', *Chroniques Yéménites*, no. 14, 2007, pp. 89–107.

Mounia Bennani-Chraïbi and Olivier Fillieule (eds.), *Résistances et protestations dans les sociétés musulmanes*, Paris: Presses de Sciences Po, 2003, p. 419.

Jonathan Benthall and Jérôme Bellion-Jourdan, *The Charitable Crescent: Politics of Aid in the Muslim World*, London: I.B. Tauris, 2003, p. xii–196.

Romain Bertrand, 'Plus près d'Allah' L'itinéraire social et idéologique d'Imam Samudra, terroriste et militant islamiste' in Annie Collovald and Brigitte Gaïti (eds.), *La démocratie aux extrêmes: sur la radicalisation politique*, Paris: La Dispute, 2006, pp. 201–222.

Robert Bianchi, *Guests of God: Pilgrimage and Politics in the Islamic World*, Oxford: Oxford University Press, 2004, p. xvii–358.

Isa Blumi, *Chaos in Yemen. Societal Collapse and the New Authoritarianism*, New York: Routledge, 2010, p. 224.

Laurent Bonnefoy, 'La guerre de Sa'da: des singularités yéménites à l'agenda international', *Critique Internationale*, no. 48, 2010, pp. 137–159.

——— 'Les identités religieuses contemporaines au Yémen: convergence, résistances et instrumentalisations', *Revue des Mondes Musulmans et de la Méditerranée*, no. 121–122, 2008, pp. 201–215.

Laurent Bonnefoy and Marine Poirier, 'The Yemeni Congregation for Reform (al-Islâh): The Difficult Process of Building a Project for Change' in Myriam Catusse and Karam Karem (eds.) *Returning to Political Parties? Partisan Logic and Political Transformations in the Arab World*, Beirut: Lebanese Center for Policy Studies, 2010, pp. 61–100.

Christopher Boucek, Shazadi Beg and John Horgan, 'Opening up the Jihadi Debate: Yemen's Committee for Dialogue' in Tore Bjorgo and John Horgan (eds.), *Leaving Terrorism Behind: Disengagement from Political Violence*, New York: Routledge, 2008, pp. 181–192.

Ludmila du Bouchet, 'The State, Political Islam and Violence: The Reconfiguration of Yemeni Politics since 9/11' in Amélie Blom, Laetitia Bucaille and Luis Martinez (eds.), *The Enigma of Islamist Violence*, London: Hurst, 2007, pp. 137–164.

Linda Boxberger, *On the Edge of Empire: Hadhramawt, Emigration and the Indian Ocean (1880s–1930s)*, Albany: State University of New York Press, 2002, p. 292.

Hamit Bozarslan, *Une histoire de la violence au Moyen-Orient*, Paris: La Découverte, 2008, p. 319.

Michaelle Browers, 'Origins and Architects of Yemen's Joint Meeting Parties', *International Journal of Middle Eastern Studies*, vol. 39, no. 4, 2007, pp. 565–586.

David Buchman, 'The Underground Friends of God and their Adversaries: A Case Study and Survey of Sufism in Contemporary Yemen', *Yemen Update*, no. 39, 1997, pp. 21–24.

ABRIDGED BIBLIOGRAPHY

Abdalla Bujra, *The Politics of Stratification: A Study of Political Change in a South Arabian Town*, Oxford: Clarendon Press, 1971, p. xvi–201.

François Burgat, 'Le Yémen après le 11 septembre 2001: entre construction de l'Etat et rétrécissement du champ politique', *Critique Internationale*, no. 32, 2006, pp. 11–21.

———— *L'islamisme à l'heure d'al-Qaida*, Paris: La Découverte, 2005, p. 215.

———— *L'islamisme en face*, Paris: La Découverte, 3rd edition, 2002, p. 303.

François Burgat and Baudouin Dupret (eds.), *Le shaykh et le procureur: systèmes coutumiers et pratiques juridiques au Yémen et en Égypte*, Cairo: CEDEJ, 2005, p. 335.

François Burgat and Mohamed Sbitli, 'Les salafis au Yémen ou... la modernisation malgré tout', *Chroniques Yéménites*, no. 10, 2003, pp. 123–152.

Jason Burke, *Al-Qaeda: Casting a Shadow of Terror*, London: I.B. Tauris, 2003, p. 292.

Robert Burrowes, 'Yemen: Political Economy and the Effort Against Terrorism' in Robert Rotberg (ed.), *Battling Terrorism in the Horn of Africa*, Cambridge: World Peace Foundation, 2005, pp. 141–172.

———— *The Yemen Arab Republic: The Politics of Development. 1962–1986*, Boulder: Croom Held, 1987, p. 256.

John Calvert, *Sayyid Qutb and the Origins of Radical Islamism*, London: Hurst, 2010, p. 288.

Sylvaine Camelin, 'Du Hadramaout aux Comores... et retour', *Journal des Africanistes*, vol. 72, no. 2, 2003, pp. 123–137.

Sheila Carapico, *Civil Society in Yemen. The Political Activism in Modern Arabia*, Cambridge: Cambridge University Press, 1998, p. xv–256.

Olivier Carré, *Mystique et politique. Le Coran des islamistes. Lecture du Coran par Sayyid Qutb Frère musulman radical (1906–1966)*, Paris: Editions du Cerf, 2004, p. 381.

Steven Caton, *Yemen Chronicle: An Anthropology of War and Mediation*, New York: Hill and Wang, 2005, p. 343.

Norman Cigar, 'Islam and the State in South Yemen: The Uneasy Co-Existence', *Middle Eastern Studies*, vol. 26, no. 2, 1990, pp. 185–203.

Kiren Aziz Chaudhry, *The Price of Wealth: Economies and Institutions in the Middle East*, London: Cornell University Press, 1997, p. xiii–330.

Joseph Chelhod (ed.), *L'Arabie du Sud: histoire et civilisation. Tome 3: Culture et institutions du Yémen*, Paris: Maisonneuve & Larose, 1984, p. 432.

Collective, *al-Yaman wa al-Khalij* [Yemen and the Gulf], Sana'a: Markaz al-Yamanî lil-dirâsât al-Istrâtîjiyya, 2003, p. 212.

———— *al-Islâmiyyûn fî al-Yaman* [Islamists in Yemen], Aden: al-Markaz al-'Âmm lil-Dirâsât wa al-Buhûth wa al-Isdâr, 2002, p. 384.

———— *al-Yaman wa al-'âlam* [Yemen and the world], Cairo: Maktabat Madbûlî, 2001, p. 491.

Nora Ann Colton, 'Homeward Bound: Yemeni Return Migration', *International Migration Review*, vol. 27, no. 4, 1993, pp. 870–882.

David Commins, *The Wahhabi Mission in Saudi Arabia*, London: I.B. Tauris, 2006, p. xii–276.

Michael Cook, *Commanding Right and Forbidding Wrong in Islamic Thought*, Cambridge: Cambridge University Press, 2001, p. 720.

Miriam Cooke and Bruce Lawrence (eds.), *Muslim Networks from Hajj to Hip Hop*, London: University of Carolina Press, 2005, p. xiii–325.

Ahmad al-Daghshî, *al-Khilâf al-salafî al-salafî fî al-Yaman* [The controversy between Salafis in Yemen], Sana'a: Markaz al-'Ubadî, 2004, p. 104.

——— *Ahl al-sunna wa al-jamâ'a: ishkâl fî al-fahm am fî al-mafhûm?* [The ahl al-sunna wa al-jamâ'a: Problem of comprehension or of concept?], Sana'a: Markaz al-'Ubâdî, 2003, p. 105.

Susanne Dahlgren, 'The Chaste Woman takes her Chastity Wherever she Goes. Discourses on Gender, Marriage and Work in Pre- and Post-Unification Aden', *Chroniques Yéménites*, no. 6–7, 2000, pp. 77–86.

Olivier Da Lage, 'L'émergence d'une identité 'khalijienne' (1971–2004)' in Rémy Leveau and Frédéric Charillon (eds.), *Monarchies du Golfe: les micro-Etats de la Péninsule arabique*, Paris: La Documentation Française, 2005, pp. 27–41.

Stephen Day. 'Updating Yemeni National Unity: Could Lingering Regional Divisions Bring Down the Regime?', *The Middle East Journal*, no. 3, 2008, pp. 417–436.

Fatiha Dazi-Héni, *Monarchies et sociétés d'Arabie: Le temps des confrontations*, Paris: Presses de Sciences Po, 2006, p. 363.

Natana J. Delong-Bas, *Wahhabi Islam: From Revival and Reform to Global Jihad*, Oxford: Oxford University Press, 2004, p. ix–370.

Renaud Detalle (ed.), *Tensions in Arabia: The Saudi-Yemeni Fault Line*, Baden Baden: Nomos Verlagsgesellschaft, 2000, p. 181.

——— 'Les islamistes yéménites et l'Etat: vers l'émancipation?' in Basma Kodmani-Darwish and May Chartouni-Dubarry (eds.), *Les Etats Arabes Face à la Contestation Islamiste*, Paris: Ifri / Armand Colin, 1997, pp. 271–298.

——— 'Les partis politiques au Yémen: paysage après la bataille', *Revue du Monde Musulman et de la Mediterranée*, no. 81–82, 1996, pp. 331–348.

Igor Dobaev, 'Radical Wahhabism as an Extremist Religious-political Ideology', *Central Asia and the Caucasus*, vol. 16, no. 4, 2002, pp. 128–138.

Samy Dorlian, 'Les reformulations identitaires du zaydisme dans leur contexte socio-politique contemporain', *Chroniques Yéménites*, no. 15, 2008, pp. 161–176.

——— 'Zaydisme et modernisation: émergence d'un nouvel universel politique?', *Chroniques Yéménites*, no. 13, 2006, pp. 93–109.

Leigh Douglas, *The Free Yemeni Movement 1935–1962*, Beirut: American University of Beirut, 1987, p. xix–287.

Paul Dresch, *A History of Modern Yemen*, Cambridge: Cambridge University Press, 2000, p. 285.

——— *Tribes, Governments and History in Yemen*; Oxford: Clarendon Paperbacks, 1993, p. 440.

Paul Dresch and Bernard Haykel, 'Stereotypes and Political Styles: Islamists and Tribesfolk in Yemen', *International Journal of Middle East Studies*, vol. 27, no. 4, 1995, pp. 405–431.

Paul Dresch and James Piscatori (eds.), *Monarchies and Nations: Globalisation and Identity in the Arab States of the Gulf*, New York: I.B. Tauris, 2005, p. vii–311.

Dale Eickelman and James Piscatori (eds.), *Muslim Travellers: Pilgrimage, Migration, and the Religious Imagination*, Los Angeles: University of California Press, 1990, p. xii–281.

ABRIDGED BIBLIOGRAPHY

Askar al-Enazy, *The Long Road from Taif to Jeddah: Resolution of a Saudi-Yemeni Boundary Dispute*, Abu Dhabi: Emirates Center for Strategic Studies, 2005, p. xvii–276.

Mamoun Fandy, *Saudi Arabia and the Politics of Dissent*, London: Macmillan Press, 1999, p. 272.

Sa'd al-Faqîh, 'I'tirâdhât al-salafiyîn 'alâ al-dîmûqrâtiyya [The Salafis' objections regarding democracy]' in 'Alî al-Kuwârî (ed.), *Azmat al-dîmûqrâtiyya fî al-buldân al-'arabiyya*, Beirut: Dâr al-Sâqî, 2004, pp. 67–93.

Jean-Pierre Filiu, *L'Apocalypse dans l'Islam*, Paris: Fayard, 2008, p. 375.

Ulrike Freitag and William Clarence-Smith (eds.), *Hadhrami Traders, Scholars and Statesmen in the Indian Ocean (1750s–1960s)*, Leiden: Brill, 1997, p. x–392.

Jonathan Friedlander (ed.), *Sojourners and Settlers: The Yemeni Immigrant Experience*, Salt Lake City: University of Utah Press, 1988, p. 188.

Gregory Gause, *Saudi-Yemeni Relations. Domestic Structures and Foreign Influence*, New York: Columbia University Press, 1990, p. xi–233.

Michael Gilsenan, *Recognizing Islam. An Anthropologist's Introduction*, London: Croom Held, 1982, p. 288.

'Abd al-Rahmân Tayyib al-Hadhramî, *al-Rajul alladhî uhabahu al-haram wa al-haram: batal al-jumhuriyya al-shaykh 'Abd Allâh Bin Husayn al-Ahmar* [The man loved by the sanctuary and the pyramid: the hero of the republic the shaykh 'Abd Allâh Bin Husayn al-Ahmar], Sana'a: Dâr al-Shawkânî, 1998, p. 294.

Patrick Haenni, *L'islam de marché. L'autre révolution conservatrice*, Paris: Seuil, 2005, p. 111.

————— *L'ordre des caïds: conjurer la dissidence urbaine au Caire*, Paris: Karthala/CEDEJ, 2005, p. 322.

Patrick Haenni and Tjitske Holtrop, 'Mondaines spiritualités, Amr Khâlid, shaykh branché de la jeunesse dorée cairote', *Politique Africaine*, no. 87, 2002, pp. 45–68.

Muhammad Hafez, *Why Muslims Rebel: Repression and Resistance in the Islamic World*, Boulder: Lynne Rienner, 2003, p. 253.

'Abd al-Fattâh al-Hakîmî, *Al-islâmiyûn wa al-siyâsa: al-ikhwân al-muslimûn namûdhajan* [Islamists and politics: the example of the Muslim Brotherhood], Sana'a: al-Muntadâ al-Jâmi'î, 2003, p. 133.

Fred Halliday, *Britain's First Muslims. Portrait of an Arab Community*, London: I.B. Tauris, 2010, p. 192.

————— *Nation and Religion in the Middle East*, London: Saqi Books, 2000, p. 251.

————— *Islam and the Myth of Confrontation*, London: I.B. Tauris, 1996, p. 255.

————— *Revolution and Foreign Policy. The Case of South Yemen 1967–1987*, Cambridge: Cambridge University Press, 1990, p. 315.

————— 'Catastrophe in South Yemen: A Preliminary Assessment', *MERIP Reports*, no. 139, 1986, pp. 37–39.

————— 'Yemen's Unfinished Revolution: Socialism in the South', *MERIP Reports*, no. 81, 1979, pp. 3–20.

————— *Arabia Without Sultans*, Harmondsworth: Penguin Press, 1974, p. 526.

'Abd Allâh Bin Muhammad Hamîd al-Dîn, *al-Zaydiyya* [Zaydism], Sana'a: Markaz al-Râ'id, 2004, p. 161.

Abdellah Hammoudi, *Une saison à La Mecque: récit de pèlerinage*, Paris: Seuil, 2005, p. 317.

Noorhaidi Hasan, *Laskar Jihad: Islam, Militancy, and the Quest for Identity in Post-New Order Indonesia*, Ithaca: Cornell University, 2006, p. 266.

Bernard Haykel, *Revival and Reform in Islam. The Legacy of Muhammad al-Shawkânî*, Cambridge: Cambridge University Press, 2003, p. 267.

——— 'Reforming Islam by Dissolving the Madhâhib: Shawkânî and his Zaydî Detractors in Yemen', in Bernard Weiss (ed.), *Studies in Islamic Legal Theory*, Leiden: Brill, 2002, pp. 337–364.

——— 'The Salafis in Yemen at a Crossroads: an Obituary of Shaykh Muqbil al-Wadi'i of Dammaj', *Jemen Report*, no. 2, 2002, pp. 28–31.

——— 'Recent Publishing Activity by the Zaydis in Yemen: A Select Bibliography', *Chroniques Yéménites*, no. 9, 2002, pp. 225–230.

——— 'Al-Shawkânî and the Jurisprudential Unity of Yemen', *Revue du Monde Musulman et de la Mediterranée*, no. 67, 1993, pp. 53–65.

Thomas Hegghammer, *Jihad in Saudi Arabia. Violence and Pan-Islamism since 1979*, Cambridge: Cambridge University Press, 2010, p. x–290.

Thomas Hegghammer and Stéphane Lacroix, 'Rejectionist Islamism in Saudi Arabia: The Story of Juhayman al-'Utaybi Revisited', *The International Journal of Middle East Studies*, vol. 39, no. 1, 2007, pp. 97–116.

Steffen Hertog, *Princes, Brokers, and Bureaucrats: Oil and the State in Saudi Arabia*, Ithaca: Cornell University Press, 2010, p. xii–297.

Charles Hirschkind, *The Ethical Soundscape. Cassette Sermons and Islamic Counterpublics*, New York: Columbia University Press, 2006, p. xv–270.

Engseng Ho, *The Graves of Tarim: Genealogy and Mobility Across the Indian Ocean*, Berkeley: University of California Press, 2006, p. xxvi–379.

——— 'Empire through Diasporic Eyes: A View from the Other Boat', *Comparative Studies in Society and History*, vol. 46, no. 2, 2004, pp. 210–246.

——— 'Yemenis on Mars: The End of Mahjar (Diaspora)?', *Middle East Report*, no. 211, 1999, pp. 29–31.

Zâyad Muhammad Jâbir (ed.), *Zâhirat al-tha'r fî al-Yaman* [The phenomenon of tribal vendetta in Yemen], Sana'a: Saba, 2004, p. 257.

Sa'îd 'Ubayd al-Jamhî, *Tanzîm al-qâ'ida: al-nashâ, al-khalfiyya al-fikriyya, al-imtidâd. al-Yaman namudhajân* [al-Qaeda organisation: establishment, ideological background, contiguity. The example of Yemen], Cairo: Madbûlî, 2007, p. 556.

Gregory Johnsen, 'The Expansion Strategy of al-Qaeda in the Arabian Peninsula', *CTC Sentinel*, vol. 2, no. 9, 2009, pp. 8–11.

——— 'The Resiliency of Yemen's Aden-Abyan Islamic Army', *Terrorism Monitor*, vol. 4, no. 14, 2006, pp. 4–5.

——— 'Profile of Sheikh Abd al-Majid al-Zindani', *Terrorism Monitor*, vol. 4, no. 7, 2006, pp. 3–5.

Uwaidah Al-Juhany, *Najd Before the Salafi Reform Movement*, London: Ithaca, 2002, p. x–213.

Gilles Kepel (ed.), *Al-Qaida dans le texte*, Paris: PUF, 2005, p. 440.

——— *Jihad: expansion et déclin de l'islamisme*, Paris: Gallimard, 2000, p. 452.

——— *Le Prophète et le Pharaon: Les mouvements islamistes dans l'Égypte contemporaine*, Paris: La Découverte, 1984, p. 248.

Anwâr Qâsim al-Khadrî, *al-'Unf fi al-Yaman* [Violence in Yemen], Sana'a: Markaz al-Jazîra al-'Arabiyya lil-Dirâsât wal-Buhûth, 2008, p. 135.

Moussa Khedimellah, 'Jeunes prédicateurs du mouvement Tabligh: la dignité identitaire retrouvée par le puritanisme religieux?', *Socio-anthropologie*, no. 10, 2003, pp. 5–18.

James Robin King, 'Zaydis in a Post-Zaydi Yemen: 'Ulama Reactions to Zaydism's Marginalisation in the Republic of Yemen', *Shi'a Affairs Journal*, vol. 1, 2008, pp. 53–84.

Amira Kotb, *La Tarîqa Ba'Alawiyya et le développement d'un réseau soufi transnational*, Masters' dissertation, Aix-en-Provence University, 2004, p. 131.

Alexander Knysh, 'The Tariqa on a Landcruiser: The Resurgence of Sufism in Yemen', *Middle East Journal*, vol. 55, no. 3, 2001, pp. 399–414.

——— 'The Sâda in History: A Critical Essay on Hadramî Historiography', *Journal of the Royal Asiatic Society*, Third Series, vol. 9, Part 2, July 1999, pp. 215–222.

——— 'The Cult of Saints and Islamic Reformism in Early Twentieth Century Hadramawt', *New Arabian Studies*, no. 4, 1997, pp. 139–167.

——— 'The Cult of Saints in Hadramawt. An Overview', *New Arabian Studies*, n°1, 1993, pp. 137–152.

Stéphane Lacroix, *Les islamistes saoudiens: une insurrection manquée*, Paris: Presses Universitaires de France, 2009, p. 360.

——— 'Between Islamists and Liberals: Saudi Arabia's new 'Islamo-Liberal' Reformists', *Middle East Journal*, vol. 58, no. 3, 2004, pp. 345–365.

Henri Laoust, *Pluralismes dans l'islam*, Paris: G. Geuthner, 1983, p. 512.

Bruce Lawrence, *Messages to the World: The Statements of Osama Bin Laden*, New York: Verso, 2005, p. 292.

Rémy Leveau, Franck Mermier and Udo Steinbach (eds.), *Le Yémen contemporain*, Paris: Karthala, 1999, p. 459.

Brynjar Lia, *Architect of Global Jihad: The Life of Al-Qaida Strategist Abu Mus'ab al-Suri*, London: Hurst, 2008, p. ix–510.

Laurence Louër, *Transnational Shia Politics: Political and Religious Networks in the Gulf*, London: Hurst, 2008, p. 256.

Anh Nga Longva, 'Keeping Migrant Workers in Check: The Kafala System in the Gulf', *Middle East Report*, no. 211, 1999, pp. 20–22.

Abdullah Lux, 'Yemen's Last Zaydi Imam: The Shabab al-Mu'min, the Malazim, and Hizb Allah in the Thought of Husayn Badr al-Din al-Huthi', *Contemporary Arab Affairs*, vol. 2, no. 3, 2009, pp. 369–434.

Saba Mahmood, *The Politics of Piety: The Islamic Revival and the Feminist Subject*, Princeton: Princeton University Press, 2005, p. xvi–233.

Peter Mandaville, *Global Political Islam*, London: Routledge, 2007, p. xv–388.

——— *Transnational Muslim Politics. Reimagining the Umma*, London: Routledge, 2001, p. 235.

Ibrâhîm Ahmad al-Maqhafî, *Mu'jam al-buldân wa al-qabâ'il al-yamaniyya* [Dictionary of places and tribes of Yemen], 2 volumes, Sana'a: Dâr al-Kalima, 2002, p. 1943.

Muhammad Khalid Masud (ed.), *Travellers in Faith: Studies of the Tablighi Jama'at as a Transnational Islamic Movement for Faith Renewal*, Leiden: Brill, 2000, p. lx–268.

Roel Meijer (ed.), *Global Salafism: Islam's New Religious Movement*, London: Hurst/Columbia University Press, 2009, p. xix–463.

Anne Meneley, 'Fashions and Fundamentalisms in Fin-de-siècle Yemen. Chador Barbie and Islamic Socks', *Cultural Anthropology*, vol. 22, no. 2, 2007, pp. 214–243.

Pascal Ménoret, 'Fighting for the Holy Mosque'. The 1979 Mecca Insurgency' in Christine Fair and Sumit Ganguly (eds.), *Treading on Hallowed Ground: Counterinsurgency Operations in Sacred Spaces*, Oxford: Oxford University Press, 2008, pp. 117–139

——— 'Le cheikh, l'électeur et le SMS: logiques électorales et mobilisation islamique en Arabie Saoudite', *Transcontinentales*, no. 1, 2005, pp. 19–33.

——— 'De la rage à l'enthousiasme: parcours d'un jeune électeur saoudien', *Chroniques Yéménites*, no. 12, 2005, pp. 121–139.

——— 'Le wahhabisme, arme fatale du néo-orientalisme', *Mouvements*, no. 36, 2004, pp. 54–60.

——— *L'énigme saoudienne: les saoudiens et le monde 1744–2003*, Paris: La Découverte, 2003, p. 260.

Franck Mermier, *Le cheikh de la nuit. Sanaa: organisations des souks et société citadine*, Arles: Actes Sud, 1999, p. 253.

———, 'L'islam politique au Yémen ou la 'Tradition' contre les traditions?', *Maghreb Machrek*, no. 155, 1997, pp. 6–19.

Brinkley Messick, *The Calligraphic State. Textual Domination and History in a Muslim Society*, Berkeley: University of California Press, 1993, p. xii–341.

Brinkley Messick and Michael Powers (eds.), *Islamic Legal Interpretation: Muftis and their Fatwas*, Cambridge: Harvard University Press, 1996, p. x–431.

Yahya Michot, *Mardin: Hégire, fuite du péché et demeure de l'Islam*, Paris: al-Bouraq, 2005, p. 176.

Flagg Miller, *The Moral Resonance of Arab Media. Audiocassette Poetry and Culture in Yemen*, Cambridge: Harvard Centre for Middle Eastern Studies, 2007, p. xxiv–525.

——— 'Metaphors of Commerce: Trans-Valuing Tribalism in Yemeni Audiocassette Poetry', *International Journal of Middle East Studies*, no. 34, 2002, pp. 29–57.

——— *Inscribing the Muse: Political Poetry and the Discourse of Circulation in the Yemeni Cassette Industry*, Doctoral dissertation, University of Michigan, 2001, p. 423.

——— 'Yafi' Has Only One Name: Shared Histories and Cultural Linkages Between Yafi' and Hadramawt' in, Mikhaïl N. Souvorov and Mikhaïl A. Rodionov (eds.), *Cultural Anthropology of Southern Arabia: Hadramawt Revisited*, St Petersburg: Museum of Anthropology and Ethnography Peter the Great, 1999, pp. 63–77.

Nasr Taha Mustafâ, *Humûm âkhir al-qarn: al-Yaman wa al-tahawwulât al-siyâsiyya al-kubrâ* [End of century issues: Yemen and great political transformations], Beirut: Riyâdh al-Rayyis, 2004, p. 262.

Vitaly Naumkin, *Red Wolves of Yemen: The Struggle for Independence*, Cambridge: Oleander Press, 2004, p. xxi–393.

William Ochsenwald, 'Saudi Arabia and the Islamic Revival', *International Journal of Middle East Studies*, vol. 13, no. 3, 1981, pp. 271–286.

Awad Al-Otaibi and Pascal Ménoret, 'Rebels Without a Cause? The *tafhit* Groups in Saudi Arabia' in Asef Bayat and Linda Herrera (eds.), *Being Young and Muslim. New Cultural Politics in the Global South and North*, Oxford: Oxford University Press, 2010, pp. 77–94.

Mohamed Ould-Mohamedou, *Contre-croisade: origines et conséquences du 11 Septembre*, Paris: L'Harmattan, 2004, p. 184.

Sarah Philips, *Yemen's Democracy Experience in a Regional Perspective: Patronage and Pluralized Authoritarianism*, London: Palgrave Macmillan, 2008, p. 241.

Marine Poirier, 'Yémen nouveau, futur meilleur? Retour sur l'élection présidentielle de 2006', *Chroniques Yéménites*, no. 15, 2008, pp. 129–159

Madawi Al-Rasheed, *Contesting the Saudi State: Islamic Voices from a New Generation*, Cambridge: Cambridge University Press, 2007, p. xxii–308.

―――― (ed.), *Transnational Connections and the Arabian Gulf*, London: Routledge, 2005, p. xii–189.

―――― *A History of Saudi Arabia*, Cambridge: Cambridge University Press, 2002, p. xvii–255.

―――― 'The Shi'a of Saudi Arabia: A Minority in Search of Cultural Authenticity', *British Journal of Middle Eastern Studies*, vol. 25, no. 1, 1998, pp. 121–138.

―――― 'God, the King and the Nation: Political Rhetoric in Saudi Arabia in the 1990s', *Middle East Journal*, vol. 50, no. 3, 1996, pp. 359–371.

Madawi Al-Rasheed and Robert Vitalis (eds.), *Counter-Narratives: History, Contemporary Society, and Politics in Saudi Arabia and Yemen*, New York: Palgrave, 2004, p. 272.

Bernard Rougier (ed.), *Qu'est ce que le salafisme?*, Paris: Presses Universitaires de France, 2008, p. 271.

Olivier Roy, *Holy Ignorance. When Religion and Culture Diverge*, New York: Columbia University Press, 2010, p. 288.

―――― *Globalized Islam: The Search for the New Ummah*, New York: Columbia University Press, 2004, p. 320.

―――― *L'échec de l'Islam politique*, Paris: Seuil, 1992, p. 251.

Susanne Hoeber Rudolph and James Piscatori (eds.), *Transnational Religion and Fading States*, Boulder: Westview Press, 1997, p. viii–280.

Muhammad al-Rumayhî and Fâris al-Saqqâf (eds.), *Mustqabal al-'ilâqât al-yamaniyya al-khalîjiyya* [Future of Yemeni-Gulf relations], Cairo: Matâbi'at Anwâr al-Yâsîn, 2002, p. 270.

'Abd al-Karîm Qâsim Sa'îd, *Al-ikhwân al-muslimûn wa al-haraka al-usûliyya fî al-Yaman* [The Muslim Brotherhood and the fundamentalist movement in Yemen], Sana'a: Maktabat Murâd, 1998, p. 158.

Edward Said, *Covering Islam. How the Media and the Experts Determine How We See the Rest of the World*, London: Vintage, 2ème édition, 1997, p. lxx–200.

Ghassan Salamé, 'Islam and Politics in Saudi Arabia', *Arab Studies Quarterly*, vol. 9, no. 3, 1987, pp. 306–326.

Hasan Nâsir Sarâr, *al-Shawkânî wa Sayyid Qutb wa al-ab'âd al-hadhâriyya* [al-Shawkânî and Sayyid Qutb: matters of civilisation], Sana'a: Wizârat al-thaqâfa, 2004, p. 583.

Fâris al-Saqqâf, *Ilghâ' al-ma'âhid al-'ilmiyya wa tawhîd al-ta'alîm* [The suppression of the Scientific Institutes and the unification of instruction], Sana'a: Markaz Dirâsât al-Mustaqbal, 2004, p. 49.

―――― *Mustaqbal al-'ilaqât bayn al-jamâ'ât al-islâmiyya wa al-sulta fî al-Yaman* [The future of the relations between Islamic organisations and the government in Yemen], Sana'a: Markaz Dirâsât al-Mustaqbal, 2002, p. 42.

'Abd Allâh Hâshim al-Sayânî, *al-Ikhwân al-muslimûn wa al-salafiyûn fî al-Yaman* [The Muslim Brotherhood and the Salafis in Yemen], Sana'a: Markaz al-Râ'id, 2002, p. 144.

Jillian Schwedler, *Faith in Moderation: Islamist Parties in Jordan and Yemen*, Cambridge: Cambridge University Press, 2007, p. xxi–252.

Robert Serjeant, 'Yâfi', Zaydîs, Al bû Bakr b. Sâlim and Others: Tribes and Sayyids', in Robert Serjeant (ed.), *Arabian Studies*, Cambridge: Cambridge University Press, 1990, pp. 83–105.

Robert Serjeant and Ronald Lewcock (eds.), *San'â' an Arabian Islamic City*, London: World of Islam Festival Trust, 1983, p. 566.

Yoginder Sikand, *The Origins and Development of the Tablighi-Jama'at (1920–2000): A Cross-Country Comparative Study*, New Delhi: Orient Longman, 2002, p. 310.

Diane Singerman, *Avenues of Participation: Family, Politics, and Networks in Urban Quarters of Cairo*, Princeton: Princeton University Press, 1995, p. xx–335.

Thomas Stevenson, 'Migration, Family and Household in Highland Yemen: The Impact of Socio-Economic and Political Change and Cultural Ideals on Domestic Organization', *Journal of Cooperative Family Studies*, vol. 28, no. 2, 1997, pp. 14–53.

——— 'Yemeni Workers Come Home. Reabsorbing One Million Migrants', *Middle East Resort*, March-April 1993, pp. 15–20.

Jamal al-Suwaidi (ed.), *The Yemeni War of 1994. Causes and Consequences*, London: Saqi Books, 1995, p. 124.

Nâsir Muhammad al-Tawîl, *al-Haraka al-islâmiyya wa al-nizâm al-siyâsî fî al-Yaman. Min al-tahâluf 'ila al-tanâfus* [The Islamist movement and the political system in Yemen. From alliance to competition], Sana'a: Maktabat Khâlid Bin al-Walîd, 2009, p. 498.

Hélène Thiollet, 'Nationalisme d'Etat et nationalisme ordinaire en Arabie Saoudite:la nation saoudienne et ses immigrés', *Raisons Politiques*, no. 37, 2010, pp. 89–102.

Dominique Thomas, 'Les salafistes et la communication: quand les 'vertueux anciens' s'emparent du Net' in Yves Gonzale-Quijano and Tourya Guaybess (eds.), *Les Arabes Parlent aux Arabes. La révolution de l'information dans le monde arabe*, Arles: Actes Sud, 2009, pp. 224–239.

'Abd al-Wahhâb al-'Uqâb, *Tatawwur al-'ilâqât al-yamaniyya al-su'ûdiyya 1948–1970* [Evolution of Yemeni-Saudi relations 1948–1970], Aden: Isdârât Jâmi'at 'Adan, 1998, p. 361.

Nicholas Van Hear, 'The Socio-economic Impact of the Involuntary Mass Return to Yemen in 1990', *Journal of Refugee Studies*, vol. 7, no. 1, 1994, pp. 18–38.

Daniel Varisco, 'The Elixer of Life or the Devil's Cud: The Debate over Qat (Catha edulis) in Yemeni Culture' in Ross Coomber and Nigel South (eds.), *Drug Use and Cultural Context Beyond 'The West'*, London: Free Association Books, 2004, p. 101–118.

Alexei Vassiliev, *The History of Saudi Arabia*, London: Saqi Books, 1998, p. 576.

Robert Vitalis, *America's Kingdom: Mythmaking on the Saudi Oil Frontier*, Stanford: Stanford University Press, 2007, p. xxvii–353.

Gabriele Vom Bruck, 'Regimes of Piety Revisited: Zaydî Political Moralities in the Republic of Yemen', *Die Welts des Islams*, no. 50, 2010, pp. 185–223

―――― *Islam, Memory, and Morality in Yemen: Ruling Families in Transition*, New York: Palgrave, 2005, p. xix–348.

Richard Warms, 'Merchants, Muslims, and Wahhabiyya: the Elaboration of Muslim Identity in Sikasso, Mali', *Canadian Journal of African Studies*, vol. 26, no. 3, 1992, pp. 485–507.

Eric Watkins, 'Islamism and Tribalism in Yemen' in Abdel Salam Sidahmed, Anoushiravan Ehteshami (eds.), *Islamic Fundamentalism*, Boulder: Westview Press, 1996, pp. 215–225.

Lisa Wedeen, *Peripheral Visions. Publics, Power and Performance in Yemen*, Chicago: Chicago University Press, 2008, p. 320.

Shelagh Weir, *A Tribal Order. Politics and Law in the Mountains of Yemen*, Austin: Texas University Press, 2007, p. 410.

Quintan Wiktorowicz, 'Anatomy of the Salafi Movement', *Studies in Conflict & Terrorism*, vol. 29, no. 3, 2006, pp. 207–239.

―――― (ed.), *Islamic Activism. A Social Movement Theory Approach*, Bloomington: Indiana University Press, 2004, p. xii–316.

――――, *The Management of Islamic Activism. Salafis, the Muslim Brotherhood, and State Power in Jordan*, Albany: State University of New York, 2001, p. 205.

―――― 'The New Global Threat: Transnational Salafis and Jihad', *Middle East Policy*, vol. 8, no. 4, 2001, pp. 18–38.

Andy Worthington, *The Guantanamo Files. The Stories of 774 Detainees in America's Illegal Prison*, New York: Pluto Press, 2007, p. 352.

Mai Yamani, *Changed Identities. The Challenge of the New Generation in Saudi Arabia*, London: Royal Institute of International affairs, 2000, p. 170.

Ayman al-Yassini, *Religion and State in the Kingdom of Saudi Arabia*, Boulder: Westview Press, 1985, p. xii–171.

Nâsir Ahmad Yahyâ, *al-Tatarruf wa al takfîr fî al-Yaman* [Extremism and excommunication in Yemen], Sana'a: Dâr al-Kutub al-Wataniyya, 2003, p. 190.

Mohamed Zabarah, 'Yemeni-Saudi Relations Gone Awry' in Joseph A. Kechichian (ed.), *Iran, Iraq, and the Gulf States*, New York: Palgrave, 2001, pp. 263–280.

Malika Zeghal, *Gardiens de l'islam: Les oulémas d'al-Azhar dans l'Egypte contemporaine*, Paris: Presses de la Fondation Nationale Des Sciences Politiques, 1996, p. 381.

Al-Tayib Zein al-Abdin, 'The Yemeni Constitution and its Religious Orientation', *Arabian Studies*, no. 3, 1976, pp. 115–125.

Selection of Primary Sources Published by Islamic Scholars:

'Umar 'Abd al-Salâm, *Mukhâlafat al-wahhâbiyya lil-qur'ân wa al-sunna* [Wahhabism in contradiction to the Qur'an and the sunna], Beirut: Dâr al-Hidâya, 1995, p. 92.

Amîn Abû Zayd, *al-Wahhâbiyya wa khataruhâ 'alâ mustaqbal al-Yaman al-siyâsî* [Wahhabism and its danger for the future of political Yemen], Beirut: Mu'assasa al-Basâ'ir, 1991, p. 71.

Abû 'Abd al-Rahmân 'Abd al-Raqîb al-'Alâbî, *al-Îdhâh fî al-farq bayn da'wat ahl al-sunna wa da'wat hizb al-islâh* [Clarification on the difference between the call of the ahl al-sunna and the call of the Islâh party], Bayhân: Markaz al-Sunna, 2004, p. 4.

'Abd al-Rahmân Bin Muhammad Âl 'Umaysân, *al-Hujaj al-salafiyya li-dahdh shabah Abî al-Hasan al-hizbiyya* [Salafi arguments to refute those who would argue that Abû al-Hasan favours attachment to parties], place, publisher and date unknown, p. 8.

Muhsin al-Amîn, *Kashf al-irtyâb fî atbâ' Muhammad Bin 'Abd al-Wahhâb* [Clarification regarding suspicion against the partisans of Muhammad Bin 'Abd al-Wahhâb], place and publisher unknown, 1991, p. 429.

Mustafâ 'Abd al-Rahmân al-'Attâs, *al-Salafiyya al-mu'âsira: usûluhâ wa asâlîbuhâ* [Contemporary Salafism: origins and methods], Singapore: Karjây al-Mahdûda, 1992, p. 46.

Muhammad 'Amîr al-'Awlaqî, *Limâdhâ akhtart al-qâ'ida?* [Why did I choose al-Qaeda?], place unknown: al-Malâhim, 2010, p. 78.

'Abd al-'Azîz Bin Bâz, *'Awâmil islâh al-mujtama'* [Factors of the reform of society], Riyadh: Dâr al-Watan, 1998, p. 32.

'Abd al-'Azîz al-Bura'î, *Takâtuf al-mutasâqitîn* [The alliance of losers], place and publisher unknown, 2004, p. 12.

Ahmad Farîd, *al-Salafiyya: qawâ'id wa usûl* [Salafism: rules and foundations], Cairo: Dâr al-'Aqîda, 2003, p. 48.

Sâlih al-Fawzân, *al-Jihâd: anwâ'uhu wa ahkâmuhu* [The jihad: its forms and modalities], Riyadh: Dâr al-Imâm Ahmad, 2005, p. 48.

——— *al-Ijâbât al-muhima fî al-mashâkil al-mulima* [The important answers to the acute problems], Riyadh: Maktabat al-Rushd, 2005, p. 344.

Abû 'Abd Allâh Muhammad Bâ Jammâl al-Hadhramî, *Bayân al-'afin fî akhlâq ra'îs jam'iyya al-taqwâ al-hizbiyya Abî al-Hasan* [Declaration on what is rotten in Abû al-Hasan's manners who heads the political association al-Taqwâ], Tarîm: Masjid al-Sunna, 2003, p. 23.

'Abd al-Hamîd Bin Zayd al-Hajûrî, *Tawjîh al-muslimîn ilâ al-tarîq al-shar'iyya fî al-ta'âmul ma'a al-khawârij min ashâb tanzîm al-qâ'ida wa al-hûthiyin* [Guidance for the Muslims towards the legitimate path for dealing with the khawârij of al-Qaeda organisation and the Hûthis], place and publisher unknown, 2010, p. 56.

Yahyâ al-Hajûrî, *al-Tawdhîh lamâ jâ' fî al-taqrîrât al-'ilmiyya wa al-naqd al-sahîh* [The clarification concerning scientific declarations and the authentic criticism], place and publisher unknown, 2009, p. 84.

——— (ed.), *Mukhtasar al-bayân al-mawdhah li-hizbiyyat al-'Adanî* [Summary of declaration proving the partisanship of al-'Adanî], Dammâj: Dâr al-Hadîth, 2009, p. 79.

——— *Mushâhadâtî fî Britânyâ* [My experience of Great Britain], Sana'a: Dâr al-Âthâr, 2005, p. 19.

Hikmat al-Harîrî, '*Zâhirat al-Hûthî fî al-Yaman* [The Hûthî phenomenon in Yemen]' *al-Sunna*, no. 138, 2004, pp. 85–98.

Mustafâ al-Harîrî, '*al-Yaman ilâ ayn?* [Yemen to where?]', *al-Sunna*, no. 39, 1994, pp. 38–42.

Husayn al-Hidâr, *al-Tahdhîr min khatar al-takfîr* [Warning on the dangers of excommunication], Sana'a: publisher unknown, 2003, p. 217.

Sultân al-'Îd, *al-Irhâb bayn al-tadmîr wa al-tabrîr* [Terrorism, between destruction and justification], Riyadh: Dâr al-Imâm Ahmad, 2005, p. 32.

Muhammad al-Imâm, *al-Hizb al-ishtiraki fi rubu' qarn* [The Socialist Party during a quarter of a century], Sana'a: Dâr al-Âthâr, 2008, p. 48.

――― *Tanwîr al-absâr bimâ fi al-rimâyya min al-manâfi' wa al-adhrâr* [Clarification on the judgement on fire arms, their advantages and their drawbacks], Ma'bar: Dâr al-Hadîth, 2004, p. 128.

――― *Tanwîr al-zulumât bi-kashf mafâsid wa shubuhât al-intikhâbât* [Clarification [Clearing away obscurity through the revelation of the ravages and the uncertainties of elections], Ma'bar: publisher unknown, 1996, p. 252.

――― *Tahdhîr ahl al-îmân min ta'âti al-qât, al-shamma wa al-dukhân* [Warning to people of faith against qat, shamma and cigarettes], Ma'bar: publisher and date unknown, p. 115.

Mustafâ Bâdî Abû al-Lawjarî, *Afghânistân. Ihtilâl al-Dhâkira* [Afghanistan. Occupation of Memory], Sana'a: publisher unknown, 2007, p. 125.

Muhammad Bin Muhammad al-Mahdî, *al-Zaydiyya fi al-Yaman: hiwâr maftûh* [Zaydism in Yemen: an open discussion], Sana'a: Markaz al-Kalima al-Tayiba, 2008, p. 98.

Abû al-Hasan al-Ma'ribî, *al-Tafjîrât wa al-ightiyâlât: al-asbâb, al-âthâr, al-'ilâj* [Explosions and assassinations: reasons, effects, and solutions], Riyadh: Dâr al-Fadhîla, 2004, p. 295.

――― *al-Fatâwâ al-shar'iyya fi ahdâth Sa'da* [Legal opinions concerning the events in Sa'da], Ma'rib: Dâr al-Hadîth, 2004, p. 27.

――― *al-Tankîl limâ fi khitâb al-shaykh Rabî' al-Madkhalî min al-abâtil* [Refutation of what is vain in the discourse of shaykh Rabî' al-Madkhalî], Ma'rib: Dâr al-Hadîth, 2003, p. 31.

Ahmad Hasan al-Mu'allim, *al-qubûriyya fi al-Yaman: nashâtuhâ, âthâruhâ, mawqif al-'ulamâ' 'anhâ* [The cult of saints in Yemen: its practices, effects and the position of the 'ulamâ' on the matter], place, publisher and date unknown, p. 448.

Sharaf Luqmân, *al-Irhâb fi muwâjahat al-irhâb* [Terrorism faced with terrorism], place, publisher and date unknown, p. 129.

Rabî' al-Madkhalî, *Adhwâ' islâmiyya 'alâ 'aqîdât Sayyid Qutb wa fikrihi* [Islamic clarifications on the creed of Sayyid Qutb and on his doctrine], place, publisher and date unknown, p. 250.

――― , *Intiqâd 'aqdî wa manhajî likitâb 'al-sirâj al-wahâj fi bayân al-manhâj'* [Contractual and methodological disapproval of the book 'The Bright Light of the Declaration of Method'], Sana'a: Dâr al-Âthâr, 2002, p. 48.

Rabî' al-Madkhalî (ed.), *Nasîhat al-shaykh Rabî' al-Madkhalî li ahl al-Yaman* [Advice of shaykh Rabî' al-Madkhalî to the people of Yemen], Tarîm: Jâmi' al-Sunna, 2004, p. 40.

Zayd al-Madkhalî, *al-Irhâb wa âthâruhu al-sayyi' 'alâ al-afrâd wa al-umam* [Terrorism and its negative impact on individuals and nations], Cairo: Dâr al-Minhâj, 2003, p. 128.

Abû Bakr al-'Adanî al-Mashhûr, *al-Khurûj min al-dâ'ira al-hamrâ* [Leaving the red circle], Aden: Ribât al-Tarbiyya al-Islâmiyya, 2002, p. 159.

Fahd al-Qahtânî, *Majzarat Makka: Qissat al-madhbaha al-sa'ûdiyya lil-hujjâj* [The butchery of Mecca: the story of the Saudi massacre of pilgrims], London: al-Safâ, 1988, p. 488.

Hasan al-Raymî, *Irshâd al-barriyya* [The way of the pious], Sana'a: Dâr al-Âthâr, 2000, p. 235.

Muhammad al-Sa'îdî, *Sa'da limâdhâ?* [Sa'da, why?], Beirut: Dâr al-Basâ'ir, date unknown, p. 19.

Umm Salama al-Salafiyya (ed.), *al-Rihla al-akhîra li-imâm al-Jazîra* [The last journey of the imam of the Peninsula], Sana'a: Dâr al-Âthâr, 2003, p. 350.

Muhammad Bin 'Abd Allâh al-Salûmî, *al-Qitâ' al-khayrî wa da'âwâ al-irhâb* [Benevolent associations and accusations of terrorism], Riyadh: al-Bayyân, 2004, p. 614.

Hasan al-Saqqâf, *al-Salafiyya al-wahhâbiyya: afkâruhâ al-asâsiyya wa judhûruhâ al-târîkhiyya* [Wahhabi Salafism: its essential ideas and its historical roots], Amman: Dâr al-Imâm al-Nawâwî, 2002, p. 157.

'Abd al-Malik al-Shaybânî, *al-Yaman fî al-Kitâb wa al-sunna* [Yemen in the Book and the Tradition], Sana'a: Maktabat Khâlid Ibn al-Walîd, 2003, p. 170.

Abû Mus'ab al-Sûrî, *Da'wat al-muqâwamma al-islâmiyya al-'alâmiyya* (Global islamic resistance call), 2005, p. 1600.

Unknown author, 'Al-shaykh Ibn Bâz wa sîrat Hayâtihi [Shaykh Bin Bâz and his biography]', *al-Faysal*, no. 273, 1999, p. 2–8.

Unknown author, 'Mawqifunâ min ahdâth 'Adan al-akhîra [Our position on the latest events in Aden]', *al-Sunna*, no. 42, 1994, pp. 9–15.

Muqbil al-Wâdi'î, *Mushâhadâtî fî al-Mamlaka al-'Arabiyya al-Su'ûdiyya* [My experience of the Kingdom of Saudi Arabia], Sana'a: Dâr al-Âthâr, 2005, p. 32.

―――― *Tuhfat al-mujîb 'alâ as'ilat al-hâdhir wa al-gharîb* [Precious responses to questions from one who is present and one who is absent], Sana'a: Dâr-Âthâr, 2005, p. 504.

―――― *Ijâbat al-sâ'il 'alâ ahamm al-masâ'il* [Answer to those who ask the most important questions], Sana'a: Maktabat al-Athariyya, 2004, p. 591.

―――― *Ghârat al-ashrita 'alâ ahl al-jahl wa al-safsata* [The attack of the audio-cassettes against the people of ignorance and sophism], Sana'a: Maktabat al-Athariyya, 2004, 2 volumes, p. 1008.

―――― *al-Makhraj min al-fitna* [Leaving dissension behind], Sana'a: Maktabat al-Athariyya, 3rd edition, 2002, p. 214.

―――― (ed.), *Tarjamat Abî 'Abd al-Rahmân Muqbil Bin Hâdî al-Wâdi'î* [Biography of Abî 'Abd al-Rahmân Muqbil Bin Hâdî al-Wâdi'î], Sana'a: Maktabat al-Athariyya, 1999, p. 224.

―――― *al-Dîbâj fî marâthât shaykh al-islâm samâhat al-shaykh 'Abd al-'Azîz Bin Bâz* [The silk in the funeral oration of the *shaykh al-islâm*, his excellency shaykh 'Abd al-'Azîz Bin Bâz], Sana'a: Maktabat al-Idrîsî al-Salafiyya, 1999, p. 100.

―――― *al-Suyûf al-bâtira li-ilhâd al-shuyû'iyya al-kâfira* [Sharp swords for the unholy communist heresy], place, publisher and date unknown, p. 339.

―――― *Maqtal al-shaykh Jamîl al-Rahmân al-Afghânî* [The assassination of shaykh Jamîl al-Rahmân al-Afghânî], Sana'a: Dâr al-Âthâr, 2006, p. 42.

Sa'îd al-Mashûshî al-Yâfi'î, *Anbâ' al-fudhalâ'* [News of noble people], Sana'a: Maktabat al-Athariyya, 2002, p. 28.

Sâlih Bin Muhammad al-Yâfi'î, *al-Mawâqif al-râhina fî al-Yaman min tatbîq kitâb Allâh wa sunnat rasûlihi* [The current positions in Yemen as concerns the application of the book of God and the Tradition of his Prophet], Riyadh: Maktabat al-Mu'ayyad, 1993, p. 163.

Muhammad Surûr Zayn al-'Abidîn, 'al-Mihna al-yamaniyya: asbâbuhâ wa natâ'ijuhâ [The Yemeni challenge: causes and effects]', *al-Sunna*, no. 40, 1994, pp. 2–22.

——— 'al-Islâm al-rasmî [Official Islam]', *al-Sunna*, no. 21, 1992, pp. 2–7.

INDEX